La Raza

THE MEXICAN AMERICANS

La Raza

THE MEXICAN AMERICANS

Stan Steiner

HARPER COLOPHON BOOKS
Harper & Row, Publishers
NEW YORK, EVANSTON, AND LONDON

Chapter XXIV was first published in *Vogue* in somewhat different form as "'The Cultural Schizophrenia' of Luis Valdez."

Excerpts from *A Cross for Maclovio,* © 1968 by Rodolfo Gonzales, and *I Am Joaquín,* © 1967; by Rodolfo Gonzales, are reprinted by permission of the author.

First HARPER COLOPHON edition published 1970 by
Harper & Row, Publishers, Inc.

LIBRARY OF CONGRESS CATALOG CARD NUMBER: 77-83622

And the Pope said to the conquistadors: Go forth and create La Santa Raza! The Holy Race! In a cantina, a bar, nowadays a man will say to another, "Say, Eduardo. How's the wife and kids?" And the other man will say, "We had another kid. Now we got six!" So the first man will laugh, "You old goat! Creating La Santa Raza, eh?"

—In the café of the de Vargas Hotel in Santa Fe, one morning over coffee, a man from the northern mountains explaining the meaning of La Santa Raza

I wish God had made people blind. Then a touch of the hand, a word of the mouth, would be all they would need to know their neighbor. People now judge each other by how they look, not by how they are. If God can perform miracles why can't He make people blind? Why can't we have perceptions like radar antenna to judge with? Our eyes betray us.

—EDUARDO PÉREZ, a community leader
in the barrios of Los Angeles

Contents

PART THREE

Illustrations

The following are grouped after page 114:

The following are grouped after page 242:

La Raza

THE MEXICAN AMERICANS

PROLOGUE: Cleofas, the Man of the Earth

"I love to be poor. I would rather be poor than rich. Yes, I think so. I have been poor all my life. I don't feel it any more. I am immune to being poor."

Cleofas Vigil's face is lined by the dry earth of the village of San Cristobal and the cold winds of the Sangre de Cristo—the Blood of Christ—Mountains. But his face is not hard. He is not poor that way. There is a warmth in his eyes. "I live with the weeds," he says.

He leans on his shovel. The digging is hard. But this stubborn land has known his family intimately for generations, they are buried here, and it welcomes his shovel. Still, he breathes heavily. It is not easy work to dig an earth cellar.

"It is a good feeling when you rub your fingers in the soil that produces food for life," Cleofas says.

He is a tall man, with the set jaw of a farmer. In the village he is a respected citizen: the head of the Cattle Growers Association and the Water Users Association. Where a herd may mean ten head of cattle and a ranch may mean less than forty acres, these are positions of honor, not of wealth. "I own a few acres in this beautiful valley of San Cristobal," he modestly says. "Our country here, the mountains, I think it is one of the most beautiful mountains and villages in the country of the United States. But it is one of the most poor."

Cleofas is the poet of his village. He is a musician and a wood carver and a singer of *corridos* and *alabados*, much sought after for weddings and baptisms and burials—a poet in the older tradition, that of the village chronicler and seer. He is a sophisticated man who knows that the truth is as cruel and beautiful as the earth.

"I will tell you a story," he says. "There were two men. One of them had a pocket full of money. He was rich. But the other man, he had nothing but some tortillas in his hand. He was poor. These two men were traveling together. And they went to many towns, and whenever they came to a restaurant, the man with the pocket full of money he bought himself a big dinner. But the poor man, he sat outside and ate his tortillas, because that was all he had to eat.

"And they came to a desert. It was a real desert. There was no town on it. No restaurant either!

"And the rich man, with his pocket full of money, was more and more hungry, he had nothing to eat. But the poor man, he ate his tortillas. The tortillas were very dry tortillas by now, and very hard. But they were still good to eat.

" 'Will you sell me one of your tortillas?' the rich man asked the poor man.

" 'Eat your money,' the poor man said.

"And the rich man, he died. But the poor man, he got across the desert.

"That is a story my grandfather told me. That is fiction, you know. It is what you call an example. But it is the truth. The Anglo, he does not understand that story."

Once more Cleofas digs. He says, "I will tell you what the Anglo, he understands. Money! Money! Money! Money! Money! Money! Money! Money! Money! Money!" And he laughs.

Cleofas' way of sanctifying the poor has little to do with poverty. He is saying something else, something quite ancient. The act of being poor symbolizes the villagers' acquiescence to nature, the peacefulness of the earth, and humility before God. As long ago as 1629 the scholarly Fray Alonso de Benavides wrote of the settlers in the villages along the valleys of the Rio Grande, "As long as they have a good crop of tobacco to smoke, they are very content, and wish no riches. It seems as if they have taken a vow of poverty." The good priest believed there were valuable ore deposits in New Mexico, but when he suggested this to the villagers "they laughed at him"—an unheard-of thing for Spaniards to do, he wrote sarcastically, "who out of greed for silver and gold would enter Hell itself." But the villagers did not wish wealth.

Nowadays being poor is a way of life. The fields of the village lie fallow. In a time of supermarket farming it hardly pays to plow the tiny plots. Many of the houses in the village are empty. Not abandoned, just empty. The families have gone to the cities in search of work. On the small farms throughout the Southwest there is quietude.

The waiting houses, the empty corrals, the decaying fences, the ruins of adobe walls as old as history, and the silent churches are everywhere, not merely in the village of San Cristobal.

The gate of the church is broken. The priest comes only on Saturday, if he comes at all.

"Our road was dirt in my grandfather's time," Cleofas says. "It has not changed. The dirt is the same dirt, but maybe it is not as good as it was. Maybe it is worse."

Where the old road breaks off and falls, like a river of mud into the valley, it forks and winds through the juniper woods to the ranch of D. H. Lawrence, where the real Lady Chatterley's lover had lived. He wrote here in the Sangre de Cristo Mountains of his search for the "pagan sun" of the Southwest; but now he is buried in a whitewashed shrine kept by the University of New Mexico for the tourists. His ashes are entombed under a Mexican altar guarded by the dogs of a gatekeeper and a poet-in-residence, a few miles from the Vigil farm. In the dust outside the shrine is the grave of Lawrence's wife Frieda.

"I did not know him," Cleofas says. "But I helped dig the grave of his wife." The farmer was a boy then. He does not remember these tourist writers too well; so many lonely intellectuals come from Taos, from the East, to the village, on pilgrimages to the earth.

One summer the hippies wandered into the valley and stayed a while. They built tepees in Arroyo Hondo and tried to set up a tribal community. They came to San Cristobal, too. No one bothered them in their gypsy camp on the mountainside at first, and then they wandered off again. "I think they are good people," Cleofas says of the flower children. "But why do they wear their hair like babies? Are they babies? They harm no one but themselves."

Cleofas feels sorrow for the hippies. They have no people, no land, no memories, he says, so they are trying to invent a way of life in their minds. "Where will they go?" he says. "Where are their people?" These people who come like refugees from the Anglo way of affluence, searching for roots in his poor land, fascinate Cleofas. He has compassion for them, but he is troubled by them. "Why are they so alone?" he asks.

"Always they say 'Dig.' If they want roots why don't they dig? That is where roots are," he says. "That is how to be together with other men.

"Old-timers, like my grandfather, they were very much together, they weren't divided the way we are now. They believed in helping each other. And their trade was different from what it is now; they traded one product for another. Like beans for potatoes, and potatoes for lentils, and lentils for carrots, and cabbages, and so on.

"In those days when a man's harvest was ready he did not say to his neighbor, 'Come, help me.' His neighbor watched the field of his neighbor, and he knew when it was time to go and help. He did not have to be asked. Now the field of my neighbor is almost ready, and when it is ready I would like to go to him and help with his harvest. That is the way it should be. A man should help his neighbor without being asked.

"In those days we had a mill in the valley. Someone stole the millstones. They use them for doorsteps, you know, in Santa Fe.

"Who can bring back the old ways? Sometimes people say to me, 'You want to bring back the old ways.' No, I cannot. Not with an ox. Not with a bull. I cannot. No one can. The tractor is a blessing. The water in the kitchen is a blessing. The airplane is a blessing. I do not oppose new things because they are new. But only when they are bad.

"In those days that I remember, everything was in harmony, everybody was in harmony. What I would bring back is the harmony."

He remembers that the village was no richer then, but that the people were more religious and happier. The land was freer and the forest was unfenced. "The old-timers, like my grandfather and father, they lived from their little farms, from their little land, land our ancestors left us. The freedom they had in the forests in those days! Our ancestors made a better living because they had more free land, they had more freedom.

"Our lands are small," Cleofas says, "so we naturally need the forests, our common lands, to graze our herds. We can't graze ten head of cows on our small land."

In the village of San Cristobal every family has a small plot, some of less than ten acres. The plots are cut in narrow strips, from the bottom land along the river that cuts through the valley, so that every inch of the fertile, flat earth can be farmed.

The village lies close to the little river that nourishes the land. In the high deserts, where the rain is scarce, the water is sacred. And the plots of the villagers have traditionally been small. Even in the days of the huge land grants long ago the actual farms were small. As late as 1855 the largest farm in New Mexico was said to be 1,721 acres, belonging to a *rico* (rich) family in Bernalillo County.

Yet the common pastures in the forests and mountains, which belong to everyone in the village, are vast. The cattle of the farmers have always roamed free here.

It is sometimes thought that these common lands originated in the land system of feudal Spain. But it was not wholly European, nor was it wholly feudal, to divide the land this way.

Under the ancient kingdoms of the Aztecs there were such common lands—the *calpulli.* A "dividing of the inhabited lands into suburbs, or calpulli, each with a set amount of land; this land belonging not to the inhabitants as individuals, but rather being granted to a family, or tribe" (*El Derecho Agrario,* by Gabino Fraga), was the way the Mexican Indians planned their villages. In the Laws of the Indies the kings of Spain protected these communal lands of the Aztecs. When the Españoles Mejicanos settled in New Mexico they brought this system of common lands with them. The viceroys of New Spain perpetuated the ancient Indian way of holding land in common by their communal land grants to whole villages in New Mexico.

The communal village with its common lands once was the accepted way of life in the mountain villages of the high valleys.

Once. But no longer. "The Government of the United States took it away, our lands, turned more than half of our lands into National Forests. For what?" Cleofas says.

When Cleofas was a young man, in 1938, the surveyors of thc U.S. Soil Conservation Service counted 358,019 acres in the National Forests of Taos County, New Mexico, where the village of San Cristobal lies at the forest's edge. These very same National Forests had grown, by 1965, to 451,245 acres, an increase of 93,226 acres (29.1 per cent) in the federally fenced land.

Where did these "new" National Forests come from? The lands were taken largely from the public domain, the *ejidos*, or common pastures, where the villagers' herds had grazed for centuries as freely as the wild deer.

Now, the villagers must get permits to graze their herds on what was their own land. If the confused cows wander into the wrong part of the forest by mistake, they are impounded and imprisoned in the corrals of the forest rangers. "Either you pay a fine, or you lose the privilege of putting that cow in the forest the next year," Cleofas says. "If you have a permit for twelve head of cows and they impound two, the next year you will have a permit for ten cows. A fellow with ten cows, maybe that same guy used to have thirty or forty head. Now they don't allow that. Every year they cut you more and more.

"Ten head of cows! You can't make a living on that! How can we feed our families?"

In San Cristobal there were 350 grazing permits for cattle issued to the ranchers in 1947; there were 140 permits in 1967: a reduction of 60 per cent. The "free permits" for milk cows, bulls, and horses have been eliminated. Cattle who were fortunate enough to be permitted into the forests have to graze most of the summer, until August 1, "on land where there is practically no grass; and rather than allow animals to starve to death, the men are selling them or butchering them. . . ."

It is the same in every village. The La Jarita allotment of permits has been cut from 839 to 420; at El Rito, 4,000 lambing permits have been withdrawn from the sheepherders; in Rio Arriba the permits were reduced by 65 per cent in one year (1965); while in Canjilon more than 1,000 year-round permits for cattle have been withdrawn entirely.

"Our poverty is made and created by the Government of the United States," Cleofas says. "The problem of the poor is that the Government of the United States creates this poverty in the villages."

In the state of New Mexico the largest landowner is the United States Government. "The federal government owns 34.9 per cent of the state's acreage," says the New Mexico State Planning Office. That is 27,150,000 acres. With the Indian reservations—6.8 per cent of the land—and the land of the state of New Mexico—12 per cent—the federal- and state-controlled lands total 53.7 per cent of New Mexico.

Of this vast terrain the Forest Service has been entrusted with control of 9,046,789 acres, almost six times as much land as was owned by the fabulous King Ranch in Texas.

The National Forests that surround the village of San Cristobal, and its brother mountain hamlets, comprise one of every three acres in the northern counties. In Taos County these federal lands are 44.3 per cent of the area. No wonder the village farmer, with his few acres, feels overwhelmed by the landlords in the government!

Once the forests may have been a refuge to the iconoclast of the frontier, who was known as a pioneer, but no longer. The explorer, the hunter, or the village farmer who has not paid for his permit is a trespasser, according to the law. Forests, that is, National Forests, are no longer free to the public.

"The law treats Forest Service land as private land," says W. D. Hurst, a regional forest official. Hurst is a wilderness bureaucrat who seeks to govern nature by the regulations, not by the seasons of mating. "Under the law a man is supposed to keep his stock where they're supposed to be," the forest administrator says, reasonably. "The regulations say repeated trespass [by animals] is grounds for reduction." Reduction is officialese for saying a cow will not be allowed to eat the berries of the forest.

A man like Cleofas is puzzled by this. He does not understand a law that tells a cow where to nibble the leaves of what berry bush, and then banishes the cow from the forest because it is enticed by an out-of-bounds berry.

"These are questions in which there is a legitimate difference of opinion," said former Undersecretary of Agriculture John A. Schnittker, after a flying tour of the villages and forests, where Cleofas and a dozen Hispano cattlemen cornered him, unexpectedly, and surrounded him with their vocal grievances.

"You give more land to the rabbits than you give to us poor people," Cleofas told the Undersecretary.

"We are almost in a concentration camp," Cleofas said. "The Forest Service is fencing all around the villages, so that in a few years we will all be in a concentration camp. In other words, we are oppressed. As a matter of fact, I think we are."

He rages at the fences. The forest rangers are fencing the forest with barbed wire, to keep the villagers' herds from "overgrazing" on the forage of the wild life. Cleofas says in outrage, "I don't feed my family with the elk."

He has heard of one village fenced so well by the barbed wire that the villagers tell him that they, not their cows, are being fenced in.

"One day I see a forest ranger, who I know, posting signs on my land," Cleofas says. "He is my friend, so I say to him, 'Why are you posting signs?' And he says, 'Cleofas, you have to move your fences. These signs tell where your land ends and the National Forest begins. You have to move your fences.'

"I say, 'Not me.'

"He says, 'Our surveys show that your fences are in the wrong place.'

"I say, 'Maybe your surveys are in the wrong place. You move your surveys, not my fences.'

"And I see in the north his signs are twenty feet inside my land. In the south his signs are a little bit outside my land. So I say to him, 'If you want my fences moved, you move them. But I tell you this: If you move my fences one inch inside my land, you better watch out! I will get my gun!' "

Cleofas' eyes grow cold. "I will make an army of one man if they touch my land.

"Sometimes I believe this. I believe these people in power are trying to *inoculate*, to contaminate, the poor farmer," he says. "They want to take away what little we own, our forty acres, to really take it away from the poor farmer and let the big, rich people come and relax in this beautiful country. They would rather have us on the welfare rolls. Sometimes this is the way I think. Let's say, I 'suspect.' A lot of people suspect this."

The suspicion of the stranger is widely held in the northern villages. And it is not a rural myopia. Yearly more than 15 million "strangers" were visiting New Mexico by the mid-1960's. That's fifteen "strangers" to every inhabitant. Worth more than $300 million annually, tourism is a cherished industry pampered by the state. "More than 10,000 sites of historic significance" have been officially "inventoried" by the Governor's Commission on Historic Sites, for the sightseeing pleasure of those the villagers call the "stranger."

Every village has its designated historic site. The poor and quaint villages are merchandised by "scenic tours"; although the guides scrupulously avoid pointing out the "TIERRA O MUERTE" *("Land or Death")* posters on the crumbling adobe walls.

Hospitable as the villagers are by tradition, they have become cynical and hostile. The spectacle of the vacationers with their expensive equipment coming into the dusty villages and enjoying the dense forests from which their own herds have been barred is too much for even the irony in the Hispanos' souls. On occasion their quiet antagonism has erupted into fights with the forest rangers.

A local Catholic priest voices the villagers' feelings: "I think the Forest Service is more interested in where the middle class take their vacations than where the poor people graze their cattle."

A farmer, Delfín Quintana, of the village of Cebolla, told Undersecretary of Agriculture Schnittker, "I think it is the unwritten policy of the Forest Service to get rid of the poor farmer."

A young man from Rio Arriba County, who heads a statewide project of village self-help and redevelopment, Alex Mercure, writes sardonically of the "great expectations" that some officials have "for the development of the natural resources of the rural areas along tourist and recreation lines." But then he adds, "This reflects the middle-class bias of the planners. Taos County is ranked fourth in tourist activity, but it also has the second lowest per capita income in the state. What tourist development has taken place has been of benefit only to commercial interests." How many sheepherders can ski, Mercure asks. The old villagers cannot even afford the hunting, fishing, camping, and parking permits. So they violate the laws and get arrested, and they curse tourism.

"Why do I pay to fish where I always fished?" says Cleofas. "Like a stranger?"

"Tourism and recreation projects which would take water away from the small farmer and land from the small rancher do more harm than good," says Father Robert García, himself a former village priest and past director of the state of New Mexico's Office of Economic Opportunity. "The poor, uneducated owner of a small herd, upon which he depends—partly—for bare subsistence does not understand. . . . Range management may be necessary, but these permits represent financial income and food for people in extreme poverty conditions. The huge gap between the Forest Service and these people is appalling."

Cleofas is more pithy and angry. "In the Latin American countries what do the governments do with the people's land? Year after year they have been dividing lands to many poor farmers so that they can make a living. Here in the United States they are taking the land away instead of dividing the public lands among the people.

"What they will do next I don't know. But I think they are going to succeed and not let us do anything. Just wait for the welfare check. That's all. They take away our land and give us federal projects. In the old days nobody dreamed of federal projects, nobody dreamed of welfare. We don't need anything like that. We don't want alms from anybody. We need some of our lands back. All the people need is more land. More freedom. More elbow room."

Yet he stays on in this valley of his anger. Why doesn't he pack up his family and get into his pickup truck and escape down the highway into the city? Why does he stay?

Once he left the village, he says, like so many others, but like so few he came back. He did not like it in the city.

"I lived in Denver. Yes, I work there for about twelve years. My two daughters and my son were born in Denver," he says.

"When we went to Denver you know what I worked for? Eleven dollars. Eleven dollars a week! And my wife, when she was going to give birth, we lived in one room. Just a shack. Then one day it burned down, our shack. Everything we owned was in that shack. My wife only had the dress she was wearing. And I only had the pants, the dirty pants, I was working in. We had nothing. I didn't own anything in Denver but a job. And I wasn't too sure of the job, either. I didn't like the city for myself, but also for my children. When they were old enough to go to school I decided to come back to my humble land. I wanted my children to know how to work with soil, with the land."

In a battered wheelbarrow Cleofas mixes a tubful of cement with his shovel. Then he pours the cement into the mold of old boards that shapes the foundation of his earth cellar. "To keep vegetables for the winter," he says.

The rows of chili and beans and corn in his fields are few. His ancient trees bear fruit that is no longer sweet. But the land is patient. "It waits until I need it."

Up on the high slopes of the mountains the autumn is gathering. Summer is dying. The bluish air of the coming frost bites at Cleofas' lips as he talks. He talks of plowing before the earth freezes. In his nostrils there is the odor of the coming snow. He knows it is too late to plow. He stands in his weedy and unseeded fields, thick with sagebrush and snakeweed and yellow stickleaf, and talks of plowing the stubborn earth nonetheless. He is a stubborn man.

A gust of mountain wind blows through the fields. It rustles the weeds. Cleofas looks up and lays his shovel down, squinting knowingly at the dark clouds that hover above the Blood of Christ Mountains.

"We better go in maybe," he says.

In the pleasant and warm house we sit and sip coffee, while the television set tries vainly to bring the news of the world outside the valley into the village parlor. The image is out of focus on the screen. Blurred soldiers are dying before the cameras.

"You think Cleofas is crazy!" he wryly says. "Who is crazy? Am

I crazy? In times of war it's prosperity all over the country. But as soon as the war stops, depression comes. And I feel that by owning my few acres of land, if war stops, I will have something to eat. I can survive without food from the supermarket. On the land there is always food. I am getting ready.

"During the depression the people of the cities starved," he says. "We had food. We did not starve, like the people of the cities. We had food enough to feed the birds."

The night wind comes down the mountain. It rattles the windows. When it is dark the wind sounds louder than in the daytime.

"I must go," I say.

Cleofas walks to the door with me. "There is a saying of our ancestors: 'Whoever sells his lands sells his mother,' " he says. "It's a true saying. Land is what keeps you and me and everybody else. That's why we value our land. That's why I stay on my land.

"Up in these mountains, these rough mountains, there is places that no human has touched. I have gone to a few. There is where there is peace, is quiet. And I believe there is where you get a touch of the Almighty God. Because it is clean.

"See where the land, it's messed up by humans? In these beautiful parks that the Forest Service creates for the tourists, how messy they are.

"I can take you to some areas in these beautiful mountains, these high mountains that we have, that no humans have touched, and you will love to stay there—forever."

Cleofas Vigil has written an ode to his land. He calls it, "Mother of All Life—The Earth":

> Ah, you who do not have false pride,
> Ah, brave companions,
> Though we have no money
> We travel hand in hand;
> Though barefoot we are happy
> With our belly heavy
> Full of green beans
> And gray Verdolagas.
> The poor man's heart rejoices

When the fields are green
With the delicious food
That never wearies the hungry;
The rounded tortillas
Prepared in every style,
Ah, what a tasty mouthful
The fields provide for us.
The sublime aroma
Of green chilis in the hot embers,
Cooked with gusto,
Ready to be plucked;
How it stirs the appetite
Of a tired chicano.
In the morning he awakes
And goes into his garden;
He quickly works up a sweat
When he sees his crops
Grow before his eyes;
It delights his heart,
He comes alive, knowing
The earth, his mother
Is going to feed him.
My brother this is your mother,
Mother, fertile and fruitful;
If anyone takes her from you
You will be an orphan;
And from whose breasts
Will you drink sweet milk,
Be it of goat,
Or be it of cow?
The earth is your food, and your mother:
I tell you once again.

PART ONE

Conquistador on a Motorcycle

The village of Antonchico is still. Not a goat goes out in the midday sun; it is too hot. Not a man walks on the street. The buzz of the flies and the whine of the supersonic jets are the only sounds in the white sky. Six men squat in the dust of the village. They talk, in whispers, of violent deeds that they intend to do to defend their ancestral lands and their manhood. They talk of murder. They talk, but not a man shifts an inch from his squat in the shadow of the adobe house.

"We are men of silent violence," says a farmer.

On a lazy old mare a young boy rides down the main street, the only street, of the village. The boy on the horse rides by in slow motion, as though he is asleep. The houses hide from the blazing sun. Even the gossiping women are sequestered behind the thick walls of adobe, for it is the time of siesta, and it is uncivilized to work, or walk, or talk loudly at the noon hour.

A priest squats in the dust beside the villagers. He is wearing an open shirt and dirty Western chinos. He balances himself expertly, so that the seat of his trousers is poised safely above the prickly sagebrush.

"It is so peaceful," I say to the priest.

"So is a volcano," he replies.

He is a hothead, this priest, so they say. I scoff at his intense words, but he merely smiles and says, "Do not be fooled by the silence."

The old farmer who squats beside us listens to our talk, but pretends not to hear. His eyes are alert as a small bird's and his face is innocent.

"He is peaceful," I say to the priest.

"In the village they say he has killed two men," the priest says matter-of-factly.

The old man gazes into my eyes with a kindly and distant look. He says nothing.

"Who did he kill?" I ask skeptically.

The priest whispers, "It is what they say. Some men tried to kill him. He killed two of them. Who knows?"

A young farmer who has heard this looks up. He breaks a twig in his hand and he jabs the broken ends into the earth, hard. "That is the way it is here," he says, then is silent once more.

"In the night I hear a rifle shot," the young farmer says, after a pause. He is answering a question no one has asked him. "And then there is this telephone call. A man says, 'If you don't watch your step we will kill your son.' He hangs up and they cut the telephone wire. My wife, she is frightened." His face is troubled by the memory. "That is how it is here."

"They cut my fences. And they steal two of my cows," says another farmer. He smiles with tight lips. "If they come again, I kill them."

A boy who has been silent among his elders—he is a student working in the village during the summer—says very seriously, "If it were up to me I would go to them with a gun and kill them. Probably I would do that."

Who are *they?* None of the villagers will say.

"I do not say who," says a third farmer. He is taller than the others, maybe stronger, with a pebbly face and hands made of bones. "But I tell you this," and his words are hard. "The Spanish people are angry now. Now all the Spanish people have a good rifle. I visit many villages and I tell you this. Everyone has a rifle now."

The old man among them speaks. He speaks in quiet Spanish that cannot be translated. What he says is something like this: They have taken our land and stolen it. They have taken our crops and stolen them. They have taken our manhood, and broken it. They have taken our Spanish language, and dirtied it. They have taken our children into their schools, and made them rude.

"We have been under the feets of so many of the stranger," the old man suddenly says in English.

"The stranger?" I ask.

"Yes," he says, "the stranger who came from the East. Who took our land. Who pushes us around. They have done dirty things to the people of these villages. They did it to my ancestors. They keep on doing it to me. And they think that they are going to do it to my sons and grandsons, but they have another think coming. I tell you they will fight."

"Now, we will all fight," the old man says.

Each man is lost in his own shadow. In the other villages do the men feel this way? No one will say. How can they tell me what they think in another village? Every village is different. "Is any man like any other man?"

"Who can speak for me?" a farmer says. "No one but me. That's who I speak for."

In the city the officials tell me that these village men are not "typical" of the men of Antonchico and that the men of Antonchico are not "typical" of the men of the villages. Some of the villagers are defeated, apathetic, and torn by self-anger and humiliation. Some of the villagers are easygoing, immune to the outside world, and tend to laugh off history. These things are more "typical" of the villagers' feelings, they say.

"Typical!" spits a farmer, when I tell him of this analysis. "You know who is typical? In the city *everybody* is typical, because you can't live in the city unless you are typical of everybody else."

"But not everybody is as angry as here."

"I am not angry." He laughs. "When I am angry I will not talk about it. Then it will be too late to talk. Angry? We are just thinking, how do you say, out loud? Yes, a man who talks about what he will do will not do it."

The farmer's words become a whisper. "We are not the black man. If we do something, we will not tell *you* about it first."

"What will you do?"

"Ah. Who knows?"

The haze of the sun diffuses the houses of the village. It looks unreal and faded. Quaint as a picturesque postcard the houses of Antonchico rise out of the adobe mud. But the adobe is cracking. Some of the houses are collapsing into the earth from which they emerged generations ago.

Hours of the afternoon fall upon the six men who squat and talk. It grows later, it is three o'clock. Who knows the time? In the sky above the village the mirage of time shimmers and is gone. The wrath of the squatting men evaporates in the sun, but they hardly notice it vanish, for they are watching the village come to life again, as it always does after the noon.

El Viejo, the oldest man, is whittling the statue of a saint. Or is it the head of J.F.K.? He uses a daggerlike knife, almost as his grandfather did. The children run barefoot, for their sneakers are under a bush. On the adobe walls the strings of red chili ripen in the sun. The chili is hung from a television wire. In the yards of the houses the goats are separated by fences of twigs and branches tied by nylon cord. The road has been paved. But it is full of holes. Now the village has three stores and a not-quite-new school and some of the adobes have tin roofs and the inevitable television antennas. Since the old days things have changed. But not much. The village still looks like a village in Old Mexico, not New Mexico.

Six hundred people lived here when the army of General Kearny conquered New Mexico, and today the number of villagers is about the same. The same families live in the same houses. The farmers plow the same fields their fathers, and grandfathers, and great-grandfathers, and great-great-grandfathers plowed.

The saying in the village is "*Lo Que Puede*"—That Which Can Be Is Enough—for this is the land of "*Poco Tiempo,*" the land of Pretty Soon, and the land of "*Que Importa?*"—What Does It Matter? The sun does not change, it merely turns. Nothing stirs the seasons of the sun but the Almighty—"As God Wills."

In a mountain village of southern Colorado near the New Mexico border there are turnstiles on the gates of the City Hall, to keep out the cows. The villagers say that when the king of Spain issued a royal land grant to their ancestors, hundreds of years ago, he ordained that the town plaza be a common pasture where every man's cows could graze freely. The highway has since been built through the village, and cows are rare on the highway, but the wishes of their ancestors must be obeyed. Cows are free to graze on any grass that is left on Main Street. If a cow is clever enough to get through the turnstiles on the lawn of the City Hall, that too is her pasture.

Ah, the sleepy villages of the Southwest. The life of the unhurried villagers is romantic to the dreamer. Most of all to the stranger.

Eighty years ago a Victorian dropout from Harvard wandered into these villages. He was enchanted by the land where "nature does little more than sleep." The romantic vision of Charles F. Lummis has since become one of the lovelier stereotypes of the Southwest. In his *The Land of Poco Tiempo*, written in 1884, he rhapsodized: " 'Picturesque' is a tame word for it. It is a picture, a romance, a dream, all in one. It is a land of quaint, swart faces, of Oriental dress and unspelled speech; a land where distance is lost and the eye is a liar."

Journeying to the land of enchantment from the old Trinity Parish in the Wall Street area of New York, where he was curate, the Reverend Ross Calvin was equally charmed by the villages, half a century later. The Episcopalian minister thought he had discovered a never-never land where "the motto of the people [is] mañana, mañana," and "where mañana is like the yesterdays." Calvin, in *The Sky Determines*, written in 1948, was sternly critical of the "unproductive indolence [that] flowers the quality that endears Mexicans to travelers, artists and writers—their quaintness." He was charmed, nonetheless. "Living among them, one grows at length to comprehend with compassion their backward indolence, their credulity and gaiety," he wrote. Where Lummis thought the villagers to be "dreamy," Calvin thought of them as "adorable."

Romantic dreams persist, as romantic dreams must, not merely in the idyls of the exiles from the East, on the travel posters, and in the fiestas for the tourists, but also in the dry scholarship of the social scientists, who need to dream too. The image of "the romantic, the picturesque, the charming" villagers of New Mexico has reappeared, as late as 1967, in the foreword written by Professor Joan Moore, Associate Director of the University of California's Mexican-American Study Project, to an otherwise realistic paper called *The Spanish Americans of New Mexico.*

"Let them dream their dreams," says a farmer when we talk of this. "When you sleep on a dirt floor you dream a different dream. It is not so much romantic."

Some of the villagers are starving. In the adobe huts the old people sit in the dark, with no electricity, no water, no food, waiting for "the welfare." Half of the families do not earn enough to reach the government-approved "poverty line." The farmers often work as migrants on the farms of the "strangers," for the village has lost more than two-thirds of its ancestral land to these "strangers." Many who own land do not farm at all. They are too poor to buy tractors or seed. They, too, are hungry. It is the cruelest irony to starve in farm country.

The village is too poor to afford a doctor. Or a dentist. In one village the sick have to go ninety miles to the nearest doctor. But the sick of Antonchico are more fortunate. A doctor comes once a week.

One of every two village families is poor in New Mexico, if they are Hispanos. So low is the income of these families that more than half —53.3 per cent in the rural areas and 57.9 per cent on the farms—earn less than the poverty level of $3,000 yearly.

In the rural regions there is "widespread physical and mental weakness, from hunger, malnutrition and poverty," admits Governor David Cargo. Poverty is endemic; but in nearby Mora County an unbelievable 68 per cent of the Hispano families exist below the poverty line. The New Mexico State Employment Security Commission, after surveying the six "hunger counties" designated by the National Citizens Board of Inquiry, reports the condition "shameful."

Rio Arriba County, in the mountain country, is a "pocket of hunger" so abysmal, the State Commission reports, that "the existing nutritional deficiencies, the need for dental, medical, correctional physical therapy, corrective eye lenses, and cases of retardation because of lack of improved home diets, are of major concern."

A school principal in Rio Arriba County tells the investigators that many students in his school say "the only full meal they eat" all day is the meager school lunch. He clinically notes that children are "fatigued" in school "because of their weak condition"; they are starving.

In the village of Ojo Caliente eye doctors do a random check of sixty-one schoolchildren. The Commission reports that fifty of the children are found to need eyeglasses but cannot afford them. Medical examinations are given to thirty of these poor children; fifteen are discovered to be in immediate need of medical attention, and three children are hospitalized at once. Half of the children "received clothing to continue in school."

Some of the children have such decayed teeth that they "cannot eat their school lunches," it is reported. Almost all of the village children show some signs of malnutrition.

In Taos County an educator reports a "problem of malnutrition" that he "compares [to] living conditions of some war-ravaged families [he had] seen in Korea."

Unemployment in the rural villages is so much an accepted fact of life that it often goes unreported. In the winter of 1965 the unemployment rate in Taos County, for example, was officially stated to have "decreased" to 17 per cent. But that winter an investigator for the State Employment Security Commission, David Sandoval, personally conducted a house-by-house survey of 887 adult villagers in Taos County, and found almost half of them, 431, were jobless, and "currently seeking work." They were "too proud" to report their lack of jobs, or did not see the point in bothering, or were ignored by the official statistics.

"Lack of employment was cited as a big factor in malnutrition," dryly comments the Albuquerque *Journal.*

One school nurse in Sandoval County tells of visiting the poor family of a schoolchild in a rural village who had hung a sign on the door of their house that simply said:

WE ARE HUNGRY

"We live in a conspiracy of silence," says Fecundo Valdez. He is a rural organizer in the mountain villages of New Mexico. One of that new breed of university graduates, wearing a Pancho Villa mustache and a dashing sombrero on whose brim he has pinned a "Grapes of

Wrath" button, Valdez travels the dirt roads to the hidden villages, for the agencies of the government and the universities. He comes from such a village himself.

"The people have a distaste, an anger, a hostility, to the things that have been done to them. But they say little," he says. "In the past these villages were not allowed to participate in real decision making. So they withdrew into their own circles, into silence. If you don't have the means to actively resist what is done to you, then what happens is that you become passively aggressive. It is a basic resistance. It may be dormant, it may be apathetic, but it may be harnessed.

"Silence is a way of resisting, you know," Valdez says. "It has been the way of the villages—until now."

The visitor who drives off U.S. Highway 84 into the village hears only the silence. He will think he has entered a valley of pastoral peace. He will not see the circle of men who squat in the dust of the adobes.

Even if he did, their low voices would be stifled in the dust, as silent as the heat. Now, in whispers, every man boasts of a feat of his fists. He tells of fights fought in the daylight in highway bars and in the dark of night on country roads, real and imaginary. Every man tries to outboast his neighbor, and succeeds. "In the mountains the people reflect the personality of the mountains," the priest says. "Life can be ruthless and violent in the mountains."

He tells a tale:

"In a village meeting there was a man who came from the government who spoke, and he promised the people work in a new factory that would soon be built.

"An old man in the back of the room, a very old man, got up. The old man said, 'You say you are going to bring us a factory. We don't even have a paved road. Why don't you bring us a paved road? Our people watch the TV. We see the four-lane highways in Santa Fe. We see our dirt road. We are not dumb dogs. So why do you talk to us like dumb dogs? We do not believe you.'

"The old man said, 'Listen to what we ask, don't tell us what we need. It may take arms, I think, before you people will listen to us.' "

And the young priest bows his head, upset by his recitation of the old man's words. "What the hell drives an old man to say a thing like that?"

"Here, in northern New Mexico, the people of the villages react slower than the people of the ghettos," Valdez says. "The distances are greater. The problem of communication from village to village is more difficult. But if something isn't done to help the rural villagers, it will happen here.

"You will not see riots," Valdez says. The farmer will not burn down his own village, his own house, his own fields! Valdez nods: "It might be the forests. In the ghettos it is the slums that go up in flames. Here it might be forests of the government. Lots of people are talking about this. If they can't get access to their grazing lands in the [National] forests, they say: 'We will set fire to the forests.' "

The six men squatting in the dust stir. Such talk in a public place makes them uneasy. When I repeat these thoughts of Valdez there is no response.

"We are not people that believe in violence," the old man says. "I suppose that's why we have been pushed around so much. The Anglos might think we are coward. But the Spanish-speaking people have shown how coward they have been on the battlefields, in the First World War, the Second World War, Korea, and now Vietnam. We are not coward. But we are not people of violence. I hope that will never happen. For myself, I don't believe in that.

"I don't know, but the people in the future might have to get violent."

The young farmer inscribes a circle in the dust with his twigs; his circle grows smaller and smaller until he jabs the sticks into its heart, like two spears. No one says another word. Even the young and volatile priest is still.

One man arises. In the circle of squatting men, he has spoken the least, for he is the spokesman of the land-grant heirs of the village of Antonchico—the man they call H.H.

"We are a little angry," he says softly.

H. H. Mondragon is a sparse man, with a slight body. It is difficult to know what he has been thinking, for his face is somber and his lips are smiling. Nothing about him seems imposing, not even his height as he stands; yet there is a dignity in his bearing, and the men seem to respect him.

"I will tell you why we are angry here," he says. "Come to La Loma, to my house." It is all he says.

Striding off, he mounts a bright-red motorcycle, like a young man. The Japanese motorcycle, new and shining in the sun, was given him by his son, the one who is a priest. H. H. Mondragon revs the engine until it roars, professionally, dons his blue crash helmet with a modernized thunderbird on its crest, tightens the leather strap under his chin, and goes thundering off down the dirt road. The descendant of a conquistador on a Japanese motorcycle.

He shatters the silence. The dust rises, like a storm, in the village of Antonchico.

11 The Black Swords of H. H. Mondragon

The blackened blades of H. H. Mondragon's swords are crossed on the adobe wall of his cottage. On the wide and thick blades are written the words "Charomagno" and "Bonaparte," for Charlemagne and Napoleon. In the crux of the crossed swords is an offering of palm leaves from the Mass of Palm Sunday. Christ's pale face gazes at these instruments of death and resurrection from across the room.

In the house of an ordinary farmer these swords might be an incredible sight. Not here; they seem entirely proper to this gentleman who graciously welcomes his guest with a diffident bow. "Forgive the house of a man who lives alone," he says—a needless apology, for his rooms are as neat and fastidious as he. He is dressed for the occasion in the formal Spanish tradition of the West, wearing a bright-red cowboy shirt and highly polished workboots.

H. H. Mondragon excuses himself; in a moment he returns bearing a tray of coffee cups that he sets down on a wooden crate.

"Come, seat yourself. Who can have words without coffee?"

When I lean back in the chair an annoying fly buzzes in my hair. Looking over my shoulder I see that the fly is a revolver hanging from the hatrack in its holster. On the wall is a hunting rifle.

He sees that I am uneasy about the guns, especially the revolver snout that nuzzles my ears.

"Rabbits," H. H. Mondragon says. "It is an old gun, but faster than the rabbits."

"And the swords?"

"The swords are memories."

H. H. Mondragon is a man who lives in history, as some men live in dreams. Not a dream of the past, for the past lives in him. History is one of his few luxuries. It is his indulgence in dignity. Like the black swords, it is visible on his walls, it is in his bones, it is even under his bed. Kneeling on his adobe floor, he gropes in the dark under his bed.

"What are you looking for?"

"I will show you why the people are angry." He kneels, cursing in the dark. "Here I have the deeds. Somewhere."

"The deed to your land?"

"Our land!" says H. H. Mondragon. "They have taken our land away—one-quarter of a million acres they have taken from us in this valley. It is the truth. The President of the United States signed our deed himself." He at last finds what he is searching for. "You will see," he says.

Under the high old-fashioned bed, with its curlicued headboards of iron, there is an ancient trunk. He bends low and tugs at it. The trunk is heavy with the burden of his memories. In the trunk are faded photographs and mildewed newspapers. He takes out a folder mottled by weather and age. On the cover are the words:

ANTON CHICO LAND GRANT DOCUMENTS
1822 = 1878
PROPERTY OF H. H. and R. A. MONDRAGON

He fondles them with his fingers and reluctantly hands them to me.

"History of our land," he says.

"But why hide them?"

"We are liars they say. We dream it. We imagine it is our land. Here are the proofs," he says. "So, I have to guard them."

"Under your bed?"

"I sleep with the revolver beside my head sometimes. No one will come here."

The documents are old court records decorated with the gaudy penmanship of the 1800's in the scrolls of a quill pen.

One of the oldest papers tells of the coming of the earliest Mexican farmers to the valley of Antonchico. It is dated the 22nd of January in the year of 1822. That day "Salvador Tapia and sixteen others" arrived with a land grant in their saddlebags, but were "driven off by Indians," it says. Undaunted, the settlers returned in the spring, and the antique document tells of how on the 2nd of May the "Governor Melgaris is purported to have granted the land to Manuel Rivera and thirty-six men, and directed Manuel Baca, the Constitutional Justice of El Vado, to place the parties in possession, which was done. . . ." The land grant of Antonchico is then marked "APPROVED" by the "Surveyor General's Office, Santa Fe, July 15, 1859. William Pelham, Surveyor General."

Stone by stone the land grant of Antonchico was measured. The Mexican Government had awarded these farmers, who dared venture into what was then Comanche territory, a small kingdom of 378,570 and a half acres. Exactly.

The ancient trunk of H. H. Mondragon is a modern Pandora's box of real-estate myth. In its musty recesses is a curious document of six and a half long and single-spaced pages that details the vastness of the land grant. Inch by inch, measured by the links of a chain, the acreage is itemized. Walk, the deed says, "seven miles, eight link [of chain], to a sandstone, thirty-six by twenty-four by five inches in size, marked A.C.E.B., on facing grant, with stone mound, the same being due South of Sabino Springs, two chains and twenty links from a cottonwood twelve inches in diameter, bear north nineteen degrees west, ninety links distance a cottonwood, thirteen inches in diameter . . ." and so on and on and on.

In the end it proclaims: "In Testimony Whereof, I Chester A. Arthur, President of the United States, have caused these letters to be made Patent, and the Seal of the General Land Office to be hereunto affixed. Given under my hand at the City of Washington this twenty seventh day of March in the year of Our Lord one thousand eight hundred and eighty three, and of the Independence of the United States, the one hundred and seventh, by the President Chester A. Arthur." And it is signed with a flourish.

"So I do not lie, you see."

"It is impressive."

"Pieces of paper!" he laughs in disgust. "What good are these old papers? What happened to this land grant is not written on pieces of paper."

"Where is it written?"

"In my blood," H. H. Mondragon says, as to a child. "The land has a long history of blood. I do not know it all. No one knows it; the history of blood cannot be written on pieces of paper. The lawyers of the Anglos think history is pieces of paper. So I keep these deeds."

"Who knows the history of blood?"

"Listen, I will tell you a little," says H. H. Mondragon. "I know a little of one little man in one little village."

Coronado passed this way. It is known that he came into the valley of Antonchico in 1541. The conquistador, a young man not quite thirty and wearing plumed armor overlaid with gold, led his motley army of 256 Spaniards, 1,000 Mexican Indians, and an African—"the most brilliant company ever assembled in the Indies to go in search of new lands"—through the "Journey of Death," onto the buffalo plains of the Comanches, and into the valley that spring. He was a medieval soldier, of whom it was said he raped the Indians' land and seduced the Indians' women. He left a trail of blood, the Spaniards' blood, in the waters of the Pecos River and the red clay of Antonchico. Seeking the fabled Seven Cities of Cibula, the General Francisco Vásquez de Coronado found himself instead on the prosaic prairies of Kansas. That discovery so disheartened him that he hurried back, through the valley of Antonchico, and into history.

The hunters of the Comanche tribe pitched their summer camps on these riverbanks while hunting the herds of buffalo that covered the plains to the east. Coronado was guided by these Comanche trails. Without these his soldiers might have died. It was brutal country of deathly deserts and bleak mountains and fierce suns that shone without mercy on the armor of the explorers. Men were known to drink their own blood to wet their lips.

Was it the conquistadors who christened the mountains—the Blood of Christ, the Sangre de Cristo? It is not known. But the old villagers say that long, long ago the village of Antonchico was known as Sangre de Cristo.

It is known that when Don Juan de Oñate settled and seeded the Kingdom of Nuevo Mexico in 1598, he too journeyed through the valley of Antonchico. He too led a pilgrimage in which the Indians outnumbered the Spaniards, though history forgets this. A penitent of the Third Order of Saint Francis, he was as cruel as the land. He once ordered that every Indian man of the Acoma Pueblo who fought his benediction have his right foot cut off. Yet, de Oñate brought the first Spanish farmers to New Mexico.

Whether there was a Mondragon in the bravado army of Coronado, or in the agony of de Oñate, is unknown. H. H. Mondragon has no ancestral memory of it, though it may be. It is known that not long after, the Mondragon family entered the history of Nuevo Mexico officially on a piece of paper. In the Archives of the Indies in Seville, Spain, the brittle papers are inscribed with the name of a Juan Alonso Mondragon, who in the year of 1629 rode as escort on the wagon trains of supplies that journeyed into the Kingdom of Nuevo Mexico. He became a captain in the king's army and later the high sheriff of Santa Fe. And in the National Archives of Mexico there is mention of a Juan de Mondragon, who may or may not have been the same man, who was Regent of Santa Fe in 1637—a "poor man" it was written of him even then.

When the Pueblo Indian revolt of 1680 drove out the Spaniards, he was an old man. He fled with the refugees as he had come, in poverty, a conquistador of dubious conquests.

His son, Sebastian Mondragon, who was a native-born New Mexican, returned with the Reconquest, in 1689, when the army of Don Diego de Vargas recaptured the land and resettled the burned-out villages. Sebastian's intimacy with the life and languages of the Indians he grew up among earned him the difficult job of interpreting for the triumphant army of de Vargas.

The young man looked Indian. A description of Sebastian Mondragon in 1681 as a man of "medium build, swarthy complexion, with black hair" might be that of the twin of H. H. Mondragon in 1968.

"I think there is Spanish and Indian blood in my veins," says H. H.

Mondragon. "Some blood runs thin. One grandfather of mine was French, but that hardly tells. My grandmother, who I remember well, very well, had black hair to her waist and black eyes. She must have had much of Indian blood.

"Some blood runs thick. My Indian blood is thick, I think."

The irony of Sebastian's intimacy with the Indians was that in the midst of his wedding feast, on December 27, 1693, the Tanos Indians decided to join the festivities by revolting once again against the dancing Spaniards in the old plaza of Santa Fe. Poor Sebastian and his bride barely survived their wedding day.

After that the Mondragons left town. In the early 1700's, the family sought solace in the cloistered mountain villages of Pojoaque and Santa Cruz. When the new government of Mexico sought to exercise the independence it had won from the Empire of Spain, in 1824, by imposing a land tax, the villagers rebelled. Taxes on their sacred lands? What sacrilege! The Chimayo Revolt of 1837 erupted in the very villages where the Mondragons had gone seeking peace; there are still Mondragons living in Chimayo. In an almost bloodless uprising, the Hispano farmers and Pueblo Indians defeated the lackadaisical army of the Mexican Governor, Albino Pérez. His Excellency, in fleeing the battle of Santa Cruz, was captured by the Indians of the Santo Domingo Pueblo. And his captors cut off his head and sent the trophy by special messenger to the victorious rebels. Encouraged by the headless state of affairs, "the rabble of mixed bloods," as one historian called them, marched on the capitol of Santa Fe, occupied it, and installed their own governor, an Indian of Taos, José Gonzales.

It was one of the few times in American history that armed rebellion of the poor overthrew a government. And it was perhaps the only time that an Indian governed the equivalent of a state.

Among the rebels were the Mondragons. "We always have been a stubborn family," says H. H. Mondragon. "I was born stubborn, too. Maybe it is my Spanish and Indian blood."

When the rebels were overwhelmed by the successive onslaughts of the Mexican Army of General Manuel Armijo and the United States Army of General Stephen Kearny, they withdrew into their villages. Not for long, however. The Revolt of Taos broke out in 1847. Once again the Hispano farmers and Pueblo Indians joined arms, this time in opposition to their newest conquerors, and killed the newly appointed American Governor, Charles Bent, in the Governor's Mansion. The United States Army ended the rebellion when it besieged and leveled the Catholic Church—the Mission of San Geronimo (Saint Jerome)—and the Taos Pueblo, where the insurgents were thought to be hiding. In truth, the revolt of 1847 and that of 1837 had been secretly led by some of the young Spanish priests in the villages. Father José Martínez of Taos was the best known, but there were many more rebels in robes of the Church.

Leaders of the rebellion were executed. "The Spanish and Indian people hung together," says Fecundo Valdez. "Literally, they were hung by the neck."

It was out of this tumult that the family of the Mondragons came into the valley of Antonchico.

Where the Pecos River spurts out of the Blood of Christ Mountains it twists onto the treacherous dry plains to Texas. The red water flows swift and shallow through the alkaline flats of the Llano de Estacado, the treeless and stark plains that early explorers named "The American Sahara," for the wastes of the Llano stretch upon a plateau of sixty thousand square miles. It is a country unto itself. Captain Randolph Marcy, who surveyed the terrain for the United States Army in the 1840's, declared it the "great Sahara of North America." He despaired of the "illimitable desert prairie," where "even the savages dare not venture to cross . . . except at two or three places where they know water can be found."

The Llano was the highway of the conquistadors, the hideout of the Comancheros, the battlefield of the Texans, and the new home of the Mondragons. No wonder the Hispanos named it the Llano de Estacado—literally, The Flat Plains Staked Out for Fighting Duels.

Into the Llano, a few years after the farmers of Antonchico settled on their land grant, came the Texans. The Republic of Texas had decided in 1836 that all the land east of the Rio Grande—half of New Mexico—was really part of Texas; and that included the village of Antonchico. When the villagers ignored their annexation, the Texas Legislature went further, voting in a Joint Resolution of both Houses in 1842 that the boundaries of Texas were hereby extended across all of New Mexico, to include upper and lower California, Arizona,

Sonora, and Chihuahua, and large parts of the Mexican states of Tamalulipas, Coahuila, Sinaloa, and Durango. In all, the Republic of Texas had grown by 500 million acres in one Joint Resolution. It legalized the fantasy of the President of Texas with the wonderful name of Mirabeau Buonaparte Lamar, who in his inaugural address of 1838 had envisioned Texas as stretching "to the Pacific and away to the Southwest as far as the obstinacy of the enemy may render it necessary for the sword to make the boundary." Old Sam Houston, who was President of Texas in 1842, when the fantasy was voted, vetoed it as "visionary" at that time.

The villagers of Antonchico heard the rumors of war and corralled their sheep and daughters. In fact, the army of Texas had invaded the Llano in 1841, five years before the war against Mexico. General McCleod led that invasion to establish "commercial relations" with Mexico. He attempted to cross the Llano, "well armed with artillery." But his men nearly died of thirst and hunger, and the army of General Armijo easily defeated the invaders. Once captured, the remnants of the Texas army were led under arrest into the village of Antonchico. Old-timers recalled later how the village "boys climbed the corn cribs and brought down ears of corn for the hungry Texans."

Less gracious was the Hispanos' welcome for the army of General Kearny, when the conquest of New Mexico was begun in earnest.

"It is one of the big myths of American history that General Kearny came to New Mexico and took it without firing a shot," says Fecundo Valdez, the rural organizer. "You can still find older people here who can relate the experiences of their fathers and grandfathers who fired shots. In the town of Las Vegas there was fighting. In the village of Mora the people burned the village down and fled to the mountains. In Taos, you remember, Governor Bent was killed.

"History is a lie if you know only one side. The people in the villages resisted where they could."

The guerrilla warfare divided New Mexico for years thereafter. So intense were the tensions between the villagers and the invaders that for four years the Territory of New Mexico remained under the military rule of the United States Army.

After General Kearny marched his army of the West into New Mexico, he responded to the hostility of the Hispanos by lecturing to them. In the village streets of Las Vegas, he climbed on top of an adobe building, and to the villagers—most of whom understood only Spanish—he said in English, "We come among you for your benefit, not for your injury." Later the General implored the people of Santa Fe, "We come as friends, to better your condition. . . . You are now become American citizens. . . . I am your governor."

Juan Bautista Vigil, the Mexican Governor, as courteously as he could, replied to the General, "Do not find it strange if there has been no manifestation of joy and enthusiasm in seeing this city occupied by your military forces. To us the power of the Mexican Republic is dead. No matter what her condition she was our mother. What child will not shed abundant tears at the tombs of his parents?

"We are aware of the unfortunate condition of the Poles," Governor Vigil said, alluding to Czarist Russia's conquest of Poland, an allusion that Kearny's dragoons from Missouri must have thought peculiar.

And yet what could not be done by war alone was at last won in the violent peace that came in the war's wake. The cowboys were to conquer the land where the soldiers had only occupied it.

The huge cattle herds in western Texas had by 1870 so depleted the prairies that the seas of grass were eroded by dry gullies. Droughts and blizzards forced the ranchers to seek rangelands further westward. "With range growing scarce efforts were made to open new lands to grazing," wrote Edward Everett Dale in his *Cow Country.* And then, in 1875, the barbed-wire fence was brought to Texas.

Barbed wire, recalls the old Hispano folk saying, marked the beginning of the end of the unfenced freedoms of the West, and the death of Hispano society: *"Cuando vino el alambre, vino el hambre"* ("With the coming of the wire, hunger came").

Cowboys riding into the Llano were on their last roundup. When the cattle entered the unfenced sheep pasture of the Hispanos of the Llano, one family, the de Bacas, had flocks of more than one million sheep, and they fought the intruders with a small army. The range wars that erupted between the sheepherders and the cattlemen were in reality battles between Hispanos and Anglos; in a sense these battles were an aftermath of the War against Mexico; and in some ways they were bloodier. It was guerrilla war, not merely range war.

"Sheepmen?" says a villager. "That meant us, the Spanish, the

Mexicans. In the old days they say we smell like sheep, we act like sheep, we make love with sheep, we are sheep."

"That is because they were wolves," says H. H. Mondragon.

One of these guerrilla wars was the Lincoln County War in New Mexico, which lasted from 1876 to 1878. The hostilities were halted by the United States Army, under the rule of Governor Lew "Ben Hur" Wallace, but before it was over, the hired gunmen of the ranchers had hanged or shot dozens of Hispano vaqueros and Anglo cowboys, burned hundreds of barns and farm buildings, and ravaged whole towns. President Hayes finally had to call out the federal troops to restore order and ensure the victory of the cattlemen. The Lincoln County War shaped a myth when it catapulted a paranoiac killer into our folklore—William H. Bonney, known more affectionately as Billy the Kid. He had been the hired gun of the ranchers.

The Kid came to Antonchico afterward. He was just one more cowboy passing through, but villagers remember that he did stay long enough to steal a few horses before he was chased to Stinking Springs, where he was captured and killed.

As always, the village of Antonchico was on the crossroads of history. Will Hale, a cowboy chronicler of the range wars in Lincoln County, where he fought with Billy the Kid, tells of his riding "to a Mexican town named Antonchico" looking for a village to shoot up to relieve their tensions.

"We had not been there long until about twenty Bar Z boys came in and shot the town up and ran most of the Mexicans out," Hale writes. "The Bar Z was a cattle brand and their ranch was close to the town. Then the men they had were Americans and the people said it was a common thing for them to shoot the gambling house full of holes. It was funny to me and Dixon [a cattleman] to see them shoot around the town."

The killing of Mexicans was an even more popular sport than shooting up a town. Once when his father, a rancher in West Texas, was hunting for Mexicans, Hale recalls in his book *Twenty-four Years a Cowboy and Rancher,* "I wrote father a letter telling him I wanted to come out and help him shoot Mexicans and Indians, but father wrote me back a letter saying it would be better shooting crawfish than Indians and Mexicans."

Historian A. M. Gibson, in homage to the naïveté and honesty of this reminiscence of the "uninhibited West," writes, "Killing a Mexican was like killing an enemy in the independent war that apparently each Texan waged, and since it was a conflict with historic scores to settle, the killing carried a sort of immunity with it. . . . Just as the mores of frontier folk, pastoral and agrarian, sanctioned a free destruction of Indians, so the mores of the border must have done the same in regard to Mexicans."

One by one the sheepmen lost their pastures, and if they fought back they lost their lives. It was then that the villagers returned to the ancient tactics of the Indians. Some of them became Comancheros.

Men who had been Comancheros were, until recently, still alive to tell of those days. "El Cuate" was one of these. He was the ranch cook on the de Baca estates, and in her *We Fed Them Cactus* the daughter of that noble family, Fabiola Cabeza de Baca, recalls this tough and belligerent old-timer who "was so much part of the land of the Llano that he might just have grown from the soil." The aging vaquero, with his leathery skin and long red mustache, relived the rough days of land wars.

"It took courage to face the Llano," El Cuate said. His nickname, El Cuate, meant A Man Who Cannot Be Equaled; and his recitation demonstrated why he had been nicknamed. "The Comanche Indians had been friendly with the *ciboleros*" (a diminutive of vaquero, meaning little Mexican bulls), the old man said. "The Comanches resented the moving of the Texans and the other stockmen with their cattle into their land. Stealing cattle was a means of revenge which the Indians used against the cattle owners. The Comanches would meet us at our camps along the buffalo country. There we exchanged our goods [rifles] for cattle and horses that the Indians had driven from the unfenced lands of the cattle kings."

"The Americans around were the real racketeers in the business," El Cuate complained. "They did the buying from us and would drive the loot to Colorado, Kansas, Nebraska, and California, where they sold it at a great profit."

Banditry did not, however, halt the herds. The fences of the cattlemen moved westward.

In the village of Antonchico and the villages nearby the farmers cut the fences. The cattlemen brought the barbed wire with them; and when their lawyers filed deeds for the open range, they fenced it in. Wearing white hoods over their faces and riding their fastest horses, the villagers would go forth at night not only to cut fences, but to burn corrals and barns. In the mornings the cattlemen awoke to "miles and miles of their pasture and farmland fences cut into fragments."

The villagers who fought back were branded "bandidos." If they were sheepherders lacking in legal guile and were caught, as they usually were, justice was so swift that they were often hanged with their hats on. The *Weekly New Mexican* of Santa Fe printed a typically casual notice of such a hanging in the spring of 1872:

"One Pablo Padilla, who has been for a long time engaged in stealing stock, etc., was overtaken on Saturday by a fit of remorse (or something else) and hung himself on a tree near Peralta."

"Los Gorras Blancas," the hooded night riders were called—the White Caps. When they rode out on a raid in some villages they prayed at a lay mass, as was fitting, for their costumes were based on the hooded robes of the Spanish Inquisition of the sixteenth century.

On the Llano some of the villagers founded "Los Caballeros de Labor," The Gentlemen of Labor. They organized a clandestine political party, "El Partido del Pueblo"—The Party of the People—to support, by day, the peasant army of Minutemen, who fought by night. Some of the Hispanos who sought to compromise with the Anglos, to re-establish peace, founded their own party, the Union Party. Life in the villages became tense and communities divided. The *corrido* singers sang: "They divided you within."

In the village of Antonchico the night riders were among the boldest, they say; for year by year the farmers were losing the land grant. "We lost it," Mondragon says.

"What happened to the land?" I ask.

"It's gone. It's washed away. Someone else got it," he says. "The strangers have bought it away, leased it away, stolen it away, swindled it away. Our own people are so poor sometimes they have to sell their land for the candles and a coffin when someone dies. Land for candles and a coffin! Is that right?"

He stands up and he walks to the doorway. He gazes out at his "garden," as he calls his land. The farm is small, but it is the only inheritance that he has left of the history of his family, and he talks about it as though it was his child.

The courtyard is a quagmire of blood-red clay, for it has rained heavily in the night. His battered pickup truck is splattered with drops of the red clay. So is his new Japanese motorcycle. The red rivulets of clay are trickling between the bean plants. It is as though the earth is bleeding.

"Whenever it rains it is like this," he says. "The rain washes the land clean. My garden is small, but it is green. How beautifully green it is after a rain. If I had enough water and enough land, how beautifully green I would make it.

"A few years ago this was still open range," he says. "Every man could run his cattle—he just turned them loose. Every man could plow wherever he could water. Then the United States Government started the money loans to the strangers. And the strangers began to buy up our cattle and lease our lands. When we opened our eyes our land was leased. The strangers had it all.

"If we had our land we wouldn't need no welfare, no OEO, no Community Action Programs. We want our land back. It's our land.

"Some say it is time for the White Caps again. Some say we must become Los Gorras Blancas again. I hope not. We have legal ways. We have lawyers. We have everything but justice." He stands looking at his "garden." "Who will do justice?"

III The Stones of the Poor

On the little hill of La Loma not far from the village of Antonchico there is an old schoolhouse of stone. It has stood for one hundred years or more on the windy hilltop. With thick stone walls and a bell tower on its peaked roof, it was once a fortress where the villagers sought refuge from the raiding Comanches and invading Texans. The schoolhouse has been empty for years. Ever since the village schools were consolidated it has been unused. Horses graze in the schoolyard.

The men of the villages, illiterate men, now have occupied the schoolhouse.

Stone by stone they are building a new kind of school. It will be a school where the poor villagers will teach each other. Unlike "the school of the stranger" this one will "belong to us," they say; and so they are building it with their own hands.

"We dig the stone, by hand. We cut the stone, by hand. We lift the stone, by hand," H. H. Mondragon says. "Sometimes it takes two men to lift a stone, it is so heavy."

There is cruelty in a stone. Hewn from the hills, by hand, and lugged by oxen in the old days, and nowadays by pickup truck, the stone is the bone of the earth and resists the hands of men. Yet the hands of these villagers have outwitted the stones before by joining hands.

"I always say we have to work together," says H. H. Mondragon. "Now, with these stones, we have no choice. We have no machines. We have just our hands."

"Nature is a wise teacher," the old farmer says.

"Our old schoolhouse has lasted forever, until now," says Piácomo Ortega, a vigorous young farmer who is the elected director of the La Loma school. "We want to build well. So the new school lasts as long as the old one did."

"These stones will last forever," H. H. Mondragon assures him.

In the schoolhouse the "students" are farmers and so are the teachers. Some of the old men have never been inside a classroom before. The young men, sons of farmers, have come to teach their fathers. One of the young men has returned to the village from the university. He says, "I am learning more than I teach."

"Why did you come to a village school?" he is asked.

"School? It is not just a school. It is one battle in our fight for self-determination. *La Raza arriba!*" the university student says. "Our people arise!"

On the scaffolding of the school they are building the villagers sit with workboots caked with red clay and study. The lesson for today may be carpentry, or village power politics, or use of an electric saw, or citizenship, or how to run a cooperative store. A classroom may be anywhere. There are hammers in the classroom, instead of books. "How do you spell hammer? In English? In Spanish?" There are boxes of medicines, shovels, tape recorders, and movie screens; for these are the textbooks of a guerrilla war against ignorance.

"If you fight poverty with education you have to fight whatever and whoever keeps you poor," says Piácomo Ortega. "Education cannot lie. Education cannot serve the hypocrite."

"Revolutionary!" writes the local newspaper.

The schoolhouse is besieged, once more. Not this time by the Indians and the Texans, but by the respectable citizens of the village. Curses and accusations are hurled in village meetings. The local newspaper at Santa Rosa has charged that "revolutionary" agitators have come into the quiet villages to "upset the status quo." Death threats have been made, the villagers say.

José Tenerio, in his slouch hat and worn workclothes, is teaching three men and a small boy how to mix mortar for stone masonry. The stones are his textbooks. The lesson he is teaching seems to be: if you want a new school in your village then learn how to build it yourself. His pupils will graduate with honors if the roof they build does not fall in.

"Our people have to help themselves," says Alex Mercure, who directs the statewide Home Improvement Education Program—HELP—a self-help and self-education project for rural villages that guides the work at La Loma and fifty other villages. "If you want to help people, let them tell you what they need. Let them decide; never impose your needs on them. It won't work."

"Farm workers have to tell you what they want," Mercure says, "and they have to learn how to do that, whatever it is, by themselves."

Even as they work, they study. They work two hours for every hour they study, for studying is the harder labor to these farmers. They earn one dollar an hour for going to school—thirty dollars a week. They are men of the earth, practical men, and what they learn to do, they do. What good is education to them if it is not of use to them?

"You can't plant seeds with talk," Mercure says.

In the village of Antonchico "the students" have opened a cooperative store, where they practice what they have been taught. "LOWER PECOS VALLEY FARMERS–CONSUMERS COOP STORE INC." says the sign on the old adobe. Inside are a few shelves of meager canned goods, sacks of flour, soda pop, and tobacco; by the screen door an archaic cash register; and at the roadside is an old-fashioned gas pump, circa 1930. The poorest of the villagers come to buy, and hesitantly join the Coop. It costs $15 a family. But everything sells for pennies less than elsewhere in the village; gas is five cents less per gallon.

One farmer, in shabby overalls, comes in with his welfare check. He owes almost the whole amount to a merchant in town for last month's groceries; but he pays his $15 to join the Coop, half a week's subsistence, before going off to pay his debt.

"I am always in debt," he says. "Now maybe I can be free of debt?"

The merchants are furious. "Socialistic" is their epithet. The Abercrombie family, whose store has been the largest in the village for nearly a century, charges that the Coop is "destructive" of the "established businesses." So does the Santa Rosa *News*, the "official paper" of the City of Santa Rosa, County of Guadalupe, New Mexico, that editorializes: ". . . it seems obvious that they [those who run the Coop] are dedicated to upsetting the status quo in Anton Chico, in the hope of getting what they call a better deal for the area's poor people." Federal antipoverty funds are being used to support this "disturbing new element" of "idealistic firebrand[s]." The editorial charges that the villagers had "every right" to run a Coop, but were they not taking "unfair advantage" by letting VISTA volunteers (who draw $7 weekly expense money from federal funds) watch the store "in direct competition with local Anton Chico business?"

"One night I think they will try to take our Coop and our school apart, stone by stone," says Piácomo Ortega.

Every village has its general store. In Antonchico it is "the Abercrombie place." The Abercrombies established their first mercantile store in the village. The four generations of the family have since been the local benefactors and bankers, merchants and mercenaries, patriarchs and pariahs. The emporium of the family is a treasure house of dry goods and foodstuffs and hardware and farm equipment. Amid the transistor radios and saddles can be found all the needs of the farmers. The Abercrombies not only retail and wholesale the scenery, but help many a village family through the rough winter, with neighborly credit. Some say the merchants have helped the village survive. And some say it is the merchants who have kept the village poor.

The small-town merchant family reigns like benevolent merchant princes. Patriarchs are hated, as well as envied. In the village they point with anger to the family ranch of five thousand acres where they live like country squires. Where did they get all that land, when we have none? they say.

Inside the schoolhouse there are violent voices; the Abercrombies have come to investigate the curious doings of the farmers of La Loma. The merchants are members of the Board of Directors of the village's War on Poverty agency, the Community Action Program. Led by David Abercrombie, they question, a bit nervously, what the farmers are up to:

Merchant: I understand you have a crop program. For what purpose?

Farmer: The purpose of this program is to teach this people a little more about farming.

Merchant: If and when you have any produce from this crop program, how will it be disposed of?

Farmer: The seed was bought by the people, so the produce goes to the people. And the produce will be sold, at a minimal price, for the benefit of the people.

Merchant: To whom?

Farmer: To the people.

Merchant: Who's selling it? Will these farmers sell it?

Farmer: If we can farm something besides a little alfalfa we can make a little money.

Listening to the voices, Piácomo Ortega and H. H. Mondragon grin at one another. "It is a tape recording," Ortega says. "Last month we had that meeting, a fight. I said, 'I like you all on tape so I can show your intention is to undermine any project we have for the poor.' "

H. H. Mondragon says, "The merchants did not come because of our crops. But because of our Coop store. I was on our local Community Action Program board, and the merchants didn't care what the poor did, at first. They got interested when we started the Coop. They wanted to keep things tight in the village. They are rich men who don't need poverty programs.

"They can't eat the hay, but they won't let the horse eat it," he says.

Saying the folk saying in Spanish—the villagers have a proverb for all occasions, but a Spanish proverb can be said only in Spanish—H. H. Mondragon translates his words reluctantly, saying, "Of course, this I cannot translate."

"Now we have two Community Action Program boards," he says. "Theirs and ours."

In the gentler era of the old *patrón* this dispute would never have happened. The welfare of the poor villagers, before there were any community action and county welfare programs, was the responsibility of the village itself, of the *patrón*.

The most esteemed, often the wealthiest, and at times the wisest man in the village, the *patrón* ruled neither by election nor by inheritance, but by the consensus of the villagers. He was counselor, godfather, spokesman, and even priest to the villagers. He was "expected to be generous, hospitable, brave, courageous," writes Dr. Clark Knowlton, director of the University of Utah's Center for the Study of Social Problems, who lived for some years in northern New Mexico. "He settled disputes between families, provided employment, assisted the poor and helpless, called out the villagers for communal endeavors, arranged for care of the church—later the school—and sponsored village fiestas."

He was known as El Jefe, the Chief. The *patrón* has been compared to a lord of feudal Spain. But in the villages of the Southwest the comparison is dubious. The *patrón* was not the master of serfs, nor was his house a castle; it was more likely a simple adobe. Unlike the elegant dons of the haciendas of Old Mexico the village leader was not a great landowner; he had no awesome power of life and death.

The old-timers talk of village life as a unity of communal Christianity and fierce individuality. Both of these tend to nullify the stereotype of the *patrón.* He was more probably like an Aztec lord or Apache chief. In personal matters his power was that of a wise father, and in political matters his voice was that of a tribal chief, or leader of a familial band. Whatever power he held could be taken from him by the unspoken consensus of the villagers—as in an Indian tribe. Even his title had to be renewed by deeds, or he lost his position of respect.

Later, the old-style *patrón* was replaced by the *jefe político.* His prestige has been traduced to that of a rural ward heeler, or local sheriff, for his power comes from outside the village; it was based on the political system of "the stranger."

The merchants have sought to become El Jefe. Most of them Anglos, some of them Texans, they have aggressively tried to assume the prestige and power of the *patróns,* if not their benevolence, not in the traditional manner, but through the commercial means they know best, by extending credit and becoming the English-speaking middlemen for the Hispano villagers. They are the commercial *patróns.*

"The *patrón* system has been acculturated," says Alex Mercure. Nowadays the *patrón* "works within the Anglo's structure and the Anglo values. He buys loyalty," as Mercure puts it. "Like the traditional *patrón* his attitude toward people is one of condescension. He treats them that way, and they react that way."

In one village the merchants buy cedar posts from the farmer for 25 cents and sell them for one dollar. The villagers complain, but they feel obligated to sell to the merchant, for they are indebted to him, and fear to "insult" him, thereby incurring his anger.

"Last summer we were without water," says Piácomo Ortega, citing another incident. "For two days, three days, we were without water. The farmers petitioned the local Community Action Program for help. We had in mind a water tank. If we could get a loan we would erect it ourselves. I have a letter that says someone in the Community Action Program went and withdrew our application. He lost it. He was one of the merchants here."

One of the merchants of Antonchico responds, "We have enough money to buy a water tank, if the people want it." He ignores the farmers' plea for a loan to build their own community water tank, as though it is an insult to his fatherly concern.

The righteous indignation of the commercial *patrón* whose motives have been questioned is recorded in the compassionate outburst of Mr. Marquez, the Hispano owner of the second and smaller store in the village of Antonchico.

"In answer to your question of what I have done for the poor: here's a few of them," Mr. Marquez begins. "They have been done with the political push I have in this part of the country. I worked to get this road paved to Antonchico. I worked to get that community association of the well. I worked to get Rural Electricity in here. I used my own pocket money. I wasn't getting no per diem, no mileage. I talked to different political big shots in the state and I got that bridge in Antonchico. That I have done out of my own self. I haven't collected a penny on it from nobody and made a penny on it. I had a lot of trouble."

Piácomo Ortega replies, with diplomatic politeness, "Thank you, Mr. Marquez. I am sure with the political push you have we can get a lot of things done."

"Lots of members of the Coop store owe me money," Mr. Marquez goes on, the implied threat obvious. "I loan them money when they need it. I even loan a certain individual five hundred dollars, and I didn't ask him to write a note or anything. He never paid me back a penny. Ninety per cent of your Coop owe me money. When they need groceries, when they were unemployed, when they didn't have no money to feed their family, I feel sorry for them and I decided to help them," the merchant says.

"Mr. Marquez, I feel sorry for you," replies Ortega. "I am sure these people would pay you if they could buy groceries a little cheaper."

"How can I sell cheap, and charge it, and not collect it?" says the merchant. "I am the cheapest store in the whole United States."

On the recording of the fight in the schoolhouse the voices grow shrill and the lines of the conflict sharply defined.

Merchant: There's a man here in Antonchico, he's not too wealthy, or anything, I think he receives food stamps; well, he had his house burned down about six months ago. Did any of you people lift a hand to help him?
Farmer: Did you?
Merchant: Yes, I did. I gave him a little credit.
Farmer: Who is that man you're talking about?
Merchant: You know him.
Farmer: I know him. Do you know what he makes with his animals? He is not considered poor.

The poor are jealous of their poverty. Among these farmers to be poor is no dishonor, it is a hard-earned misery. They do not trust those who profess their love of the poor, or who make their living from helping the poor, or the politicians of poverty.

A stone, they say, that is what poverty is. It is a stone on the heart of a man to be poor. He who is poor must bear the burden with dignity.

It is his sense of pride as much as, if not more than, the fears of the poor villager that has preserved the quiet of the countryside. The reticence of the Hispano was, in part, due to this inbred dignity. A political leader says of the villager, "He is proud—not humble."

H. H. Mondragon has a more sophisticated way of phrasing this paradox: "It is mostly the humbleness of the poor that lets them be tricked. But the poor can be tricky, too. They may be humble, but they are shrewd. They know how to protect themselves by expecting nothing. They are seldom disappointed."

Once the villagers of La Loma had begun to rebuild their own community, with their own hands and their own ideas, stone by stone, their pride grew to stubbornness. The attacks of the stranger bewildered them.

"The people in the village try to do something to better themselves, and what happens? Everybody in power tries to stop them," exclaims young Arthur Sandoval, who is a VISTA volunteer and clerk in the Coop store. He is a likable young man, with serious eyes and a quiet, moody manner. "I always had food on my table when I was a boy. My family wasn't poor," he says, almost apologetically. "These people have nothing." A young Chicano coming home to his village from the world of affluence brings with him the sense of dedication of a penitent. "He considers himself well paid in the intangible gains to the status and well-being of the people he has volunteered to serve—the poor people of his native New Mexico," the Santa Rosa *News* comments. He is, says the newspaper, one of the "revolutionary" ones.

"Revolutionary?" Sandoval says. "I spend most of my time selling cans of soup!"

He says little among the village elders. In the meeting in the schoolhouse, with the merchants, the youth says not one word at first.

"May I say something?" Sandoval begins in a small voice hardly audible on the tape. "I would just like to say, you, Mr. James Abercrombie, are asking the HELP director what he's done to help the poor when right before your very eyes, your very eyes, there is a cooperative store that will help these people. You on the Community Action Board might be asked the same question: What have you done to help the poor?

"I will tell you," the young man goes on, his voice rising in pitch. "You haven't done a damn thing!"

"Wait a minute! Wait a minute!" James Abercrombie yells into the din that arises. He is stung by the youth's insolence. He calms himself sufficiently to say solicitously, "Did you eat your meal today? At noon?"

"I don't have to ask you that," Sandoval replies. He will not be hedged. "I can see you did."

Now there is uneasy laughter among the farmers. In the village no one insults an Abercrombie to his face so brazenly.

"Do you know that what you eat somebody works for?" the merchant says coolly. He is talking of the government money that pays for the VISTA volunteers.

"Do you know I also work for what I eat?" Sandoval is belligerent and petulant at once.

The merchants turn from the youth in annoyance, as though he is a mosquito, and turn their questions to the village leader, Piácomo Ortega.

Piácomo Ortega is more than the director of the Center of HELP. He is the rural Chicano, a man of sturdy build and toughness, whose boyish face hides his unexpectedly quick tongue. When he is crossed, he strikes back. He has that "Spanish temperament." Under his mild manner there is that residue of anger common to the rural village leader.

"Why don't you help your people, instead of these coop stores to fight the established businesses?" David Abercrombie asks him.

"You have a misunderstanding. We're not trying to fight anybody," Ortega says. "We're trying to help the people. And if we can get them together, to unite, they can help themselves by helping one another."

"I think we've all done these things for our community," the merchant says. "We've done everything we could to help the people of the community. Everything constructive, not destructive, as you are trying to do."

"Very well stated, David," Ortega says with sarcasm. "Constructive —for yourself!"

"For the community," the merchant insists.

"For yourself," Ortega says. "You help these people for the money they pay you. You don't help them because you're such a good soul, David."

There is silence. There is nothing more to say. In the school of stones the young farmer and the wealthy merchant glare at each other. The social abyss that has been hidden under the calm surface of the village for generations of poverty has been exposed. It is ugly to see, the distrust, the hatred. The men are both disturbed and silenced by the sight. The stones of the poor have shifted the weight of power, ever so slightly. The village is divided, publicly.

"I will tell you something," says a farmer. "We are angry. If the men of Tierra Amarilla came here, with their rifles, I would follow them. And, I think, I would not be alone."

"When is Tijerina coming?" he asks.

IV The Lion and the Cricket

On the grassy fields the sun is gentle. Police cars are parked by the roadside. The officers stand off to the side, in a tight group, their revolvers hung loosely at the hip, uneasy as cowboys inside a rodeo corral. Whenever a car passes on the highway their eyes follow it with suspicion to see if it will turn onto the country road. The officers are strangers in a strange land.

The State Police have every reason to be wary. In one of these cars Reies Lopez Tijerina may be riding.

Barely two months before, at a remote village crossroads not much different from this, four State Police cars were shot full of holes, two officers were wounded, and the county courthouse was invaded by an armed band of villagers said to be followers of Tijerina. They are out of the state penitentiary and heading this way. They say Tijerina is coming to speak at the schoolhouse in Antonchico.

"*He* is coming," they say in the village. "El Tigre," the tiger, Tijerina.

A small handbill has been surreptitiously passed about the village for days, read aloud in whispers, with disbelief, awe, curiosity, and mockery. The handbill reads:

U.S.A. IS TRESPASSING IN NEW MEXICO
U.S.A. HAS NO TITLE FOR NEW MEXICO
THE TREATY OF GUADALUPE HIDALGO IS A FRAUD AND INVALID
ESTADOS UNIDOS NO TIENE JURISDICCION EN N. MEX.
ALL TRESPASSERS MUST GET OUT OF NEW MEXICO! NOW!
ALL PIRATES GO HOME
ALL SPANISH AND INDIAN PUEBLOS ARE FREE FOREVER
ALL TRESPASSERS WILL BE PUNISHED BY LAW
VIVAN LOS PUEBLOS REPUBLICAS LIBRES DE NUEVO MEX.

At the crossroads there is a church with a large cross of wood, chopped out of logs by a woodcutter's ax. One old cow lies down in the middle of the road as the cars detour around her. A chicken is hit by a pickup truck. It seems to be just another Sunday.

On Sundays there are always cars on the road. The families on the outlying farms come to Mass and stay to visit relatives. But this afternoon the cars and pickups of the farmers disappear as soon as they come into the village, leaving the street deserted.

The Sheriff drives by. He circles the village and the one street, four, five, six times. He too is waiting for Tijerina. But the doors of the schoolhouse are locked. The janitor has disappeared with the keys and cannot be found. The meeting will not happen after all.

A Hispano policeman walks up to the car of one of the village elders parked in the shadows. He extends his hand, palm upward, through the open window of the car. In his palm is the missing key.

"I am with you, fellows," the policeman says. He walks away.

The village elder opens the schoolhouse doors. He is a very old man in a rumpled, unpressed suit and faded cravat, but his best for this important occasion, wearing a crucifix and a tie clip inset with a gaudy miniature of the Virgin of Guadalupe. The elder leads the way and a few younger men follow him. Most of the villagers wait to see if Tijerina will really come.

"*He* is come," someone says.

"Where?" a man asks.

"In the black car," says the elder.

The large, black car roars to a halt. A group of young men in business suits get out; these are the stalwarts of the Alianza—the Alianza Federal de Los Pueblos Libres—the Federal Alliance of Free

City States. In the midst of them is a young man in his shirtsleeves, his dark hair flying, with a tense and preoccupied look. He is Reies Tijerina.

Hundreds of villagers suddenly appear. They come in pickup trucks, cars, and farm trucks and on foot. In minutes the schoolyard is jammed by dozens of vehicles and hundreds, perhaps three hundred, villagers.

An old man in a weary cowboy hat kisses Tijerina on both cheeks. They have never met before, for they say Tijerina has never been in this village. The elders of the village go forward to welcome their guest, but not a word is said. Ranchers and farmers are men of few words. They gather in a circle of silence about Tijerina. He embraces them, one by one. The younger men, who have waited stiffly and politely, shake his hand. It is a wordless ritual.

When the welcome is done, Tijerina strides into the schoolhouse in what looks like a religious procession. The men walk after him, and the women after them, to the lunchroom, where the meeting will be held. Half of the village is crowded onto the benches, the tables, the window sills, the kitchen stoves, expectant, watching Tijerina, who sits facing them.

It is not yet time to begin. The village women bring pots and cauldrons full of green chili and beans and hot dogs. Four homemade layer cakes elaborately decorated and iced, one covered with red hearts of sugar, are set out on the tables.

A *corrido* must be sung. George Jaramillo is the village singer, a bull of a man who sings with much gusto. His is but one of the songs written for Tijerina; the popular band leader and vocalist Rudy Martínez has recorded a ballad, "The Robin Hood of the North," that is a hit song on the jukeboxes in cantinas throughout the Southwest. One of the best known of the *corridos* is that of Cleofas Vigil of San Cristobal, whose verses celebrate the advent of the "God-sent" Tijerina:

Reies Lopez Tijerina
blessed with courage
they put him in jail
but he showed no fear.

He spoke for Justice
with reason, and what he said
to them, in truth,
is the purest truth.

Ay, Mexican Indian
born of Spanish blood
you begin to bestir
and shed your humiliation.

Reies Tijerina rises. There is no applause. He has said nothing and the farmers do not applaud for nothing.

He begins with a parable: "We are like the cricket. The cricket is a very small insect. It is said that one night the King of the Beasts, the great lion, heard the cricket yelling and making noise. The lion laughed at all the yelling the cricket was doing.

"The lion said, 'It is a shame to be King of the Insects. You have no power. Nothing to be proud of.' He insulted the cricket's pride.

"The cricket challenged the lion to a fight to decide who was the strongest. And the King of the Beasts was ready to swallow the cricket in one bite. The cricket got into the lion's ear. He tickled and he itched him. The lion started scratching with his claws, to get the cricket out of his ear. And he bled himself to death! And the cricket won the battle.

"Humble people, weak people, small people, who are surrounded by empires, have no other resort but the wisdom and strategy of the cricket.

"We are a very meek people. We don't stand a chance against an empire. Though we are weak and small, the day is very close when this great giant, the United States, the King of the Beasts, with its economic strength, its political power, its ruling the world, with the claws of the lion, will either give in to the cricket, or bleed himself to death, by scratching his own ears.

"The great lion can't afford to do that, to bleed himself to death."

He says this softly. Reverend Tijerina—he was an evangelical preacher—talks from a podium as though it is a pulpit. In gentle tones he begins a sermon. Without warning his voice rises to a shrill cry:

"Justice is catching up with the United States. Justice is catching up with all the great empires that have suppressed the cultural rights and property rights of the small and weak people such as we, ourselves. The rich and the unjust are being swept away. The rich and the unjust have no place any longer, and they know it. It is why they are desperate against us, but history is against them. The poor and the humble will have their day under the sun. The poor and the humble will rule. Mankind will rule mankind.

"It is never too late for justice. This is the time. The time is ripe. There is a time for everything under the sun. Solomon the Wise said that. Our time has come."

The whispers of the women stir for a moment, then subside. The men sit stunned and unsure. It is good talk, but it is easy to talk.

He tells of the uprising of the farmers in the mountains to the north, in the village of Tierra Amarilla, where poor men, like themselves, decided they were ready "to fight, to go to jail, to die" to win back their land.

"The Spanish people matured in those few days, they grew up," he says. "We are more determined than ever to win back dignity, to preserve and revive our culture. We can never go back now. We will fight to the end. We will win back our land."

The land! This the men of the village do understand. He tells them of history through the land. In a booklet published by his Alianza it says: "For as long as the ownership of property is the basic foundation of our society, everyone has a vested interest in the protection of property. . . . Therefore, every person has a vested interest in seeing to it that not only his, but his neighbor's, property is adequately protected, *so that the thieves will not inherit the earth.*" Yet, the thieves, the Anglos, have stolen your land, Tijerina says. The men of the village lean forward, intent.

He recites the Treaty of Guadalupe Hidalgo of 1848, signed by the United States after the war against Mexico. Article VIII of that rarely reprinted, little-remembered treaty states, "In the Name of Almighty God":

Mexicans now established in territories previously belonging to Mexico, and which remain for the future within the limits of the United States, as defined by the present treaty, shall be free to continue where they now reside, or to remove at any time to the Mexican Republic, retaining the property they possess in the said territories. . . .

In the said territories, property of every kind, now belonging to Mexicans not established there, shall be inviolately respected. The present owners, the heirs of these, and all Mexicans who may hereafter acquire said property by contract, shall enjoy with respect to it guarantees equally ample as if the same belonged to citizens of the United States.

He recites the decisions of the Supreme Court of the United States, going back to Chief Justice Marshall, reaffirming property rights guaranteed by international treaty (*U.S.* v. *Percheman*):

It may not be unworthy of remark, that it is very unusual, even in cases of conquest, for the conqueror to do more than to displace the sovereign and assume dominion over the country. The modern usage of nations which has become law would be violated; that sense of justice and of right which is acknowledged and felt by the whole civilized world would be outraged if private property should be generally confiscated and private rights annulled. The people change their allegiance; their relations to each other and their rights of property remain undisturbed.

Our rights, says Tijerina, were held by the Supreme Court to be "consecrated by the law of nations," for "the treaty stipulation was but a formal recognition of the pre-existing sanction of the law of nations" (*U.S.* v. *Moreno*).

He recites these texts from memory. When he talks he quotes dozens of documents from memory. He is a walking lawbook. Not often does he misplace more than a word.

"We are people of little knowledge," Tijerina says. "We remember our history, however."

He tells the villagers that he has visited the "United States Government in Washington" in pursuit of justice. "I have been to the State Department two times. I had an invitation from a lawyer in the Legal Section of the State Department. He objected to the treaty. He stated the treaty holds no water because the signature of Nicholas P. Trist, who signed it for the United States, was not official, was no good, and there are records that Congress refused to ratify the treaty on those grounds. However, President James Polk persuaded Congress to ratify the treaty because of the coming elections. So they signed it the way it was.

"Now, the way we stand with the State Department is—they refuse to recognize the treaty. They refuse to recognize the protocol. They claim the United States has 'the right of conquest.'

"Our blood, our culture, our destiny, our property right depend on the treaty," says Tijerina. "The treaty is binding on the United States, just as the Treaty of Guantánamo Bay with Cuba, just as the Treaty with Vietnam. It is a treaty!"

In the Southwest, the lands ceded by Mexico to the United States, under the Treaty of Guadalupe Hidalgo, range across Texas, New Mexico, Arizona, California, Nevada, Utah, Colorado, and north into Wyoming. The vast lands constitute one-third of the nation, an area larger than that of any nation of Europe (except the Soviet Union) and greater than that of the majority of the nations of the world. Whether the property rights guaranteed by the treaty are held to be legally valid would appear to be no small real-estate matter.

Of these lands much, if not most, belonged to land grants known to number at least 1,715, given by the Spanish and Mexican governments to early settlers. Land grants in New Mexico alone may have covered half of the state. No one will ever know. The archives of Santa Fe were destroyed, burned, and sold for waste paper by order of the Territorial Governor, William A. Pike, from 1869 to 1871. Hardly one-fourth of the historic documents and land-grant records were ever recovered. Ten years later, in 1880, Adolph Bandelier, the Swiss traveler-writer, visited the ruins of the archives. They were in "horrible condition," he wrote. General Lew Wallace, the then governor, told Bandelier that his predecessor in office had "thrown them [the archives] into an outhouse to rot" amid the dung; but it was done "through ignorance," the governor thought.

The rector of St. Francis Cathedral in Santa Fe believed the truth more evil. Governor Pike had been a land speculator whose destruction of the archives "was done on purpose to destroy Mexican claims" to the land, the Catholic priest said. Pike was, in fact, an owner of the Maxwell Land Grant and Railroad Company, together with the Surveyor General of New Mexico, T. Rush Spencer, and the cohorts of the "Santa Fe ring."

Curiously, at the time that the archives of Santa Fe were being stuffed into an outhouse, the archives of Guadalajara in Mexico were damaged by fire, an intriguing coincidence.

Encouraged by their fellow conspirators of fire and feces, the "Santa Fe ring" fleeced the Hispano sheepherders of their lands. The "ring" leaders, Thomas B. Catron and Stephen B. Elkin, were lawyers so ingenious that within a few years "over 80 percent of the Spanish and Mexican grants were lost to their owners" (*The Public Domain in New Mexico* by Victor Westphall, past president of the Historical Society of New Mexico). One "ring" leader acquired pieces of seventy-five land grants, owned 2 million acres outright, and was part owner, or lawyer, for 4 million more acres. The Maxwell Land Grant, one of the "ring's" prizes, ranged over entire mountains and whole villages for 1,714,764 acres. Although this empire was the private property of half a dozen men, it had cost them but a few dollars. They did not buy it; they simply "patented" it in their own names, with the approval of the U.S. Government's Land Office.

"He who steals a million is a financier," wrote the Rio Abajo *Weekly Press* of Albuquerque, in 1863. "He who steals half a million is only a defaulter. He who steals a quarter of a million is a swindler. He who steals fifty thousand is a knave. But he who steals a pair of boots or a loaf of bread is a scoundrel and deserves hanging."

The land seemed to be for the taking. After all, the villagers did not occupy much of their land grants, the forests were *ejidos,* the common pastures, and the villages were far away in small, neighborly valleys. Most of the land was uninhabited, by the definitions of Anglo-Saxon law. It was simple to claim the land by merely filing a "patent," or deed.

In this way the lands were lost. A Catholic Sister of Charity who lived in New Mexico at this time described one method of legal land theft. Sister Blandina Segale, in her *At the End of the Santa Fe Trail,* wrote:

> In the early days of Anglo settlement in New Mexico the unsuspicious and naive Spanish Americans were victimized on every hand. When the men from the states came out west to dispossess the poor natives from their lands, they used many subterfuges. One was to offer the owner of the land a handful of silver coins for the small service of making a mark on a paper. The mark was a cross which was acceptable as a signature by which the unsuspecting natives deeded away their lands. By this means, many a poor family was robbed of all their possessions.

In the village of Villanueva the farmers told Dr. Clark Knowlton ("Land Grant Problems Among the State's Spanish-Americans," in *New Mexico Business*, a publication of the School of Business Administration, University of New Mexico) of still another "typical" method of land theft:

> Several Anglo-American lawyers living in Las Vegas cast their eyes upon a large community land grant rich in grazing lands. A lawsuit was brought against the village, challenging its land title. The panic-stricken villagers employed lawyers to defend their claims. The lawyers agreed to take the case provided they were paid in land. . . . After several years of court action, the village won. The defending lawyers had taken as their fee the best grazing land from the village *ejido* and divided the land with the challenging attorneys.

The farmers did not understand this business of written deeds and lawyers' fees. Not because they were simple-minded, but because their philosophy of land ownership was too complex and ancient. In a sense the Hispano villagers thought of the land as did their Indian ancestors. Were not the fields a blessing of the Almighty God for which all men had a common moral obligation unto Him? Land was a parcel of eternity; it could not be reduced to the size of a piece of paper.

"One thing that is not commonly understood or known is that the philosophy of Anglo-American law [of the land] is very different from New Mexico's Spanish philosophy of law," says Father Robert García, a former village priest. "Anglo-American law is legalistic, highly technical, aggressive. The law that they (the New Mexican villagers) were used to was humanistic and based on tradition, *de facto* ownership, and a consideration for the right of every individual to own property and earn a living. Much consideration was given to the good of the family, inheritance, and the good of the community. The failure of the people to understand a new system of laws imposed on them by the Anglo-Americans has caused the collapse of their rural economy."

The profits on these land grabs were as large as the land grants. Catron, "The King of the Santa Fe ring," in a state of euphoria had legalized the expected return on land sales when he personally wrote a law that approved interest on bank loans in New Mexico of up to 20 per cent a month, or 240 per cent a year. His license for usury was passed without debate by the Territorial Legislature.

"He left his scars, this man, on each one of the land grants," Tijerina says of Catron.

Not until 1891 was a Court of Private Land Claims established to deal with the conflicts over the land. Thought of as the belated offer of justice to the poor villagers, the court rulings justified the theft of their lands. Land grants of 34,653,340 acres were brought to the court, often by village men who traveled for days and weeks by wagon and horseback, but the Court of Private Land Claims validated title to only 1,934,986 acres, and denied the rest. Ninety-four per cent of the claims of the villagers were dismissed.

Tijerina tells the villagers that the courts were "death traps" for the poor. There were no Mexican judges in this court. There were no Mexican lawyers.

"We can detect ill will," Tijerina says of the court. "By refusing us judicial protection; by the governor destroying our titles, and then the court denying justice, there were ill intentions on the part of the United States."

In Texas the Spanish and Mexican land grants may have covered 20 million acres or more. No one knows, or will ever know. Here, too, the archives of the Land Office were reportedly "badly damaged during the difficulties under Joaquín de Arredonde in 1813." These land grants prior to 1813 that were destroyed, unfortunately, belonged almost exclusively to Mexicans. But those given to Texans by the Mexican Government in the 1820's and 1830's to entice settlers were not damaged by natural catastrophe. Unsatisfied by their good fortune, the Anglo land speculators and cattle ranchers persuaded the Texas State Legislature to insert an article in the Constitution of 1876

—Article XIII, Section 4—that decreed that all Spanish and Mexican land grants not duly recorded by that year were invalid. The Texas Supreme Court ruled Section 4 was unconstitutional, but even this has not ended the dispute over the ashes of the lost land grants.

"The end is not in sight," one authority on the Texas land fights reports. In the barrios and *colonias* of Southwest Texas, Tijerina's Alianza is recruiting the heirs to the land grants.

"We will get our land back," says the scion of an old family in San Antonio; he is a conservative leader of the community. "One day this will be the country of Mexicans again," he says. "We have the legal right to the land and soon we will have the political power to enforce the law of the land. We will then get back our stolen land."

Up in the San Luis Valley of Colorado, the fight for the land grants has been violent. In the late 1950's, long before the advent of the Alianza, the cowboys of the cattlemen and the Hispano farmers engaged in a gunfight over the grazing rights on the mountain pastures near Alamosa. The land-grant heirs said it was their common pasture. Several cowboys were shot and beaten. The gunfight flared into the headlines of the local newspapers, but then died away as the courts wondered aloud about what jurisdiction they had over land grants issued by the Court of Queen Isabella.

The fight is quieter in Arizona. Long before the coming of the Americans, the warring Apaches had driven the original land-grant owners out of the deserts.

Land grants in California, however, may have come to tens of millions of acres. How many acres is again unknown. The lands have never been accurately surveyed; the results could lead to embarrassment for ranchers in the valleys and real-estate men along the freeways.

Under the Spanish rule the lands were sparsely settled, mostly on the coastal plain. The missions were few, after almost three hundred years of colonizing. There were but twenty ranchos in all of California. In 1821 the independence of Mexico changed all that. From 1821 to 1846 at least 630 land grants for private ranchos were given by the Mexican governors. When the war against Mexico began, in 1846, most of the fertile land up to the Sacramento Valley was owned by

Mexican land grantees in ranches of from 4,500 acres to well over 100,000 acres.

In 1851 the new State of California decreed that land-grant titles had to be approved by its courts. "This measure resulted in heavy court expenses drawn out over a period of years and ultimately deprived the Mexican people of some of their aristocracy, as well as their lands," the *California Almanac* records. "This measure, as it was carried into effect, clearly violated the spirit of the Treaty of Guadalupe Hidalgo which guaranteed the conquered Mexicans the ownership of their lands and ranchos."

Whenever Tijerina talks in a village, he tells something of this history. He may talk for one hour, two hours, three hours. It depends on where he is, what village, how angry the village is, and whether this talk is welcomed with silence, or "*Vivas.*"

In the village of Antonchico the talk goes on all afternoon. The yells of "*Viva!*" that applaud grow louder and more frequent.

He tells the villagers that the thieves have inherited their land: "All in all, we feel there was an organized plan not only to destroy our culture, but our property rights. We have proofs, documents, petitions, writings with dates. The lands taken away from us belong not to individuals. They belong to the pueblos, the villages. Just like the Pueblo Indians. The United States respected the Pueblo Indians, but *he* has denied us. Why?

"These land grants are not dead. These lands belong to the pueblos and the pueblos are alive. These pueblos have never been legally dissolved; therefore, we ask our government to recognize these pueblos and return our lands, so that we can make our living out of the land, the water, the forests, the minerals, as The Almighty God intended. So that we can live."

If they will fight for their land, he tells the villagers, they will have to join together, to join with their neighbors, to join his Alianza.

"We represent the dreams, the reality of the dreams of the Spanish Americans," he says. "We represent the inner feeling and cry of the Spanish Americans. We represent the faith of the Spanish Americans. We represent the Treaty of Guadalupe Hidalgo. We represent the culture of the New Breed. We represent the future, the spirit of the future."

The skeptics have speculated that the land-grant movement has anywhere "from 300 to 30,000 followers," the *New York Times* has reported. When the New Mexico State Police seized the membership lists of the Alianza the newspapers reported that 13,000 names or more were in the card indexes. The idea of "card-carrying" heirs to ancestral lands brings smiles to the villagers.

In the villages an heir needs no membership card in his history. That would be meaningless. Rituals of organization do exist, and they are religiously adhered to, but the itemized and computerized method of evaluating political strength that is normal to the nameless voters in the cities is unnecessary, and absurd, in the rural villages. Everyone knows his neighbor's politics, intimately. He remembers the beliefs of his great-grandmother just as well. "We don't need membership lists," explains an old village leader. "We don't need elections."

The villages are organized by history, in unseen ways. By old family groups, blood and compadre ties, the ancient lineage of marriage and heirship claims, and the secret societies of church and politics that outsiders rarely see, there is an elaborate hierarchy of power. Yet it exists beneath the surface. In every village there is either a Brotherhood of Penitentes, or an Order of the White Gloves, or the White Caps, or a Red Horseman posse of night riders in one southern mountain town, or the renowned Mano Negra—the Black Hand.

Reies Tijerina and his Alianza did not organize these villagers. He merely reflects the generations of hidden and complex organization that has always existed. When "the Prophet" comes to a village no organizer has to go ahead of him as an advance man. The villagers decide on their own, in their own way, whether or not to listen to their "spokesman." He is chosen not by vote, but by an unspoken consensus.

The Prophet is an unelected leader. He may be deposed at will if he betrays the faith, or violates the beliefs of the villagers. When such a leader is rejected no one may tell him. He learns of the decision when his faithful followers turn away. He is laughed at and he is abandoned.

In the village of Antonchico when Tijerina talks that afternoon there are times when no one seems to be listening. The old men gossip in whispers. Children run about. A young mother nurses her infant. He is telling the villagers what they already believe, so they hear him with half an ear, and nod occasionally in approval to reassure him. He is simply the catalyst between the villagers and the world, the voice of their silence.

He does not make a speech; he enacts the history of the village. He performs all the roles in the historical pageant he recites. He is the lawyer, judge, victim, preacher, sufferer, farmer, oracle, avenger, and holy prophet. When he performs the ritual that everyone knows by heart he embodies all the voices, in falsetto, in basso, in *sotto voce*, in heroics, in anguish, in English, in Spanish; for he suffers the history of La Raza for everyone in the audience, as they have always told it themselves.

The style is more than the man. His being is the organizing tool of the Alianza. No one hands out membership cards, no committees and subcommittees are formed, no dues are collected, there is no table for printed propaganda, and nothing is said publicly that has not been whispered privately for generations.

But a prophet cannot stick to an old script. Suddenly the voice of Tijerina has brought the conflict of the twentieth century into the village. He jars the audience awake.

"We cannot get our land back just by being nice and polite. We have to demand it. We have to fight for it," Tijerina exhorts the villagers. "We have to be willing to die for it, like those patriots, George Washington and Benito Juárez."

"Look at the black man," he says. "He has become free, free in spirit. He has lost his fear of the 'white power.' He is clean of fear and terror. And when you become free of these things you become filled with anger. You strike out for freedom. Anger is a manifestation that you know you are right and you wish to tear down the system that enslaved you."

He offers not hope, but anger. The villagers, at first, are stunned, then enthralled. "Viva Tijerina!" they yell.

The hot dogs and green chili and cakes with the little red hearts are served. In the schoolhouse lunchroom there is an air of celebration. One by one the villagers shake Tijerina's hand. The old men embrace him, again. He is offered a slice of the cake.

It is late afternoon when the meeting ends. The white sun is turning yellow. Soon it will be orange and red. On the road that leads into the village from the highway the state policemen wait, yawning and sweaty from the relentless hours in the sunlight.

Evening comes to the quiet village. Nothing has changed.

v The Fall of the Bastille of Yellow Earth

When the men put their rifles and pistols in the back seats of their cars that morning it looked like a storm was brewing.

The sky was uneasy. In the mountains rain was threatening that Monday, June 5, 1967. But by the time they drove into the village the sun was shining. They thought it an omen. They entered the courthouse, pointing their guns. They had come to make a "citizen's arrest" of the District Attorney, they said, but they captured the Rio Arriba County seat instead, in a wild-West gunfight. They were headlines across the nation by daybreak.

"ARMED MEN SHOOT UP COURT IN LAND CLAIM," one newspaper wrote. "SHOOT OUT AT TIERRA AMARILLA," proclaimed another. The headline in the New York *Daily News* was more prosaic:

LAND GRABBING MOB
GUNS DOWN 2 COPS

No one had heard of them before. Until that day the village of Tierra Amarilla—Yellow Earth—was hidden in a green valley, behind the mountains where the anger of the villagers had been asleep for generations. In these mountains there are forests where the wilder beasts outnumber the humans. There is only one paved road.

Where the road turns into the village there is an "Official State Historical Marker" that reads:

TIERRA AMARILLA
Founded 1858

POP. 1,246 ELEV. 7,460

THE TIERRA AMARILLA LAND GRANT COMPRISING ALMOST 600,000 ACRES WAS GIVEN TO JOSE MANUEL MARTINEZ BY THE MEXICAN GOVERNMENT IN 1832. MANY DESCENDANTS OF JOSE MANUEL MARTINEZ STILL LIVE IN THE AREA.

One man took it all away. The hundreds of thousands of acres of the land grant of Tierra Amarilla were taken from the villagers in the 1880's by the shrewd lawyer and land speculator Thomas B. Catron. He acquired the land merely by "patenting" it in his name at the Land Office and bribing a few officials. He became the owner of 593,000 acres with a single piece of paper.

"We were naïve," an aged farmer sighs in a bar in Tierra Amarilla. "Our grandfathers did not know anything about deeds, but only about the soil they held in their hands."

The villagers were landless. Yet they knew the land was theirs. It had always been their home. It was nonsense, surely, for a stranger to wave a piece of paper in their faces and say, The land is mine! He could not plow with his piece of paper. Then the cowboys came and put up barbed-wire fences. At first the villagers did not believe the stranger, but they believed the barbed wire.

And then the little villages were stripped of their governments as easily as they had been stripped of their lands.

In those days every village had its Mayor and Common Council—its Alcalde and Ayuntamiento—that governed the land grants. Some of these elected bodies were as old as the New England town meetings; some were older. The Territorial Government of New Mexico, in 1882, ordered these ancient village governments dissolved by issuing a decree. Recently lawyers for the villagers have questioned whether a federal official had the constitutional right to abolish an elected local government. But in 1882 there were no lawyers in the villages to question anything.

The village of Tierra Amarilla was legally abolished. It was ordered to "incorporate" under a new law, but as in many villages the order was ignored for years. The people thought, We have our own government. So why do we need another. In the meantime the strangers from the East "incorporated" new villages in the place of the old ones.

Las Vegas, a stubborn mountain town that is north of Santa Fe, has been divided ever since the decree of 1882 into two governments, two city halls, two mayors, two city councils, two police and fire departments. One is Hispano and one is Anglo. The villages that were divided in this way were separated by what the Santa Fe *New Mexican* has called a "tortilla curtain."

The lament of Dr. Sabine Ulibarri of the University of New Mexico is perhaps more acute: "A dynamic and aggressive Anglo culture has come between the Hispano and his past." Without land and without political power the villages began to die. The zest and vitality of rural life atrophied. The gregarious and boisterous Hispano villagers withdrew into the shadows of neglect, suspicion, poverty, and resentment. The deserted villages became backwaters of history.

So the stage was set for the dramatic raid of the armed and angry farmers on the courthouse of Rio Arriba County, and the fall of the bastille of Tierra Amarilla.

Once it was a beautiful village. In the bower of the mountains Tierra Amarilla was the county seat of Rio Arriba. It boasted the most imposing courthouse in northern New Mexico, an attempt at rural Greek Revival that succeeded in looking like a too-large mausoleum, and was therefore all the more imposing. The stores on its Main Street were garish and too large for a small village; the houses resembled small hotels, elaborate and rambling wooden buildings of Western baroque, with porticos and columns embroidered by Spanish woodwork.

The courthouse is today a rural slum. Its paint is peeling and refuse heaps surround it. The fine houses tilt and sag. The great columns of the porticos are askew. The old stores are boarded up. On one of the abandoned stores there remains a sign, "THIS IS THE PLACE," but underneath is the inevitable litany of architectural decay, "FUCK YOU! FUCK YOU! FUCK YOU!" The village is surrounded by National Forests and has not enough pasture for its sheep and cattle. Its people are hungry.

Rio Arriba County is a "hunger county," one of the poorest in the Southwest. Of the 23,000 residents there are 11,000 on welfare. In Tierra Amarilla the conditions are so poor they say it is a "ghost town." There are 600 villagers left of the 2,200 who lived there in its days of splendor.

"Some of us are pretty desperate," a farmer in Tierra Amarilla wrote to the Albuquerque *Journal* in July, 1964. "We have tried to be good citizens, and our reward has been no justice in the courts and powdered milk from the Welfare. We don't want Welfare, we want enough of our land to graze a milk cow."

The life of the ghost town is volatile. It goes on underneath the faded façades and repressed history. The villagers have become muted, irritable, cynical, and self-destructive. When they get drunk they explode with hatreds. "They are not violent by nature. They are very patient," said Governor Cargo. "They are a people that is quiet and reserved." But the angers within them eat at them like their hungers.

When Reies Tijerina first came to Tierra Amarilla he was met with suspicion. He told the hesitant villagers about the Alianza—the Alliance of Free City States—which he had founded to regain the Spanish and Mexican land grants. It was time, he told them, to reclaim their lost land and to re-establish their village government. They listened with one ear. He told them of his prophecy of the "New Breed," who would inherit the earth of their ancestors; "Justice shall reappear on earth, like Christ," he told them.

One by one the villagers shook Tijerina's hand. They did not wholly trust the prophetic stranger—he was an "outsider"—but if they did not do something they would have nothing. And their children would starve or run away.

The villagers went on a pilgrimage to see the then Governor Jack Campbell in the summer of 1966, bearing petitions that politely, with formality, asked for an investigation of their land claims. Marching on the superhighway from Albuquerque to Santa Fe, for sixty miles, they chanted, "We want justice, not powdered milk!" It was a peaceful march. Led by the stranger, Reies Tijerina, they had come reluctantly. His beautiful daughter, Rosa, rode before them on a white horse; it was a splendid sight to see. On the outskirts of the state capitol they camped in a field, one hundred tired marchers. At last word came that the Governor would hear them. He praised the villagers for "exercising a basic American right in such an orderly democratic fashion" and he promised to read their petition, and give it to the President of the United States.

"Incidentally," wrote the Albuquerque *Journal*, in 1966, they have "a good moral case. They say their march has stirred up much support all across New Mexico. We can see how that might be true. We would imagine it is also stirring some consternation among present land owners. And it will be interesting to see what comes of it."

Nothing came of it. "We do not demand anything," Tijerina told the Governor at that time. "We just want a full investigation." There was no investigation. "We have written to the Presidents—Eisenhower, Kennedy, Johnson—and to the State Department, all with no success," Tijerina recalled in frustration.

A bold deed was decided upon. *El Grito del Norte* (The Cry of the North), the newspaper of the mountain villagers, reported, "The Alianza looked for a way to . . . bring before the courts this entire land issue, and force the U.S. Government to prove its right to the land."

Several hundred villagers gathered that October at the Echo Amphitheatre, in the Carson National Forest, for a camp-out, or rather a camp-in; for "a picnic." The site was the old San Joaquin del Rio de Chama Land Grant, of some 600,000 acres. In the midst of their picnicking they "liberated" the forest, "In the name of God Almighty" and the "Peoples' Republic of San Joaquin." They "arrested" two forest rangers for "trespassing" and in an impromptu "court," in the picnic area, found them guilty and "confiscated" their jeeps. "As they confiscate our cows," a villager said.

Bemused by the "trial" of the two rangers, a state police officer, Martin Vigil, asked, "Why are you doing this?"

From the picnic table, where he had climbed to watch, Tijerina shouted, "Publicity!"

There was only laughter. "King Tijerina," the newspapers mocked. He was dubbed a "jet age Pancho Villa" and a "Mexican Elmer Gantry" and a "would-be Castro" and a "disgrace to New Mexico." Few people took the villagers, or Tijerina, seriously. Voicing the attitude of those beset by the more troublesome affairs of state was the offhanded comment of New Mexico's Attorney General Boston Witt, "We considered Tijerina merely a rabble-rouser." He was an after-dinner joke.

"Nobody is listening," the newly elected Governor Cargo later said. "They've got problems and nobody is listening. No one has time to listen."

"The Governor will hear us, we thought," Tijerina said. He led the villagers once more to the state capitol. It is said that the young Governor is something of a maverick, a liberal Republican in austere Goldwater country; he has a degree in literature as well as law. Independent and unorthodox he has married into an old Hispano family. The Governor's lady is a member of the Alianza of Reies Tijerina. "So with open heart we went," the land-grant leader said.

On the morning of the audience two hundred villagers came to the Governor's office. The Governor was out. The no longer reluctant villagers, whose angers have become public knowledge, held a protest meeting in the middle of the great marble lobby of the new *palacia* of the Governor.

"I never speak in public," a woman said. Her demurring was in proper deference to the Hispano men. "But, after all, this building and the land it was built on belong to us, too. The Negro people show their anger. The whole world listens. Are our grievances not worthy to be heard?"

"Let's enter his office by force," the woman shouted. "He'll have to listen."

In the Land of Poco Tiempo of not so long ago such words would not have been spoken by a woman, or a man. At the Governor's arrival, five hours late, he was apologetic. "We are not able to swallow, to tolerate, discriminatory procedures any more," Tijerina told the Governor.

"Violence never gets you anywhere," the Governor said.

"Yes? What about Vietnam?" said Tijerina.

The Governor's offer to appoint a commission, "in the near future," to investigate the land grants did little to soothe the frustrations of the villagers.

"We have held back our hands for a hundred and eighteen years, and where did it get us?" the woman had said.

In the courthouse of Tierra Amarilla the villagers gathered again in May, 1967. Most of the village was there, almost five hundred men and women. They had come to hear Tijerina talk of yet another conference, in early June, to be held in the nearby village of Coyote, where the Alianza would plan a statewide campaign, and of course have a barbecue. But the villagers were tired of talk. Then and there, in the old courthouse, they voted to re-establish the Pueblo Republica de San Joaquin that had been dissolved by the decree of 1882.

An *alcalde* (mayor) was elected. The military chief, the ancient title from the days of the Kingdom of New Mexico, was then chosen, along with a sheriff and the town council.

They proclaimed the Free City-State of Tierra Amarilla. If the little village had declared war against the state of New Mexico the incredulous officials in the capitol would not have been more shocked. Had the villagers gone mad? One by one the old land-grant villages might re-establish free city-states, as Tierra Amarilla had done, and a peaceful revolution would sweep through the mountains. And what of the land? Who knows what these village alcaldes might decree, or do, to restore the land grants?

In Santa Fe the rumors spread. The men of Tijerina were ready for a "showdown," one newspaper warned; it would begin with a "takeover" of the National Forests. Roadblocks manned by rifle-toting farmers were envisioned. And the summer tourist season was just beginning!

State police were ordered to Coyote to halt the barbecue and meeting of the Alianza Federal. The District Attorney of Sante Fe County, Alfonso Sánchez, issued the orders, it was reported. Governor David Cargo was out of the state. "I didn't order any arrests be made. I had nothing to do with it," he later said. Sánchez was, however, a "special enemy of the Alianza," declared *El Grito del Norte.* He had been a lawyer for some of the land-grant claimants before becoming District Attorney; his former clients said he had advised them to cut the National Forest fences and simply graze their cows. He perhaps regretted these indiscretions of his youth and now condemned the angry farmers as "a bunch of Commies."

"I wish the public did not think that all of us are like *him,*" Sánchez said of Tijerina. "Already the public has the wrong image of our people."

The barbecue of Coyote was never held. On Friday, June 2, the posses of State Police and local sheriff's deputies surrounded the mountain village and the ranch where the farmers had gathered with their children, and rounded up the picnicking guerrillas. Eleven men were arrested.

On that quiet day "ten Spanish Americans were arrested, probably illegally, for unlawful assembly," the *New York Times* observed. "There had been no violence." James Thompson, who was to replace Alfonso Sánchez as District Attorney, later declared, "The raid [on the courthouse] was frustration precipitated by the action there at coyote . . . the action [of the police] was apparently mishandled."

Under the mountain skies the frightened picnickers fled to the village of Canjilon, where they camped in a sheep pasture. On Monday morning, June 5, the Mayor of the Pueblo Republica de San Joaquin, and the Free City-State of Tierra Amarilla, issued orders for a citizen's arrest of District Attorney Sánchez. Those who had been arrested for "unlawful assembly" were to be arraigned at the courthouse that morning.

The posse of twenty armed Hispano farmers, ranchers, and loggers was deputized by the Vigilance Department of the Pueblo Republica de San Joaquin.

It was quiet in Tierra Amarilla that day, as usual. A flock of sheep grazed on the weeds behind the courthouse. The old man who walked down the middle of Main Street did not look up, for there was no traffic. The Valley Movie Theatre, a dilapidated building with barnlike wooden doors, was playing the usual Mexican melodrama, such as *La Amor, La Gloria y el Muerte:*

LOVE, GLORY AND DEATH!

In the shabby blue and muddy courthouse were not only the offices of the sheriff and the state police, but also, in its dirt-floored cellar, the County Jail, and up a flight of worn, splintered stairs, the Department of Welfare. These were the pillars of power in the village—the court, the police, the jail, and the welfare office.

The men approached the courthouse with ancient fears. To them it was the village Bastille.

Sheriff Benny Naranjo dismisses the courthouse as "obsolete." In the dank cellar the earthen floor of the jail is strewn with debris, the iron bars on its windows are rusted and ripped off, and the odor of urine is like that of a cesspool. "The jail's not fit to keep animals in, let alone humans," the Sheriff has said. "The jail would be condemned, except there is no other place to keep prisoners."

Men of the village who had been imprisoned in the jail have said it was "like being buried." It was fear of this, too, that made the villagers come armed on that day.

Reies Tijerina has said, "These people whose rights have been abused see the courts only as death traps. Innocent people become pale, weak, their joints freeze [in court]. That is the spirit that has developed over a hundred and twenty years, when people have lost all their money and their homes."

On the bulletin board of the courthouse were signs of these fears, but mostly there were notices of village boredom:

WANTED—HAY HAULED
HAY HAULER WITH TRUCK
CALL—LOUIE ARCHULETA

And urgent pleas from the government offices:

NEW MEXICO STATE GOVERNMENT NEEDS YOU!
The New Mexico Department of Welfare
urgently needs case workers

And one ominous note:

NOTICE OF INTENTION TO IMPOUND
TRESPASSING LIVESTOCK

Notice is hereby given that all livestock found trespassing upon lands owned or controlled by the United States within the LabatoCH Allotment, El Rito Ranger District, Carson National Forest, State of New Mexico, will be impounded by the United States Forest Service . . .

After impounding owners of trespassing livestock may regain possession thereof only by first reimbursing the United States in full for the expense incurred in gathering, impounding, feeding, or pasturing said livestock and for the forage consumed during the period of said trespass. All impounded animals not redeemed within 5 days after impounding will be offered for sale at public auction. Animals not sold at public sale will be sold at private sale or condemned and destroyed, as required by the regulations of the Secretary of Agriculture.

Signed at El Rito, New Mexico
This 17th of February, 1967
Jack P. Miller, Acting Forest Supervisor

The impounding notice is beside a poster of the "TA Community Action Program" that proclaims in bold letters:

GET TOGETHER
SPEAK OUT!
COMMUNITY ACTION IS YOU
WORKING TOGETHER TO SAVE YOURSELF

When the gunfight in the courthouse began that afternoon they say a bullet ricocheted off the wall beside that exhortation "COMMUNITY ACTION IS YOU."

In his dismal office in the old courthouse Benny Naranjo leaned back in his chair and dozed that afternoon. The state policeman, Nick Saiz, lounged in the lobby by the peanut-vending machine. Judge Scarborough had just freed the jailed men of the barbecue on bail. It was three o'clock by the courthouse clock.

At that moment the villagers burst into the dreary building. The gunfight erupted at once. The state policeman, Saiz, was told to drop his gun. He reached for it, he says, and was shot in the chest. A man who was there, Fabian Durán, later swore that the state policeman drew his gun first. Judge Scarborough locked himself in the toilet of the Judge's chambers. Some of the court employees escaped through the windows. One who jumped was Deputy Sheriff Elogio Salazar. He was shot twice before he reached the earth.

Later, that winter, Elogio Salazar was found murdered in his blood-stained car on a lonely mountain road. He had been beaten to death by unknown assassins.

In spite of the noisy gunfire at the courthouse only two men were wounded. The villagers held the building and searched the corridors but could not find Alfonso Sánchez, the man they had come to arrest. The District Attorney was not there.

The Mexican American, a staff report prepared for the United States Commission on Civil Rights in 1968, had this to say about the raid on the courthouse of Tierra Amarilla:

> Recent cases in Northern New Mexico have aroused particularly wide-spread resentment among Mexican Americans throughout the Southwest. In June of 1967, an organization formed to press Mexican American claims to ancestral and land grants, had scheduled a rally to be held in the country-side. The district attorney of Rio Arriba County [sic] warned leaders that the meeting would not be tolerated; as Mexican Americans arrived he arrested them on a variety of minor charges, including mistreatment of animals, and held them incommunicado for several days before dismissing the charges. In reprisal, a group of Mexican Americans attempted a citizen's arrest of the district attorney at the Rio Arriba County Courthouse in Tierra Amarilla. In the ensuing melee the attackers wounded two officers. Following this episode, 50 Mexican Americans, including women and children, were held in an open sheep pen for 36 hours, with no charges against them, then or later.

At dusk the villagers escaped to the high mountains, led by Tijerina himself. He was later to swear that he came to the shoot-out at the courthouse after the gunfighting had started in order to halt it. But State Policeman Saiz is equally adamant that he saw the land-grant leader with "a rifle strapped to his arm [that] looked like an AR-15." The county clerk, Cipriano Padilla, thought it was a "Thompson machine gun."

The orders for the arrest of the villagers and land-grant leader were prompt. The charges: twenty-four counts of kidnaping, three counts of assault with intent to kill, and one count of attacking a courthouse.

Reies Tijerina was himself later to be charged with fifty-four criminal acts because of the incident!

Led by an M-42 tank destroyer a small army of National Guardsmen, under the command of General Jacob Jolly, Adjutant General of New Mexico, invaded Tierra Amarilla. The soldiers, numbering 350, were joined by 80 members of the New Mexico Mounted Patrol, dozens of state policemen, sheriffs and their deputies from all the northern counties, and the officers of the New Mexico Game and Fish Commission. In all an armed force of more than 2,000 lawmen.

The roads were barricaded. Jeeps crisscrossed the mountain passes with machine-gun units, but the raiders had escaped.

In Canjilon, where the families awaited the return of their menfolk, the M-42 tank destroyer blocked the road. The old men, women, and children left in the camp were surrounded by soldiers who herded them into a muddy sheep pen and imprisoned them overnight in the barbed-wire enclosure.

"They're bait," a National Guardsman said. "The brass expects that Mexican cat will come back in here tonight to try to free these people."

"Let's don't get involved in civil liberties," General Jolly told the *New York Times.*

"In these high mountains no one could ever find us," said a villager. "We know these mountains. They could never find us. No, they could not find Reies, he gave himself to them. The army would never find him. All the National Guard could not find Tijerina and twenty men.

"Here in these mountains they would never find anyone," he said. "What would happen if a Castro came into these mountains?"

After the arrests of the "Robin Hood of New Mexico" and his Alianza men, and after the trials had begun, the villagers listened to the news reports with sullen anger. The state police complained, "No one will talk. They are afraid."

But in the villages it was not fear that silenced the farmers. "You mark my word. They better not hurt that man," said a village leader. "If they hurt that man there will not be enough guards to protect someone in high places. I do not say who!"

The trial of the land-grant leader and his followers was to be held before Judge José Angel. After weeks of hearings the judge dismissed half of the charges and many of the defendants.

Infuriated, District Attorney Sánchez impaneled a new Grand Jury, in another county, which is legal under New Mexico's statutes. The original charges were reinstated. Sánchez decided to prosecute the case himself (he has an "emotional involvement" in the case, said James Thompson, who defeated Sánchez for District Attorney in the next elections) and the death penalty was sought for Tijerina, on the charge of kidnaping. In response Tijerina dismissed his lawyers. He would defend himself. The Prophet explained to his followers, "I had to be *un hombre completo*, a complete man, for those who follow me. I had to show I was not afraid."

"I stand before you like David before Goliath," Tijerina told the court. "I'm not an attorney. I'm just a man against a political conspiracy, a conspiracy by the government, the political machinery, and the press."

He denied that the raid on the courthouse was an attempt to begin a violent "revolution of Tierra Amarilla." He was there simply to help make a citizen's arrest. So were the armed farmers, who were after all deputy sheriffs of the Pueblo Republica de San Joaquin. He charged that the "violence of the law" had been directed against the villagers. He accused his prosecutor, Alfonso Sánchez, of "murdering my unborn child," by ordering the arrest of his pregnant wife, who had a miscarriage while in the state penitentiary. He told the jury, "Yes, we are guilty of wanting our lands. We are guilty of believing in the Treaty of Guadalupe Hidalgo. We are guilty of uniting the North. If I deserve to be punished for what I am doing for the poor people, then do it. But you cannot get rid of the land problem by putting Tijerina in jail."

In the trial the under sheriff of Tierra Amarilla, Daniel Rivera, the man Tijerina was accused of kidnaping, faced with the impassioned rhetoric of the defendant, blurted out, "I'm not blaming you for anything, sir."

Sánchez was adamant. He accused the land-grant leader of organizing and guiding the assault on the courthouse, of kidnaping the under sheriff, of deliberate violence and murderous intent. He asked for life imprisonment for Tijerina, at the very least.

"The State wants you [the jury], based on this crooked, biased charge, to send me to the State Penitentiary so they can, like Pilate, wash their hands and say, 'Well, they [the jury] did it,'" Tijerina told the jury.

On the wall of an abandoned gas station in Tierra Amarilla someone had written in huge letters, during the trial:

IF TIJERINA GOES TO JAIL
WAR!

The jury deliberated briefly. It found Reies Tijerina not guilty.

Soon after his triumph Tijerina was jailed. He was seized by New Mexico state policemen and United States forest rangers, at gunpoint, as "a danger to the community." Led by Ranger James H. Evans, armed with a special paratrooper carbine, and State Policemen Robert Gilliland ("I always shoot at the head. I don't shoot to maim. I shoot to kill"), the prophet of the land-grant movement was surrounded in *High Noon* style at the scene of a burning of a National Forest signpost by his followers, on June 8, 1969, near the faithful village of Coyote, where it had all begun. It was two years, almost to the day, since the raid on the courthouse of Tierra Amarilla.

The burning of National Forest signposts has replaced the burning of barns in the villages of northern New Mexico. But Tijerina was not arrested on that charge. His bail on an earlier charge—stemming from the picnic at the Carson National Forest, where the Forest Rangers were "arrested" by the land-grant heirs—was revoked.

Reies Tijerina was sent to the Federal Penitentiary at El Paso, Texas.

El Grito del Norte wrote angrily: "Reies Lopez Tijerina is in jail. A political prisoner, in Texas. And the white racist world which put him there now attempts to breathe deeply, safely, closing its eyes to the ugliness of its lies, turning its face from the foul smell of its 'justice.' The smell of the *chota* (the police) is everywhere. There are many ways to assassinate a man."

Yet before their leader was jailed once more the villagers held a political fiesta for "the man who defeated the courts." Joyously they feted the innocence of their prophet. And they danced to his prophecy.

In a victory celebration at the barren Lito Ballroom, on the dusty

Main Street of Tierra Amarilla, Tijerina was exultant. He still faced fifty-one of the fifty-four charges brought against him. And his fellow defendants had not yet been tried at all. Yet, he was joyous. "Our victory in the court was a symbol," he told the villagers. "Everybody in the world [now] knows about Tierra Amarilla."

On the village street the dust blew about the gloomy courthouse. He pointed toward the building where the drama began. "We don't believe in violence, but we believe in Jesus Christ. The revolution of Tierra Amarilla was like Christ entering the temple and cleaning out the Pharisees.

"When the jury brought in its verdict that Tijerina was innocent, the justice of God fell on the heads of the powerful," the Prophet thundered. "The sky fell on their heads."

VI The New Breed

"I went to sleep, and in the morning the sun woke me and that white, how do you say, dew, had covered me, had covered me all over. That night I asked God to show me the future of my life. It shaked me, shaked me like this, it shaked all my life. From there I turned to New Mexico. I saw frozen horses, they started melting and coming to life in a very old kingdom, old walls. Then I saw three Angels of Law, and they asked me to help them. They said they had come from a long ways, had traveled the earth and come for me. Those tall pines I saw meant New Mexico. . . ."

He was reborn in his vision. Reies Tijerina tells of his becoming a prophet of the mountain villages as an act of divine revelation. At the moment of his vision he was a fugitive from the jail of a small town in the Arizona desert, hiding amid the cacti on the scorched slopes of the barren Tortilla Mountains. He was hungry and pursued. But that hardly mattered. The frozen horses of snow who beckoned to him from the fiery desert sky in that spring of 1957 were a "sign" that he dared not doubt, or disobey.

The Lord had chosen him on the mountain. He had no choice but to follow the frozen horses. He offered himself as a martyr to the prophecy, and he went over the mountain to New Mexico, to his destiny, or his death.

"He will be murdered!" one of his faithful followers says. "Reies is a sacrifice. He knows it, too."

In the brief years since that moment Reies Tijerina has become one of the mythic leaders of La Raza. He is "the Most Hated Man in New Mexico," a television network announces to the nation. He is also the most beloved, and the most feared. Attempts are repeatedly made to kill him.

On the night of April 16, 1968, a former sheriff's deputy of Bernalillo County, William R. Fellion, bombs the office of the Prophet in the headquarters of the Alianza—the Alliance of Free City-States. The awkward assassin falls on his dynamite and blows off his right hand, trailing blood down the streets of Albuquerque in his escape. Police capture him, finding another stick of dynamite in a lunchbox in his blood-splattered car. Municipal Judge James A. Maloney, later New Mexico Attorney General, dismisses the "deadly weapon" charge. And a Bernalillo County grand jury clears the former sheriff's deputy of a "dangerous use of explosives" charge. He is sentenced to work for sixteen hours in the County Medical Center.

Rifle shots from a speeding car shatter the office windows on another night, during a meeting in the winter of 1968. There are no arrests. In June, 1969, the crowded hall is shot up again by terrorists.

Still no arrests. There "are repeated bombings, shootings and rock throwings—what amounts to a campaign of crime and terror against the Alianza," comments the *New Mexico Review and Legislative Journal.* Houses of land-grant heirs are bombed. Cars are shot up on the downtown city streets. Ranches are burned. The arsonists set afire the villagers' health clinic of the Rio Arriba Cooperative in Tierra Amarilla. The children of Tijerina's followers are threatened with kidnaping and murder. The members of the Alianza are gassed when powdered tear gas is secreted in their cars; one man is hospitalized and eight others affected by the gas attacks. Yet, when asked about "any suspects" or anticipation of "any arrests," the Deputy Chief of the Albuquerque Police, Albert T. Swallows, shrugs: "I'd rather not comment." In two years of terrorism there is not a single arrest.

In the midst of these attacks the leader of the extremist Minutemen, Robert DePugh, and his chief assistant, Walter Peyson, are caught by the F.B.I. in a hideout in a small New Mexico town, south of Albuquerque. The cache of arms and bombs captured is so large that a listing fills twenty-four pages. It includes dynamite, grenades, homemade pipebombs, hundreds of fuses, an armory of rifles, shotguns and revolvers, twenty-five cans of cyanide gas, bows and arrows equipped to carry bombs, aerial maps of the land-grant villages, and thousands of rounds of ammunition. The Albuquerque *Journal* mentions "a lengthy Minuteman membership list," which vanishes. Local law-enforcement men are rumored to be on the list.

Fabian Durán, the Assistant Security Chief of the Alianza, tells reporters that his informants on the police force have warned him that the opponents of Tijerina are "going to pay someone" to assassinate him. After their arrest, in the summer of 1969, the Minuteman leaders are hurriedly whisked out of the state.

The office of the Prophet is bombed three times in a few months. He escapes injury, but one bomb explodes within a few feet of his wife and children. Curiously, no one is ever injured. "Very accurate misses," someone says.

A guard is posted at the Prophet's door. He is a taciturn, tall man wearing the wool vest of a shepherd. Wherever the leader of the land-grant movement goes he is accompanied by a bodyguard. On the roof of the headquarters there are men with rifles stationed at night, like sentries.

The meeting hall of the Alianza is quiet as an empty garage. On the wall is a sign: "CABALLEROS DE LAS INDIAS"—the "Gentlemen of the Indies." But for this it is an unpretentious and nondescript building. The windows, broken by bombs and bullets, have been bricked and boarded up. Nowhere is there any visible fear. Inside the hall some old men are laughing at the antics of a psychedelic band on the television set.

On his desk Reies Tijerina has a bust of Socrates. A small flag of gold, red, and blue with the single word "Justicia" is beside the philosopher's head. The shabby walls are covered with a fascinating array: a map of "Spain in the History of the United States," a facsimile of the Declaration of Independence, an informal portrait of the late John F. Kennedy and his wife, a rosy-cheeked calendar Christ, and a roadsign used when the villagers of the Alianza "liberated" the Kit Carson National Forest and re-established their independent republic:

PROCLAMATION
IN THE NAME OF GOD ALMIGHTY
PUEBLO REPUBLICA DE SAN JOAQUIN
DEL RIO DE CHAMA

Reies Tijerina appears from the rear of the hall, where he has been napping. He brushes a mop of hair from his stark, handsome face. He is younger than one expects, almost boyish.

"I was having a rest," he apologizes.

"You look weary."

"Sometimes there is no rest."

"Politics can kill a man."

He looks surprised. In his face there is a sadness. He smiles and says simply, "If I die, I die."

A man dies, and is reborn, many times in his life. Reies Lopez Tijerina was born in a farm worker's shack. "I was born in the Depression days," he says. "All my life a migrant." The memory of poverty blots out much. He was actually born in 1927. He was a child of migrants, whose family picked cotton in Texas and sugar beets in Colorado, as he did as a boy. He traveled in the jalopy caravans of the Okies and he grew up in the migrant camps. It was an ordinary childhood.

Untaught by the schools, he was a pupil for only three years. He remembers his brief schooling with the bitter taste of the garbage pails he rummaged in for his lunches on the way to class. As a child he learned about life from life; he is still suspicious of textbook knowledge. "What learning I got I learned by candlelight. There was no chance for me, the son of a migrant, to get an education."

He was born again in the Bible. "I learned to read by reading the Holy Bible," he says.

When he was twelve someone gave him a Spanish Bible. He taught himself to read "by studying the Psalms and Proverbs." The biblical language has stayed with him, even in everyday conversation.

At nineteen he attended an Evangelical Bible School, at Ysleta de

Sur, Texas. He became a circuit preacher in the Assembly of God Church, a fundamentalist sect. Journeying from town to town throughout the Southwest with his wife and children, he preached in bare village churches, barrio homes, and revival tents and on street corners.

"I saw the miserable situation of my people," Tijerina says. "I gave my life to them."

He was born a third time in a town named the Valley of Peace. In the deserts of Arizona there was a handful of poor campesinos who had bought an arid piece of land on the irrigated flat between the Maricopa Indian Reservation and the Tortilla Mountains, which they hoped to farm cooperatively. The Reverend Tijerina came to preach in the town they optimistically named the Valley of Peace. It wasn't. The buying of land by the landless upset the old landowners. A few of the houses of the Mexicans were burned in the night. The families were run off their land, and the Reverend Tijerina and his parishioners landed in jail. Not comprehending why they were jailed when it was their houses that had been burned, they broke out of the jailhouse. Tijerina, who had remained in his cell, was rearrested for engineering the jailbreak. He says his life was threatened when he was released on bail, and he quickly left the Valley of Peace.

Sheriff Coy De Arman of Florence, Arizona, declared, "Tijerina should be considered extremely dangerous. He is known to be an escape artist."

"I have nothing to be ashamed of," Tijerina says. "Unless to save your life is wrong."

Although he had jumped bail and landed in the headlines, the local authorities did not extradite him, and the charges against him were permitted to expire. They did not seem unhappy to see him go over the mountain. They wanted the land, they did not want him, the troublesome Reverend now thinks.

The roots of the trouble were in the earth, Tijerina decided. Land was the soul of the poor villagers. He would search for the roots—"the soul of my people"—in order to be able to preach the message of their salvation. In digging into the history of the land he unearthed the lost land grants that the Spanish and Mexican governments had once given to original settlers of the Southwest. He was amazed. "I dedicated my life to research to make sure these land grants were legal." And he explored the old archives in Mexico and Spain for proof. In the villages of northern New Mexico he discovered farmers who still had memories, and copies, of their land grants. He decided that in these mountains he would make his stand.

"Destiny and the cry of the people were calling for a man who would take over the land-grant struggle." He merely answered the call.

He left his church, but not his pulpit. "I have not left the fear of God," Tijerina says, "the ways of truth I still feel. The kind of justice I pursue, I found the first taste of it in the Bible, but not fully. It was in the world among my people, among the struggles of my people, that I found the virtues of justice.

"So I am proud and have no regrets. I was of little use to my people as a preacher. There were too many preachers."

On February 2, 1962, Tijerina founded the Alianza Federal de Mercedes to fight for the land. He recalls there were fifteen or so who came to his meetings in what was then a printshop. "It was like talking to a block of ice. They sat there like a block of ice. My words chipping away on that block of ice for three years. Three years!" One man who was there in the beginning called it "El Sueño Loco"—The Mad Dream.

"I had discovered the lost identity of my people," Tijerina says. "Where? It is in the Laws of the Indies that I had discovered the place for my people in history.

"We were born out of a law. It was the Law of King Philip II, of Spain, that he established on October 19, in the year of 1514: Law II, Title I, Book VI, of the Laws of the Indies. This was the strongest of all the Laws of the Kings of Spain. It was to legalize the matrimony, by marriage, between the Indians and the Spaniards. Through this marriage we were born.

"The Indian was our mother. The Spaniard was our father, yes, but the Indian was our true mother.

"Our father, the Spaniard, left us. We decided to stay with our mother, the Indian, here in New Mexico. This was our country. The land was our birthplace. We were a New Breed. As all New Breeds, we were born as the consequence of a conflict of races and cultures, when the Spaniards discovered, explored, and christianized this continent. Out of that conflict came a New Breed, a new people. This new people is sometimes known as *los peones*, the peons. Sometimes we are known as La Raza, which is The Race, The People. But the name we are known by does not matter. We are a New Breed.

"We are like the Hebrews in Egypt. It is said that when they went into Egypt the Hebrews were a weak people, they were in bondage; but now they are a strong people, many millions of people. After four hundred years of bondage we consider ourselves a strong, big, multiplied people. For the last four hundred years we have been growing and developing. Until now, like many other people in recorded history, we have our beginning. I think we are just beginning to live, just beginning to taste life.

"Like the Hebrews in Egypt we are just now becoming free of our bondage," Tijerina exclaims.

The Prophet envisions the genesis of his people in his mind; he is exhilarated by his thoughts. He talks with a religious ecstasy. Words pour forth with such excitement that he seems to be experiencing his prophecy at the very moment he is talking.

In his voice there is a fanaticism that has frightened his enemies. One of his close friends says of him, "Reies is the product of a medieval age and pentecostal eschatology." Yet, within the fury of his messianic vision he retains a remarkably calm belief in the inevitable cycles of life that is strangely Indian. He goes from biblical exhortation to the folk wisdom of migrant camp and mountain village in one breath.

"My grandfather and my father would talk of a time when all things would be right, when everybody would be friends with everybody," he says. "Though they were ignorant people and had no education, very little, they had the natural feelings of the animal world. The animal world has an instinct; they can feel when a storm, or flood, is coming. Especially the sheep. They get together, every animal. Well, the poor people of the world, the New Breeds, somehow, it is hard to explain, they can feel when something is changing, when a great change is coming about.

"We are expecting this great change. The Negroes are expecting this great change, they feel it. That's why they are jumping, breaking the barriers, and yelling, and respecting *nothing* that gets in their way. Because the Negroes can *feel* the future. And so can we, the New Breed.

"I say, We got all the time in the world. We are in no hurry. We are clean of national crimes. We have never been a nation. We have not oppressed anybody. We have not stolen the lands of anybody. The New Breed is ready to be just, to be used by justice, to bring justice. It is hard for justice to reveal itself to an old, corrupt power. But it is easy for the New Breed.

"So we are not in a hurry. We need more time to develop. Time is running out for the United States, for Russia, for England, for the old powers. But not for us.

"A people with this belief will go a long way. They will sacrifice everything. They will sacrifice money. They will unite with the Indian, with the Negro, with everybody. They will work hard to establish harmony between the races and people, to destroy barriers, to bury hatred, and to pursue justice without accumulating hatred, and to avoid the mistakes that every nation has committed in ruling empires with hatred.

"Our intent is to put a stop to hatred between people. We don't need hatred. We are not afraid of anybody.

"We are not alone. We are just a small picture of the universal and cosmic picture," Tijerina says. "We are just part of history and of this continent. In a very few years there will be 600 million Latin Americans south of the Rio Grande. These are our brothers. Yes, we are but a small grain of sand belonging to a great mass, a great people. Even though we are few, the whole world will force the United States to negotiate with the Latin American people, under the Latin American peoples' terms. That is, under terms of justice.

"Even though the United States has played the ignorant, the role of the ignorant, ignoring us, ignoring our pleas, our marches, our activities, our claims, our demands, we feel that eventually the United States will have to heed our cries. The whole world is the jury. The whole world is looking toward the United States."

In a booklet of his Alianza there is a sharper warning: "The days of hopelessness of the Spanish people of New Mexico are numbered. The Anglo should read this handwriting on the wall and make allowance for it in their hearts and lives. The Anglos should not forget the Mano Negra (the Black Hand) movement in New Mexico, earlier in the century. Vigilance committees and vendetta movements are always terrible for both sides. But if the Alianza loses the confidence of the Spanish people [it] can no longer guide them upon a proper course of action within the law. . . ."

"Do you agree with this threat?" I ask Reies Tijerina.

"What threat?"

"It sounds like a declaration of war."

"Yes, there will be a war of races," Tijerina replies quietly. "Hatred will build up. There will be a great clash of race against race around the world. Yes, a war of races. After that we will live like brothers. Like one family of races, I believe."

He is not talking of riots and rebellions. The Prophet is talking of nothing less than the Armageddon.

"Communist!" is the accusation hurled at his biblical rhetoric. The former District Attorney of Santa Fe County, Alfonso Sánchez, has gone so far as to publicly accuse Tijerina's followers of being trained in the political guerrillaism of Fidel Castro's "Cuban Communism." Sánchez has implied that the mountain villagers of the Alianza may be training in northern New Mexico for a revolution.

"I don't know much about Communism or Marxism," Tijerina scoffs. "Communism is just another European political system to me, just as corrupt as any other political system. We don't need it." He condemns the "Russian Empire," as he does the "British Empire." "The old powers are dying," says the Prophet. "We are being born.

"The Communists are no threat to the rich, the oppressors, in New Mexico. We are a threat to them."

The contempt with which Tijerina dismisses the political conflict dividing the Western world is echoed by as different a man as Luis Valdez, the poet of El Teatro Campesino of California's farm workers.

"Marx and Hegel were European. What have they got to say to us?" asks Valdez. "The Aztecs had a communal society before Communism was ever heard of in Europe. I think Motecuhzoma has more to teach us than Marx. Our ideology is in this earth, this continent."

In Los Angeles a young leader of the Brown Berets, Carlos Montes, agrees. "Communism? That's a white thing. It's their trip, not ours."

"La Raza has its own political ideology," Tijerina says. "We don't have to borrow anybody's secondhand politics." The belief of the Prophet is in his prophecy, in any event, more than in his politics. He is a messenger of divine revelation, whose text he has witnessed himself, whose message he bears.

Politics is religious to the Prophet. When he briefly campaigned for Governor of New Mexico, Tijerina began his political drive with a pilgrimage, on foot, to the miraculous Sanctuary of the Black Christ of Chimayo. He journeyed to the historic shrine of the Penitente Brotherhood to "demonstrate the sincerity of his political intentions." He told reporters, "Many go to Rome, or to the Shrine of the Virgin of Guadalupe, in Mexico. I come here to Chimayo, on foot. I have no other way to tell the people that I serve them."

"To serve the people is to serve God," Tijerina said. It is his political credo.

His prophecies mix religion and politics rather freely. The middle-class Hispanos of Santa Fe and the suburban barrios of Albuquerque are uncomfortable with his rhetorical visions. "Reies Tijerina? He is a clever faker," they say. "He is a revival-tent politician," and "He embarrasses the respectable Mexican Americans, the way he speaks."

They joke about his land-grant demands:

"I talked to Tijerina," says a low-ranking official, of an old Hispano family, "and he offered me the City of Santa Fe if I will support him."

"That's nothing," says another. "He offered me the State of Texas."

"What did you say?"

"Reies, I said, let's make a deal. *You* keep the State of Texas. Then I will support you."

In the days of the *caudillos*, the Mexican warlords, and the desperados of Pancho Villa, he would have had his place, they say. The Savior turned dictator is out of place in the sophisticated politics of today. One of the directors of the Community Action Programs of New Mexico, Rudolph F. Baca, says archly: "Many people say Tijerina is an effective spokesman of the people. All I can say is that we disagree on the basic issue—how a program is run. His movement is not democratic. It is a one-man show."

Some of the Hispano officials go further. He is nothing but a bandito to them, a rabble-rouser and a "tool of the Communists." The man is a charlatan; he is too intelligent to believe the nonsense he tells people; his prophecies are a ruse to fool the village fools.

"I consider him an enemy of the country," says United States Senator Joseph Montoya (Democrat of New Mexico). "When he calls this nation of ours a prostitute, I say he's a damned liar, and if he doesn't like the nation and what it stands for he can get the hell out." Tijerina is an "exploiter, discredited charlatan, impostor, and racist," says the New Mexican Senator; and as for his land-grant movement —it is "just a racket."

"He takes the savings of people who follow him in order to fatten his purse."

Tijerina's reply is a shrug: "Of course they have a right to ask, 'What's in this for Tijerina?' But for me I wouldn't even stop to give an answer. They do not know what justice is. They think in terms of money or land. Many people tell me, 'If we win, Mr. Tijerina, we the people of Antonchico, we the people of Tierra Amarilla, will give you so many acres.' I don't even answer. I don't want to hurt their feelings. But to me, it's nonsense. I don't think in terms of land or money. If I can see, with my own eyes, justice taking over the State of New Mexico, that will be my reward.

"I am a patriotic son and child of the United States," he says. "I love my country as much as anyone does, but the Constitution doesn't compel me to go along with the actions of every U.S. agent, or U.S. Senator."

The landed Hispanos and the official politicians do not all ridicule the land-grant prophet, or fear him. The resentment toward the Easterners' real-estate zeal has been after-dinner talk for more than a century. In the genteel society of New Mexico, among the scions of the old families, hereditary bankers and gentlemen ranchers, and even among the Hispano officials (some of whom publicly prosecute Tijerina), there is often delight and quiet laughter at the embarrassment that Tijerina has caused the Anglo establishment.

One such man is Paul Vigil. Vigil has a Texan's leathery, sun-dried skin (though he would bridle at the word Texan), his red hair whitening, his eyes hard as a prairie hawk's, his hands sure of themselves. He was a rancher in eastern New Mexico, near the Texas line.

"I ran a big herd. Sold $60,000 a year in cattle, some years. Well, I guess I spent twenty-seven years of my life building that place before I was run off," he says.

"I was alone there, the only Spanish rancher. There were neighbors I had for years, and they turned against me. Even my banker, he was an old friend, a good man, he cut off my credit. He told me they made him do it, those Texans. We had a Cosa Texas there, or maybe we have a Nuestra Texas here. Well, I know some kind Anglos. Not the Texans, though. The Texans want power. Power is all they are interested in: power and money."

Vigil has a decisive voice, the sort that is used to giving orders and not being crossed. He says, "They say the Spanish wouldn't know what to do with the land if we did get it back. I am going to curse now, forgive me. Well, I say to that, bullshit!

"I say we were cattle-ranching before they came here. There are things I could still teach the Texans about ranching."

He is one of the faithful of the Alianza. There are many like him who have been denied the inheritance of their land and who feel they have been disinherited. Few of these support Tijerina, but they are sympathetic to his movement.

In the days after the courthouse insurrection, a high La Raza politician confided to a friend, "You know what that bastard Tijerina has done to me? He has questioned my whole life. All my life has been based on my denying I am a Mexican to myself. My life has been a denial of what I am. Now I have to decide whether I am lying to myself. Now, there are two sides of me and I have to decide which one I am."

The politician cursed. "I hate that bastard for that. Who appointed him my conscience?"

It is a personal thing. Unforgiving of those who have made it out of the barrios, away from the villages, and who look back with alms and guilt upon those they left behind, Tijerina has been known to turn the back of his hand on their offers. He is hard on his benefactors.

The turmoil that catapulted the Prophet into the headlines brought many offerings. One "Luncheon Club" of La Raza businessmen and professionals in a Southwestern city offered the Alianza hundreds of dollars in support. Tijerina was so touched he told his benefactors he would speak at their "Luncheon Club," in gratitude. No, that would not do! came the startled reply: If the local newspapers heard that Tijerina was addressing them, they would be ruined! Would the Alianza send another speaker! Tijerina refused their money. The deceits of ordinary politics do not appear to interest him. What he says is, "I have no time for this."

"Sometimes when we are discussing tactics and organization, I see he is not listening," one of the young admirers of Tijerina says. "I look at him and know by his eyes that he is thinking of something else."

An older man, a veteran of New Mexican politics and sympathetic to the land-grant movement, though not a member, says, "Reies is limited in his knowledge of organization. It is something he has to learn, or they will cut him to ribbons. He is not political enough. He does not know what to do next. He is the greatest leader we have in New Mexico. There is no question about that. But he has to learn organization."

"He trusts too much," says one of his supporters. "He trusts the truth too much. I tell him, Reies be careful, they will betray you; but he trusts 'the truth of justice,' he says, and will not listen."

"Our belief is founded in justice, in one God, in punishment for the evildoer after resurrection," Tijerina responds. "Justice is a power. Justice will synchronize the creation as it was thousands of years ago. Justice will finally settle the scores of the rich and the poor. Justice is the only weapon left for the poor people, the humble people. Justice has no need of bullets and bombs. Justice has accomplished more according to recorded history than all the empires that have used powder and the sword to conquer, to enforce their law and order. Justice is the law of God.

"Justice will become human, become incarnated. Like the Christ who was born in the likeness of man, a human being. That is how justice will appear to us. That is our strong belief. Like the uranium-238 that was discovered and converted into energy to explode bombs and generate power, we discovered the energy; the moving spirit of the people is in justice. It is a power so strong that it can kill you or make you strong. But it needs cultivation.

"We have to materialize justice! Justice will become life within our life. Our belief in justice is so strong that we can see and hear justice being transformed into human beings. We can feel the elements, the power of justice, using our mouths, our feet, our eyes, our hands, our hearts. We can equate justice with the common needs of mankind—like the oxygen, the air we breathe. Mankind should build a monument to justice as evidence that for the first time in history justice has become human."

The Prophet knows that he has shaken the status quo of poverty with his prophecies. Wherever he has gone—leading the Poor People's March to the nation's capital, helping found the La Raza Unida (The United People) movement in South Texas, preaching "the power of justice" to the Chicano university students of California, or by defying and defeating the courts of New Mexico—Tijerina has become the incarnation of his own visions.

"It doesn't matter what he (Tijerina) does, it doesn't matter what he says, it doesn't matter if he never runs for office. Everyone has to be for, or against, anything he says or does. He has driven a wedge into the political setup in this state, and maybe the Southwest," says Governor David Cargo, of New Mexico. He disagrees with the methods and he doubts the goals of the land-grant prophet, the Governor quickly explains. But, he adds, "I tell you, Reies Tijerina is the man to beat in this state."

The Governor leans back in his leather chair beneath the gigantic Seal of New Mexico. He contemplates the seven figures of Santos that cast a peculiar calm about the tumultuous executive office. "I don't say Tijerina did it by himself. But the people in the villages will never be the same again. They want to be independent. They are tired of being told what to do by politicians.

"Maybe—" the Governor smiles—"they are tired of listening to Tijerina, too."

A sense of history has followed in the footsteps of the Prophet, so closely that sometimes it overwhelms him. He is weary. He realizes that the young men who have come after him, into the breakthrough he has made, will be able to go further than he did, more confidently and with more sophistication. "Revolutionary movements go far beyond the goal conceived by their original theorists," says Jesús Silva Herzog, a Mexican political writer and former director of the School of Economics of the University of Mexico.

It has already happened to Tijerina. The villagers have begun to create their own farming cooperatives, educational programs, and land-reform campaigns without him. The disciples of the Prophet—the mountain youth of the Comancheros del Norte, the Brown Berets in the barrios of Santa Fe and Albuquerque, the Chicano activists of the United Mexican American Students (UMAS) at the University of New Mexico—have begun to dispute his messianic style of politics, argue with his rhetoric, and challenge his leadership. "He is old-fashioned," a student leader complains. "Our movement has outgrown his revival tent."

"The force of the collective drags the leaders beyond their purposes. If they try to oppose that irresistible force, the power of the mass will either eliminate or destroy them," declares Jesús Silva Herzog.

Reies Tijerina is philosophical. Yet he is bitter. He jealously holds onto his prophecy. He does not understand the etiquette of democracy; a prophet rarely does. "Betrayal" becomes a favored word of his vocabulary. The inner circle of trusted lieutenants around La Mesa (The Table) that directs the Alianza grows smaller and smaller, as the organizations of La Raza in New Mexico become more numerous and varied. He knows he is creating the very forces that seek to depose him.

"I am no longer organizing villagers," he says. "I am organizing organizers. I am organizing organizations."

"What will happen to you?" he is asked.

"A man is just one man. I will die for what I believe," Tijerina says. "The other men, maybe they will die for something else."

Once more he will become "the outsider," the wandering preacher, the son of a migrant. "All my life a migrant."

"Christ was an outsider, too," he says.

"Like the Christ who was born in the image of man, a human being, justice will be born in my people, the New Breed. I hold fast to the dream of our rebirth."

In the world of Reies Tijerina the advent of justice will be like a cosmic epiphany. He foresees the sweep of history in his prophecy. He shakes his fists and yells to the heavens when he talks, imploring the Almighty God to hear his voice. If no one listens to him in his audience, he does not hear them.

"He talks to God," the villagers say.

VII The Death and Resurrection of the Rural Village

One cold winter not too long ago a young reporter journeyed into the villages in the state of New Mexico. He saw death. The houses were boarded up, half of their people gone. "A man splits wood for his stove. And only a dog hears the noise of his ax," Peter Nabokov wrote in the Santa Fe *New Mexican.* "The villages are dying."

Years before the coming of mechanized farming the villages were "doomed." In the colonial Spanish era in the old Southwest it was evident that "beyond a mere livelihood incentive stopped, bowing to a stone wall of inevitability. And a dry rot set in," the Reverend Ross Calvin wrote twenty years ago in his *Sky Determines: An Interpretation of the Southwest.* His requiem was the usual one of the Anglo for those whom he had conquered: "A stronger race came and took away their inheritance."

And yet what else could one expect from the "illiterate, half savage proletariat," as the historical writer Harvey Fergusson has contemptuously described the Hispano villagers of the Southwest.

In the villages the earth too was dead. The earth was no longer sacred: it was fertilized by chemicals, not by the sun, plowed by machines, not by men, measured by market prices, not by its own beauty.

The strangers, many of them, were city men before they came into the wilderness. Who among them worships the gods of the earth? The Hispano villagers of New Mexico do. So do the Mexican farm workers of the Southwest, the descendants of Indian and Spanish farmers, who lived in communal villages, with a reverence for the earth. They sowed seeds to grow food, not to profit. They were outmoded, bypassed by progress.

"The destruction of the Spanish American village economy and social structure" is at hand, Dr. Clark Knowlton of the University of Texas informed a recent meeting of the Rural Sociological Society. His gloomy view, so common among the knowing, beholds the villages as "a large distressed region marked by poverty, functional illiteracy, unemployment, high rates of welfare payments, poor educational features, emigration, apathy and ethnic bitterness." Elsewhere Dr. Knowlton has questioned the "continued existence" of the villages. "Problematical," he guesses.

It is true that emigration from the farms to the cities in the past twenty years has been greater than the flood of European immigrants into the ghettos during the peak years of the exodus—1896 to 1915. The refugees from the countryside numbered 17.5 million from 1940 to 1960. And still they come at the rate of almost one million a year. Mostly the young and restless, they fill the new ghettos with longing and discontent. Lopsided crowding has squeezed 70 per cent of the people into 3 per cent of the land. The trail of the refugees is everywhere the same as in the Southwest.

The folks down on the farms have decreased from 32 million in 1910 to 12.3 million in 1965. So, too, have the farms disappeared in those years, from 6,361,502 to about 3,000,000 today. Half of those remaining are barely subsistence farms, whose crops account for a mere 3 per cent of the agricultural market. Jobs in rural areas have evaporated. In the years before World War I one-third of the people labored on the land, but by the mid-1960's only 6 per cent of the people had rural employment.

In a doomsday prophecy titled "The Decline and Fall of the Small Town," in the emporium of social scientism *Trans-action* (April, 1967), two moody sociologists, William Simon and John H. Gagnon, dissected the corpus delicti of three small towns in Southern Illinois —with little glee but no regrets. Simon and Gagnon, senior researchers at the Institute for Sexual Research at the University of Indiana —where they are specialists in the study of "adjustment of male homosexuals"—deviated from their normal scholarly pursuits to excoriate the ghosts of small-town life. They tried, but they failed.

Life in these small towns is "doomed," the sociologists decided. The "local amenities must deteriorate," the towns themselves "will become isolated and decayed," and soon only "the aged, the inept, the very young—and the local power elite" will be left on the dilapidated and dying Main Streets.

Not that the small towns cannot compete with the cities, but they won't, the sociologists wrote. "Redevelopment is not a promise but a threat to the ideologies of small town life."

Quiet and neighborly concerns, the belief in traditional ways, and "a strongly anti-urban system of values," such as a "rejection of purely mercenary values," convinced the sociologists that small towns were a drag on progress, an anachronism that had to succumb to history. "They must lose their best people," who presumably do not believe in these outmoded ideas, and those "who return will be failures," who are satisfied with "the second best in our competitive society."

The perverse and bygone literary farmer from Texas, Stanley Walker, extended this harsh view into the countryside. In his tirade of a few years ago, *The Myth of the Family Farm*, he wrote: "Far from being sturdy, valiant yeomen who should be preserved these people are for the most part born leeches. They hate their work. They make rural slums."

The requiem varies, yet it is everywhere the same. The ghost towns of the old mining camps in the Rockies, the abandoned farm towns on the Dakota plains, the deserted country crossroads in the cotton delta, the decaying adobes of the Hispano villages—these are all ruins of a dying way of life. Our countryside has become a cemetery of beautiful memories. . . .

Alex Mercure, a quiet man not given to outbursts, is nonetheless angered by the prophecies of doom. He is the State Director of the Home Education Livelihood Program (HELP) of New Mexico, probably the most successful attempt at the revival of village economy and pride in the whole country.

"Villages are not dead," he says. "Some of the experts believe that rural life is no longer functional. That rural society has collapsed beyond any possibility of rebuilding. It is not so!

"What do the experts know of our village life?" Mercure scoffs. "Our villages have many human resources. People!" They know how to organize and run their own Cattle Growers Associations, and how to manage Water Users and Ditch Associations. They practice their own village democracy. They have religious strengths. They have the framework of strong families, though these have been weakened by the welfare system. They have their native skills—woodworking and weaving—that could be profitable for them. Most of all, says Mercure, "they know how to enjoy life."

"Communal life still exists in the villages," Mercure says. "It is not entirely the shadow that the experts see from the outside. It is a reality. And that communal life may be our greatest strength. These are the seeds of the revival of village life. Can these seeds be regenerated? I think so.

"Gandhi in India advocated a cottage industry. That may have been all right for India. But not here. What is cottage industry in an industrial country such as this but handicrafts and art crafts? That benefits just one man. And a Gifte Shoppe. It is archaic. It won't help a whole village. Look what the government's Indian Arts and Crafts program has done to stop poverty on the reservations. Not much.

"We need village industry," he says. "Small village industry that can revive the village. A village does not need a large plant, or huge investment. That would only destroy the village completely. No, we need native industry that would employ maybe ten, or twenty, people. Because ten jobs would feed one hundred people. That will mean more jobs in the grocery store, the post office, the gas station, the tavern. That's all a village needs to survive."

More than fifty village industries and cooperatives have been begun by the HELP project. Established in 1965 under the sponsorship of the New Mexico Council of Churches and the Roman Catholic Archdiocese of Santa Fe, and supported by Ford Foundation and OEO grants, HELP seeks to aid "the poorest of the poor" in the villages, who "never had a true sense of community." Its aims are straightforward and simple. The training of job skills "based on the skill needs of the community" is a prosaic enough beginning. So too is its second goal: the setting up of farming cooperatives to help stabilize "small family-sized farms." And finally, it hopes to help "small business enterprises to utilize existing handcraft skills."

"We are rebuilding the villages," Mercure says. "You know why we are succeeding where so many have failed? Because we practice old-fashioned democracy. I am very conservative about that."

"The most conservative program in existence today," Governor Cargo of New Mexico agrees. But the old ranchers, with hard-lined faces, are leery of HELP's program to encourage the self-reliance of the Hispano villagers. They cite an accusation of nefarious subversion, "The Communist Plot to Grab the Southwest," by Alan Stang, that appeared in *American Opinion*, a supposed John Birch Society publication, which implied that Mercure and the HELP program were part of a "plot" to "grab" the land of the Anglos.

"I thought the conservatives would support us," Mercure says, shaking his head with a bewildered smile. "All we are doing is encouraging individualism and free enterprise and old-fashioned initiative. Isn't that what everybody always says they want?

"Everybody is suspicious of our 'power.' What power? Look at our directors," he says. "On the Board of Trustees of HELP are six farm workers, five church lay leaders; in the villages, two ministers, one banker, one businessman, and a Catholic nun. What's suspicious about that?"

In the villages the self-help programs are run by the villagers themselves. One village has a woodworkers' cooperative where they make chairs for kindergartens; another makes wooden crates. There are farm-machinery cooperatives and apple-marketing cooperatives and vegetable farmers' cooperatives. There are health clinics that the villagers build and run. In one village famous for its weaving, until recently a dying art, the craftsmen are encouraged to establish a weavers' cooperative. The villagers decide on their needs and develop solutions that the farmers and artisans wish.

"Too many decisions are forced (on the poor) and consequently are resented rather than responsibly met," Mercure says. His philosophy is simply to help the villages decide what to do, with capital loans and technical aid. Eight of these villages have set up credit unions run by and for the poor farmers and farm workers.

"If you want to help people let them tell you what they need," Mercure says. "Let them decide. Never impose your needs on them. You are only fooling yourself that you are helping them. You aren't fooling them.

"All this middle-class nonsense of trying to teach people to be middle class on $1,500 a year. What good does it do?" The urban programs thought up in government offices by middle-class planners just confuse the villagers, he says. "Rural people don't need them. Learning to push an elevator button! Now what good does that do a farmer?" Even though these programs may be offered with the best of intentions he feels they stifle the initiative of the rural poor.

"'We want to do something *for* you,' they say. They can't do anything *for* us. They don't understand that," Mercure says.

In the beginning of the War on Poverty he thought these government programs might offer new hope. He fears that hope has been betrayed, as do many others. "We thought that they would be of some service to the people," says Fecundo Valdez, who too has worked on OEO projects. "But as it turned out, on many occasions they have been a deterrent. In a way the War on Poverty has speeded up the actual displacement of people in the rural areas."

The frustrations of villagers brought about by governmental promises and congressional withdrawals has been picaresquely portrayed by Lauro García, a young village leader in the farm workers' community of Guadalupe, Arizona:

"It's like having a beautiful woman. She excites you. She entices you. You are ready. Then she closes her legs. And you get nothing. Just frustrated. You feel humiliated. You feel like killing her. That's the way you get frustrated by the promise of these government programs. Because they don't deliver what they promise. And you are left holding the bag.

"We have a saying for that in Spanish," says García, "but it's not polite."

The Lord giveth and the Lord taketh attitude of the agencies dealing with the Hispano villages is not the creation of the OEO. It is the traditional way of the government. "Our people do not trust the government. *Gobierno!* That's almost a curse word," says Fecundo Valdez; the *patrón* and the peon have too often been preserved in the attitudes, procedures, and institutions of the government.

Much of the rural Southwest, and most of all New Mexico, is treated like a colony by the rest of the country, Mercure says. "We export our raw materials and we import the finished products. Isn't that the way it is in a colonial country?" he asks bitterly. "Like poor colonials we are kept in a state of dependency and indebtedness. And condescension is the political expression of this.

"I told this to the Executive Committee of the New Mexico Legislature," Mercure says. "I told them, Do you know that of all the hides of all the cattle in this state not one hide is tanned in this state? Do you know that all the hay and straw that is grown for brooms, that the villages could make into brooms if they had small industry, that all this hay and straw is sent out of the state? Do you know that we import 70 per cent of the food we eat in this state, though this is an agricultural state?

"We *are* a colonial country. That's why we are poor. And we will have to change that ourselves."

The villages are not dying, says Fecundo Valdez: the villages are being methodically and deliberately killed by the urbanization policy of the government. "It's a sociological murder!" he says.

"No effort is really made to increase the land base of these people. Their lands are taken from them. Why? Because all government programs are geared to complete urbanization," Valdez charges. "Not just by the centralization of bureaucracy, but of rural life. Services are further and further removed from the villages. The villages are depleted. If the schools are consolidated, for example, that means the people in the rural areas have to move nearer the schools. Why? Because there are no roads, good roads, in many of these villages. The government builds superhighways that bypass the villages entirely and kill the small businesses. But they are reluctant to build country roads. Yes, we have more of these micro-urban cities. And the extended villages are killed.

"Bureaucratic bumbling? Yes, but it is also a conscious effort to displace the people from rural areas," he says.

In an article written for *Fortune* magazine, "The Southern Roots of Urban Crisis" (August, 1968), Roger Beardwood searchingly explores "the malaise of the rural South." He finds it no economic accident. "Since World War II, U.S. agricultural policy has encouraged the sweeping mechanization of farming in the South," Beardwood writes. "The resulting migrations are inexorable results of policies and programs devised by the agricultural committees of Congress in which white Southerners have long had a dominant voice. Encouraged and financially aided by the Department of Agriculture, southern farmers are using modern technology that constantly raises the productivity of both labor and land. But abundance produces surpluses. To reduce them, the department pays farmers not to cultivate some of their land. On the land they do cultivate, white southern farmers need less labor each year. On the land they take out of production, they need almost none."

For the large farmers and urban consumers these "policies have been beneficial," Beardwood writes. But what of the rural poor?

"So far, government and business have focused their problem-solving powers on urban problems, and blinkered themselves to rural ones," Beardwood concludes. "But every additional migrant is another burden to the cities, and the urban crisis will not be cured, or even arrested, until the South becomes more attractive to its black population than the urban North. The slums are in large part a result of the malaise of the rural and smalltown South; the violence in northern streets is a product of frustrations born in the southern fields."

It is merely necessary to substitute brown for black, and the Southwest for the South, to depict the migrations and the miseries of the Chicanos in the barrios of Los Angeles, Phoenix, or El Paso.

The vanishing farms have been helped into oblivion by the Census Bureau. In the mid-1950's the statisticians eliminated hundreds of thousands of farms, and thus Department of Agriculture services to them, by moving a decimal point. Farms of less than ten acres were declared not to be farms any more, and were not counted. Tens of thousands of the Hispano farmers in New Mexico, and throughout the

Southwestern *colonias*, with their garden plots and small pastures, were thereby rendered nonexistent.

Alex Mercure is neither infuriated nor dismayed by the plight of these villagers. "The villagers are stubborn people," he says. "So am I." He was born into this troubled world. "I come from a rural village," he says. Lumberton, the mountain community where his family lives, is in the midst of the old Spanish land-grant country. The Jicarilla Apache Reservation is nearby. "I grew up with Apache boys," he says. The strength of these Apaches is in his patience.

When he became a schoolteacher he stayed near his village, teaching in Chama, a lumber town in the mountains. Even when he went to the university to study business administration and economics he kept close to the way of the villagers. "I was even a local bartender," he says.

"Now I can go into any village and the people will say, 'You come from Lumberton. You are one of us.' A man has to begin with himself. He has to know himself. He has to know where he comes from and know who he is."

Mercure lives in the suburbs of North Albuquerque now, in the farthest-out community he could find without leaving the city. "I got as near to the farms as I could." Along the wall of his driveway he grows rows of corn, and by the patio behind his suburban home there are patches of strawberries. On the wire fence that separates his lawn from the irrigation ditch, he has planted grapevines.

The village has not left him, though he has left the village. His philosophy is still that of a villager: Like an old man the earth may grow tired. Unlike an old man the earth cannot die. In the spring every seed is an act of resurrection. Men may erode, cut up, fence in, sell, and disfigure the earth. But the earth will outlive them. This is his belief.

"Our allegiance is to the land. The villager couldn't care less about politics in the United States, or even Mexico. He cares about his land. Sometimes people will ask me why the villager doesn't move. There is nothing in the village, they say. There are no jobs. That may be so. But it is our homeland. It is the land we were born on, and where we have lived for hundreds of years."

He tells the story of a man from the village of Portales. The man was asked if he would like to relocate to Albuquerque, where there were jobs, since there were no jobs in Portales. His way would be paid. The man said, "I have been to Albuquerque." He thought about it for a while longer, then he added, "I would rather *live* in Portales than *work* in Albuquerque."

The man from Portales is not alone. A national opinion poll has shown that the majority of people who work in the cities would prefer to live in the country—if there was work. Urban living was the preference of a small minority. Irving Kristol, citing this poll in a critique of urban "myths," feels that it indicates that rural life is not merely an idyllic memory; it is a living reality in the minds of most city dwellers. The "myths" of urban utopias are tenuous, Kristol writes in the *New York Times;* for the better the job the urbanite has, the farther away from the city he tends to live.

The exodus to the cities has been slowing down in the last few years, Mercure believes In the most recent statistics of the Census Bureau this estimate is affirmed; the "urban boom" has begun to level off, the *New York Times* reports, and fewer rural immigrants are on the roads. At the height of the trek to the cities, in the 1960's, more than 30 per cent of the people still lived in the rural areas. That population is "becoming more stable," Mercure says, "and the people are not moving from the villages as *eagerly* as they once did. They are returning to their villages more often. I think more would return if we had village industries. Jobs!

"Life in the villages may be a resource for the entire country," Mercure says. "Cybernetics and the computer revolution may soon mean that most workers won't have anything to do. Then we will be in a real crisis. We may be in it already. We, in the villages, may then have to teach the country how to live in leisure.

"Riots in the cities may be a symptom of this age of cybernetics. The ghetto people who have 'nothing' to do, who have no jobs, are taught to feel ashamed and useless, to feel guilty. So they try to assert their manhood, to do something, anything. They riot. It's this neurotic idea city people have that 'doing nothing' is somehow a crime.

"In the villages we know how to 'do nothing.' To live at a leisurely pace. To enjoy life. No one has to teach the villager how to live in the age of cybernetics. He is ready, willing, and able. He is not neurotic about 'doing nothing.' That's one of the strengths of the village, and one of the reasons the village has endured. So, if the villages disappear our nation may lose its most precious resource—the solution to its urban problems.

"The villages had better be rebuilt," Mercure says, with matter-of-fact severity. "Where else can urban man go to find peace of mind?"

Fecundo Valdez has an equally disregarded rural view of urban crisis: "The root of the riots, ghetto poverty, and crime is the decline of rural life. And that's something all these Presidential Commissions on urban problems just ignore. Unless something is done at the roots it's just going to get worse and worse. I think it's high time that a serious attempt is made to halt the growth, break up and decentralize our industrial cities.

"If we wish to save our cities, we will have to save the villages," Valdez says. "But who will do that?"

In the village of Penasco, high in the Sangre de Cristo Mountains, wedged in between the 13,102-foot peak of Truchas Mountain and the 11,947-foot Cerro Vista, the farmers no longer bemoan the "doom" of their village. They are too busy sowing seeds.

The farmers of Penasco have formed a Vegetable Cooperative. In the past these farmers were too poor to buy tractors, and their plots of land were too small to be profitably farmed in an era of supermarket farming. Every year the families left the village to seek work in the cities. Now they farm cooperatively to compete with the factory farms and save their village.

"We don't say, Wipe out the fences. Instead we say, Let's join hands, cooperate, and work together to make it feasible to farm the area. Instead of buying forty tractors, we'll buy four, and all forty farmers can use them," says Alex Mercure, who helped organize the Penasco Vegetable Cooperative, with the aid of HELP. He foresees a time when the poor farmers' farms, whose meager harvests bring $25 to $50 an acre, will increase their harvests to $250 to $1,000 an acre. "These farmers could earn $4,500 a year."

Across the high mountains, in the village of Tierra Amarilla, where the men of Tijerina had come with their rifles two summers before, the farmers are building their own agricultural cooperative. They have laid down their rifles and have taken up their plows.

In the spring of 1969 there were several meetings in the mountain village. The winds of March had not blown away the snow and frost when the farmers began to gather to talk once more of Zapata's dreamed-of *"La tierra le pertence al hombre que trabaja, con sus propias manos"*—"The land belongs to those who work it, with their own hands." Couldn't they reclaim their land?

Some of the farmers were skeptical. How could they, who had nothing, finance a cooperative? A few thought the cooperative would fail. "It is a mistake to give our sweat to a dream that will evaporate," one man said.

They had no money. A farmer offered his tractor. One villager donated his *molino* (a grinding mill for flour and cornmeal). Still another gave "a squealing pig." Acre by acre the farmers of Tierra Amarilla gathered their land together, until they had offered two hundred "well-rested" acres to begin their cooperative with.

If they cooperated, one village could help another, said young Pedro Archuleta, a leader of the Comancheros del Norte. Velarde, a nearby village, had lost all its fruit the year before. The apples, pears, and peaches had "dried up" on the trees, because the market prices were so low the farmers let the fruit rot. "We could trade beans, potatoes, and pumpkins for the fruit of the Velarde people," Archuleta explained, if the villages would cooperate. "That way, we could have both vegetables and fruits."

In the villages of Coyote and Las Vegas, and the cities of Española and Albuquerque, the women put up "donation boxes" to gather food for the cooperative farmers. Every week they collected canned goods and dried meat so that the workers in the fields would have something to eat during the long summer, before the harvest was gathered.

"Our ancestors could make it pretty well; then we can now," declared a village woman, Señora Juan Martínez.

A woman in the village of San Cristobal, the dark and intense Enriqueta Longeaux de Vasquez, who is a voice of the cooperative movement, wrote in *El Grito del Norte* ("The Cry of The North"):

"Land is a beautiful part of man's relationship to nature. I see land as something that belongs to everyone. Land is like air and life. It is part of each and every one of us."

"The gringo doesn't understand the way we feel about the land," the villagers' newspaper editorialized. "He uses the land to make money from. The land for us is not to make money. Nor is the water or the trees. *'Ellos son de Dios'* These are of God! He gave them to us to feed our families with, and not to make a lot of money.

"Our people in Tierra Amarilla are going to revive the old traditions of working together to feed our people, because this is the revolution, also," wrote *El Grito del Norte.* "What good is it to fight for the land when our children grow up without food? Without a culture? Our children belong to the tomorrow when our revolution will bear fruit."

And so the farmers voted to set up their "COOPERATIVA AGRICOLA DEL PUEBLO DE TIERRA AMARILLA." They issued a proclamation: "We are going to work together this summer to grow such crops as beans, potatoes, wheat to grind for flour, onions, garlic, and squash: just to name a few vegetables. We are going to work together so our children will not go hungry next winter. Our people are hungry and have to practically beg for food from the government. We beg the same government which took our land, or supported those who took it. We don't want to beg any more. We want to grow the food we need, so we don't have to go on welfare, or to the store which robs us in credit charges. We will store the food we grow and next winter give it to those of our people who helped grow it and to those who are hungry."

As the summer approached the call went out to the mountain villages: "The Tierra Amarilla Co-op needs volunteers. Come work with your brothers and sisters. Work! So that people may eat. Work! For unity and power. Work! To be independent of the bloodsuckers."

In *El Grito del Norte* the beautiful Enriqueta Longeaux de Vasquez wrote: "Let's go back to being more self-sufficient. Why do we have to support Mr. Safeway, whoever or wherever he may be? Let's work the land. Then the land will come back to the people and it will belong to those who plant the seeds, water the fields and gather the crops."

The defiant slogan of the farmers, in honor of the hero of the Cuban revolution, had been rewritten. Once it had read: "Che Is Alive and Hiding in Tierra Amarilla." Now it had been changed to:

CHE IS ALIVE
AND FARMING
IN TIERRA AMARILLA!

PART TWO

VIII La Junta

It is a long, hot summer afternoon. Four young men from the poorest barrios of East Los Angeles lounge about beneath the lazy palm trees. In the suburban house of shabby elegance, mocked by once-gracious lawns and broken garden urns, the young men of the streets eat cheese sandwiches and drink beer and philosophize about bygone Aztec kingdoms and utopias of brown power and poetry they have liked and the police who have beaten them up. Summer days inspire dreams. And these "young toughs," as the police call them, are romantic and wistful.

Who are these young dreamers? They are the Chicanos of La Junta.

All summer the Los Angeles Police Department has feared trouble in the barrio from these youths. "The *placas* [police] have treated us like '*pendejos*' [literally, 'pubic hairs']," the Chicanos say, "because they do not understand us." These young men are rebels, but are philosophical about their rebellion.

José: "If you have a rebellion you have to have something to rebel against. So you may become racist. Stone racist. Is 'brown power' racist? No, 'brown power' is cultural. So it doesn't have to become racist."

Hector: "I wonder. Why do militants create a lot of alienation in their communities?"

José: "Man, we're not rebelling. We're building something. We're trying to create less alienation and more community unity. A man without knowledge of his people is like a tree without a root. What we're trying to do is get people this cultural consciousness. Brown power is to know your culture."

Roberto: "I agree with him. Brown power has to be different from black power because we are not black."

Hector: "I don't agree with that. You ask a black man, What is black power? He's going to tell you, well, black power is like the black man being able to take over his institutions, running his own thing. It's black institutions run by black people for the betterment of black people. That's what he'll tell you. You know, basically, we want that."

José: "I think we have to go farther than that! Brown power has to be our cultural heritage. So we can get those values that were inherent in the Indians of ancient Mexico. And we can take those same values and same culture and use it in our lives and our movement. The way an Indian would relate to his family, to his tribe; the pride he had in his Indian nation. Brown power is first of all nationalism. But it isn't nationalism that we have to learn from reading what some intellectual says, like black people do. This is nationalism that we know existed among our people thousands of years ago. It was true then, today, and it will be true a hundred years from now."

Hector: "Our people have been saying brown power for hundreds of years—only we have been saying it in Spanish."

Chuck: "Like before anything ever started, we used to get together, some dudes where I live at, we used to drink and all that, and we used to be talking—before black power, before they had the riots and everything. Viva La Raza! and Chicano power! and Brown Power!—about things like that. So if you ask how come we copy the black people? It's just we didn't come on until later on. We didn't do all kinds of demonstrations. But we always had it. We always said it. Among ourselves."

Once these young men were Brown Berets and wore the defiant caps with the insignia of the Holy Cross and two crossed rifles. "The brown beret was chosen because it is a symbol of the love and pride we have in our race, and in the color of our skin," the manifesto of

Villagers from the Sangre de Cristo Mountains of New Mexico come to Washington, D.C., on the Poor People's March, in 1968. After a century, the discontent, poverty, and repression in Hispano villages erupt in national headlines. *Photo by George Ballis*

Reies Lopez Tijerina, prophet of the land-grant movement and a torrential orator; his Alianza Federal de los Pueblos Libres (Federal Alliance of Free City-States) leads a legalistic and religious rebellion, aimed at regaining the lost lands of the original settlers of the Southwest. *Photo by George Ballis*

In the village of Antonchico, Tijerina is greeted by Hispano farmers and ranchers. Unlike urban political movements, his cause–La Causa–arises in seeming spontaneity out of the family groups, religious ties, and ancestral memory of village life. *Photo by Stan Steiner*

The cross of Christ and the cross of the Electric Company symbolize the changed life of the rural village, side by side, on the crossroads leading to the Antonchico bridge, where, in 1541, Coronado crossed the Pecos River. Don Juan de Oñate, Billy the Kid, and Reies Tijerina also passed this way. *Photo by Stan Steiner*

Where the cultures meet, American-Spanish-Chinese food results. In the uranium-mining town of Grants, New Mexico, the Uranium Café serves tortillas as a side dish to chop suey. *Photo by Stan Steiner*

An old wooden carreta abandoned in the trash beside a gas station, near Socorro, New Mexico; the supply trains of the conquistadors were made up of such oxen-drawn carretas during the Conquest, four hundred years ago. *Photo by Stan Steiner*

Under a portrait of Benito Juarez, the Indian who became President of Mexico, an old farm worker in the Lower Rio Grande of Texas ponders the degradation of La Raza; his ancestors established the Republic of the Rio Grande a few generations ago and liberated the region from Texas. *Photo by George Ballis*

In the Lower Rio Grande Valley of Texas, dozens of poor *colonias,* like this, have no water, no sewers, no electricity, no city services, and a standard of living that is "lower than Mississippi's." *Photo by George Ballis*

A farmer of the Cooperativa Agrícola del Pueblo de Tierra Amarilla (Agricultural Cooperative of Tierra Amarilla) plows the several hundred acres, fallow for twenty years, that were donated by local villages to their own communal farming project. "CHE IS ALIVE AND FARMING IN TIERRA AMARILLA," says their poster. *Photo by Maria Varela*

Mrs. Gregorita Aguilar, president of Tierra Amarilla's Cooperativa Agrícola, feeds baby goats from Coca-Cola bottles. All the animals in the village cooperative, where a few years ago Tijerina led his raid on the county courthouse, have been donated by local villagers. *Photo by Maria Varela*

"Cholo graffiti" on the walls of a house in the farm town of Visalia, California, the traditional form of protest in the barrios. Political slogans, manifestoes of love, and suicide notes form a mosaic, in a lettering unique to the Chicanos of the Southwest. *Photo by George Ballis*

the youth group declares. A barrio "Self-Defense" unit in the beginning, it was established "to keep a watchful eye" on the police and to protect the rights of Chicano youth "by all means necessary."

In their pockets the Brown Berets carry "calling cards" with the motto "To Serve, Observe, Protect," and the message at the bottom, "You Have Just Been Helped By," with space for the bearer's name. Newspapers have compared the Brown Berets to "a Mexican imitation of the Black Panthers." In a national magazine the youth group was described as a "highly disciplined" and "paramilitary organization." "We have information that they are receiving semimilitary training," an intelligence officer of the Los Angeles Sheriff's Department was quoted as saying. He talked of "bayonet drills." One latter-day dime novel forecast a "Brown Beret Revolution," with the fearful words, "the revolution is on," because the manifesto of the Brown Berets asserts their right to bear arms: "We demand the right to keep and bear arms to defend our communities against racist police as guaranteed under the Second Amendment of the United States Constitution."

These young men have left the Brown Berets. "It is not enough to rebel," one says. They are searching for something more lasting, to build something new.

Roberto: "I don't really know what brown power is. To me it's a new feeling I have."

Hector: "Brown power means liberation to me. I don't want to be outnumbered by Anglos ten to one. I don't want to conform to what they want. Some little old lady in Pasadena is figuring out right now what us wetbacks will be doing next week. What freeway is going to run through my home. I don't go for that. I want to determine what is right for me."

Roberto: "It's not a racial thing."

José: "You see, we have some black Mexicans. We have some Mexicans with blue eyes and blond hair and white skin. He's a surfer, you would think. He's not. He's a Mexican. He can take it any way he wants. The blacks can't do that because their color is so obvious no matter what they do. What I'm saying is that brown power is not a black power sort of thing. Even though we are in the same condition, like brothers, we are not the same. I mean this is *our* motherland."

Hector: "You are using the white people's words. English, you see. English is a racist language. That's why they sound the same—brown power, black power. In Spanish we don't say a color. We say, the power of the people—La Raza."

José: "I grew up in San Diego. Well, I used to think I was a good citizen. They say, you be a good citizen and you help your Uncle Sam. So I volunteered. I wanted to be the best, so I volunteered for the paratroopers."

Hector: "Man, he asked what brown power is and you're talking about the paratroopers."

José: "Brown power! That's me!"

In his boyhood José was a paratrooper in Vietnam. He became the "Field Marshal" and elder statesman of the Brown Berets; a thoughtful, toughly philosophical young man of poetic words and a fragile sadness. Hector, with his perpetual dark glasses, talks tougher. He is preparing for college, training himself in intellectual self-defense. Carlos, called Chuck, is sullen and silent. When he talks his thoughts are flat and matter-of-fact, and he does not give himself away. Roberto, the youngest, talks the toughest, but he has a cherubic eye and he shyly whispers that he is a poet. (The poet laureate of the La Junta!)

"Man, don't mention our names," says the former "Field Marshal" José. He feels that the Los Angeles Police Department is trying to harass and arrest the Brown Berets and to destroy their group. The young men agree; no real names.

José: "I'm nervous. Man, I don't know what I'm saying. The thing is I wanted to be a good citizen. Later on after I finished trade school I found out there's something wrong with me. I'm brown! So I started saying, the devil with these people. I'm brown, fine! I don't melt into this big pot, this melting pot *you* call 'America.' You know, oil and water don't mix. So I *have* to float to the top, where I came from, to the top of the pot."

Hector: "We're not in the melting pot sort of thing. Chicanos don't melt."

José: "In this country it's real hard. If you want decent bread you got to go to college. So you get a job for the government. So I have this poor Chicano in front of me and I have to send him to jail for stealing. Hell, the white man stole this whole continent, but white people never think of that. Did the white man ever get punished? No! He got rich. But my duty as a good citizen is to nail my brother! My brother! Why my brother?"

Hector: "There's a lot of Mexicans that are identifying with the Anglo. But the Anglo don't really accept them. In most cases they look down on them too."

Roberto: "So we are like the man with a sword in his chest and nowhere to step back. We are pinned against the wall."

It began in the office of the mayor of Los Angeles. . . .

The Mayor's Advisory Youth Council had just selected an "outstanding high school student" and "exemplary young man" as its chairman for 1966—David Sánchez; a boy of sixteen. Los Angeles' Mayor Samuel Yorty welcomed and congratulated the young man personally and gave him a gavel.

One of David Sánchez's projects was the Young Citizens for Community Action. "A bunch of nice kids," Eliezer Risco, the editor of *La Raza*, says, "that began reading about community issues and began setting up community projects, like taking kids to camp, or going to Delano and raising food for the farm workers. At one point they decided to have a coffeehouse." The hope of the coffeehouse, says a Youth Conference Report of the University of California, was simply to attract teen-agers "and give them something to do instead of just walking the streets and hanging around street corners and smoking pot or indulging in what we call 'the grapes of wrath.'"

But, Risco relates, "the sheriff decided [the coffeehouse] was a bad place, because the kids drew a picket line in front of the sheriff's station where there had been a case of police brutality. So they [the police] went at it—every night, every night, every night. They would shine their lights into the coffeehouse, they would come in and pick up people for selling coffee without a license; the band that was playing there for nothing would be given a ticket for entertaining without a license, and anybody under eighteen would be picked up and held for six hours before they would release them, and [they would] tell the parents not to allow the kids to go there because they were Communists, they were dope pushers, they were addicts."

David Sánchez, bitter and bewildered, tells what happened to him: "I was jumped by the fuzz. They had me at the jail for some minor kid thing and I didn't want to get booked. I said I hadn't done anything and I didn't want to sign. One cop got me in a judo hold and another came up behind me from the back and knocked me flat. When I woke up they were booking me. So I began to change my mind about things. I began to see something was wrong with America. Things were no longer Stars and Stripes. We formed the Brown Berets, and one of our main jobs is to keep an eye on the cops."

The chairman of the Mayor's Youth Advisory Council, David Sánchez, became the Prime Minister of the Brown Berets. "Who organized them? The police organized them," Risco says.

Hector says, "I don't know what's wrong with white people."

José replies, "Man, the name of the game is racism. The white man is a racist. It's a colorful country."

Hector: "If people are racist, then something made them racist. So we get into the thing: why do we have racism? Mostly everybody says it's economics. Who brought the slaves here? In Mexico they enslaved the Indians purely for economic reasons, to get gold out of the mines. It's greediness that created racism."

José: "If you figure out how the West was won, it was just that. Racism is the democratic tradition."

Hector: "In my mind, this country was built on violence, built on blood. Like the way it's being done in Vietnam, it's the same thing that's always been done here to the people—black or brown. As a matter of fact, wasn't the Cuban revolution fought against the same owners of the same farms that now we're fighting in the San Joaquin Valley?"

José: "You say, Why is the world turning bad on me? The world is sick and tired of being good citizens. The world wants to eat, that's all."

Hector: "Sure. I believe there will be armed conflict in this country between the races."

José: "There's going to be armed conflict. But we won't start nothing like that. We would be wiped out. We ain't that crazy, man."

Hector: "I hear people talk about violent overthrow of the government. And setting up a new system. But the way I feel things are changing. Very fast. So whether it's violent or nonviolent there is going to be something new to replace the old."

Chuck: "Violence is violence."

Hector: "You don't have to be an intellectual to see it like that, man."

José: "It may not have to go to violence. Say we set up cultural nationalism right now. It becomes part of our lives. We get certain values we can believe in. We get a new system and new institutions. And we have a new country, see."

Now that they have formed La Junta, it is with a sad ceremony that the youths hang up their brown berets. They have a nostalgia for their days as street fighters, the *vato locos* of the barrios. "The *vato loco* has truly been at the forefront of the Chicano Revolution, but without realizing it," they say. *Vato Loco* is untranslatable, meaning something like "crazy mixed-up kids," but said affectionately. "The *vatos* have been the victims of the most jacked-up schools, shitty jobs, and messed-up *chantes*. We have no choice of making decisions that affect our lives. The only way we could express our pride in La Raza was putting our *placas* [insignia, or graffiti] on walls, buses, and other places. Today the *placas* still go up on walls, but we are also learning other ways," says the La Junta manifesto.

La Junta is one of the "other ways." It is "a group of *vatos* from different barrios" who "know who is their real enemy."

Hector: "People say the country is in a revolution. We've always been in a revolution. If burning a television store is revolution, what is it when the Ku Klux Klan burns a church?"

José: "Well, different people have different interpretations of what revolution means. John F. Kennedy, you know, talked about *his* American revolution. Man, *his* revolution wasn't ours."

Hector: "On our continent the white people are a minority. And your minority just happens to control the rest of us brown people. That's what we're fighting. Just saying self-determination isn't enough any more. See, we'll never have self-determination in this country as long as the Man runs *his* electricity into our homes, as long as he sells us *his* cars, as long as we're *his* boys. Well, you know what I'm getting at."

José: "I'm fighting as the Indian fought—for motherland."

Roberto: "If our white brothers won't accept us we'll go back to our ancestors. Our brown brothers."

José: "We're going back to our old culture. Now we don't want none of this Hispano stuff no more. The Spanish were murderers. They murdered our ancestors. It's not that we don't want to be white. We know we are part white and part Indian. It's just we have made up our minds who we want to be."

Hector: "One thing we want our people to see is America isn't a country. The United States is a country. But America is a continent. A *brown* continent."

José: "This is motherland. God put the brown man on this continent. Just like God put the black man on his continent, he put the white man on his continent, he put the Asian man on his continent. But this is motherland. I come from the part of motherland that is called Mexico—the part, it's not a country. I don't see Mexico no more as a country. I'm not talking about Mexico. I'm not talking about the United States. Now it's all just motherland to me."

Hector: "It's hard to understand what we're saying. We haven't discussed it yet, so maybe we better not talk about it."

José: "Now, in this country, we get eaten all the time by the wolf. All of a sudden the wolf figures out he can't eat you no more, so he comes dressed as a fox. But it was the white man that put the fox in it. We didn't have foxes before the white men came."

Hector: "Once there was no poverty. There was no poverty upon another man. I read the Indians of Mexico, they worked just forty-five days out of the year. It was the perfect society to them. The wheel was invented here, you know. The principle of the wheel. Why didn't they use the wheel? Because they didn't want to go no place. Everybody was happy. But no! The white man has to come along with his 'progress.' "

José: "Where Geronimo used to hide out, that's where they exploded the A-bomb. It is ironical."

Chuck: "Man, that's 'progress.' "

José: "What are we going to do? What are we going to set up? I think we have to study what our ancestors had. So far we haven't studied that, because we no longer have our real, true culture, because we were made slaves and indoctrinated with a bunch of bull. If we say we're studying what our ancestors did, they start calling us Communist! You know, everything belonged to the tribe, you know, communal."

Hector: "The witch doctor belonged to the tribe. So you had socialized medicine."

José: "I think we have to go back to what we had before. That doesn't mean we're going to walk around barefoot, half-naked, in Los Angeles. It's just that things that existed then can exist now. The family ties. The tribal ties. Everybody thinking they're part of the tribe and everybody working for the betterment of the tribe.That's what Chavez is doing in the fields. That's what Tijerina is doing in the villages. That's what we can do, the same thing, in Los Angeles, in our communities. That's what no white man can do for us because the Man don't know where that's at."

The young men have come from the public library with arms full of books. In the summer afternoon they sit and read aloud to each other from the poetry of the Aztecs, Mexican history, and the culture of La Raza. "We are going back to our beginnings," José says, "so we know where we will go in the future."

One youth comes upon the words of Jaurez. He reads the passage loudly, with the excitement of discovery. His black eyes are luminous. These men of La Junta have dark, sensitive, moody faces and gentle voices. If humanists can rise from the ghetto streets these barrio youths are the living images of Ralph Waldo Emerson's "scholars of the gutter." Their manifesto says:

> It is the purpose of La Junta to spread cultural consciousness among our people by setting up Chicano Libraries in the barrios which will carry books dealing with the History, Heritage and Culture of La Raza; by setting up educational classes; by setting up programs of community involvement; by working in the creative arts such as the Teatro Chicano, Music, Poetry, Painting and Film. . . . We will stress pride in our people not only by teaching and learning our history, but by showing the great contributions of La Raza to civilization. In working towards our goals we will conduct

ourselves and La Junta in a free and democratic manner, in keeping with the great traditions of the Americas.

In the streets nearby the police cars patrol, looking for trouble.

IX Exodus

Good-bye, my beloved land,
Now I am going away.
I go to the United States
Where I intend to work.

For I am not to blame,
If I abandon my land;
Poverty is to blame,
That holds us in misery.

He comes an exile, from himself; a refugee, a wanderer, a pilgrim, a seeker. But at the border he is merely an alien, a wetback, another "dirty Mexican."

In the old *corrido,* "An Emigrant's Farewell," the Mexican sings as he goes into exodus:

Good-bye, my beloved land,
I bear you in my heart.

On any of the bridges over the Rio Grande, for 2 cents or 5 cents, anyone can walk across. The river is so shallow much of the year that in many places you can wade through the water without getting your back wet. "Wetback" is an unnecessary insult; for hundreds of miles there is no river at all. Like the wild steers and jackrabbits, anyone may cross the legal line in the sand who dares brave the deserts and the jeeps of the Border Patrol. And that, too, was unnecessary a generation or two ago, when there was not even a fence on the border line.

The rites of passage to exodus have never been physically difficult, but they are "humiliating." It is a "process where a human being is asking permission to enter the home of another," Antonio Gómez, a young Chicano in East Los Angeles, writes in *Con Safos: Reflections of Life in the Barrio.* "The latter thinks over this request very carefully. He asks for formal proof of his neighbor's character and sends him for a medical examination, to rule out the possibility of contaminating his household."

Old and young braceros were medically examined for "tuberculosis, venereal disease and infestation of lice." It was an insult to a man's dignity. The Mexican, more than most wanderers, likely traveled with his entire family, and because of this he was especially sensitive. He is not a man to be shamed before his wife and children.

"What was I? An animal?" are the words that still enrage the memory of so many who crossed over.

How much easier it is to walk across the International Bridge and not go back. To cross the water on the raft of a *coyote* at night, hiding from the Border Patrol, is preferable to being numbered and questioned. At least, that takes some courage. To bribe an official and defy the customs is better still, for that way a man may face some of the perils to his manhood that ennoble the journey, yet he may laugh at the governments. To laugh at the *gobierno* is after all a poor man's luxury.

I go sad and heavy-hearted
To suffer and endure;
My Mother of Guadalupe
Ay, grant my safe return.

Crossing the border line is legally traumatic and inhuman. "Every poor Mexican is familiar with [his] powerful neighbor, and it is the dream of many to emigrate to the 'land of opportunity,' " writes Antonio Gómez. "However, the dream of many is the reality of few, for it is no easy task to enter the United States legally." The purgatory of the emigrant is not merely one of bureaucracy, red tape, fees, quotas, and petty bribes. He knows that all too well from Mexico.

It is more "humiliating" that he must do all this to cross an all-but-nonexistent border, into a land that was settled by his forefathers. He goes to what he calls "conquered Mexico."

"Where is the border?" says Eduardo Pérez, a community leader in East Los Angeles, who has been secretary of the State Committee of the Democratic Party of California. "There is no border to many of our people. There is no border in their hearts. It seems the same country, the same desert to them. There is only a border for our government officials.

"For hundreds of years our ancestors lived in the Southwest," Pérez says. "This was conquered Mexico. It still is. History cannot just be wiped clean of blood."

"You are in Mexico!" Pérez exclaims, lounging in his office in the Institute of Industrial Relations of the University of California, Los Angeles. "Sometimes I think, Is this the University of California, or the University of Northern Mexico?"

"The journey to the United States for Mexicans, particularly to the Southwest, where most Mexican Americans live, is a trip to another part of 'their' country," says Hector Abeyta, the director of California's Manpower Opportunities Project of the U.S. Department of Labor. "The Southwest was once Mexican. It retains language, culture, and physical resemblances. The next-doorness of Mexico, the ease with which the border is crossed and recrossed, reinforced these resemblances; for there is the seemingly bottomless reservoir of poor from Mexico."

The emigrant knows. "To the Mexican American in the Southwest, *this is his land* and his roots are sunk deep in it," says Maclovio Barraza, the president of the Council of Mexican American Unity and an officer of the United Steel Workers in the Southwest. "In many, if not most cases, he [the Mexican] preceded those who have exploited and are exploiting him."

It is the homeland of the Chicano. He is native to it. By his Spanish ancestry, before the English landed on Plymouth Rock, and by his Indian ancestry, before either England or Spain existed, the Southwest was his mother country. Now he looks around, and he knows that memory has become a myth. He sees only a trace of his ancestry in the history books, the land offices, or the traduced names of cities. *This is his land,* by ancestry; yet, he comes as an alien.

In a day, in a year, how many millions of men, women, and children cross the border "in their hearts"? Who can say?

It has been estimated that on an ordinary day more than 150,000 Mexicans "officially" come and go across the border. In an ordinary year, say 1964, there were estimated to be 67,200,000 border crossings, to and fro, by citizens of Mexico who checked through the few dozen customs stations.

These impressive figures do not include the millions who crossed "unofficially." Nor the Mexican Americans who are citizens of the United States. They do not include either "the first entry of immigrants [or] agricultural contract workers." They do not include "wetbacks," those who simply do not bother to go through the customs stations on the desert-and-river border that stretches for 1,600 miles across half a continent.

It was estimated by the Commissioner General of Immigration, in 1911, that the discrepancy between "unofficial" and "official" immigrants from Mexico was *ten or twenty to one.* During the first decade of the century the Annual Report of the Commissioner General reported that while 24,000 Mexican immigrants were "officially" noted in the years 1900 to 1910 (with inevitable inaccuracy another estimate was 49,000), the "unofficial" count was perhaps 500,000. The Commissioner wrote that "at least" 50,000 were arriving in "normal years," but these uncounted Mexicans were dismissed as "nonstatistical" aliens.

Years before that all Mexicans were "nonstatistical." In the late nineteenth century and the early twentieth century, the Immigration "Reports" specifically excluded "citizens of British North America and Mexico coming direct therefrom by sea or rail." The Mexican was not yet an "alien," wrote a contemporary writer. The "nonstatistical"

Mexicans were even then thought to number half a million.

Later, these "nonstatistical" Mexicans increased. In the years from 1950 to 1960 the exodus of Mexicans who "officially" crossed the border as immigrants numbered 293,469. Yet during that same decade 4,078,655 Mexicans, who had apparently immigrated "unofficially," were deported. Though "official" immigration averaged 30,000 a year, in two years—1953 and 1954—1,910,282 men, women, and children were deported to Mexico.

These masses of immigrants do not include the braceros, 3,485,786 in that decade. Braceros are laborers contracted for work in the fields. Statistically these men and women are not aliens, even though thcy are brought across the border outside of the quotas. But their passage is not illegal. The agreements between the United States and Mexican governments render them legal—if "nonstatistical." Every year thousands of braceros simply disappeared.

"The Immigration Service had not the facilities to keep count of this hegira," lamented the Immigration Service in the 1930's. It never has had the appropriation nor the inclinations to do so, says Dr. Ernesto Galarza, who has devoted a lifetime of scholarship to attempting a cultural count of the exodus; the Mexican and United States governments have agreements regulating the flow of everything from glass beads to water, says Dr. Galarza, "but never, as far as I know, with regard to the flow of working men, women and children."

"One of the major mass movements of people in the western hemisphere," Dr. Galarza has written of these great migrations of the poor that have not yet ended.

Like the Pharaohs of Egypt the lesser officials have neither the will nor the power to halt the exodus. Or even to count it. "It is perhaps the greatest peacetime invasion complacently suffered by a country under open, flagrant, contemptuous violation of its laws," complained the overwhelmed Assistant Commissioner of Immigration, Willard F. Kelley, who had charge of the Border Patrol.

Why, then, the legal quiescence? It is odd that the quotas of immigration, meticulously contrived by Congress and chastely enforced by customs at all ports of entry, should be so oblivious of millions of Mexicans. "Migrations unguided and unaided by any national or state policy," the Bureau of Agricultural Economics in Washington, D.C., has termed it.

In the years of 1953 and 1954, there was a wave of deportations. Under the shadow of the economic recession that befell the country after the Korean War, and influenced by the mood cast by the restrictive McCarran-Walter Immigration Act of 1952—which has since been rewritten and liberalized—a Special Mobile Force of the Border Patrol was launched into the barrios as far north as Chicago and Spokane. It was named Operation Wetback.

The barrios were terrified. People were confronted "at home, or in the street, or other public places"—even while at the movies—and arrested. If their papers were not in order, they were deported. Some with "long residence status in this country were apprehended and sent back to Mexico," reports Dr. Leo Grebler in *Mexican Immigration to the United States* (UCLA Mexican American Study Project).

One *corrido* laments:

> I could not run away,
> Not knowing the country.

In the years of 1953 and 1954 there were 1,910,282 deportations of Mexicans. Operation Wetback was a success.

Yet in the very next year 380,091 Mexican aliens registered under the Alien Registration Law in the state of California alone. By 1959 there were 528,275. This, despite the fact that fewer than 200,000 Mexican aliens were legally admitted into the United States from 1956 to 1960. Operation Wetback was a failure.

During the mass deportations Congress was cutting the appropriation for the Border Patrol. The Senators and Congressmen from the border states led the fight for the cuts. In disarming, if somewhat disingenuous, words, Willard F. Kelley, whose Border Patrol executed the deportations, sought to explain the *non sequitur* of immigration policy: "We do feel we have the authority to permit to remain in the United States aliens who are agricultural workers, whether they are here legally or not!"

"Out of a total farm work force of 1.6 million in this country, illegals account for at least 20 per cent," James D. Lorenz, an attorney for the

California Rural Legal Assistance (CRLA), told the Senate subcommittee on Migratory Labor in August, 1969. Lorenz testified that the Border Patrol deported 151,705 Mexican aliens the previous year. He quoted Labor Department estimates that "at least one, probably two" illegal emigrants worked in the fields "for every one caught."

Growers knowingly employed these "illegals," let them harvest the crops, then reported them to the Border Patrol so that they were arrested before they were paid their wages, Lorenz said. The Border Patrol "is running a revolving door, probably the most expensive travel agency in the world," the attorney told the Senators.

The exodus has had beneficial results for many. The reservoir of fearful, low-paid, non-union, and once-grateful Mexican laborers who helped build the Southwest have been largely the "nonstatistical aliens." Keith Mets, the president of the Imperial Valley Farmers Association, said: "Every farmer from Brownsville [Texas] to San Diego [California] uses these people."

The hard-rock miners of the Southwest traditionally have been Mexicans. In Arizona there are copper pits where more than 90 per cent of the miners at the pit faces are Mexicans still. The railroads, too, have used La Raza. It was partially at the request of the railroads in World War II that the government inaugurated the bracero program and, in those years alone, employed more than 60,000 Mexican aliens.

> They told me dollars
> Lay about in heaps

"It is the poor who come," says Luis Valdez, the director of El Teatro Campesino of the farm workers of California. "The poor and illiterate, not the rich and powerful. Where are they going? They come from the fields of Mexico and they are still in the fields here. And they still do not know where they are going.

"They keep coming. Eighty thousand, one hundred thousand, a hundred and fifty thousand a year, they come across," Valdez says.

> The cockroach, the cockroach,
> Can no longer walk

"Migration is the failure of roots." It is more, for migration is the seeking for roots as well, and to say "displaced men are ecological victims," as Dr. Galarza does, is to tell but half of a man's story and demean the rest. "Lay down the choice: move or die," and some men will die. Those who "are able to break away, leaving a hostile world behind to face an uncertain one ahead," as Dr. Galarza says in tribute, are courageous men, and their trek into the exodus is no less heroic because they are barefoot, ignoble, earthy, ill, and unschooled workers in the fields.

"La Raza has a tradition of migrations," Luis Valdez says, "starting from the legend of the founding of Mexico." Huitzilopochtli, the sun and war god, prophesied that if the ancestors of the Aztecs would march south they would found a mighty kingdom. "In that march he prophesied that the children would age and the old would die, but their grandchildren would come to a great lake. In that lake they would find an eagle devouring a serpent, and on that spot they would begin to build a great nation. The nation was Aztec Mexico." It is still the symbol of Mexico, the eagle devouring the serpent that is on the national flag. When the descendants of the Aztecs marched north again, to the fields of California, he says, the Farm Workers Union put that eagle on *their* flag.

"We put our old history on wheels of jalopies," says Valdez. "Culture of the migrants! It is nothing but our Aztec heritage of migrations, mechanized."

In 1168, the year of Genghis Khan's first birthday, the Aztecs set forth on their pilgrimages. The year was marked on the calendar of the People of the Sun with precision, for their exodus was a religious migration, led by the god of sun and war himself.

Huitzilopochtli said to the people: "Verily, I shall lead you where you must go. You shall go only where you see me, the sun, and when you come to a land where it shall seem good to me that you stay, there I shall come down to earth, and shall you see me there." In simple words, Go, follow the sun. The Mexican migrant still does just that. But he no longer is guided by the gods.

An old migrants' *corrido* says:

Oh, land of the sun,
I sigh for your sight—
Now I am so distant
I go without love—
I go without life—

On their pilgrimage the Aztecs were tested by the gods. The offering of two bundles was made to the tribal elders, one bundle concealing a jewel and the other nothing but sticks. Whoever chose the bundle of sticks was judged by the gods to be wisest. The moral being: When on a pilgrimage through hundreds of miles of wilderness, jewels are useless.

The legends of the exodus of the Aztecs are many. One tells of seven tribes that went in search of "the promised land" of their Sun God. Six tribes went directly to Anahuac, "The Land of the Ring," that was in the Valley of Mexico City. But not the Aztecs. Like Indian Jews they wandered for generations. The biblical migrants even then, they journeyed from kingdom to kingdom, through war and ordeal, before they finally reached their second homeland, in 1216. When the priests saw this land they cried, "Now we have reached the promised land, now we have seen what comfort and rest has been bestowed on the Mexican people. Nothing more remains for us."

It was a land of dazzling whiteness, says one legend: white cypress, white willows, white frogs, white watersnakes. But there was no land like this in the Valley of Mexico. It is thought that the whiteness of the Aztec vision was a memory of their old homeland.

The name Azteca is derived from the Nahuatl word *Aztlán,* meaning the "white land," or "land of white reeds." Knowing this, some scholars say the tribe migrated from the Sonora desert of northwestern Mexico, and some say they came from the white sands along the Rio Grande or Colorado Rivers. Francisco Javier Clavijero, who studied the origins of the Aztecs in the early 1700's, thought the tribe may have come from north of the Colorado River, in the deserts of the Imperial Valley of California, or the deserts of Arizona—the "white land" of their name. He knew they came from the north.

If this is so, "the promised land" of the exodus of the modern migrants is really the homeland of their ancestors, the Aztecs. Exodus is a homecoming, in the Bible. It is not the tragedy of the wanderings of the Hebrews in exile, but is a celebration of their return to the land their God "promised" them. Perhaps that, too, is the story of the Mexican migrants.

"Many years before, the Aztecs had walked their own walk in search of a place to live," writes Dr. Octavio Ignacio Romano, in *El Grito: A Journal of Contemporary Mexican-American Thought.* "Now the refugees of the Revolution were walking. They walked to the north, to another country. They too walked in search of a place to live. And this too was a long walk.

"This is how the long walk began anew. Or was it that it had never stopped?" Dr. Romano writes.

"We are all migrants," says Luis Valdez. "We always have been." So the *corrido* of the migrant laments in the endless refrain:

To see myself alone
Like a windblown leaf—
I would like to cry,
I would like to die,
Because of grief.

"Good-bye Revolution—Hello Slum!" writes Dr. Romano.

X The Man with the Guitar

It is four o'clock in the morning on the Mexican border. The lights of the Border Station flicker on the deserted streets. A truck parks in a dark alleyway. The driver lights a cigarette, and waits. Hundreds of people with small bundles move noiselessly past the yawning border guards. The driver spits contemptuously at the ragged ones. These are his human cargo.

One by one the men and women crawl under the loose tarpaulin on the back of the truck. No one talks. When the truck is full the driver stomps out his cigarette and roars northward. He drives one hundred, two hundred, three hundred, four hundred miles without stopping, except for gas. The local city ordinances along the way are not gracious to truckloads of Mexicans. He knows the police will not stop him if he does not stop.

Inside the truck there may be thirty or forty men and women. The stagnant air is nauseating. Even the breeze under the tarpaulin of sweetly sick desert dawn does not help. An old man may urinate in tension; his fear pollutes the crowded, stifling truck.

"Are you sick?" someone says.

"Yes," the old man says.

They nod. What is there to say when there is nothing they can do?

Going to the fields, in every truck I have been in, there is a man who can sing. He may have a harmonica or he may have a guitar. It doesn't matter. If he sings at that lonely hour he sings to himself.

When I left Hermosillo
My tears fell like rain,
But the little red flower
Consoled my pain.

I am like a coyote
Who eats poppies, and goes
Trotting off sideways—
Where? Nobody knows.

The migrants are put in windowless trucks and the doors are locked. Where they are going? They do not know. They do not all get there. In San Antonio one locked truck was abandoned on the highway in the summer of 1968. The men and women who were imprisoned inside—more than three dozen—cried out for hours until their lungs gave out, pounded on the steel walls that muffled their shrieks until their fists were bloodied. When help came, several had died. They had suffocated in the truck that was to deliver them to jobs in the fields.

The brave men have died.
Every good man passes.
The shameless are left—
Who eat corn mush.

The open, rumbling trucks of the *coyotes* and the old buses, abandoned by the regular companies, are not all that bad. Like the village buses of ancient vintage in old Mexico they wheeze through the deserts of the Southwest. Every year one or two of these fail to make it across the railroad crossing, somewhere on a country road, and the campesinos are flung out, like chickens, to die beside the highway.

One ordinary morning in the little town of Calexico, in the Imperial Valley of California, there are twenty-three trucks and old buses waiting for their human cargoes. In one hour, from 4:00 to 5:00 A.M., Dr. Samuel Yellen, a city councilman from nearby Brawley, using a hand counter, clocked those who crossed the border at that single customs station. He counted 1,404 campesinos, in that dim, predawn hour.

"These are poor people," says Dr. Yellen. "In Mexico the farm workers earn fifteen cents an hour, those who are lucky enough to get jobs. The corporations—Litton Industries, Fairchild Camera, Hughes Aircraft—who have factories south of the border pay their workers as little as two dollars a day. So naturally these poor people think that working for fifty cents an hour in the United States is paradise. It's worth the suffering, they think."

And so they come, singing of sorrows and nostalgia. The exodus goes on. It is the same in every border town, on every morning, from Brownsville to Tijuana.

"The most deprived classes of Chicanos are constantly replenished by new immigrants, both permanent and temporary, from Mexico," says Hector Abeyta, the director of California's Manpower Opportunities Project of the U.S. Department of Labor. "Almost all of the immigrants are from the poorest people in that country, who come north in search of opportunity.

"Mexican Americans have a higher proportion of foreign born than any other ethnic group in the United States," Abeyta says.

It is whispered in the barrios that tens of thousands of people are neither citizens nor legal residents of the United States. "They jump!" says Eduardo Pérez, a community leader of East Los Angeles. "They disappear. They vanish into the barrios. They live like anyone. They don't hide in this Disneyland of the U.S.A.," says Pérez. "They are bold."

The old *corrido* says:

Who puts water in his wine
Makes it thin and weak;
Who never has known life
Of living may not speak.

And yet the emigrant is fearful. The rites of passage across the border of legality are Kafka-like. One young man, a Chicano student at UCLA, says, "Kafka would be at home here. If Kafka had more *macho* [masculinity], more passion, he could be Mexican. He knew what he was writing about when he compared a man to a cockroach. 'La Cucaracha'—that's us."

"La Cucaracha" was the hymn of the Mexican Revolution, but the man with the guitar sings it differently. He *is* a cockroach. He is invisible. Not only the memory of his illegality, but the ever-present reality of deportation.

It is officially guessed that as many as 40,000 Mexican citizens come to Los Angeles alone yearly. (The population of San Antonio is estimated to increase by 50,000 every year.) One barrio leader of East Los Angeles says that he unofficially guesses the annual influx in that city may be 100,000. He is asked, Why, if this is so, is the population of the barrios not many millions? "The border is a two-way street," he says. "Maybe 100,000 come; maybe 100,000 go."

Once he has crossed over, he is in jeopardy. He may be "cowed and thankful" for his family's safe arrival. "After all, isn't he, the Mexican immigrant, a guest, an *ensimado,* and an *arrimado,* a parasite?" writes Antonio Gómez in *Con Safos:* "Is it not unthinkable for a guest to complain about the lodgings and odd jobs that his host has given him? What voice does a guest have in operating the host's household?"

The migrant is ridiculed by the Chicanos. The young Los Angeleans sometimes refer to the newcomer contemptuously as a "TJ." Literally the nickname means that he comes from Tijuana. Where he crosses the border does not really matter so much as his awkward manner, unfashionable dress, and servility. He is cowed by the affluence of the city and overwhelmed by the speed of the freeways. The poorest of the poor, the TJ has no choices. He must accept the lowest jobs, live in the worst barrios, suffer the insults of both Chicano and Anglo. He has only his family to help him. Life is precarious and work is scarce.

An emigrant to the barrios has to know how to laugh at his dilemma.

I went to the border
To see who knew me:
And at eleven that night
The police arrested me.

They arrested me
In the American style:
As if I was a criminal
With pistol in hand.

He is jailed for "being a fighting cock," the emigrant of the *corrido* laments. In his cell he is offered "a recipe of the House of Congress," the warrant for his arrest. "Do you know why you're in prison?" asks the judge. He doesn't. The emigrant replies seriously, putting on a formal manner, "I don't expect a temple or crystal palace." But the judge is not amused; he sentences the emigrant to jail, and to himself the emigrant thinks, I have been arrested "because of my stupidity." He laughs at himself.

> I come from Morelia
> Dreaming of the dollars,
> Bought shoes and a hat,
> Even put on trousers.

Hundreds and thousands of *vaciladas, corridos,* ballads, serenades, *posadas, aires de la tierra,* and popular tunes tell of the journey of the migrants and of living in the barrios. In the life of an "unlettered people," words are music and history is sung. "Wherever you go, you shall go singing," Huitzilopochtli, the war and sun god of the Aztecs, had commanded. It is still so. The odyssey of the migrants into the urban cities is rewritten by every man with a guitar. "Out of poverty, poetry; out of suffering, song," is the old Mexican proverb. Songs are the true history of the migrations of La Raza.

> Now I am confused.
> I am a shoemaker.
> But here I am a camel,
> With a pick and shovel.
>
> What good is my trade
> If machines are faster;
> When I make two shoes,
> They make one million.
>
> They told me the money
> Lay in the streets
> Like girls and theatres—
> A utopia of sweets.

Laughter of the *vacilada* is cruel, yet not bitter. "It hurts. Like the old clown, we laugh on the outside and connive on the inside," says Eduardo Pérez The song of the *vacilada* is the song of irony; it has many meanings. It is the tale told by the *corrido,* set to music of a madrigal, with the moral of a hallucination.

> Damn the black clothes!
> And the scissors and thread!
> My sweetheart wears mourning!
> But *I* am not dead!

He is complex, the man with a guitar. He is the troubadour of the exodus. The *corrido* and *vacilada* are the Mexican spirituals of the barrios.

And yet these songs are as different as the sunrise and the twilight. The *corrido* is a musical fiesta of barrio life and love and death, the newspaper of those who do not read, sung in the cantina and plaza by the village chronicler. Its melody is familiar to all, every verse is as rounded and predictable in form as a tortilla, and every line is rhymed. The *vacilada* is a blasphemy. It is the song of the refugees from the dying villages. Sung by the urban villagers, on the highways and in the barrios, its words have the mocking tone of a Mexican Bob Dylan, haunting and questing. Nothing of how a *vacilada* will end is known when the singer begins, except that it will end in a tragicomic way. It always does. Even death is mocked, not lamented. The singer twists the words any which way he wishes. The melody is unsettled and nervous, with lines that rhyme and lines that conflict.

Strangely, the words of the *corridos* that the man with the guitar sings sound more and more like those of the *vaciladas.*

> The cactus is bare
> Where my fish was sweet;
> So worry no more
> About girls I meet.

Often the wanderer works for a season, pockets whatever he has saved in the fields, and goes home again, to his sorrow:

My green tree has fallen
Where my dove cooed;
If I go home again,
Will I find a blonde brood?

The hut of adobe is gone
Where my machete hung;
Everything I owned
Is buried in dung.

Like the troubadour of old he goes down the road not quite knowing where he is going. He knows only he has nowhere else to go. He goes singing.

In the back of a truck or in a broken bus he rides with his family. He goes into the fields or into the cities. Wherever he goes he momentarily becomes a nonentity, one of the unknown and nameless ones who leave their identity behind and seek a new life. He is invisible. There is safety in not being seen, in the ghetto, in the barrio, where he is one of many in what seems a hostile and unfriendly society.

He may sing to himself:

Where am I to go? Where?
The road is here.
The road to the Gods.
Well, who counts men here?
Here where all lack a body?
At the bottom of the sky?

XI In the Barrios of the City of Angels and Seven Hells

The Urban Villages

On the hills of the City of Our Lady of the Angels there are tiers of little houses, like the strings of villages on the sea coasts of Spain or Italy or Mexico. The houses are painted in dime-store shades of yellow and white and lavender and pink. In between the houses are fig trees, and cypress, and cedars, and old cars and palms rise like questioning fingers out of the flower beds of poverty in between freeways. The sky is blue as the Mediterranean, or gray as a dirty window when the smog does not stay downtown where it belongs.

"Wonder at this scene of many-colored houses! The houses of our city make us, who are miserable, see light among the flowers and songs and see beauty. Where it gleams forth in fourfold rays, where the fragrant flowers bud, there live the Mexicans, the youth." So a poet wrote of the capital of the Aztecs, hundreds of years ago.

In the barrios of Los Angeles the modern descendants of the Aztecs have built a suburb of that ancient city. The metropolis is a paradox composed of oldest Mexico and the newest technological gadgetry in the United States.

Signs of that paradox are on the walls of the barrios: "VIVA KENNEDY!" "ABAJO DODGERS!" "GO, DODGERS, GO!" "EL BAZAAR DE MEXICO": a dry-goods store that sells workclothes and bikinis. "ROPA USADA": the secondhand clothing store with a surfboard and a pair of water skis in the window, beside used brassieres. "VOTE FOR REAGAN!" "GRINGO, GO HOME!" "THE JOKER'S DEN": the hamburger joint with "FINE MEXICAN FOOD." Tacos and Cokes. "TORTILLERIA": Wholesale and Retail. "JOIN THE U.S. MARINES." "CHICANO POWER."

Old women in black mantillas and floral dresses from Sears buy bananas from an open fruit stall. Across the street, in Spanish, the sign in the real-estate office entices the old women: "Naturalization Papers" and "Income Taxes Prepared."

Here is the religious store: *Artículos Religiosos, Herbas.* Candles to the Virgen de Guadalupe. Candles to the Infant of Prague. Candles to Christ. Candles to "Papa Julius." And candles to a huge, ominous Indian chief in blood-red wax.

Here is the secular shrine: the storefront mission of the Remedial Education and Cultural Opportunity for the Rurally Deprived (RECORD, let's call it), where a Berlin café skit by Bertolt Brecht is advertised in Pachuco slang, underneath a plastic piñata made by the Sunset Years Club of retired farm workers.

Here is the "Extermino La Cucaracha" sign in every drugstore window. In sunny California the cockroaches grow healthy and strong. Exterminating cockroaches is the main sport of the barrios' hunters. Who remembers that "La Cucaracha" was the anthem of the Mexican Revolution?

The barrios of Los Angeles are the third largest Mexican city in the world. Guadalajara and Mexico City alone have greater populations. No one knows for certain, but barrio leaders say that from 800,000 to 1,000,000 Mexicans live in Los Angeles. Either population is larger than the population of Washington, D.C., or Cleveland, Ohio. The people of La Raza in the city, by themselves, constitute one of the ten largest cities in the United States.

Los Angeles is the capitol of La Raza. It is to the Mexicans what Boston has been to the Irish and New York City has been to the Jews.

Many people are extremely poor. And yet there is a beauty in the barrios. Roses entwine the junked cars in the backyards, much as the tropical flowers cover the poorest Indian hut in Mexico. In one of the cities in the San Joaquin Valley, there is a Community Poverty Council that has a eucalyptus tree on its front lawn, a lemon tree at its back door, and roses blooming on the window sill of the "welfare lady's" office, where the poor come for their alms. The poverty of a rural home is not visible from outside, especially when the home is in a city.

Ever since the Aztecs built the City of Mexico the people of La Raza have been people of the cities. The conquistadors thought their city as magnificent as any in Europe. Bernal Díaz del Castillo, the chronicler of Cortés, wrote: "Some of the soldiers among us who have been in many parts of the world, in Constantinople and in Rome, said that so large a market place and so full of people and so well regulated and arranged, they had never beheld before." And Spaniards, too, were of the city: "The civilization of Spain is an urban thing," one historian says. "In America it is the one city that symbolizes the rule of Spain," another writes. It is not surprising, then, that 85.4 per cent of the Chicanos of California live in urban areas.

In the Southwest the number of city dwellers is but slightly less; only in New Mexico are the urban Chicanos a minority—little more than one-third of the state. The population of La Raza in urban areas from Arizona to Texas ranges from 69.3 to 78.6 per cent. The Chicano population of Los Angeles, Denver, and Phoenix is 10 to 20 per cent of the city; in Albuquerque it is 25 per cent; in San Antonio and El Paso 40 to 50 per cent; in Laredo 85 per cent.

Even so, the barrios of the Chicanos are not like the gray tenement tombs of the ghetto. The barrios sprawl over the hills and into the arroyos and valleys, amid the weeds and flowers, like wandering Indian villages. They are a paradox that defies easy comparisons.

Ghettos are the refuse dumps of the industrial city.

"Who creates the ghetto?" asks Eliezer Risco, the editor of *La Raza*, the newspaper of the barrios of East Los Angeles. "The ghetto is where you are forced to live by housing discrimination. But La Raza has been living in the barrios for hundreds of years. No one has forced us. The barrios are not ghettos, although we do have ghettos in the barrios. There are suburbs and there are skidrows; there are ghettos of the poor and there are neighborhoods of the rich. We have everything here that you have in the larger city, but one thing—you, in the larger city, govern us. We do not run our own lives because you do not let us. You run the barrios and you don't know how."

"Barrio" is a Spanish word that simply means "neighborhood." In the colonial era of Mexico the Spanish rulers subtly changed the meaning by using barrio to designate the "native quarter," where the Indians lived. It was a word of contempt. The word barrio, as it is used in the United States to designate the Mexican or "Spanish" neighborhood, is a modern version of that colonial term; except that today the Chicanos have once more changed the demeaning meaning of the old colonial word to one of pride.

It is a city within a city within a city. Wherever the outsider sees one barrio, there are not one but many barrios within the boundaries of family ties, origins in Mexico, or simply street-map geography. Each barrio has its own loyalties, churches, local shrines, shopkeepers, gangs of boys, customs, history, and old village patriarchs.

"Urban villages" may be a better definition of "barrios." In these communities the Chicanos try to live in the best of both worlds: those of the village and those of the city.

"Why do you still live in East Los Angeles?" a man on the street is asked by *La Voz,* the newspaper of the Community Service Organization. "Just a matter of being in a place something like the old country," one man replies. Incongruous? Where in Los Angeles is Mexico? He feels it is in the barrios.

Men and women who come from the rugged mountain towns of northern Mexico and the rural valleys of the Southwest to seek jobs in the city do so warily. In self-protection they bring their village ways with them. The rural feeling of independence, the little gardens, the religious ecstasies, the large and comforting family loves, the communal ways of life—all of these give the urban villages and villagers a resilience that resists the numbing conformity of the concrete streets. None of these human exuberances fit within the confines of gray ghetto walls.

In the old days a goat and a vegetable garden were more of a necessity for the survival of a barrio family than a car port. Some of the barrios are still derisively referred to by outsiders as "Goat Hill."

"Years ago Los Angeles was rural. It was all farms," says Eduardo Pérez, a barrio leader. He remembers that it was just one generation ago. "Where I was born, in East Los Angeles, there were Japanese farmers. Hundreds of vegetable farms. In World War II the Japanese farmers were put in concentration camps. And their land was confiscated. Up to then the Mexican people used to come to Los Angeles to work on the farms."

It was not simply out of migrant camps that the barrios grew. The people of the Sonoran deserts and mountains on both sides of the border could have moved into the ghetto tenements, but they would have been suffocated. "We need open sky," Pérez says, "or we would die.

"Our people in northern Mexico are rural people," Pérez says. "We're in the mess we're in partly because of that. Mexicans coming to this country head for the countryside. We're always going to the rural towns first to work in the fields, to do stoop labor. We're being displaced by automation on the farms. So we go to the cities. In the barrios we know our countrymen will help us. We're desperate. Where else can we go?"

The Masks of the Invisible Men

On a fertile riverbank where a tribe of Indians had built a village of mud and reed huts, a strange band of brown, black, yellow, and red men appeared one day in 1781. These travelers decided to settle amid the native Californians. Industriously they built mud and reed huts of their own, and then proclaimed the tribal village to be a city—*El*

Pueblo de Nuestra Señora la Reina de los Ángeles de Porciuncula. In other words, L.A.

The old faded records of the "Patron de Los Angeles" in the Bancroft Library of Berkeley list these "Spanish settlers" who were the founding fathers of the city:

Nine Mexican Indians
Eight Mulattos
Two Blacks
Two Espanoles
One Mesitzo

And there was the gentleman widower by the name of Antonio Rodríguez who alone had come without a wife. Rodríguez was Chinese.

Of the twenty-three "Spanish settlers" who founded Los Angeles only two were Spanish. The earlier expeditions into the Southwest by Don Juan de Oñate, Father Kino, Don Juan Bautista de Anza, and Father Garces had found few white faces. When the lost party of Cabeza de Vaca wandered for a decade through the Southwest in the 1530's, one of those bedraggled men found was Estévanico, the black Moor. One of the first Europeans to set foot in the Southwest was thus an African. On the expeditions of the Spaniards, the men and women recruited from the barrios of Mexican Indians and African slaves outnumbered the Spaniards by two and three to one.

The pueblos they built around quiet plazas were more like those of the Indians than the grandiloquent style of baroque Spain. In their leisurely old houses descendants of the Españoles Mejicanos, the Mexican-born "Spanish," lived for hundreds of years. Nowadays all that remains of the memory of the original settlements is the tourist attractions: the "Old Town Plaza" of Albuquerque and Olvera Street in downtown Los Angeles, but the heirs of the founding fathers have long since been deprived of their cultural inheritance and their property.

History has all but obliterated our dark-skinned forefathers, who, after all, do not fit the romantic image of Spanish courtiers who, in the mythology of the textbooks, settled the Southwest.

"Old Spanish families are an invention of the gringos," wrote Arnold R. Rojas, the descendant of a generations-old Los Angeles family, in his *The Vaquero.* "They are a myth which paisanos have come to believe themselves as Sancho did his enchantment of Dulcinea in *Don Quixote.* . . . The *Californiano*—writers on California to the contrary—called himself a *Sonoreno.* [Sonora, the northernmost province of Mexico once embraced California.] I have heard third and fourth generation descendants of members of the De Anza expedition (in 1777) say, '*Nosotros somos Sonorenos. Sonora es nuestra tierra.*' We are Sonorans, Sonora is our motherland.

"When the gringos took over the land," wrote Rojas, "the paisano —if he did not migrate to Mexico, Chile, or Spain—gathered what few cattle were left him and disappeared into the most distant and isolated places he could find in the West, as far away from the marauding bands of gringos as he could get. Where is he now? Ask the lonely canyons and deserts of the far places. They could tell if they could talk."

In coming to the cities the rural villagers were returning to the homes of their forefathers. They rebuilt the barrios, in the style of the twentieth century, but they were strangers in their own cities.

"Who's got the land? Who's got the money? Who's got everything?" asks Eduardo Pérez. "You Europeans who came here have taken our land away by conquest, have taken our jobs away with machines, have taken our women with false promises. We do not give up our women, but you take them. You have taken everything from us but our color. And you probably are working on that."

The newcomers from the East who had driven the Mexicans out thought of the original settlers as "foreigners." They viewed the "Little Mexicos" of the cities with a mixture of fascination and fear, hatred and envy.

In the twenties, there was an uproar over the barrios. The isolationism of the times, as the country recoiled from the traumas of World War I, and the uneasy peace that was haunted by the specter of the Bolshevik Revolution, had culminated in a national hysteria against the "foreigners." Cries of "The World Is at Our Portals" and "Guard Our Gates" were echoed in the Southwest as "Keep Out the Mongrel

Mexicans" and "Lock the Back Door." The mounting revolutions of Mexico, from the fall of Porfirio Díaz in 1910 to the triumph of Pancho Villa in 1917, had frightened newcomers to the Southwest and terrified the real-estate developers.

The rhetoric of racism was voiced nationally by the warning of a Justice of the Supreme Court of New York, Norman Dike, who proclaimed, "Diseased, ignorant and belonging to a greatly lower class, the Mexican elements are lowering the standard of our population as far north as Wyoming." The Mexicans, said the Justice, were "the most undesirable of all of the peoples."

Justice Dike's was one of the more somber voices. The chorus of exclusion reached its highest pitch in a book called *The Alien in Our Midst,* published in 1930. William Green, the president of the American Federation of Labor, and John E. Edgerton, president of the National Federation of Manufacturers, called in unison for those "who are American in blood" to "call the roll of the armies of gunmen in our cities . . . worst criminals . . . anarchists, communists, foreign language newspapers and other lists of disturbers containing unpronounceable or exchanged names" (Edgerton); and "To guard our gates" and ensure that "the Country contains at all times a great preponderance of those of British descent" (Green); for, as the president of the Immigration Study Commission, C. M. Goethe, wrote in that volume, the "Mexican menace to our homogeneity" threatens "our race purity."

On a fact-finding trip into the barrios of East Los Angeles, during 1927, the historical novelist Kenneth Roberts was shocked to find not only "Mexican half-breed Indians," but "negroid blood" in the "chocolate-colored Mexican peons." In *The Alien in Our Midst* (edited by Madison Grant, Chairman of the New York Zoological Society), the disturbed novelist wrote that the Mexican "mixed breeds [are] unfit to enter the United States," for "they are inferior to immigrants from Central and Southeastern Europe, and incompetent to advance, or even sustain the civilization already established in the United States."

Late that winter Roberts accompanied a "Relief Mission" of East

Los Angeles "through two Mexican sections"; he wrote, " . . . in no part of Poland or Southeastern Europe has ever been seen a more ignorant and more destitute class of people than the Mexican peons packed into shacks and hovels that have spread out over those former truck garden districts. . . . The signs are in Spanish, the names are Mexican. They are an acute plague sore on the body politic." Roberts then quoted Professor S. J. Holmes of the University of California: " 'The Mexican is prone to various diseases . . . he brings in various maladies. . . . They are a constant menace to our physical welfare.' "

In the 1930's the barrios were of less interest to the civic authorities. The building booms of the Southwest collapsed in the money-tight depressions, and the lands of the "Little Mexicos" were no longer needed. Many emigrants decided to return to Mexico rather than face the humiliation of bread lines, and for several years the tide of immigration turned. Even the "Lock the Back Door" advocates were silenced by the unexpected turn of the poor away from the promised land.

"I remember back thirty years," says one woman, reliving the Depression years in East Los Angeles. "The leaders of the community in those years were what I call hard-core Mexico Mexicans who did sort of well. They had stores, you know. In those days we had a community organization where there would be dancing and vino and 'Viva Mejico!' and the 16th of September and Cinco de Mayo, and the men drunken as the dickens and the gringos, they would be watching, and it would embarrass us. So we decided to keep away from those people. You see, at the time we thought a Mexico Mexican was something to be ashamed of."

There was little hope in the barrios in the dim thirties. The poor stayed within the safety of their homes and fought about scarce jobs and Cinco de Mayo dances; few entered into the upheavals of that decade that shook up the cities.

Life was in limbo until the post–World War II building boom exploded in the barrios. That upset the quiet forever. The old cities of the Southwest, from Texas to California, doubled and tripled and quadrupled in size and population in the wake of the affluence that swept through the deserts after World War II. A sleepy, Sonoran desert town like Tucson, Arizona, moved from 45,454 in 1950 to 236,877 in 1965; old Albuquerque, New Mexico, from 35,500 in 1940 to 201,200 in 1960; the metropolitan area of San Antonio, Texas, from 525,852 in 1950 to 787,000 in 1960.

Once more the old barrios stood in the way of progress and suburban developers. "Very rapid urbanization of the Southwest brought the absorption of [the] Mexican American barrios whose history can be traced to their function as former agricultural labor communities," says the report *Residential Segregation in the Urban Southwest* of the UCLA Mexican American Study Project. Some barrios were bulldozed. The oldest barrio of San Antonio in the heart of the city was leveled to rubble, and the 1,200 families that lived there were evicted to make way for the HemisFair of 1968.

The nemesis of the barrios of Los Angeles has, of course, been the freeways. Chavez Ravine, an old barrio that was bulldozed to make way for freeways, parking lots, and the Dodgers' Stadium, still echoes with the bitterness of the cry painted on the walls: "Remember Chavez Ravine!"

"Naturally they built it in our backyards," Grace Olivarez, a former state leader of Arizona, says of Highway 80, which curves through the backyards of the barrios of South Phoenix, Arizona. "Would you expect them to build a highway through the lawns of Scottsdale, or Goldwater's swimming pool?"

Hemmed in from the outside by the heritage of anti-Mexican racism and built up from the inside by the cultural pride of La Raza, the barrios were a paradox of poverty and strength. The barrios have existed for generations as communities with their own ways of life, their own leaders, their own language and culture and histories. Few outside would see, or would recognize, these hidden resources. The disguises of a colonial people are excellent.

"No one looked 'Mexican' to me when I came to East Los Angeles," Father Luce, a popular Episcopalian minister in the barrios, reports. "In the streets everyone looked so Anglo it startled me. I was determined to find out where the 'Mexicans' were hiding."

Even poverty is hidden. "I didn't know what poverty was until I found out that I was poor," says young David Sanchez, the prime minister of the Brown Berets, who grew up in the barrios of East Los Angeles. A university student, Frank David Cervantes, revisiting the barrios of his childhood in San Antonio, has the same startled thought. "I felt mostly shock and shame seeing this wasteland of poverty in which I had grown up. Until that moment I had never realized my family had lived in a 'slum.'" A judicious observer, Paul Bullock of the Institute of Industrial Relations, University of California, writes in *Poverty in the Ghetto*, "No one can deny that poverty is less 'visible' in Los Angeles."

"Society doesn't want to see us," says Eduardo Pérez. "Technology in the United States is so highly perfected that you cannot see anything you don't want to see. A computer is as blind as the technician who runs it."

La Raza is still referred to as "the invisible minority" in official reports. The barrios are largely unknown and misunderstood by outsiders, even those who devote years to studying them; for the heritage of a colonial mentality blinds outsiders to the reality.

It is no mystery to Eliezer Risco. "When you live in a hostile environment you learn to disguise yourself, so that you are not conspicuous. You wear a mask."

The Quaint Starve

On the ruins of the oldest barrio of San Antonio, beneath yellow and pink umbrellas, with the flags of Texas, the United States, and the Holiday Inns flapping in the scorching August air, the one thousandth motel in the chain is opening.

The Holiday Inn chairman is given a scroll declaring him an Honorary Alcalde of La Villita—the Mayor of the Little City—and the Urban Renewal Award of San Antonio. Where the motel gleams in the sun there was formerly "one of the densest slum areas," says Roland Bremmer, president of the city's Urban Renewal Commission. "This shows what is being done throughout our great country to change the downtowns of America."

Where have the people of the barrio gone? Into "the quaint, the picturesque Mexican life on the Westside" as a tourist guide, *San Antonio*, by Charles Ramsdell, describes it.

The *Inferno*, a La Raza newspaper of San Antonio's Westside, sees these barrios differently:

"With roofed-over corrals for homes and chutes for streets, San Antonio's Westside is like a stockyard; its residents treated with less humanity than cattle. Perhaps as many as 200,000 Americans of Mexican descent are herded here, in what is one of America's largest ghettos. . . .

"Roosters crowing, followed by barking dogs, then wailing youngsters, herald each new day on the Westside. It is the day of hard, dirty work for long hours and little pay. The Westsider is a hearty individual who has endured much.

"One son is drafted into the Army to fight in Vietnam. Another son is sent to prison for breaking open cigarette machines. Yet the Westsider endures. His wife is in the hospital awaiting birth of their ninth child and the blessing of the Church, while his 12 year old daughter is receiving treatment in another ward for venereal disease. Yet the Westsider endures. He waits mostly for Saturday night when he can get drunk at the cantina with his friends who like himself are the wretched refuse of affluent America."

These are "The great unwashed, the unloved, their souls are mortgaged and their tongues are locked with fear; yet they see and they feel and they wait for their redemption," says *Inferno;* ". . . the despair of the people is ever deepening as magazines and movies from the 'outside' show them all they are missing."

The hearings of the Citizens' Board of Inquiry into Hunger and Malnutrition in San Antonio produce expert testimony that 150,000 people or so are hungry. Dr. Vera Burke, director of Social Services for the Bexar County Metropolitan Health District, which includes San Antonio, is questioned about the accuracy of this figure:

Do you, or do you not, agree with that as a general figure?
I would agree that this is probably true.

Sixteen people starved to death in the barrios of San Antonio during 1965, James Kazen, the director of the Economic Opportunity Development Corporation, reports, although starvation is a statistic of death not officially recognized by the coroner.

In the hearings of the Citizens' Board of Inquiry into Hunger and Malnutrition in San Antonio, Sister Mary Rachel testifies:

Would you try to just give a guess as to how many people you think in the San Antonio area might be in a state of need in regard to food?
I think I could say about 25 per cent, probably. Maybe more.
What would that be in numbers, Sister?
I guess around two or three hundred thousand.

"Malnutrition on the Westside relates to that of underdeveloped countries," writes Patricio Tamez, in *Inferno.*

In the same hearings another woman testifies. Her name is Theodora Hernández:

Raisins are the only fruit you get?
Yes.
No eggs? No vegetables?
No.

Another comes as a witness. Her name is Mrs. Julia Gonzales:

How often do you get meat?
Once in a while.
And milk?
Weekly. Sometimes we can, sometimes we can't.
Do the children ever go to bed hungry?
No.
How about yourself? Do you ever go to bed hungry?
I feed my children.

"Often children are brought in [to the Robert B. Green Hospital] weighing less than their birth weight," Dr. Vera Burke says. Expectant mothers are so anemic and undernourished that they are automatically given blood transfusions as part of the hospital routine.

Dr. Charles Bernard Hilton of the Robert B. Green Hospital testifies:

Are you a pediatrician?
Yes sir.
You are also associated with the Robert B. Green Hospital?
Yes.
How long have you been in San Antonio?
Six years.
Will you tell us something about what you have found here with children?

I have seen children at the Robert B. Green, just as any doctor who has worked there has seen children, three, four, five years old, all weighing twenty pounds. In my Well-Baby Clinic I know of at least ten children who came to us at the age of two or three months, and they all weighed the same as their birth weight.

Almost half the men in the barrios are subemployed. Studies by the U.S. Department of Labor and the Texas Employment Commission of the "slum arca of San Antonio" (84 per cent Mexican American) in November, 1966, showed that the national unemployment rate was 3.7 per cent, San Antonio's 4.2 per cent, and the barrios' officially 8 per cent: the subemployment rate was "a startling, sobering *47.4 per cent.*"

"Subemployment" meant those working part time, although looking for full-time work (7.2 per cent of all men between twenty and sixty-four); those working full time but receiving low wages (below the poverty level—44.5 per cent); labor force dropouts who are not working and have given up looking for a job (8.9 per cent); and "those who are known to be present in the community but who do not show up at all in a survey" (15 per cent). These men—"the truly invisible people of our society"—are omitted from traditional "unemployment" statistics; the Labor Department reported, therefore, that "national measurements of unemployment are utterly irrelevant" to the barrios.

"No conceivable increase in the gross national product would stir these backwaters," said the Labor Department; "inferior education, no skills, discrimination, fatherless children, unnecessarily rigid hiring practices and hopelessness" isolate the barrios. The family income in the barrios that year averaged $2,876 compared with the national average of $6,300—less than half.

In the hearings, another woman testifies:

Mrs. Roma, how many children do you have?
Six.
Where do you live, please?
I live with my father-in-law.
How many rooms do you have to live in?
One.
One room for the eight of you?
Yes.
Do you do your cooking and everything in this one room?
Yes.
Do you have enough to eat?
We have $25 a week to spend on food.
What does this food you eat consist of?
Beans, potatoes, eggs, string beans, or peas.
Do you see meat in your house at all?
Oh, yes. Sometimes chicken.
Tell me more about this one room you live in. Do you have cooking facilities?
Yes. A kerosene stove.
What do you use for heating when it gets cold?
The kerosene stove.
Do you find the $25 a week is enough to feed your family?
No.
Would you say that the children go hungry?
Yes.
Do they get milk, the small ones?
No.
No milk at all?
No.
They are not getting any milk?
No.

In his journeys the Holiday Inn chairman had visited Jerusalem. He had walked in the site of the stable where Christ was born. "That's why we're building Holiday Inns," Kemmons Wilson tells his guests at the festive opening of the beautiful motel where once there was a barrio of the poor. "So there will always be room at the Inn."

The Communal Colony

In the irrigated desert water is life. But in the barrio of Wasco in the thirsty fields of the San Joaquin Valley, the water is filthy. The city has its own water system, for its white residents. On the edge of the fields the barrio of the brown residents has a separate water system. For years it tasted foul. The clothes washed in the water were stained. Nonsense! the city officials replied, had the water analyzed, and pronounced it clean.

Sixty-seven of the barrio residents sought the help of lawyers at the California Rural Legal Assistance office in nearby McFarland, who had the water analyzed by a private chemist. Chemical impurities, was the chemist's report. The water is dangerous to drink. The lawyers filed complaints with the California Board of Health and the city's Public Utilities Commission. Long conferences were held, until it was finally agreed that steps would be taken. The residents received refunds of $3,000 for water bills paid for the impure water, from July, 1966, to May, 1967.

"Our water didn't smell any better," says a barrio resident. "But after that it tasted just a bit sweeter."

Life in the barrios is like living in "a colony" to Esteban Torres, director of the East Los Angeles Labor Community Action Committee and an International Representative of the United Auto Workers. He believes the second-class citizenship in city services is due to the lack of the communities' control of their civic life. Usually the barrios are on the outskirts of the cities, beyond the concern of the city halls. The streets may be poorly paved, or unpaved. Sewers do not always extend to the edges of the barrios. Even the mail deliveries do not always reach into the streets where people are so poor they cannot afford mailboxes. There is little native industry and few but menial and manual jobs. There is less local capital. If there are businessmen in the barrios with money to invest they must go outside of the barrios to invest it.

Torres says: Our money flows out rather than in, and this leaves the barrio impoverished. "East Los Angeles is a colony," he says, because it has no "community control" over its economic and political life.

"Much of industry's alleged 'open-door policy' [for the barrios] has been nothing but a well-planned Madison Avenue 'smoke screen' to impress federal compliance officers," complains the director of East Los Angeles' Mexican American Opportunities Foundation, Dionicio Morales.

Jobs offered to barrio youth are usually of the dead-end sort, Morales says. The subtle and overt discrimination in industry frustrates any economic advancement. Agencies such as Jobs for Progress (SER), sponsored by the American GI Forum, the League of Latin American Citizens, and the Community Service Committee, financed by a $5 million federal grant, have made little dent in the economic wall that surrounds the barrios.

"We have a colonial mentality?" says a barrio leader. "Of course! You treat us like colonials."

Ironically, the United States Commission on Civil Rights itself has been accused of job discrimination against Chicanos by one of its former employees, Nicolas Vaca, a graduate student at San Francisco State College. He testified that the Commission on Civil Rights "has systematically, knowingly and insidiously practiced discrimination." At a Los Angeles hearing he charged angrily that in its ten years of existence the civil rights body had not employed a Mexican American on its Washington, D.C., staff of 115. Nor had it issued a single report on the civil rights of the Spanish-speaking in all those years.

"We, regretfully, do not find concerted willingness on the part of industry or government to give the employment needs of the Mexican American serious and sufficient attention," Dionicio Morales has observed. Economic problems of the barrios "are increasing in both magnitude and complexity."

From 1960 to 1965 because of inflation, the "purchasing power, or 'real income' of the average East Los Angeles family fell off by nearly $400 annually."

The late Senator Robert Kennedy compared the dilemma of the poor caught in this economic squeeze to that of an "underdeveloped nation within our nation." He recommended enlisting "the power and resources of our private enterprise system." But the *Wall Street Journal* was cautious, and less than enthusiastic, about what it called "a Marshall Plan for the city slums": "There is a built-in limit on business efforts. We think the private economy does indeed have broad social responsibilities, but those responsibilities cannot supplant the business of doing business."

Frustrated and disillusioned by the repeated failures of outside agencies, barrio leaders have begun to seek economic solutions within the barrios themselves.

A group of Hispano businessmen in Albuquerque, New Mexico, discuss the prospectus of a La Raza bank that would reinvest its funds within the barrios with "low interest loans to our people who have difficulty getting loans from the Anglo banks."

In El Paso, Texas, a shopkeeper and former head of the Community Action Programs, Jesús Terrazan, draws up an ingenious plan for a chain of Cooperative Shopping Centers to utilize the handicraft skills of barrio artisans. He proposes they be built like modernized village marketplaces of Mexico.

In Denver, Colorado, a plan for Chicano control of barrio economy is offered by Rodolfo Gonzales of the Crusade for Justice: "We demand that businesses serving our community be owned by the community. Seed money is required to start cooperative grocery stores, gas stations, furniture stores, etc. Instead of our people working in big factories across the city, we want training and low-interest loans to set up small businesses in our own communities. These industries would be coops with the profits staying in the community."

In East Los Angeles a Civic Improvement group submits architectural plans for a barrio housing project to be constructed on communal lines to accommodate the large Mexican family groups. The units are to be built around little plazas, with families living together in clusters of apartments. The City Fathers reject the plans in favor of a high-rise apartment skyscraper, which the barrios' leaders in turn reject.

A campaign to re-establish East Los Angeles as a "separate city" nearly wins: "We tried to incorporate the barrios as a separate city a few years ago," says Eduardo Pérez. "East Los Angeles ought to govern itself. But the unions opposed us. It's not good for economic reasons, they said; you know, not enough industries, and so on. So we lost, by just three hundred and some votes. One day we will win."

"Water?" scoffs a former teacher in the urban barrios near the city of McAllen, Texas: "We have to buy water in jugs, or bring it home in barrels. No water! No sanitation! No drainage in the streets! No sewers! People don't have a damned thing when it comes to city services. My neighbor has no electric lights, right in the middle of the city. Across the street, in that house you see, half of the floors are earth. The good earth! Housing in these barrios is ten times worse than the worst slum in any northern city. It's worse than Mississippi. I tell people in the university what it's like in these barrios and they don't believe. You know, things are not supposed to be that way in this country."

Esteban Torres foresees industries, stores, and banks, "such as cooperatives, credit unions, etc., controlled and run by the community." They will "resolve the social, economic, and political grievances of the community."

For centuries before the coming of the Anglos the barrios had "community control." The sloganized cry for brown power, or Chicano power, is not new. The unique and communal life of the villages, the *ejidos*, and the *patrón* benevolences on the frontier gave La Raza its distinctive character in the Southwest.

"What are the alternatives?" asks one of the wealthiest Chicano businessmen in the Southwest. "You control us? That's the way it has been, but our young people won't stand for that any longer. We control you? That's too foolish to talk about. No one suggests such nonsense. We control ourselves? That's the only solution that makes any sense, or will do any good. That's what we want to do, and we will decide how we will do it."

Dionicio Morales indicates the sobering alternatives: "I say to the nation: Look around you! See what is happening! People must work, they must belong, or they will start appropriating what they have long been told is theirs rightfully as American citizens. The Mexican American has not yet been strongly militant. I pray that he will not have to resort to molotov cocktails to focus national attention on his economic need."

Evening in the Barrios

"It is more beautiful at night," Risco muses.

Evening has come. On the twilit street little children play Bat Man in the patios of Pachuco. The tropical flowers around the pastel houses close their petals against the night smog. In the sky the neon lights of the Taco-Burger stands explode like fireworks. Where the supermarkets are like rural fairs, the men push shopping carts full of pinto beans, Coca-Cola, frozen tortillas, and TV dinners. On the marquees of the movies there is a nostalgia of Mexico that is so near, less than a few hours distant, but beyond reach. On the curbs the old cars gleam brightly as color television screens, the piñatas of the urban villagers.

The barrios do not sleep well at night. It is too late to talk, but it is too early to sleep. It seems a million miles away. Wistfully the young man closes his eyes. He lifts his head for a moment, letting the night breeze bathe his face and dry the sweat of the summer day. Eyes wide, he peers into the darkness.

"I see clearly at night," says Eliezer Risco, young editor of *La Raza.* He sees then what he cannot see by day. He is the "tough organizer" of the barrio, "swarthy" and "mysterious," a popular magazine has written of him. The Los Angeles police have arrested him for "conspiracy." Yet, he has gentle, sad eyes. His voice is soft and thoughtful as a poet's. "If I was a religious man, I would be a Franciscan Father. The Desert Fathers—I dig that," he muses.

"You are a paradox," I say.

"Every Latin is a paradox," he says. "The Chicano is the quintessence of paradoxes."

"So is the barrio?"

"Look at this street. Would you say it is a ghetto? A slum? We say that ourselves. But there are few more beautiful places in the city than this barrio. What is more peaceful? Where is it more beautiful?"

"It reminds me of a village on the Mediterranean coast," I say.

"Well, they are Latins too. You know, when I came here they told me that Los Angeles was the graveyard of La Raza. It is a hard, paranoiac town, they told me. That may be so, but that is the Anglo side of town. That is not the Mexican side of town. Here there is a beauty, a friendliness, a communality that no one writes about on the outside, no one on the outside knows about. He is a mosaic, the Chicano of the barrio. One of these days we will put that mosaic together. Then everyone will see what beauty really is."

XII The Conquered Country

"It was a wedding dance. Everybody was dancing. These cops come to the door. One cop gives the signal to the other: Let's get him! They charge onto the dance floor, not asking anyone's permission. They knock this man down, kick him. They said he had narcotics. All of a sudden there are twenty cops breaking in the doors. Cops with shotguns, with riot equipment. Jumping on the stage. Walking on the wedding gifts. Yelling at the band, 'You stupid asses! Quit playing! This is it!' Pushing the ladies with those nightsticks. Shooting that Mace at the wedding guests."

The member of the wedding who relives the Walpurgis Night in the summer of 1968 is still dazed by it. He bewilderedly shakes his head. "People kept on dancing. They didn't want to get involved!"

On that Fourth of July weekend four hundred guests had gathered for the wedding party of Virginia Vargas and Edilberto Olmos at the El Monte American Legion Hall in the hedged and quiet community of El Monte of Los Angeles. Most of El Monte's residents are, or pretend to be, proper members of the Mexican American middle class, with emphasis on the American.

Sixty policemen, summoned from five police departments in outlying suburbs as well as that of El Monte, attended the wedding party, and circled the Legion Hall in a score of patrol cars. The wedding guests tried to flee in their flower-decorated cars, and in the confusion, several were arrested—and a passer-by as well.

In a church hall, a few days later, the wedding guests gather again to discuss the events. Mr. Vargas sits silent. He seems too stunned to speak.

"The language that the officers used was just *terrible,*" says an outraged matron. "Even if *we* don't use such language, I am going to quote it, but I can't. One officer said, 'That's what happens when we let Mexicans have a party.' Well, the guests at this wedding were respectable people."

"All Mexicans are," says a young man.

She gazes disdainfully at him. "*And* they banged on the hoods of our *new* cars with their clubs, and they cursed us. *They* cursed us."

"They sprayed Mace in my eyes. They sprayed my girlfriend in her eyes," a teen-age boy says. "We were leaving—they asked us to leave. Then they sprayed us. I had Mace in my eyes so bad I could hardly see."

"Children were crying. I saw quite a few gassed," an elderly man speaks up. "A man too, his face swelled up. His eyes were damaged by Mace. I thought it was tear gas. But who tear-gasses a wedding? 'Mace is better,' an officer told me, 'than hitting heads.' It's scientific."

"One cop shoved a kid with his nightstick. The kid said, 'I don't like to be pushed.' So the cop smashed the kid in the face." This is the teen-ager again.

"I was walking by the hall. I didn't know there was a fight," a man reports. "Then I see a friend of mine being beat up by a cop. 'Lay off him,' I said, 'he didn't do anything.' The cop screamed at me, 'Get the hell out of here!' "

"Weren't you arrested?"

"He arrested me on Section 148—'inciting to riot.' "

The matron goes on. "I *heard* one of the officers say into his radio, 'Reporting a riot at the El Monte Legion Hall.' He saw me watching him and he turned away, embarrassed. He *ought* to have been. Now, how could there be a riot when one man is fighting *two* officers?"

"I heard it too," says a young man, "the riot code on the police wave length—Code Four, I think. So I said to a cop, 'There's no riot. Why don't you call back the cars on the same wave length?' He said he couldn't do that. He won't listen. Why not?"

"Because he was lying."

An elderly man talks. "We went to the police chief to complain. He laughed. 'If we hadn't broken it up, you people might have gotten drunk and run off with the bride,' the police chief said. He laughed."

"We never caused them any trouble, so why did they attack us?" a young girl asks.

"It was a Mexican wedding," a man replies. There is nothing more to say.

There is nothing quite as happy as a Mexican wedding. Some men may even drink too much, and sing of Zapata off key. And the officers may be summoned to silence the singers. But why the riot police?

It is a Sunday afternoon. On the wall over the piano Christ hangs on His cross. There is a sadness in the church hall. Everyone knows: It is the way it is.

"*Gabachos!*" a community leader curses. "It is the white cop. The *gabacho* with the gun. He is conditioned, he is programed to treat us Mejicanos that way. He sees a lot of brown faces and he doesn't see human beings. He feels he can treat us any way he likes and get away with anything. Years and years he has been doing this.

"They are not preventing violence. They are creating it. They are not building community relations. They are building up animosity."

"But why? Why do they do this to us?" asks the suburban community leader.

It is not the behavior of the police that shocks the wedding guests —the dweller in the barrio expects to be treated like a second-class citizen. He knows he is. What shocks the wedding guests is the presumption of racial inferiority that enables the police to treat all Mejicanos with the same brutality, without seeing a difference between a wedding party and a brawl in a bar.

"We are a conquered people," says Bert Corona, the past president of the Mexican-American Political Association. "The behavior of the police toward our people will not let them forget that."

Few if any, of the white officers live in the barrio they patrol, and few know the language of the people. The barrio is not home to them, but a strange place of strangers who have unfamiliar ways and an unknown culture. "We are foreigners to them," says Eliezer Risco, the *La Raza* editor, "and they are foreigners to us." In the routine of barrio life there is mutual fear of these "foreigners." "The police [have] fear of the Mexican American and would kill him out of fear rather than out of justice," D. C. de Herrera writes in Denver's *El Gallo.*

The officers of the law are familiar strangers: abstract, respected, cursed, and feared. In the barrio they are not called *policía* in proper Spanish, but by the name of their stigma, "*placas,* pigs, *gabachos, chortas,* dog pack, *pendejos,* Mister, motherfuckers, *los muertes,* the Man."

One young man in the Boyle Heights barrio of Los Angeles tells me: "The cops are just nothing but Anglo Pachucos. Man, we learn everything we know about street fights from them. They teach us from when we were little kids. It's like basic training, except they use live ammo."

In the streets there is unseen warfare, not between gangs of boys, the Pachucos of legends—that is a daily headline—but between ordinary citizens and police. One family fight, of many, was that of the Santoyo family. The police were duly summoned, and *La Raza* reported the consequences: "The Santoyos, father, mother, and daughter, were beaten; the father into unconsciousness—he was kicked, slapped, pushed, pulled by the hair and insulted verbally with terms like 'Mexican animals!'" Five of the Santoyo brothers, mother, daughter and father, were tried and convicted, not of fighting each other, but of fighting the police.

These are minor skirmishes that do not become headlines. But from time to time there is deadly violence.

Here are a few who were shot by police in one barrio in one city in one year:

A young boy, Louis Pinedo, is killed in a dark street in Denver by an officer's bullet. Patrolman John Cain argues self-defense and is acquitted of wrongful death. "Gunshot wound, back," says the medical autopsy on the teen-ager. He was seventeen and small. The barrio leaders march on the City Fathers.

On a downtown street, Andrew García—he is twenty-three—shot

to death by an officer moonlighting as a bouncer in a bar. Two women who are walking by say they have to pull Patrolman Harold MacMillen from the body of the dying boy: he was clubbing the youth with his revolver.

In the bedroom of his home, in his girl's arms, Richard Medina, age twenty, was shot three times. He was thought to be armed, but his girl says, "While I was holding him the policeman came in and started shooting. After he stopped, Richard dropped from my arms to the floor." He did not die.

Joey Archuleta died on the street on a summer day. Patrolman Theodore Zavashlak says he tripped and his gun went off. Joey was 15. The officer is cleared, the shooting "accidental." Once more the barrio marches through downtown Denver to City Hall and the Police Headquarters.

Robert Gene Castro, age fifteen, is shot to death in his home.

The shootings were reported in *El Gallo* within a single year. Yet there are those to whom "police brutality, harassment and inhumanity is only a figment of the poor peoples' imagination," the barrio newspaper caustically wrote. "Denver has had no riot to date [the summer of 1968], but the toll of injured and killed in the Mexican American community [at the hands of the police] continues to mount. . . ."

Hardly a year after this editorial there was a riot in the Denver barrios. The police had shot still another Chicano youth, and high school students rampaged through the streets in protest, overturning cars, smashing windows, until dozens of schoolchildren were injured, or arrested.

"More Chicanos are killed by cops on the streets of the Southwest than any other minority group in the population," writes a young man in a barrio newspaper. He calls it "Chicano birth control."

Yearly "the wild-West shooting of minorities by the police" grows worse, charges investigator D. C. de Herrera, the chairman of the Denver barrio's own Police Review Board. "To the Mexican American in Denver, the Police Department presents one of the biggest problems. They have absolutely no respect for our rights. They search our homes, our automobiles, and our own persons without any search warrants and due process of law."

Police "lawlessness" is denied by the stoic, white-haired chief of the Denver Police, George L. Seaton. "Attempts are regularly made to depict officers in an unflattering manner, or to improperly charge them with misconduct," the chief complains. "Such claims tend to create a 'bad' image of policemen."

"Chief," reporters on the Denver *Post* ask, "do you feel there is any discrimination on the part of Denver policemen in dealing with Hispanos or Negroes?"

"Occasionally there may be some kind of discrimination," the police chief replies. "When I find out about it, it is stopped, or it is corrected. On a large scale—definitely not. . . . I think Denver gets along very well with their minority people."

In a speech to a luncheon of the City Club, in the Brown Palace Hotel, the troubled police chief voices his deeper concerns. By 1985 the minorities will be the majority of the population of cities such as Detroit, Chicago, New Orleans, Cleveland, Oakland, St. Louis, and perhaps some in the Southwest. "Such things as joblessness, poor education and discrimination" will be a "cause for conflicts," Chief Seaton says. "Law enforcement is attempting to cope with problems far beyond what was ever considered to be its area of responsibility.

"To these minority citizens the police are widely recognized as the most visible symbol of a system which they believe is discriminatory and unjust," the Denver police chief laments.

The apostle of nonviolence in the Chicano movement visits Denver at about this time. Cesar Chavez tells members of the Crusade for Justice that he too has suffered from the violent police: "For those who have never suffered from police brutality it is impossible to discuss the problem, and for those who have nothing is more degrading and barbarous than police brutality.

"We must draw the lines once and for all," says the gentle leader of the campesinos.

In Los Angeles the newspaper *La Raza* describes the nature of the "degrading" behavior by the police. The "frisking, harassment, name calling and brutality" is a "daily occurrence" in the streets. *La Raza* cites what it says is a typical incident on an ordinary day: One summer afternoon five young and unemployed Chicanos who enrolled in a job-training program at a "Skill Center" are having lunch. They are horsing around. Local police arrest the restless youths on "suspicion" of being high, possessing narcotics. In the trunk of one boy's car they find a tool box; so they charge him with theft of that, too. But the tool box turns out to belong to the boy's father, none of the youths has any narcotics, and they are released for "lack of evidence" after a night in jail.

The youths voice hatred of the police. "Racism!" they charge, and the barrio newspaper editorializes: "The suspicion was based solely on the fact that they were Mexican." All the natives look suspicious to an "occupying army" of colonialists, and so "the Chicano is always the criminal," a young man writes to the newspaper.

"Americans of Mexican descent are subject to discriminatory treatment by law-enforcement officers," Dr. Hector P. Garcia, a United States Civil Rights Commissioner, says flatly. Investigation in the barrios across the Southwest, by staff lawyers of the federal body, revealed a state-by-state pattern of legal and police harassment, the Commissioner asserts. These investigators report: "The most serious issue encountered in the course of the Commission's study is harassment and abuse of Americans of Mexican descent by law-enforcement officers. Such conduct ranges from unjustified arrests to insults, threats and, not infrequently, physical assaults," Dr. Garcia told the Senate Subcommittee on Migratory Labor.

In the courts the complaints of injustices suffered by La Raza defendants were equally prevalent. The "unfair legal practices" reported in the barrios, Dr. Garcia testified, involve widespread charges that Chicanos are "excluded from jury service, denied equal access to bail and adequate counsel, and [are] employed in disproportionately low numbers in law-enforcement agencies."

The legal system is often designed "to keep Mexicans in their place," the Civil Rights Commissioner concluded. He termed such practices "rather sordid."

Laws are written, laws are enforced, and laws are judged by those outside the barrio. The Chicano who obeys the law of his traditions, the moral codes of his family, and the social customs of the barrio may find himself opposed by the laws of the outside society. Even the way dispute is settled by a barrio family may violate half a dozen laws of the Anglo society. What the Chicano does may not seem unlawful to him, but he is a criminal simply by being a Chicano.

"Law and order doesn't seem to be the practice of the Los Angeles Police Department," says *La Raza.* "The Eastside [of Los Angeles] is becoming a no man's land in which the people have no protection whatsoever from the services rendered by the Police Department."

Seeking to overcome the gap of hostility, Chief Thomas Reddin of the Los Angeles Police Department holds and personally participates in a series of "Police-Community Relations Conferences." One of these is held at the Church of the Epiphany in the summer of 1967. Reddin is a forceful man of the "modern breed of police officials," who have read much sociology and who sincerely believe in honest confrontations. He talks amiably with a group of barrio youth leaders. Among them is David Sanchez, then chairman of the Mayor's Youth Advisory Council. It goes well until the barrio youth offers a petition of demands: "That an Executive Order by Chief Reddin be sent to the Commanders and men [in] all predominantly Mexican American communities to cease immediately any form of physical violence, harassment, name-calling and bad treatment by the Los Angeles Police Department," and that there be "an Executive Order establishing equal protection under the law in predominantly Mexican areas—fast response to calls, etc."

"I don't receive demands," Chief Reddin replies. "I am not susceptible to demands. I am here to explain our position."

The conference ends in hostility. Youth and police return to their homes on the opposite sides of the barrier of the barrio. In a tone of frustration, *La Raza* wrote, "Conferences, seminars, workshops, TV shows, banquets, luncheons, and what-have-you. . . . Meanwhile Reddin's 'hired hands' run amuck in the streets." It was not that communications had broken down, but that communications had widened the gap of hostility. Rather than bridge the gap, the talks had apparently increased it by revealing the depth of the differences between those inside and outside the barrio.

"Nothing has changed in the streets," was *La Raza's* final word. Succinct, too, was the later comment of John Marquez, president of the Pico Rivera Young Men's Association: "The police don't want us on the streets."

The young men now talk of self-defense, both on the street corners and in the universities. And it is not only talk.

"What is self-defense?" I asked Obed Gomez, the young leader of the Latin American Defense Organization of Chicago.

"You think of guns," Gomez replies. "That's not what we mean by self-defense. It's not the vigilante thing, or the Minutemen. Self-defense means protection of our people from the injustices we feel the police subject us to. Yes, but it means more. The defense of our people from being pushed around by housing authorities, welfare investigators, draft boards, anybody. It means the defense of the whole community."

"Civil rights, then?" I ask.

"What is civil rights in the barrio?" Gomez says. "So far we don't exist in the eyes of the law, of most of the country. First we have to be recognized as a community, respected as a people. Then we can talk about civil rights and it will mean something."

"Then what are you defending?"

"Our right to exist."

In Chicago the Latin American Defense Organization was organized after the riot in the Puerto Rican barrio in the summer of 1966. Led by Obed Gomez, a volatile and quick-tongued young Mexican, its activists are largely Chicano youth and students. Within a few years it has become one of the barrio's most militant, best-known storefront centers of community activity. Gomez's group contributed to the making of the Poor People's Campaign and the unmaking of Governor George Romney's presidential campaign in a nationally publicized confrontation. Self-defense, as Gomez sees it, extends beyond the barrio.

In Denver the Crusade for Justice was founded in the spring of 1966, in a civil rights battle. But that battle quickly developed into a wide-ranging barrio group, with self-defense one of its organizational aims. It has its own "security" force, whose aim is not only to protect the barrio but also to safeguard its activists. It was praised by police officers in Washington, D.C., during the Poor People's Campaign, for its discipline in maintaining order.

In New Mexico, the Alianza Federal of Reies Tijerina has not only "security officers" but a citizens' constabulary of Hispano rural villagers. One village, Tierra Amarilla, has publicly elected its own land-grant "sheriff," and several communities have quietly done the same.

In Los Angeles, the Brown Berets, with their motto of "Serve—Observe—Protect," were originally founded as a self-defense unit of barrio youth. Patrols of young Chicanos to maintain law and order have been suggested by Brown Beret leader David Sanchez. On demonstrations by Chicano youths, the Brown Berets have placed "our bodies between the police and the kids" to protect the demonstrators, Sanchez says.

In San Antonio an ex-convict has organized a self-defense group—MANO, the Mexican American Nationalist Organization—whose members are mostly "ex-convicts of Mexican descent," like himself. As *Inferno*, the newspaper of the old and historic barrio, describes it, their "primary reason for organizing is to curb police brutality on San Antonio's Westside." Few men know the law as intimately as these. "We have about 300 members," says the founder. Alberto "Beto" Martinez, a handsome young man, explains that "most of them don't speak English. They go to court and plead guilty to anything. Man, the deck is stacked against them." He defends the membership of "his people" in a community group dedicated to enforcing law and order: "You cannot preach freedom unless you have been denied freedom."

Beto is a legend in the barrio. He is self-taught, educated in the streets and jails. He knows "ex-con and Muslim, pimp and priest, junky and politician." He drinks and talks and fights hard.

Beto has worked with Cesar Chavez in California and Reies Tijerina in New Mexico. Of the traditional barrio leaders he says, "All these cats talk, talk, talk." He prefers to be "where the grassroots begin," where "the action is." He distrusts "the gringo in uniform," whether police or priest, *Inferno* says.

To the new Chicano leaders civil rights are more than equality before the law. "Equality is but a word," Rodolfo Gonzales writes. "Here I stand before the Court of Guilty Justice." Of civil rights, Reies Tijerina says, "Courts have been death traps for our people." And Cesar Chavez has said, "We are weak. And the weak have no rights, but the right to sacrifice, until they are strong."

Rodolfo Gonzales writes in his poem, "I am Joaquín":

> My land is lost,
> and stolen,
> My culture has been raped,
> I lengthen
> the line at the welfare door,
> and fill jails with crime.

Yes, we demand "the guarantee of our constitutional rights," *La Raza* explains, but we demand something more, "our rights as a people who have their own culture, their own language, their own heritage, and their own way of life."

Civil rights become cultural rights.

In the church hall, where the wedding guests gathered, they form the El Monte Committee for Self-Defense. They politely request the expected redress of grievances and an apology from the uninvited guests at the wedding. Let the Police Department desist from "all brutal tactics toward our people," and let "the charges against those arrested for protesting the brutal tactics of the El Monte Police be dropped," and let "there be an open investigation into the El Monte Police Department."

Then comes the wedding guests' extraordinary request, "that members of the [Police] Department receive *careful* [my emphasis] instructions in the rich heritage of the Mexican people to avoid future mistreatment of these proud and dignified people."

"Four hundred people have lost faith in the Police Department," say the wedding guests. "We were shocked by the way we were shoved, struck, Maced, and verbally abused while we were complying with police orders to disperse." The "insensitive police" were requested therefore to promise "treatment of us with the same dignity given to Anglo people." For it was by respect, not only for their civil rights but for their cultural rights, that the police would "restore our faith" that has been "lost."

Yet the thought is not that extraordinary. In the meeting with Chief Thomas Reddin of the Los Angeles Police, the Chicano youth had demanded that the chief of police issue "an executive order requiring all officers in predominantly Mexican areas to take *extensive* [my emphasis] training in the language, history, culture, and prevailing conditions in those communities."

In the *Chicano Student*, a barrio youth had written of the East Los Angeles police:

When I walk down
our street
I am afraid
I am afraid
not of the meager lights
or of the boys
grown old before their time—
But of the white helmets
that hold lead-weighted
night sticks . . .

The father of the bride says to me with dignified pride, "I always supported my local police. But no more." He joins the El Monte Committee for Self-Defense.

XIII In the Suburbs of the Spanish Myths

The ornamental hardware dealer needed money. He was a merchant of suburban baroque, and his San Antonio business was expanding. Emanuel Salias requested a $10,000 loan from the Small Business Administration. It was quickly approved, for baroque was booming in the suburbs. Then, just before Easter, 1969, a Special Assistant in the local Small Business Administration office, Albert Fuentes, Jr., met the hardware man, and the results were scandalous. In a sworn statement the merchant accused his benefactor of offering him more money than he wanted if he would incorporate his business to include Fuentes and a few friends, "and pledge them 49 per cent of the corporation."

He was shocked, Emanuel Salias said.

Congressman Henry González of San Antonio held a press conference to air the charges. He had reason to believe that Fuentes "has engaged in, or attempted to engage in, shakedowns of Small Business Administration loan applicants." The Democratic lawmaker urged that Fuentes be "immediately" suspended pending an investigation by the FBI.

The scandal has shaken the suburban barrio. Fuentes is a man of influence. He is a pillar of the middle-class community who had been the chairman of the Political Association of Spanish-Speaking Associations, a member of County Commissioner Albert Pena's staff, and the regional director of the "Viva Nixon!" presidential campaign in Texas—this last an endeavor hardly likely to make him popular with Congressman González, a loyal supporter of the Democratic ticket.

Fuentes denied the accusations. His innocence was defended by Eddie Montez, a prominent San Antonio executive and former Board President of the Edgewood School District, who publicly testified that the "49 per cent" deal was intended for him and him alone.

In anger, Congressman González attacked the Montez mea culpa: "His reputation as a wheeler and dealer is well established." The sordid little scandal became more incestuous when it was revealed that the self-confessed "wheeler and dealer," Eddie Montez, had been on the staff of Congressman González for several years, before he was fired. On the day that this news story appeared in the San Antonio *Express* a reader, C. E. Pratt, wrote the newspaper: "U.S. Rep. Henry B. González is much upset over a small item of behind-the-scenes finagling involving SBA personnel and their friends trying to grab off large chunks of small businesses . . . but since when is this anything new, or surprising?"

Yet, all of these men are respected leaders of the La Raza middle class of the city. Some of them trace their family names to the Spanish conquistadors. In a sense, they still live in the suburbs of the Spanish myths, though they have little left of that nobility but the conquest of an ornamental hardware business.

"Once you were the master of all you surveyed, and your head of cattle were countless in South Texas. As adventurous, carefree and pleasure-loving Dons, you dealt with the friendly Tejas and the savage Apaches. A Nordic cloud appeared in the north and slowly but remorselessly grew into monstrous proportions. You gallantly attempted to stem the tide, but you were swept in the current. You swore allegiance to a new country, but went on revering old heroes. The invaders, of course, brought their own customs and made their own laws. The gulf has grown so in the years that still you are a different people, merely tolerated as citizens of a nation in which you resided even before you joined the Union! Your pleasure-loving ways, your good nature have been unable to cope with the energetic, wealth-seeking characteristics of the Nordics.

"Conditions have reached a point where your neighbors say 'a white man and a Mexican!' Yet in your veins race the hot blood of adventurous Castilian noblemen, the whitest blood in the world, and the blood of the cultured Aztecs and fierce Apaches, the reddest blood in the world! So why this disgraceful slap in the face? You can hold your head up with the best, and you should do so in order to keep your ancestors from turning in their graves."

A man with the noble name of Rodolfo A. de la Garza wrote these embittered words in an essay, "Who Are You?" in September, 1932. The resentments of lost pride still enfuriate the former aristocrats and embryo middle class of the barrios. Even the decades of growing political influence and suburban affluence have not soothed the feelings of impotence and insult.

"All the Presidential conferences and protest marches in the world cannot erase one hundred and twenty years of defeat and humiliation," says a brilliant young professor with a historic Mexican name. "You know very well I could be president of this university, and to 90 per cent of the Anglos of the country I would still be a 'Spik,' 'dirty Mex,' 'Hey, Pancho,' 'a nigger.' "

"Where can we hide from you?" the professor asks. "It's your country. So the only way we can hide *from you* is by becoming *like you.* Great! That way you think that we are paying you the compliment of imitation; and you pay us a compliment by saying 'You are different.' What a farce!"

Some have fled the barrios to escape from these indignities. The memory of being "Mexican" pursues them, so they go incognito. In suburbia they leave behind their Spanish names, Mejicano accents, and Indian hearts. Even their black hair acquires a protective coloring and grows lighter in the bright sunlamps of suburbia.

> Many are darker than black tar,
> But they pretend to be Anglo,
> They powder the back of their necks,
> In order to look lighter skinned.

Actually, few "Mexicans" live in the suburbs. They are mostly "Spanish." Says a barrio lawyer, "I know of families who converted to 'Italian,' and even to 'Greek.' " The warm countries of the warm blood; has any Mexican ever "passed" as German?

> Some Mexicans don't care to speak
> The language their mothers taught them,
> And go about saying they are Spanish,
> And denying their country's flag.

Hard-working and Anglicized, those who earn enough to move out of the barrios into the suburbs may be looked upon with envy and contempt by those who stay behind. They may look back with equal contempt and envy. They have a tenuous hold on the fringes of the middle class.

One scion of a prominent Phoenix family, Joe Benitos, says of the precarious status of the middle-class Chicano in the suburbs, "He has to obey the unwritten rules. He can join the Kiwanis Club, but not the Country Club. He can eat dinner with his neighbor in a restaurant, but not in his neighbor's house. And not with his whole family. If he makes one false move, one faux pas, he is snubbed off the cliff of Anglo acceptance with a pat on the back." He is a marginal man in a social no man's land, who can sit beside the pool but can't go in the water.

In the barrios they say contemptuously, "He is a Malinche! He is a *vendido!*" Literally, he is a traitor; he has sold us out. *Inferno,* the newspaper of the San Antonio barrios, features a "Malinche of the Month." One month it is a wealthy undertaker, and one month a successful politician who receives the award for having "made out."

Malinche was the Indian woman who became the concubine of Cortés. Her name has sorrow and compassion within it, for a woman held in bondage by her love for what enslaved her is a creature to be pitied as much as hated. The curse "Malinche!" is spoken that way. For are not the modern Mexicans all "the Sons of Malinche"? asks Octavio Paz. *"Viva los Hijos de la Chingada!" (The Sons of the Sacred Whore).*

One barrio leader says: "It is shameful. We work better with someone from another ghetto—he may be black or white or green, it does not matter—than with one of our own people who has 'made it.' No one is more frightened, smug, and conservative, and harder on our people, than the typical schoolteacher or shopkeeper who has escaped from the barrios in a two-car port and king-sized bed."

The contempt goes deeper than the social gap that divides the barrios from the suburbs. It comes from the history of old Mexico. In the colonial economy of that country the middle class was the obsequious and toadyish servant of the conquerors. In *Profile of Man and Culture in Mexico* the philosopher Samuel Ramos writes: "Middle class concepts of family, religion, morality, love, and so forth, conform to the European mold."

The Mexican petty bourgeois had few native traditions, but was imitative of the foreign colonialists; and this divisiveness crossed the border with the emigrants.

"If you have a civil war between the blacks and whites, we will have a civil war between the Chicanos and Malinches," says a Los Angeles Brown Beret.

The judgment of Dr. Ernesto Galarza, of the "ideologues of affluence," as he calls the middle-class professionals, is not less severe: "In Mexico the elite has learned little from history. The country is biding an explosion of social forces not unlike the tumultuous revolution of 1910. Yet the elite are as insensitive to this as they were in 1909. Is this applicable to the United States? Our elite has been just as insensitive. Little has changed or been learned by the ideologues of affluence in the last sixty years in the Southwest either. Perhaps they are too self-centered. Or stupid."

"Mexico's middle class, like the Chicanos' middle class in the U.S., is a sham," says Luis Valdez of El Teatro Campesino, "the product of brainwashing and easy accommodation to the *patrón*'s culture, for individual gain." It is the "refuge of hypocrites."

However servile its role in the colonial world, the middle class of Mexico had a place in that world. The baroque furniture in their homes, heavy as carved stones, was a sign of the secure and immobile status they had in that society. In the barrios of the United States the Chicano middle class has no such secure place. In this country, where the middle class reigns with success and largesse, the insignificant numbers of Chicanos who "make it" to the suburbs are marginal men to both communities—their own and the Anglos'. Of the national minorities in the country, none but the American Indians have a less influential and more provincial middle class than does La Raza in the Southwest. Even the blacks in the northern ghettos have proportionately more professionals than do the Chicanos. The Census of 1960 showed a mere 4.6 per cent of the Chicanos were professionals, compared with 15.1 per cent of the Anglos; while in all white-collar jobs (professional, managerial, proprietors, sales, and clerical), nearly half, 46.8 per cent, of the Anglos, but only 19 per cent of the Chicanos, had entered that tight, white circle. Chicanos were crowded into the professions traditionally open to them—teaching, law enforcement, and small shopkeeping. In the prestige fields—like the sciences, the legal and medical professions, and the executive offices—they were few.

The old elite are even fewer. Like the faded but discriminating aristocrats of any ruling clique in a mass society, their numbers diminish and their influence grows more fragile with every generation. Yet they are durable.

It is comforting to see a daughter of the aristocracy in a War on Poverty office. The cheerful face of the matronly Mrs. Mildred Serrano is at ease amid the lean, agitated young men and women in the barrios of the poor. "Some of them are militants," she says disapprovingly, but with a mother's sigh. "They all call me Mom. I watch them like a mother. Perhaps I am like the mother of the family." Mrs. Serrano works in the barrios of Fresno, one of the poorest of the communities of campesinos in the farm valleys of California. The sparse house, the hungry children, the stinking outhouses may dismay her, but she believes the successful of La Raza owe a debt to the poorest. "Our people now need everyone's help. We are a big family." Her philosophy has a New England simplicity. "If there is a little group of Mejicanos who need help, we help them. We teach them to help themselves. If a street has no street lights, we help get street lights. If there are no mail boxes, we help get mail boxes where the postman never came. If there are no sewers, we help get sewers."

Her demeanor would be appropriate at a lawn party, or at a diplomatic dinner. In the barrios of the poor, amid hunger and disease, her gentility seems out of place. It is unimaginable that she say an unkind word, for if something has angered her she says, "I better not speak of it."

"Our descendants date back to before 1776, to the expedition of de Anza. I am a native Californian. I am really Spanish, I suppose. But my ancestors came from Sonora in Mexico, so I consider myself to be Mexican."

Her work in the barrios has taught her humility, she says. "When you work with humble people, and these are humble people, you have to learn to humble yourself a little." It is not charity work she does, but she is charitable. "I do not put myself above them," she says of the poor. Her concern for the poor "isn't something the War on Poverty thought up. We have always taken care of our own." Mrs. Serrano has pride in her heritage and a disdain for the "uncultured, self-centeredness" of the Anglo newcomers "who think they are our saviors."

"The Spanish-speaking can help themselves. Hasn't that always been the philosophy of our Community Service Organization? It has. We are simply using our own philosophy in these 'new' programs. My husband and I are charter members of the Community Service Organization, you know."

Of the civic moralities of the middle class of La Raza in California, none are more highly organized than those of the Community Service Organization (CSO). It was founded in the optimistic years of the late forties "to guard and further our democratic rights; to become more aware of our responsibilities as citizens; to better discharge our civic duty," as the constitution of the Fresno CSO chapter declares, "to the promotion of the general WELFARE in the Spanish-speaking neighborhoods."

In the lexicon of the CSO, this has meant everything from the Back Alley Project for the "beautification of the barrios" by the planting of 168 trees on a slum street in East Los Angeles in the tense summer of 1968—leafy "green power," the CSO called it—to the "nonpartisan" voters' registration drive that registered 137,000 La Raza voters who promptly voted, albeit not quite nonpartisanly: 95 per cent for John F. Kennedy in the summer of 1960. The "kid-glove approach of our nice ladies," says one young activist. "If they want to go to the political side, there is the Mexican American Political Association," says Mrs. Serrano, "and those *other* groups."

Mostly it is the cautious virtues that have been promoted by the

CSO. Save Your Money. Join Our Community Credit Union. Invest Wisely. Count Your Pennies. Join Our Buyers Club: Meat is sold at a five per cent markup. Group Insurance: At one-eighth the regular rate. Classes in How to Pass Job Applications.

The beginnings of the CSO are usually traced to the manipulations of the pioneer of nonviolent confrontation politics—Saul Alinsky. His Industrial Areas Foundation in Chicago, and especially his lean, apostolic, and selfless West Coast organizer, Fred Ross, are described as the guiding spirits of its creation. CSO's founders deny the inference that outsiders led them.

In his office in Washington, D.C., one of the founders, the graying, eloquently voiced Congressman Eduardo Roybal of East Los Angeles, reminisces about the early days. He personally called the first meeting of the CSO, he says. As he remembers it, puffing on his pipe to draw out the memory, "It was in 1947. That was when I first decided to run for the City Council in Los Angeles." Since 1881, no Mexican American had been on the City Council. But in 1946, a La Raza leader was elected city councilman in Chino, California, and that generated a flurry of political optimism and activity. "We lost that year. Some of us decided what we needed was a community group. The CSO was it. We thought of it and we organized it. Of course the others helped. But we did it."

Mrs. Ursula Rios Gutierrez, a director of the East Los Angeles CSO, whose brother Anthony Rios was one of its founders, agrees: "It was the campaigners for Roybal who began the CSO; Roybal, Rios, about ten of them. Fred Ross helped, but he didn't organize it. History organized it."

It grew out of World War II. "The war was the catalyst," says Congressman Roybal. "Why, at the original meeting there were only war veterans—ten war veterans. Someone said, 'This isn't just for veterans. This is for everybody.' At the meeting after that we brought our wives. That made twenty of us instead of ten." Even the bringing of wives to an all-male veterans group was something new.

The experiences of World War II had taught the Chicanos to confront the Anglo prejudices directly and defend their identity, rather than cower. "In the army I was assigned to a barracks full of Texans," Roybal recalls. "One of them woke up every morning and cursed

Mexicans in general. Then one day he cursed me. So, I turned around and socked him. I knocked him out. That ended the argument right there. Most of us in the service had experiences like that. And then on the battlefield, every man was equal, of course. Death does not discriminate. So we were caught between the bigotry and the officers who wanted none of it. Not because they loved us, but because they wanted things to run smoothly. It dawned on some of us for the first time that the Anglos were divided. And if we united, we could win concessions."

After World War II, the middle class of La Raza used the CSO as a political lever. Roybal was elected. But then social rigidity returned. "In California they put a ceiling on La Raza," says one of the younger Chicano leaders, Alex Mercure. "You can elect so many, no more. You can earn so much, no more." The CSO stagnated in frustration.

For twenty years the CSO held to its innovative yet cautious course. It sometimes showed boldness, but always tempered it with politeness, virtues that are ridiculed by the barrio's activists. "The CSO is a middle-class bag," says a Brown Beret. "It's O.K., but it's too Malinche." Lately its membership has fallen, from 12,000 in 1960 to 4,000 in 1968. "Our members are the older people mostly," Mrs. Gutierrez says of the East Los Angeles chapter; the CSO doesn't have "the people of the streets."

In the suburban barrios of Texas the United League of United Latin American Citizens (LULAC) has suffered a like denouement. Founded in the wake of the racist outburst of the Ku Klux Klan that swept through Texas in the aftermath of World War I, LULAC began with a proclamation of self-defensive patriotism. Its constitution emphasized the obvious: "Section 1. As loyal citizens of the United States of America: We believe in the democratic principle of individual political and religious freedom." A few years before its founding in February, 1929, the Klan had held sway over much of east Texas. The then wholly Democratic state had gone to Herbert Hoover in the presidential elections because of the Klan's hatred of the Catholic "papist" Al Smith. "We had to adopt a euphemism and call ourselves a 'League of United Latin American Citizens.' Simply because 'Mexican,' or even 'Mexican American,' was not in vogue," says Dr. George Sánchez, a former national president of LULAC.

The LULAC pledge of loyalty was meant to soothe the anti-Mexican jitters that had bedeviled Texans ever since the time of Pancho Villa. Hysteria had reigned in the Southwest. It was then that the age-old name Españoles Mejicanos—Mexican Spaniards—by which the people had referred to themselves for centuries, was replaced with the innocuous and much safer Spanish Americans, or Latin Americans.

One early president of LULAC in 1932 voiced the social pressures of the time when he described the group's goals as encouraging "people of Mexican descent now residing in Texas to assimilate as rapidly as possible." The lawn parties, Red Cross teas, barbecues in the Texas style, mariachi bands in the Army Day Parade, crowning of a Mexican beauty queen on Columbus Day, and annual baseball game against the Pan American Optimist Club, for which LULAC became known, were an attempt by its middle-class leadership to appease the blatant racism then prevalent against Mexicans and to secure peace for the barrios.

Influenced by the "Four Freedoms" of World War II, LULAC, in 1944, enlarged its goals: "We solemnly declare . . . a sincere and respectful reverence for our racial origin, of which we are proud." So dedicated, the dentists and shopkeepers were henceforth to "eradicate discrimination . . . seek equal protection under the law . . . political unification . . . participate in all local, state and national political contests." LULAC, in thirty years, became a civil rights organization.

But old habits die slowly. One of the offspring of LULAC, the League of Loyal Americans of San Antonio, dedicated itself as well to "benevolent, charitable and educational undertakings" in the barrios. In demonstrating their intent, the Loyal Americans launched a drive "to clean up the red-light district" frequented by the soldiers at Fort Sam Houston. These civic moralities were usually financed by enchilada dinners and fiestas in the local high school gyms.

"The enchilada dinner is the high point of their activity," says Fecundo Valdes, of LULAC. "They are afraid to rock the boat. They play it safe. They are polite. They are so conservative that they are out of sight."

And yet the older leadership, Knights of America and Sons of America, that united to form LULAC had driven the Ku Klux Klan out of south Texas in the early twenties. More recently LULAC has endorsed many of the demands of the new movements of Chicanos and campesinos.

"So LULAC is not militant or political," says George Sánchez, the former national president of LULAC; but, he added, "Don't make this a purely social club where we pat each other on the back, you know, and have a cocktail. I hope it's more than that."

"We are beginning to be proud of the things our people have done. As Indians, yes. As Spaniards also." Dr. Sánchez tells a LULAC Club of the middle class of El Paso: "I am very proud that I am part Indian. All of you, almost without exception, are part Indian. Wonderful! Something to be proud of! Something to point to and say, *'Soy Indio'* [I am Indian], as they used to say in Mexico just after the Revolution. Most of us can say that: *'Soy Indio. Soy Mejicano.'* We have too often tried to suppress our 'Mexicanity.' To deny our traditions. We need to reverse that trend. We are not doing that. We are letting people lead us around places here, places there. I, for one, am not going to be placed except insofar as I place myself."

He is a salty-tongued, aging, and indestructible advocate of La Raza. A teacher for forty-five years, Dr. George Sánchez (his doctorate is in education) has most recently been director of the Center for International Education at the University of Texas, where he was Chairman of the Department of History and Philosophy of Education. One of the distinguished scholars of La Raza, he has grown weary, he says, of "lost battles."

"See these gray hairs, these scars? They come from calling a spade a spade. And telling the politicians—from LBJ down—'We're tired of talk. We're tired of promises.' Let's tell LBJ that. Let's tell Governor Connally that. He says, 'Oh, I love my Latin Americans. I was raised with them down in Florisville.' Stuff! I could use a harsher word. Stuff! I don't want pretty words. Put it on the line. Deliver. Then I will judge if you are my friend or not. Not by your *lavia.* Your short talk. Your palaver.

"O.K. You are going to get your head bloodied. It's going to cost you money. But what is blood and what is money compared with this sense of pride, the sense of potency, cultural potency? We have it. And we share it. What are we waiting for? Someone to put us on the WPA?

Or the Peace Corps? Excellent undertakings. I'm for them. But are we waiting for a handout of some kind? Go and take it! It's yours. Your potency!"

Not every member of the old elite or new middle class reflects the same surety and confidence that George Sánchez does. In private, there are troubled voices among the waning aristocrats and perplexed businessmen.

Of all the social events of the gentry, *gente de razón*, the people of reason, of the Southwest, few are older and more traditional than the Fiesta de Taos. Every year, for generations, the local elite of that historic town gather at a costume ball held to commemorate the founding of the ancient Spanish settlement in the 1540's.

The Kiwanis Club of Taos sponsors that centuries-old costume ball in the summer of 1967. Elegantly gowned women with but the faintest hint of Mexican ancestry in their faces, the shopkeepers of the plaza, together with a handful of landowners and mine owners who don red sashes and ruffled blouses for the festivities, dance and drink the night away. In the Katchina Motel, opposite the Esso Station, these members of the Hispano bourgeois and remnants of the "old families" dance the old *rancheras* and fandangos. The "Latin" band, which is neither Mexican nor Anglo, has some difficulty playing the music. Its style is that of the bland "Latin" rhythms of the night clubs. An old man requests a traditional Hispano dance. "Well," the band leader says apologetically, "I don't think we can play that real pretty. But we will try, folks." He doesn't succeed.

Looking like a venerable *patrón*, the old man who asks for the dance leads a young girl onto the dance floor. He sets his own tempo, with intricate two-steps, yelling "Bravo!" to the faltering band out of politeness.

At one table the family of a mine owner sits quietly laughing and drinking. The decorum is abruptly shattered by the appearance of a young man in cowboy boots, shirt, and hat. He is very drunk. Unsteadily he makes his way through the dancers to the family table. He is a scion of the town aristocracy. The mines? He has no interest in that boring subject. "I don't know what they use the ore for," he mutters. After all, it was his great-grandfather's land. The mine owner is just an uncle.

"I've been stood up," the cowboy says, sitting down. He is shamed before his relatives.

"You're drunk," says his aunt.

Contemplating her disapproval, the young man says in self-defense, "Ah, this is a cruddy, dirty, nothing town."

His aunt says in Spanish, "It's home."

"I'm going away."

"Where will you go? This is the only decent place to live."

"I'm going away. After I have another drink, another dance, and another girl. Then I'm going in the morning. If I ever sober up."

"You're dirty," his aunt says.

"I'm honest. We are all dead here. We don't even know it. I know it."

XIV The Secret Politicians

Under the desert palms of the Imperial Valley, politics is a surrealist fantasy. The sour and sweet wind of twilight rises from the irrigated fields of the Mojave. The hot wind singes the town. It is 120 degrees on Main Street. No one is on the sidewalk. Somewhere in the town there is to be a secret meeting of the Mexican American Political Association. I have been invited by the former mayor of a border town, but I cannot find any sign of life in the County Building, where the meeting is to be.

On the back stairs, behind the building, there is a dim light. Everything else is in darkness.

In the desert town that afternoon I asked an official in the County Building for information about the meeting. "What meeting?" he says. He has never heard of the Mexican American Political Association (MAPA), he says, though MAPA is known throughout the state as the most influential electoral group of the two million California Mexicans. Known everywhere, that is, but in Imperial Valley. The poor of the barrios are 35 per cent of the county's population and the saviors of its quarter-of-a-billion-dollar agricultural crops. But the official feigns ignorance of any political activity of La Raza.

"You mean to say the Mexes are going in for voting?" He grins.

I climb the back stairs and knock. The former mayor comes out of the shadowy corridor to greet me. He ushers me into the back room, where two city councilmen and several respected civic leaders—all Chicanos—are seated quietly about a conference table talking of community affairs in hushed voices, like thieves.

Businessmen, lawyers, and city officials, they are not conspirators indulging in nefarious schemes but are discussing hospital conditions, water and tax rates, community centers, and voter registration. The Imperial Valley MAPA is an eminently proper and middle-class group whose propriety is seen in the ties and white shirts these men wear in the desert heat. No one has mud on his shoes.

Later, when I describe the surrealist meeting to Bert Corona, the imposing and powerful then state president of MAPA, he is not surprised nor outraged. "The story of our life. Many of our political leaders do not want to make their activities too well known to the Anglo. In these towns the Anglo leadership is often very conservative. They are in control. They could prepare all sorts of traps for us, extract tribute, have our people fired. Mexican Americans who work for government agencies, who are teachers, could be penalized in their personal lives and careers. It happens.

"Our people have learned after many years of hard experience to stay as far underground as possible—underground not because they are doing something illegal, but to keep their deliberations and strategy to themselves. So this kind of situation does not amaze me. It has to be so. Neither does the fact that the Anglo leadership said they did not know about it. Many of the elected leaders of a community do not want to know about Mexican political organization or power. They have ruled it out of their minds. They do not want to recognize that we exist.

"We are quietly organizing. We have not taken on the power structure yet," says Corona.

Everywhere in the Southwest the secret politicians of La Raza meet in the suburban barrios. The underground is often rather highly placed. When the quiet and hard campaigning of these political leaders becomes visible, the outside society is stunned and, at times, uncomprehending.

"Who are the local Mexican political leaders?" I say to an Anglo official in Crystal City, Texas.

"I don't rightly know," he says.

"How about the Democratic and Republican party leaders," I say. "You know, the Chicanos."

"I don't rightly know who they might be."

"You don't know the party leaders in town?"

"I can't rightly say."

The people of Crystal City, Texas, where 85 per cent of the inhabitants are Mexican Americans, had elected a city government of Chicanos a few years ago. Since the "Conquest" of 1846, few urban groups of La Raza had won so sweeping a victory. The election had startled the Chicanos and upset the balance of apathy in Texas. Paul Matta, a young teacher who was elected mayor in 1968, has called this "the political coming of age" of his people.

Nothing has changed to the Anglos. They visibly ignore the presence of the new mayor. When I visit the City Hall of Crystal City to see Mayor Matta, I am told by a white official, "Oh, he just comes in to sign checks," wouldn't I rather talk to the city manager? He, it seems, is not a Mexican.

When I ask Mayor Matta what the duties of his office are, he nods. "I sign the checks and I sign the municipal authorizations. And I lead all the official functions—you know, like parades and things like that."

Even the elected leader of La Raza is largely invisible to his colleagues. He has long been a singular and lonely figure, for there is no national minority in the United States that has had less voice in the halls of government, or fewer elected officials. It is an old tradition of undemocratic representation in the Southwest that still prevails. Proportionate to the population there ought to be at least fifteen, and possibly twenty, Chicanos in Congress. There are three: Congressmen Henry González and Eligio de la Garza of Texas, and Eduardo Roybal of California. And this is the largest number of lawmakers that has ever come from the barrios.

There is no major city in the Southwest with a Chicano mayor, despite the large barrio populations of Phoenix, San Diego, El Paso, San Antonio, Albuquerque, Denver, Fresno, and Los Angeles. There is not one state with a Chicano governor. There is but one U.S. Senator, Joseph Montoya of New Mexico, where the tradition insists on a cultural split of the state's senatorial ticket into hyphenated politics.

La Raza's numerical strength ought to elect 10 to 20 per cent of the legislatures of the Southwest. Instead the representation ranges from no per cent to a high of one per cent.

In San Antonio, Texas, where La Raza represents 40 per cent of the city's population, only two of the nine city councilmen come from the barrios. So unrepresentative is the local government that Dr. Bill Crane, Chairman of the Department of Government at St. Mary's University, has dubbed it "San Antonio: Pluralistic City and Monolithic Government"; while County Commissioner Albert Pena, Jr., has denounced the "undemocratic, decadent, and dangerous" political machine that runs the city. In El Paso, where La Raza comprises 45 per cent of the population, there is an equal imbalance. Houston, Phoenix, Tucson, and Denver have but token representation. Los Angeles has none at all.

The barrios of Los Angeles, with a population that is said to be approaching one million, have not a single Chicano representing them on the City Council. Election districts are so gerrymandered that it takes almost two votes in East Los Angeles for every one vote in West Los Angeles to elect a councilman.

Worst of the farcical *corridas de toros* of elections without representation occurs in California. In the zany atmosphere of the state's political circuses, the rigid exclusion of La Raza from the most minimal participation in government seems incredible. There may be two million Mexican Americans in California, but there was not one Mexican American in either house of the state legislature in 1968.

Although La Raza is 10 per cent or more of the population less than 10,000 of the 249,000 federal employees in California, in 1967, were Chicanos. Where there are large La Raza concentrations the invisibility is most glaring. Fresno has a barrio population that is one-fifth of the city; but "not one Chicano has been appointed to anything of significance in Fresno," says Gilberto López, a lawyer who heads the city's MAPA chapter. "In Fresno County, to give you an example, there is only one highway patrolman who is Mexican."

"As a people we are still very isolated," in Bert Corona's words, "isolated for two reasons: Our inclination to be politically isolated, and the rejection by the Anglo community—which you might say is discrimination or racial separation."

The isolation is recognized by political scientists, who nevertheless challenge the charge that racial discrimination is the primary cause. Robert W. Glascow, an editor of the Phoenix, Arizona, *Republic*, sums up the majority attitude in *Urban Politics in the Southwest* by saying, "The Mexican American until now has been passive, if not apathetic, politically."

The recognition of La Raza's own political viewpoint has been so insignificant that Lawrence Fuchs, a professor of American Civilization and Politics at Brandeis University and the editor of *American Ethnic Politics*, all but ignores the Mexican Americans as an ethnic group: "Of all the so-called 'minority groups' only Afro-Americans (and a much smaller number of American Indians and first-generation Orientals) . . . were excluded systematically from politics," Fuchs writes in his introduction. There is no chapter on La Raza in *American Ethnic Politics.*

La Raza has been excluded from politics as effectively at the polls as it has in the textbooks. In San Patricio County, a fiefdom of ranching dynasties north of Corpus Christi, a newly elected city commissioner of the town, Manuel Chavez, tells the Texas Advisory Committee of the United States Civil Rights Commission that "intimidation and other acts by election officials, police, welfare officials and employers [are] designed to reduce the turnout of Latin American voters." The commissioner itemizes his charges:

1. Welfare recipients were warned that they might be dropped from welfare rolls if seen in the 'wrong place' on election day;
2. Surplus food commodities were curtailed two or three weeks prior to the election;
3. There was harassment by police, including the ticketing of cars for minor mechanical defects on election day;
4. There were attempts by voting officials to confuse voters by implying that there were property qualifications for voting;
5. There were no voting booths as required by law and people were forced to vote in full view of others;

6. There were difficulties in getting people registered;
7. Attempts were made to take field workers to the fields early on election day to prevent them from voting.

Of such elections, fought in stifling hostility and enforced isolation, the La Raza politicians who have been elected are understandably wary. They have been few in number and they have had haphazard political support. Bert Corona has lamented these elections as "maverick accidents." Legislatively they have had little power, and too often their function is to parade before the electorate as "showpieces." Rodolfo Gonzales has contemptuously said of his own career as the upcoming Chicano of Colorado politics, "They thought they owned me. I was their showpiece." It is the sort of success "that ruins a good man and corrupts a bad one," says Commissioner Albert Pena of Texas.

Until recently, the highest-placed La Raza politician was Eduardo Pérez, the secretary of the State Committee of the Democratic Party of California, in the administration of Governor Edmund Brown. Pérez says of his ranking position, "I don't do a damn thing. They sign my name to every letter they send out. They even give me a real Mexican name, Eduardo Pérez. It's something! They wanted me to become Americanized, so they said, 'Change your name to Eddie!' So I did. Now it is more romantic to be named Eduardo again. So they changed my name back. They don't tell me what's going on. I am left out of their planning sessions, out of everything.

"Oh, I get an honor every time we're having an Executive Board meeting. I get to read the roll. That's it. It's tokenism."

"It is true we have one member of La Raza in most city halls and on almost all boards. This is just window dressing," says Fecundo Valdez of New Mexico politics. "Most of our political figures are not politically free. Most of our leaders have participated in illusory decision making, but never where the real decisions are made. Hence, whenever real leadership has emerged, it has always been siphoned off, or bought off, or silenced. They become regular turncoats."

Leaders who do not lead and politicians kept from political power may take refuge in rhetoric, verbal eloquence, the prestige of office, or the mannerisms of a *patrón.* The "leaders who are concerned about their own image," as Bert Corona says, are such men. The older generation of politicians fought their way to acceptance when the barrios were weak, ignored, and disunited. It was not until the late twenties that the League of United Latin American Citizens (LULAC) was founded, and the Community Service Organization (CSO) did not begin political activity until the late forties. Both these groups were remote from the barrio masses, were "not political," as Dr. George Sánchez has said. These were the most active barrio organizations for two generations. It was an era of "political impotence," says John Burma in *Spanish-Speaking Groups in the United States.* "On the whole, the Mexicans and Mexican Americans . . . were of little political significance before 1945." But for the abortive attempt to establish the Congress of Spanish Speaking People in the late thirties, no lasting political breakthrough was made outside the barrios. When Eduardo Roybal was elected to the House of Representatives from East Los Angeles in the 1950's, no Chicano—outside of New Mexico—was serving in the United States Congress.

If a man was to be elected, he had to be chosen by non–La Raza politicians and often by anti–La Raza politicians. The unique style of barrio leadership had to be disguised. Success in politics required subservience to the established party machinery "downtown," the imitation of its methods, and the espousing of the Anglo campaign styles. The "La Raza politico was castrated by the Anglo niceties," says a younger leader. "He was Anglicized. He lost his balls."

El Gallo of Denver calls such a barrio leader "the Green Tío Tomás" (Uncle Tom), not unaffectionately and a little sadly. "This is the man who was our leader when the gringo 'picked' our leader. But he's not our leader now. He's green with envy." Then there is "the Grey *Tío Tomás*—he is neither brown nor white. He picks up something in the Chicano neighborhood and takes it downtown. Then he gets something from the power structure and brings it back to the Chicanos. He is neither hot nor cold—and he means no good to either side."

In the barrios of East Los Angeles a roomful of community people who are active in local politics discuss the old styles of leadership. They argue about these traditional politicos:

Man: "Let us discuss about leadership. What kind of leadership have we had in the past?"

Woman: "Ineffective! To a certain degree I think they were ignorant. Not now so much as they were before."

Man: "A leader thinks, sometimes, the people are ignorant."

Second man: "You know, he thinks we can be led like sheep. You know, he is very dominant."

Third man: "The old, traditional leader seems satisfied to maintain the status quo. In other words, 'Don't rock the boat! We never had it so good! Let's keep things the way they are!'"

Second man: "In the past the traditional leaders have failed to mobilize the community. That's why we have no representation in the field of politics."

Woman: "Like a mother who has a bunch of kids who she never taught how to iron, wash dishes, clean house, and they get to being fifteen, the poor kids don't know how to do anything. She robbed them of their ability to do things. This is how the traditional leader is. There are a lot of Mexican men like that."

Man: "I wouldn't call him a traditional leader. I would call him a headman. Usually these guys are hand-picked by the power structure for other than ability, you know. These guys are in the in-crowd. They are not leaders."

Woman: "He is ineffective because he doesn't understand the times are changing. He thinks our needs are still the same; consequently, he doesn't affect the people—because they feel he doesn't understand our needs. The people just go along with him and try to keep him appeased while they go out looking for someone else."

Man: "The leader with prestige, without any power."

Leaders who are not leaders, these men are elected to represent the barrios to the outside world, not to lead within the community. "We elect him every year," says a barrio leader of a Congressman. "But we do not listen to him in between elections. He listens to us. He has no influence among the people." The barrios are governed by leaders and laws of their own making.

In every family, on every block, there is a leader who is listened to. He may simply be an old man, without any status in the neighborhood except the respect afforded him. Long life is an achievement that is valued highly; it earns him recognition as a man of wisdom. But not all old men are so respected. The qualities of the barrio leader are his tenderness, compassion, suffering, and manhood. He is the *patrón* of the urban villagers.

"The old Mr. Alvarado is such a man," says Gonzalo Cano, the former director of the El Santo Niño Neighborhood House of the CYO in East Los Angeles, talking about a mythic barrio leader; "He may be a retired railroad worker, or a farm worker whose back is too bent to bend. He is poor; he has nothing of material value to his name. Yet everyone respects him and he respects himself. Here comes old Mr. Alvarado down the street in clothes that look as old as he is, with his hat, his urban sombrero, on his head, walking with the dignity of a Senator although he may be on welfare.

"Every block has its old Mr. Alvarado," says Cano.

The urban *patrón* of the barrio is like a village elder or tribal wise man. He has no power to enforce his words. He is not elected by the laws of politics of the outside society. Legally, he does not exist. People come to him, listen to him, and go away to do as they wish. He has no wealth or indebtedness by which to bind them to him as the landed *patrón* did.

"We are not a united group, but are more like a large family," says Bert Corona. In barrio politics the entire family of the leader is often involved. Politics becomes a family affair, where loyalty to brother and cousin may outweigh party loyalty. "If you scratch beneath a political fight, you may draw family blood," an Albuquerque Chicano politician says.

In one Southwestern city there is a contest for the postmaster's job. The mayor seeks the job of postmaster. He is supported by the Democratic County Committee and the local Congressman. Opposing the mayor is the assistant postmaster, who has the support of the local Democratic Party Club.

"Our town split apart," says a councilman.

"Is it a family fight?" I ask him.

"They both have large families. Lots of in-laws that cannot be disregarded." He smiles sheepishly. "Besides, the assistant postmaster is my brother."

Man is the wheel upon which the philosophy of La Raza politics turns. The leader does not talk to the people about their problems, nor do they judge him simply by his programs. He is a man first of all. People listen to him or not, depending on how they feel about him as a man. "He is one of us" or "He is a stranger to us," they say.

"What a stranger he has become to us. He is no longer the man he was. All he is interested in is politics," a La Raza politician says of a Congressman he helped elect.

" 'Politics' remains a dirty word and accusation," declares *The New Mexican.* The common feeling in the barrios is not that politics is corrupt, but that it is inhuman. Corruption is, after all, human, and the barrio voter tends to be tolerant of the leader who flamboyantly flaunts his ego. He may be admired for the buoyancy of "his style," while the coldly efficient politician who has no feeling for the people is despised. In his discussion of the Hispanic style of politics, Salvador de Madariaga writes: "All the efforts of the political propagandists to make the Spaniard feel like a citizen have failed. He feels like a man —quoting Unamuno (the Spanish philosopher)—'nothing less than a whole man.' "

It is like this in the barrios. *La Raza* of Los Angeles voices this idea of politics in its slogan, "Viva la Causa Carnal!" ("Hurrah for the Cause of Man!") *"Carnal"* in Spanish means the flesh, the sensual. The slogan really is "Hurrah for the Cause of Sensuality in Man!" In the mountain villages of New Mexico they say of Reies Tijerina: "I think he may be a faker. He is one real scoundrel. But what a man he is! He is *macho!* He is a real man."

"We have been waiting since 1846," writes *La Raza,* "for real men." The barrio newspaper hails "El Tigre" and "Corky," Reies Tijerina and Rodolfo Gonzales, as "a new and militant type of leadership" that youth "admire and respect." "Not since the days of Joaquín Murietta and Emiliano Zapata have the Mexican people, especially the younger generation, had leaders they can be proud of." These men "have said and done things Chicanos have only mumbled and have said under their breath, but didn't have the 'Guts' or the 'Machismo' to say out loud." These men are real men: "They are both *machos.*"

The idea of the whole man has emerged from the barrios to enter the political arena. The young activists and Chicano politicians have clashed with the established, old-style leaders who have devoted a lifetime to learning how to subdue and sublimate their Chicanoismo, in order to be acceptable to the Anglos. "Many of our old-timers in MAPA are overcome with our so-called image," says Bert Corona. "The young people say, 'To hell with your image! What about the image of the hundreds of thousands of Spanish-speaking poor, the illiterate, the unemployed, and those who live in miserable housing?' The older leadership in MAPA is being pushed by the younger people."

In New Mexico one of the younger generation, Alex Mercure, the director of the village HELP programs, sees a similar trend. "The undercurrent of the last ten or fifteen years in politics is that people are seeking a new kind of leader, an honest leader. Sincerity is what they want. They are tired of the *jefe político* and the hypocritical politician. That's why so many of the new leaders you see arising are not old-style politicians belonging to either of the two old parties.

"The new political leaders tend to be nonpolitical. What party do they belong to? I think they are not geared to either political machine. They tend to be independent."

Where do the new leaders come from? In the East Los Angeles workshop on barrio politics the discussion leader, Mr. Chavarria, dates the change to World War II: "We were exposed to experiences we had never experienced before. The veterans of World War II, who, because they went away, because they were in the army, because they went to foreign lands, because they had a variety of experiences, returned with ideas, with a perspective that was different from the one they had before. They even became concerned about politics!

"The barrios had been changing, not only the young men had been changing. And this filtered down to his family. His children had been able to go to school. His children were now able to go to college. The individual did no longer grow up to just particular jobs he was going to hold. He began to choose the jobs he wanted.

"Hence we began to see a new type of leader; the leader that wanted to displace the traditional leader; not only in political leadership. So the community is changed. We are still in a confusing stage. This kind of change is never clear. It is clear only in the books of the sociologists and economists and political scientists; but as we look around us these things are not very clear.

"The new leader that issued from this cleavage, of World War II, he is a man who is no longer satisfied with the status quo. He sees our community in an entirely new way. He is a man who believes that things can be done, that he can mobilize our community, and he is going to do just that."

He is a man, a whole man. "He has *huevos!*" That is, "He has eggs! He has balls!"

Rodolfo Gonzales, in resigning from his post as a district captain in the Democratic Party of Denver, evoked this idea of political *macho.* His political act was an act of his manhood, he wrote in an open letter to the county chairman:

> The individual who makes his way through the political muck of today's world, and more so the minority representatives, suffers from such an immense loss of soul and dignity that the end results are as rewarding as a heart attack, castration, or cancer! . . . You and your cohorts have been accomplices to the destruction of moral man in this society. I can only visualize your goal as complete emasculation of manhood, sterilization of human dignity, and that you not only consciously but purposely are creating a world of lackeys, political boot-lickers and prostitutes.

The secret politicians of La Raza were coming in from the cold of Anglo politics.

xv Gracias por Nada

Wheezing and mustached, the deputy sheriff leans back in the rocker. He cocks his Stetson hat. "I don't say that you can't trust any of them. Just most!" he drawls. "Now, I'm not prejudiced to them. I worked beside them all my life." He doesn't say, some of my best friends are . . . , but he says, "Why I even got a friend who's a Texas Ranger." He grins maliciously. "Of course, I won't want my daughter to marry an Anglo!"

The deputy sheriff is a Chicano.

In the living room of a suburban home in a barrio in southwest Texas eight men sit around and plan an election campaign. Some of the group are county officials, astute students of the folkways of Texas politics whose expertise influenced the triumph of John F. Kennedy in the state, and the defeat of Lyndon Johnson's candidates. Jokingly they refer to themselves as the "Mexican Mafia." They have political power in the barrio, and they exercise it quietly, almost secretively.

"Let's run someone for mayor," a man suggests.

"We won't win," an old man—he must be seventy—interrupts him. When the patriarch of the men speaks, the younger men listen carefully and argue diffidently.

"Sometimes we win," protests the man who made the suggestion.

"The dogcatcher's job!" the patriarch admonishes him. "We win the fleas. Until we have a real two-party system in Texas we will never win control. I mean a *real* two-party system."

"Aren't you a Democrat?"

"My whole life."

"You vote for the Democrats?"

"Sometimes."

"You don't trust the Democrats, though?"

"No."

"Or the Republicans?"

"No."

"When you say 'a real two-party system,' do you mean Democrats and Republicans?" I ask the cagey old man. "Or do you mean Mexican and Anglo parties?"

The old man's eyes brighten. He says nothing for a while.

"Well?"

"Yes." He smiles. "I mean a *real* two-party system."

The upheaval in barrio politics reflects a striving for self-determination. In the most obscure town and quiet valleys of the Southwest there are new and independent Chicano movements being formed, to free the La Raza voter from tutelage to two Anglo-run parties.

In the Rio Grande Valley of Texas a La Raza "Independent Party" enters the county elections for the first time and to everyone's surprise wins several seats. "Community candidates" run for local office in the suburban barrios of Los Angeles, and lose. In San Antonio a "barrio slate" of young Chicanos brashly enters the mayoralty race, while the Crusade for Justice *caudillo,* Rodolfo Gonzales, runs for mayor of Denver on a few weeks' notice and wins several thousand votes for his "La Raza Revolution." High in the mountain villages of New Mexico the land-grant heirs are becoming politically independent. Reies Tijerina is a gubernatorial candidate. When he is ruled off the ballot he is replaced by a Pueblo Indian, José Alfredo Maestas. He is the first Indian since 1837 to seek the governorship of the state, with Hispano support. Even in the remote little towns of the San Luis Valley, in the Southern Rockies of Colorado, there is talk of a "People's party."

The attempts to create "a La Raza style of politics" are more symbolic than successful. Most of these fledgling efforts are enthusiastic fiascos; the voters are skeptical.

In the past the barrio voter was taken for granted on election day and ignored thereafter. He was a "safe" and "captive" voter. He voted, if and when he voted, in political segregation, for the memories of Franklin Delano Roosevelt and John F. Kennedy, on a straight Democratic ticket. The barrios turned out "up to 97 per cent for the Democrats," estimates Bert Corona, the past State Chairman of the Mexican American Political Association (MAPA). Election districts from California to Texas, where there were a majority of La Raza voters, in campaigns of 1956, 1958, 1960, 1962, and 1964, show a remarkably consistent vote for the Democratic Party ticket of 95 per cent—or higher. No group in the country has been as loyal to a single political party. Yet few voting blocks have had less political power or patronage.

"We have been political whores," says a highly placed Chicano politician in California. "Or, maybe, virgins!"

"And what do we have to show for giving ourselves so freely? Nothing! So now we say no more. We will not be whores any more. We are no longer virgins. We are not so easily seduced by innocence or promises of politicians.

"La Raza has to organize our own political power," he says. "That's the only way we'll get the two parties, or anyone else, to listen to us, and give us what we demand."

When the county commissioner of Bexar County, Texas, Albert Pena, attended the Democratic Party National Convention, in 1960, he was one of a handful of Chicanos. "Every group was represented except Mexican Americans," he recalls. The Chicano was unknown then, on the national political scene. He was supposed to stay in his provincial place, in the Southwest, and he did. The United States government had, after all, never had a single agency, or department, devoted specifically to the needs of La Raza, in all the years since the War Against Mexico, in 1846. Rarely did the two major parties bother to mention the Chicanos in their presidential platforms.

The lonely La Raza leader tried unsuccessfully to interest the party politicians in the anguish of the barrios. Pena testified before the Minorities Committee, headed by G. Mennen Williams, then governor of Michigan. "The governor was genial," he recalls. "He listened carefully. And then he told me he had 'never heard of' Mexican American problems before.

"I told him that Mexicans had always voted Democratic. We were considered to be in the hip pocket of the Democratic party. But we were getting fed up. The day would come when we would be independent, I told him. It has come."

Viva Kennedy!—the barrio movement to help elect President John F. Kennedy—was begun soon after that. In Texas the state chairman was Albert Pena. "We did it on our own. We financed it ourselves. And we won Texas for the President when the political bosses dragged their heels," Pena says. "We brought out the highest barrio vote in Texas history. The President recognized our work: the first Mexican federal judge was appointed—little enough, but a beginning. Then the President was assassinated, right here in Texas.

"It was as a result of Viva Kennedy! that we formed PASO. We were becoming independent of betrayal!"

PASO is to Texas what MAPA is to California. It stands for Political Association of Spanish-Speaking Organizations; it stands as well for *paso a paso*—step by step. "We wanted to get all the Mexican American political clubs together, so that we could manifest our own power," Pena says. "We don't want *to belong* to either party."

Still "political brokers" in Texas doubted that La Raza voters could organize their influence beyond the borders of their barrios, or that they could become an independent force with the "swing vote" in state elections. But then, in 1966, Waggoner Carr, the Attorney General of Texas, ran for the Senate seat held by conservative Republican John Tower. The Democrat, Carr, had angered many Mexican Americans by his refusal to meet with the Rio Grande Valley farm workers who walked 491 miles to Austin to be told that Governor John Connally and the Attorney General were out of town. One LULAC official in Texas was quoted as saying that Carr symbolized the sort of Democrats "who seem unaware of the poor housing and poor job opportunities" in the barrios.

There were quiet signs of a revolt in the barrios. In the *Journal of the Harris County PASO* a news clipping was reprinted when the Texas Attorney General held a press conference in the midst of President Kennedy's burial service at Arlington. *"Waggoner Carr no sabe portarse con dignidad,"* read the message beside the news clipping, *"La elección es en noviembre—no se olviden de los que nos insultan."* ("Waggoner doesn't know how to behave with dignity. The election is in November—we have not forgotten how you insulted us.") On the last page of the PASO *Journal* was the advertisement: "Congratulations PASO! from Senator Tower," who was photographed beside Father Antonio Gonzales, spiritual leader of the Valley Farm workers.

When election day came, Tower defeated Carr by 198,718 votes. On the same ballot, Connally defeated Kennerly, the Republican candidate, by 788,072 votes in the governor's race. Half a million voters had switched parties from one line on the ballot to the next. These voters were mostly Mexicans, who had voted 95 per cent for the Democrats in the previous election; they now voted 35 per cent for the Republicans. Curiously there had been no perceptible change in party registrations.

"We did it," Pena says simply, "by crisscrossing political lines. A minority is more important if it is the swing vote."

Sam Goddard, the Governor of Arizona, known as a liberal Democrat and "friend of the poor," was defeated in a close election by the slight shift of barrio voters, in the year of the Texas revolt. He was accused by some La Raza leaders of ignoring the housing needs of the Phoenix ghettos—one of the few major cities without a housing code requiring minimum building standards.

In New Mexico the electoral revolt was even more dramatically explicit. The "Land of Enchantment" had a generations-old tradition of La Raza participation in Democratic administrations. But it was "window dressing," Chicano leaders charged. Suddenly in 1966, for the first time in the state's history, villages that had always voted up to 90 per cent for the Democrats switched just as heavily to the Republicans. They elected the maverick Republican David Cargo as Governor. On the same ticket, in village after village, the Hispanos voted for the local Democrats.

The trend did not reach the West Coast that year, but the implications were clear. California, with its two million Mexican Americans, would be strongly affected by any independent political movement in the barrios. In that divided state the La Raza voters could be decisive. Politicians of both parties would have to bargain equally for Chicano support—an incredible prospect in a state where there was not one Chicano in either house of the legislature in 1966.

In Washington, D.C., the election results brought an immediate response. La Raza politicians, like Bert Corona, were summoned to the White House, where plans were discussed for a promised "White House Conference of Mexican Americans." The outbursts of anger and frustration by Negro leaders at the previous conference on the black ghettos had, however, made certain officials of the Johnson administration hesitant. President Johnson was himself wary of focusing the national spotlight on the Chicano revolt. It was decided to convene a more manageable meeting, at a remote location, far from the nation's capital.

On June 9, 1967, the President announced the creation of The Inter-Agency Committee on Mexican American Affairs. Since there was no precedent, and no place, in the governmental structure for such a group, it had to be attached directly to the White House. The President then appointed Vincenti Ximines—a respected La Raza politician from New Mexico, and a Commissioner of the Equal Employment Opportunities Commission—to chair the new agency composed of four Cabinet officers and the head of the OEO.

The task of the Ximines Committee, by Presidential Order, was to "hear solutions to Mexican American problems." Although the committee had little authority and no enforcement powers, its creation was a recognition that the Chicanos would no longer be the "stepchildren of the Great Society," in the words of Judge Alfred Hernández, the past president of LULAC.

When it was learned that the more outspoken La Raza leaders were not to be invited to the proposed White House conference—Senator Ralph Yarborough (Democrat, of Texas) had requested that the President invite the full spectrum of independent barrio leaders—the dispute flared so bitterly that the conference was postponed indefinitely.

It was never held. Infuriated, the state leaders of California's MAPA, LULAC, CSO, the American GI Forum, and the Association of Mexican American Educators, in the spring of 1968, expressed their "frustration, disappointment, and impatience over the long delays, inaction and indecisiveness on the part of President Johnson and his White House staff in convening a national conference on the pressing and urgent needs of the 9,000,000 Mexican Americans and other Spanish-speaking people of our country." They threatened to convene their own "grassroots White House Conference."

Hoping to placate the revolt in the barrios, the White House ordered the holding of "Cabinet Committee Hearings on Mexican American Affairs" in El Paso, Texas, in October, 1967. But these hearings merely institutionalized the rebellion.

Leaders like Cesar Chavez, who were invited by the President, refused to attend. Leaders who were not invited, like Reies Tijerina, attended, but then set up a rival La Raza Unida conference in the nearby Church of the Sacred Heart. Leaders who were featured speakers at the White House meeting, like "the dean of Mexican American politics," Dr. Ernesto Galarza, spoke at the La Raza Unida meeting as well. Leaders of the powerful MAPA of California voted to boycott the Cabinet Committee Hearings entirely, but its members were permitted to attend individually. "We have to learn to play the political game and beat the Anglo at it," explained one of MAPA's top officers.

In the Church of the Sacred Heart the young Chicanos took over the pulpit. A bumper sticker that symbolized the rebellious spirit began to appear on the cars of the officially invited delegates; it read "La Raza Unida," and showed a farmworker raising two rifles in his fist. The delegation of community leaders from Laredo, Texas, marched into El Paso bearing the sign: "TODAY WE PROTEST, TOMORROW REVOLUTION."

"We are moving forward," President Johnson told the El Paso meeting. The United Steel Workers Union leader, Maclovio Barraza, who heads the Southwest's Council on Mexican American Affairs, responded directly to the President: "It is not enough! And it barely touches the many problems that beg attention. Our people are saying that before we shout 'Viva Johnson,' there better be a 'Viva la

Gente Mexicana' (Long Live the Mexican People). Mañana is too late."

"MANANA IS HERE!" was a placard of the young Chicanos at the La Raza Unida conference. The juxtaposition of humor and anger, irony and protest, connivance and idealism, was not just a political tactic but was part of the "unique style of La Raza politics" that was developing. "Gracias por Nada!" (Thanks for Nothing!), the slogan of the protest marchers in California, voiced the same quality of bitter joking. It reflected the mood of a bicultural people who are urban and rural, ancient and modern, Indian and Spanish, Mexican and American. "Brown humor," said a Chicano organizer, "is deadly serious."

"Now, don't forget we are a culture within a culture. We are contradictory and complex. We are a conquered people," explains the MAPA leader, Bert Corona, a hard-eyed, toughened veteran of political in-fighting. He is a tall, imposing man with the demeanor of a governor, who is expert at practical politics and not given to romanticism. "We have our own life style in the barrio. We have our own culture, that we retain very strongly. You hear more and more talk about the uniqueness of the Chicano. He is not really an English-speaking, Anglo-cultured individual. He is more complex than that. Our own consciousness is coming into the consciousness of the nation. The President recognized this, and so have many of the Cabinet officers. Why? Because La Raza has begun to exhibit its own style and demand its own priorities in politics.

"If by self-determination you mean the liberty to plan and act on our own programs, in our own way, this is what we want. We want self-determination, now!

"So we cannot be just ordinary Democrats," says Corona, himself a leading Democrat, "or Republicans either, in the Anglo way. The political parties are just vehicles for our fight for self-determination. We are La Raza always."

His views are echoed by a prominent Republican, Joe Benitos of Phoenix, Arizona. Benitos, a young man who rose high in his state's GOP ranks ("They babied me," he says, "because they wanted the Mexican vote"), is just as ambivalent about party politics. "I'm not a Republican's Republican, just as I won't be a Democrat's Democrat.

Politics is only politics. My main concern is the Mexican American! La Raza! I'm a Mexican American, first."

In the tacky summer of 1968 the raucous Democratic and Republican presidential conventions pushed the newly declared independence of the La Raza politicians to an uncomfortable test. At both conventions the candidates and demands of the Chicano caucuses were ignored by the party leaders. Some of the barrio delegates talked of a dramatic walkout. The martyred Senator Robert Kennedy had been the emotional hero of barrio voters, and the *jefes políticos* knew that neither of the nominees would rally much support in their constituencies. When the ill-fated Chicago Convention of the Democrats nominated the effervescent Hubert Humphrey, who had been picketed at the El Paso meetings, the delegates from the California barrios stood on their chairs shouting, "No! No! No!"

Soon after the nominating rituals had been performed the *jefes políticos* of MAPA met in Fresno, in their traditional, rubber-stamp "Endorsing Convention." The barrio leaders voted, however, for the first time in their history, to reject the presidential candidates of both parties. In the balloting Richard Nixon received 3 votes, Hubert Humphrey received 32 votes, and 130 votes were cast for "no endorsement." The political independence of La Raza was proclaimed, by three to one.

"Neither party has given much to the Mexican American," declared Aban (Abe) Tapia, the newly elected state chairman of MAPA, who replaced Bert Corona. La Raza, which had "the swing vote for national and state elections" in California, would therefore support neither.

By withholding their support from both presidential candidates the barrio leaders would hurt the Democrats most obviously. The *jefes políticos* had been influential in the campaigns of John Kennedy and Lyndon Johnson. "It's time to hit the Democrats hard," Corona said, knowing full well the effect of a "no endorsement" vote. "We would rather stay at home and sit on our hands and not campaign for those who are not for the Mexican Americans. We don't have to beg those who come around with lip service," Tapia agreed. The revolt at the polls had reached California, and it was to cost Hubert Humphrey victory in the state.

The delegates proposed no alternative candidates or independent parties. Where could they go politically?

"Our movement is changing from month to month," says Eliezer Risco, editor of *La Raza*. "No one knows what political form it will take tomorrow. No one knows who the national leaders will be next year. All we know is that it will be our own. We will no longer take orders from anyone."

"Chicanos are not damn fools," were Corona's parting words. "At least, not any longer!"

XVI The Shrunken Head of Pancho Villa

The De-education Schools

The boy waves his hand bashfully, and the teacher tells him to come to her desk.

"Charles, what do you want?"

"I have to go," the boy whispers, in Spanish, "to the bathroom."

"Charles, speak English."

"I have to go," the boy whispers a little louder, in Spanish, "to the bathroom."

"English!" the teacher rebukes him, growing impatient. "We speak English in school, Carlos," she says in Spanish. "You ask in English, or sit down."

The boy, who is maybe ten, and small, looks up at the teacher with the awe and fear that schoolchildren of his age have for authority. He does not know what to say or do. Suddenly his eyes light up with a mischievous thought.

"If you don't let me go to the bathroom," the boy exclaims, in Spanish, "maybe I piss on your shoes."

Years later the grown man remembers the incident of his boyhood humiliation without smiling. In his village the schoolhouse was closed long ago, and the teacher is gone, but the conflict in the classroom is indelible in his memory. "That teacher, she did not like us," he says. "She was a good teacher, but for forty years she did not let children speak Spanish in her classroom. She made us shamed." And the man of fifty is angry, still.

"Why did that teacher shame us? Spanish is a cultured language. It was here before English."

Children have been taught to forget the "foreign" ways of their fathers. Children have been cajoled, enticed, threatened, and punished for speaking Spanish. Children have been beaten.

In one school in South Texas the children are forced to kneel in the playground and beg forgiveness for uttering a Spanish word. Some teachers have pupils who talk the forbidden language kneel before the entire class. A popular punishment is to have the offender stand facing the blackboard. Cesar Chavez, the farm workers' leader, vividly recalls being forced to stand in a corner for defying the order, "No Spanish in the classroom." That teaching method is still practiced in the rural schools. "Spanish detention" is another widely used punishment for speaking the native language. A wispy, white-haired teacher in Tucson, Arizona, proudly tells how she teaches English. The child who answers in Spanish walks to her desk and "he drops a penny in a bowl, for every Spanish word." She boasts, "It works! They come from poor families, you know."

One Rio Grande Valley school goes further. The teachers assign students to be "Spanish monitors," who guard its corridors, writing down the names of their fellow students who are heard speaking Spanish. The culprits are reprimanded or beaten.

Not all the methods of de-educating the Chicanos to forget their native language are nonviolent. Some of the largest school systems in the Southwest still sanction the beating of recalcitrant children if they persist in being "Spanish-speaking."

Even now, the schoolchildren of Los Angeles may be "paddled" with the official approval of the Board of Education.

When the barrio students walked out of the high schools of East Los Angeles to protest what they called "racist education," one of their pleas was that, "corporal punishment, which is carried on in the East Los Angeles schools, should be abolished throughout the district." The Los Angeles *Times* commented casually: "Corporal punishment is mostly in the form of paddling. . . . Authorization of corporal punishment at the discretion of school personnel is the board's [Los Angeles Board of Education] policy." The offhanded defense of "paddling" the Chicano high school students, by the second-largest school system in the country, was offered in the spring of 1968!

"We are teaching these kids with psychological guns pointed at their heads," angrily observed Sal Castro, a Los Angeles high school teacher. "If a kid speaks in Spanish, he is criticized. If a kid has a Mexican accent, he is ridiculed. If a kid talks back, in any language, he is arrested. If a kid wants to leave school, he is forced back. We have gun-point education. The school is a prison.

"Education in the barrio doesn't free the mind of the Chicano. It imprisons his mind," the teacher said.

One day that spring an honor student at the Sidney Lanier High School in San Antonio, Texas, was caught reciting his Spanish homework aloud, in the school cafeteria. He was taken to the principal's office and beaten with a paddle; there were several cases of young people being beaten for speaking Spanish. "Just a gentle whack or two does them good," a teacher said. When the students complained about the paddling, they were threatened with the loss of their college scholarships and suspended. In frustration there was talk of a school strike. A meeting was hastily held by the city's Human Rights Commission in the hall of a local Catholic church, where the young Chicanos cited dozens of incidents of intimidation because they dared to talk in their mother tongue.

Educators listened in silence. There were no denials; everyone knew that it had been this way for generations. Wasn't it everywhere? In Texas it is illegal, according to Section 288 of the State Penal Code, for a teacher, principal, or school superintendent to teach or conduct school business in any language but English. Textbooks have to be in English. By custom the language restriction has been stridently applied to the students as well.

The "sons of Zapata" County Commissioner Albert Pena extravagantly praised the students: "Our generation didn't have the courage to speak out. You are brave," he told them.

In the San Antonio high schools there were months of turmoil, meetings, student strikes, firings of teachers and even priests, newspaper headlines, and charges of infiltration by "Castro-trained extremists" before the high school students won the right to talk openly in their mother tongue. Until that triumph they had to whisper the language of Cervantes in the secrecy of the girls' locker rooms and the boys' urinals.

It was so everywhere. Language is a vital teaching tool in the de-education process. The banning of Spanish in the classroom is not an arbitrary act of a callous teacher. In the metropolitan school systems and in the village schoolhouses the suppression of the Spanish language and the culture of La Raza reflects the de-education policy that has been dominant in the schools of the Southwest since the "Conquest" of the region.

In the small town of San Luis in the high mountains of southern Colorado the people are mostly Spanish-speaking. Yet, there too the native language was prohibited inside the school gate.

"Until quite recently Spanish has been tacitly assumed to be an *inferior language* by nearly all of us," writes a village teacher in San Luis, Alan Davis. "Its use has been forbidden in our classrooms, and on our playgrounds, until this month [February, 1969]." Of course, the teacher adds, "we offered no courses in Spanish."

The native language of the Chicano child was treated with colonialist disdain. His voice was muted. "English is the national language of the United States, but it is not a native or indigenous language. It is one of the colonial languages," writes Dr. Vera John, in a comprehensive study of bilingualism in the schools of the Southwest. In a conquered land the institutions of culture—theaters, books, libraries, academics—may be visibly suppressed. It is more difficult to eradicate the spoken word. Language then becomes the last resource of cultural survival. "If the language goes, the culture goes with it," writes a scholar of La Raza. And so, in the schools there are bitter skirmishes over the spoken word. The children have become combatants.

"They yell at our children in school, 'Do not speak Spanish!' You are a free man in the land of the free, but 'Do not speak Spanish!' English is the only language of freedom," Reies Tijerina, the prophet of cultural revival, tells a meeting in a village schoolhouse. "It's like the story of the man who took a bird from his cage, and set it free. But first he took the pair of scissors and clipped off its wings.

" 'Fly! Fly!' the man said.

"The blue-eyed cat, the Anglo, came and ate the poor, helpless bird," Tijerina says.

In the "migrant schools" proposed by the state of California's "master migrant plan," the process of de-education by which a Chicano child is stripped of his culture is bluntly outlined. The "sample migrant school curriculum" is explicit:

> Physical education—English cultural games and activities . . .
> Creative arts and crafts—Introduction to English culture, music and song . . .
> Arithmetic—Concrete objects, English concept of arithmetic . . .
> Social Studies—Developing knowledge of characteristics of English culture . . .

Nowhere in the curriculum is there a word on the Indian, Spanish, and Mexican cultures of the Southwest. In all the classes the emphasis is upon the de-education of the Chicano child.

He has to be de-educated before he can be re-educated—as "English"? The "English" cultural games he is taught may be the old Aztec sports of basketball and handball; the "English" music and song, Western style, may have originated in the vaquero music and song of the old West; and the "English" concept of arithmetic may be based on the sophisticated mathematics of the scholars of ancient Mexico. But none of these origins is mentioned in the textbooks or the curriculum. Education of the Chicano is de-education, first of all. The language and culture of the Southwest are seen by his teachers as a prime hindrance to his progress, not only in learning English, but in "becoming an American." In the better schools the ensuing conflict may be subtle, but in the poorer schools it is vulgar and cruel.

"Schools try to brainwash the Chicanos," says Maggie Alvarado, a student at St. Mary's University in San Antonio. "They try to make us forget our history, to be ashamed of being Mexicans, of speaking Spanish. They succeed in making us feel empty, and angry, inside."

De-education is a difficult process. The culture of La Raza and the Spanish language were native to the country for hundreds of years before the coming of the Anglo to the Southwest; they are not easy to uproot. Every generation the attempt at de-education has to begin anew, for the conflict of cultures in the schools of the Southwest is an unending conflict between the conquered and the conqueror. Colonialism has usurped the purposes of education. The schools have been one of the most effective instruments of the "Conquest." "It is safe to say that the school, more than barbed wire or the plowing up of the range, was responsible for the decline of the vaquero," writes the venerable old cowboy and settler of California, Arnold Rojas. The "Yankee schoolmarm" was a more efficient conqueror of La Raza than the United States Army, Rojas writes. "The children did not have a chance."

A child goes to school to wonder. The school is where he enters the Anglo world with shy curiosity; it is a magical microcosm of society to him. The teacher is his sorcerer, a mother who is worldly-wise, knowing all sorts of facts and magic, powerful as the policeman, but human as an aunt or uncle. In the beginning that is how school seems to the child.

He is lost at the thought that he cannot enter that wonderful world because he speaks the wrong language or is the wrong color. The child is proud of his father; he boasts of his barrio heritage. He doesn't know that he is supposed to be "culturally deprived."

If the teacher ridicules the language of his father, his way of thinking, the beliefs and behavior his mother taught him, the child is bewildered. He is told he must choose between being "American" or "Mexican." It is no choice for him, for he is neither but is both. He will argue, or grow silent. Either way the child will be in conflict with the teacher. And his idyl of education is ended.

The anguish of the child from the barrio who faces a "traumatic first day" in school has been depicted by Dr. Sabine Ulibarri, Professor of Spanish at the University of New Mexico. He told the Cabinet Committee Hearings on Mexican American Affairs: "The child begins with a handicap the very first day he shows up in the first grade. English is the language of the classroom. He speaks no English, or he speaks inadequate English. He comes from a father-dominated home, and he finds himself in a female-dominated classroom. The Anglo concepts and values that govern and prevail are unintelligible to him. In all likelihood he comes from a low social and economic class, and there he is in a middle-class environment. He probably feels uncomfortable and self-conscious in the unfamiliar clothes he is wearing. He looks about him. The teacher, far from representing a mother image, must seem a remote and awe-inspiring creature. There is nothing in the atmosphere from which he can draw any comfort.

"Everything he sees is foreign," Ulibarri goes on, "the Hispano kid, José Pérez, finds himself in a hostile environment indeed. He has to be something very special, a star, a hero, in order to win."

Ulibarri, a scholarly and cultured man, is an acerbic critic of the de-educating curriculum of the schools. "The whole program is designed to make him [the Chicano student] an Anglo. He doesn't want to become an Anglo, or he doesn't know how," the professor of Spanish says. By the time the student reaches high school, "no one can blame him if he feels cheated, betrayed, and frustrated."

The malaise of the de-educated child does not come entirely from the forbidding rules of the unfriendly school, where "English, a foreign language," mutes his voice. It comes from his home as well. Many of these children are hungry. They bring their hunger to school. They suffer from malnutrition and anemia that is so severe that a health survey of the Office of Education, in Washington, D.C., has estimated that as many as 15 per cent may have their thought processes retarded due to lack of nutrition. "They may need food, or medication, or warm clothes to be able to learn," reports a barrio classroom teacher, Hercella Toscano of San Antonio. "I do stress this need because I see it every day as I visit one class after another. I see children who are listless and restless. Some are in need of better clothes and some show signs of malnutrition.

"How can we expect these children to learn, especially if they are hungry?" asks the barrio teacher.

Poverty is not measured by the IQ tests. The hunger quotient is not registered, nor is the psychological effect of poor clothing, disease, and illness computed in the surveys of the lack of motivation, educational achievement, and rates of dropout. "Our kids don't drop out," says another barrio teacher, Froben Lozada, "they are pushed out by poverty."

The depressing effect of the de-education process upon the nearly two million Chicano youth of school age has been summarized by the sad statistics of the National Advisory Committee on Mexican American Education of the U.S. Office of Education:

> . . . In the Southwest the average Chicano child has only a 7th grade education.
>
> . . . The drop-out, or push-out, rate in Texas for Chicano high school students is 89 per cent, while in California 50 per cent of Chicano high school students leave school between the 10th and 11th grade.
>
> . . . Along the Rio Grande Valley of Texas four out of five Chicano children fall two years behind their Anglo classmates by the 5th grade. (The city manager of San Antonio estimates that 44.3 per cent of the barrio residents are "functionally illiterate"; 20 per cent never went to school "at all.")
>
> . . . College enrollment is infinitesimal. In California, where 14 per cent of public school students are Chicanos, less than ½ of one per cent of college students at the seven campuses of the University of California are Chicanos.

Among the families of farm workers the process of de-education is most successful. The life on the road makes schooling difficult. The nature of the rural schools makes it worse. In the San Joaquin Valley of California, near Fresno, the results of a recent educational census show that the adult male Chicano has an average of 5.7 years of schooling.

The de-education of La Raza is indeed overachieved. Of all the children of the poor who go to school as though they go to battle to defend their cultural heritage, none come away with greater bitterness and frustration. In the barrios of the Southwest the Chicano child might echo the lament of a little Puerto Rican boy in the barrios of New York City, who told a social worker, "I am illiterate in two languages. I am an alien in two lands."

The Language of La Raza

The child of migrants and barrio dropout is heir to one of the most ancient cultures, magnificent literatures, and historic universities in the Americas. He is the descendant of learned men whose civilizations compared with the greatest in the world.

Long before the founding of the University of Mexico, in 1553, the widespread school systems of the Aztec, Toltec, and Mayan nations were teaching their children medicine, mathematics, philosophy, art, architecture, and engineering. When the Spanish conquistadors landed on the shores of the empires of Mexico they were amazed, as Bernal Díaz del Castillo, the chronicler of the Cortés expedition, wrote, by "the many books of paper" the Mexicans had. They were "large books with beautiful paintings and symbols about all the arts, from which they taught," wrote Fray Diego de Durán. "Everything was written down; they recorded their memorable deeds, their wars and victories." In the schools "they also taught astrology, the meaning of dreams, and the count of the tears," added Fray Bernardino de Sahagún; for there were "many kinds of schools" in the land—the *telpochcalli*, or houses for youth, and the *calmecac*, or institutes of higher learning.

So vast were the libraries of these Indian schools that it took the conquistadors years to ferret them all out and to attempt to burn all the books. They were not successful.

Perhaps, the Europeans had come upon "the oldest literary works in the Americas," as Leon-Portilla says in his *Pre-Columbian Literatures of Mexico.* The Aztecs religiously paid homage to a literature older than their own that existed "in a time which nobody can reckon," before the birth of Christ:

Those who
carried with them
the black and red ink;
the manuscripts and painted books,
the wisdom.
They brought everything with them,
the annals,
the books of song . . .

The archaeologists have dated, by carbon-14 tests, the "writing and calendar system" of these little-known people "at least as early as 600 B.C." In Europe there were no written languages at that time, except for Greek. Fray Sahagún, in fact, likened these Indian cultures of ancient Mexico to those of Greece and Rome. He observed a generation of learning, of aesthetics, and of scholarship that seemed to him "classical." "The same thing [as in Greece and Rome] existed in this Indian nation, especially among the Mexicans [Aztecs], whose learned, valiant and virtuous men are highly esteemed," the awed priest wrote in the sixteenth century.

The conquistadors could not eradicate all traces of such a civilization. Instead they destroyed its visible forms of power and sought to absorb, or were absorbed by, its riches and emotions and earth. In the "Laws of the Indies" the Spanish Empire acknowledged the impasse by decreeing that the Indians were "human," and that the conquerors were morally free to marry the conquered—a recognition of reality that created a bilingual and bicultural nation and, perhaps, the Indian-born Saint of Mexican Catholicism, the Virgin of Guadalupe, as well.

When the conquistadors and Mexican Indians came north they brought both cultures. In the Southwest they gave birth to the culture of La Raza, which was Indian, Spanish, *and* Mexican. The early settlers were known as Españoles Mejicanos—that is, bilingual "Mexican Spaniards," who were native-born, often of the loves legalized by the "Laws of the Indies."

On the riverbanks of the Rio Grande, in 1598, when the settlers of the de Oñate expedition performed the first play enacted on our soil, the "comedy" combined the pageantry of feudal Spain and that of Aztec ritual. The horse dramas so popular in the Southwest for hundreds of years—such as "The Christians and the Moors," later to become "The Christians and the Comanches"—continued that cultural and bilingual tradition and they added new elements.

The literature of the Southwest was equally bilingual and bicultural: Spanish and Indian. Gaspar Pérez de Villagra's poem *The Chronicles of New Mexico,* written in 1613, is widely known as the first "American" literary work, on an "American" theme, penned in "America." Yet even at that early date words and concepts in Nahuatl, the language of the Aztecs, are in the text.

In the years thereafter a rich literature—books, poems, essays, plays, histories—was created by the writers and poets of the Southwest, in an indigenous idiom. The country was then part of Mexico, where most likely these books were published and in whose universities they were studied, and where they have been forgotten.

"We have to rediscover ourselves," says Luis Valdez, the director of El Teatro Campesino. "There are years and years of discoveries we have to make of our people.

"People ask me: What is Mexican history in the United States? There is no textbook of the history of La Raza. Yet the history of the Mexican in this country is four hundred years old. We know we pre-date the landing of the Pilgrims and the American Revolution. But beyond that? What really happened? No one can tell you. Our history has been lost. Lost!

"Our generation says: Wait! Stop! Let's consider our roots! Let's rediscover our history!" Valdez says.

Upon dusty shelves, frayed and forgotten, the books of this history may still be hidden. By word of mouth, from time to time, there is word of a lost literature, in reminiscences and folk memories. But the culture of La Raza has been effectively suppressed in the Southwest. The textbooks barely refer to it; the teachers are unfamiliar with it.

In the Faculty Forum of the Lincoln High School of East Los Angeles a teacher of Chicano youth, Richard C. Davis, dismisses that history: "Before the Spanish came, he [the Mexican] was an Indian grubbing in the soil, and after the Spanish came he was a slave." The teacher's ire is aroused by a fellow faculty member, Joe McKnight, who has the temerity to suggest that "Mexican and Mexican American history should be a required course in all Eastside [Los Angeles] schools." Davis, who voices the "dominant view" of the faculty, disdainfully rejoins, "Mexican history is taught, what there is of it."

A few days after the teacher's contempt is publicized two hundred parents picket the Lincoln High School with the inevitable signs of the times: "BRONZE IS BEAUTIFUL" and "WE ARE NOT INSECTS, DAVIS! WE ARE HUMAN BEINGS!" The *Chicano Student*, an underground campus newspaper in Los Angeles, complains of "teachers who at worst have contempt for our culture, and at best have no understanding of it." Chicanos are weary, they say, of "teachers who can't communicate, books in a strange language about blond, blue-eyed strangers named Dick and Jane."

In the beleaguered school a student is more explicit: "I am a prisoner of Lincoln High School," he writes, "where Richard Davis is allowed to preach racism; he should pack up and move out of our school."

Says a Chicano youth, in Texas: "The worst thing that happened to me in my life was when I went to a blasted high school which was mainly Anglo. I was taught how great the Anglo was. Never once did a teacher tell me, Oh yes, the Mexicans did great things in the Southwest. The only time they mention Mexicans in the schools is when they talk about the Mexican-American War. And then we are the bad guys, who lost.

"They teach white history and white education," the young man says. "You're white and you're great. So if you are Anglo you are given a superiority complex, and if you are not Anglo you are given a guilt complex. It's a racist way of teaching."

The children of La Raza, humiliated by the textbooks, tongue-tied by the teachers, de-educated by the schools, have had to hold onto what they can of their heritage by themselves. In the barrios they have created their own communal culture and have invented a language of their own beyond the pale of the Anglo schools.

In an "unlettered speech" they have created an unwritten literature. The schools ignore it. The mass media does not know it.

The culture of the Chicano is *voiced.* It is voiced in the *corridos* of exodus, the chronicles of spoken history, Pachuco legends and *cholo* tales of the ghettos, *posadas,* the old, remembered church plays and the artistry of pilgrimages of religious politics, cantina love lyrics and aphorisms, and oratory in the language of ecstasy. Words of this oral language have special sensitivities and nuances. The words have an immediacy, a human vibrance and brilliance of expression that is often missing in shadowy reflections of the written words. An illiterate man may talk with direct imagery and tonal richness that the literate man has forgotten how to use, for he does not need it. He who is literate is truly illiterate in these ancient uses of language, which he nostalgically calls "poetic." When a language is primarily spoken, and sung, rather than written, like the language of the Chicano, it has to be lyrical in its rhythms, brutally exact, not abstract, and its symbols must be as living as the flesh.

So it is in the barrios. The word is the flesh. "In the beginning was the Word. And the Word was made flesh," writes Professor Ulibarri. "The language, the Word, carries within it the history, the culture, the traditions, the very life of a people, the flesh. Language is people.

"A Hispano who does not speak Spanish must choke on his chili," Ulibarri says.

Can a language personify a human being? When an educator of the U.S. Office of Education tells teachers of barrio schoolchildren, "Wave your arms! Talk with your bodies! Use your emotions!" he is recognizing the human nature of the language of the Chicanos. The words are invested with bodily emotions. The meanings are the embodiment of feelings.

Rodolfo Gonzales, the barrio leader of Denver, reflects this when he accuses the schools of "emasculating our language." And the oracle of the land-grant movement, Reies Tijerina, voices a similar concept of language when he tells a banquet of lawyers in New York City, half apologetically, half accusingly: "I do not speak to you with my heart, in English. English is a cold language, to me. Spanish, to me, is warm and alive as my body. I speak Spanish with my whole heart, not with my head.

"If you cut out our Spanish, you have cut out our heart," Tijerina says.

The importance of language to a conquered people has been recognized by the Congress, in the passage of the Bilingual Education Act.

Introduced by Texas Senator Ralph Yarborough, and cosponsored by Senator John Tower, as Title VII of the Elementary and Secondary Education Act of 1965, the bill recognizes and encourages teaching in Spanish in the schools, and was signed into law by the President in January, 1968. Spanish was no longer forbidden.

Political upheavals in the barrios brought about the legislative acts. The "Texas White House," where Lyndon Johnson then held the reins, was particularly alarmed by the disenchantment of formerly "safe" La Raza votes in the state. In the early and mid-1960's independent campaigns by Chicano politicians in Texas had caused the defeat of several Democratic candidates.

"We made demands," recalls San Antonio County Commissioner Albert Pena. "And they listened."

But the Bilingual Act was ensnared in old prejudices. Texas and California both had laws that prohibited teaching of regular classes in Spanish; in these states the legislators had to introduce bills to enable their school systems to accept federal funds for bilingual teaching. In New Mexico both Spanish and English teaching were officially recognized by the state constitution, but the practice was in such long disuse that new legislation had to be passed. Curiously, the constitution of the state of California had been originally written in Spanish, by a Mexican American, and the first vice president of the Republic of Texas had been a Tejano, a native of Mexico. But that was long ago.

Even so, "As of 1967–68 the total number of genuine bilingual programs . . . certainly does not exceed two dozen in the entire country," wrote Theodore Anderson, head of the Romance Language Department of the University of Texas and chairman of the National Advisory Committee to Title VII, in the Office of Education. The federal appropriation had been a cautious and pithy one—$7.5 million—and by 1969 some 310 school systems and agencies had requested some share of those bilingual monies. Understandably only a token few could be funded.

The bilingual classes in the schools are administered by the same school systems, in the same classrooms, and by the same teachers that the Chicanos have accused of "racism." Grotesque parodies of bilingualism soon became apparent. For instance, in one school in El Paso, where the students are taught in Spanish for part of the day, the same children caught talking in Spanish during the rest of the day are punished with "Spanish detention."

And in the Imperial Valley of California, where one-third of the children are Chicanos, mostly children of farm workers, the bilingual program is directed by the wife of one of the largest growers. The Imperial Valley classes in Spanish are among the oldest in the state. Begun in 1963, they have been run by the County School Board, which has always been almost wholly Anglo, as are the local principals, whose contemptuous attitude is expressed by one who said, "These Mexes will never learn anything anyway. So it can't do any harm to try teaching [them] in Spanish."

In a town near Fresno, in the San Joaquin Valley, when a local principal recognized that the Bilingual Act would be law of the land he sent a memorandum to his teaching staff advising them to learn "idiot Spanish."

The desire for educational reform in the barrios is usually tempered with the demand, as stated by the high school strikers of East Los Angeles, for "compulsory bilingual and bicultural education [for] *teachers and administrators* to receive training in speaking Spanish and Mexican cultural heritage." It is the teacher who has to be taught, in the eyes of the students. In his ***Bilingualism in Education***, the barrio principal of a San Antonio public school, Nick Garza, explains that the teacher "must know both languages well" to teach the bilingual Chicano child.

Unless "100,000 bilingual-bicultural teachers and administrators" are trained, the program will not become a reality, warns the Committee on Mexican American Education of the U.S. Office of Education. That retraining program, the "revised textbooks," and the classroom aids necessary would, in themselves, cost hundreds of millions of educational dollars.

In the barrios the Chicano child has gone beyond bilingualism. He is trilingual. The language of La Raza is more than "hybrid language" that unites English and Spanish. In four hundred years a new language has been developing, with a distinctive vocabulary, its own borrowed and re-created grammar, and a unique usage, which combines the

Castilian Spanish of the conquistadors and the frontier Americanisms of English with the ancient and modern languages of the Indians of Mexico and the Southwest.

Pachuco is one aspect of this language. In the California barrios the "invented" words, evocative syntax, and urbanized rhythms of rural Indian threnody with which the younger Chicanos speak is neither Spanish nor English. The language of the Pachuco is the creation of the barrios. "Placa" for "police" cannot be traced to the popular Mexican "placa" that means "baggage check," or the old Spanish "placa" that means "star, or insignia of knights," nor any English equivalent.

Even the proper Spanish spoken in the barrios is not truly Spanish. It never was. The ordinary, everyday words, such as tortilla and chili, are of course not Spanish at all, but are from the languages of the Mexican Indians, much as the Castilian Spanish of the conquistadors was interwoven with the words of the Moors.

In a Joycean vocabulary that weaves together the words of the Indian, the Spaniard, the peon, the modern Mexican, the Anglo, the Pachuco, and finally the Chicano, the people of La Raza have been creating their own "mother tongue." The words may be spoken with what Professor Manuel Guerra, of the University of Southern California, has termed "the intonation of sound patterns peculiar to Southern and Central Mexico"; but the language itself is "influenced by the environment and natural habitat" of the Southwest—"the spoken language of the deserts" and "the language of the highlands." The country's "foremost" linguists have "never researched the problem in depth," argues Guerra.

Yet, long ago, the venerable old vaquero of California, Arnold Rojas, recalls that "the Spanish of the vaquero [did] not conform to the best Castilian. The reader will, no doubt, search through Spanish dictionaries for some of the words. He will either fail to find them, or they will have definitions that do not agree with [my] text."

Similarly, the "dialects spoken in Texas are not good Spanish," writes Anderson, but " 'Tex-Mex' is authentic, natural, expressive—entirely adequate and appropriate to time, place, and to circumstance."

In New Mexico the old-time rancher "Uncle" Fred Ramsey, in his memory book, *These Are My People*, reminisces that people along the border have always spoken "not Spanish, but Mexican." He tells of his neighbor, Albino Elias, the "descendant of old Spanish settlers," who taught him the native tongue. "You see, I never learned to speak Spanish, but speak Mexican fluently," he says disarmingly.

Of this new language a new literature is being born. The young writers of the barrios have begun to create literary forms of the "unlettered speech" of their forefathers. In the modern Chicano plays of Luis Valdez and Rodolfo Gonzales, the multicultural poetry of Abelardo Delgado, Beni Luna, and Guadalupe de Saavedra, the La Raza scholarship of Ernesto Galarza, Octavio Romano, and Richard Durán, and in the barrio paintings of Manuel Martínez the infinitely varied, subtle and brutal, stark and complex life of La Raza is being transmuted into art. The pages of the barrio newspapers and literary journals of the Chicano students—*El Grito, Con Safos, La Raza, El Gallo, El Malcriado, El Paisano, Bronze*—are infused with the vibrant language, pent-up expressions, and as yet unrecognized literary force of those who have for generations been the silent people, "the invisible minority."

In the past the culture of the Chicano has been so "invisible" to Anglos that when the rural educators of the National Education Association recognized the need for teaching the language and heritage of La Raza in the schools, in 1966, and issued an impassioned appeal for bilingual education, entitled *The Invisible Minority—Per No Vencibles,* they misspelled the Spanish in the title. But then, the educators had no bilingual textbook of La Raza history or Chicano culture to study. There has been none published. Nor had the major publishers issued any of the books, nor had Broadway produced a single play that has been born of the cultural revolution in the barrios, at that time.

Just as they have had to preserve their language, by themselves, the Chicanos have had to create and publish their new literature without the *simpático* and commercial help of the educational institutions. The first anthology of modern Chicano writing, *El Espeso (The Mirror): Selected Mexican American Literature,* was published in 1969 by the independent student publication *El Grito,* outside the schools.

Inevitably, the new culture of the young Chicanos had to clash with the archaic de-education system of the schools.

The Shrunken Head of Pancho Villa

"Sorry, white man," wrote Ruben Gutierrez, a student at Woodrow Wilson High School in East Los Angeles. "La Raza has had enough." One mild day in March of 1968 some 15,000 Chicano students simply walked out of five Los Angeles high schools. By noon the strike had all but shut down classes throughout the barrio. The police invaded the classrooms and playgrounds. Swarms of sheriff's deputies blockaded the neighborhood, in an old-fashioned Western version of law and order. In an hour the arrests of students and teachers began.

The buoyant teen-agers called it a "blowout" and their hastily hand-drawn picket signs voiced their jubilant air—"EDUCATION NOT CONTEMPT," "EDUCATION NOT ERADICATION," "TEACHERS, SI, BIGOTS, NO!" "QUE PASO? FREE SPEECH!" "WE ARE NOT 'DIRTY MEXICANS,' " "OUR KIDS DON'T HAVE BLUE EYES, BUT THEY DO GO OVERSEAS," "SCHOOL, NOT PRISON," and "IS THIS A HOLIDAY?"

Enthusiasm and admiration of the adults for the young Chicanos' boldness unified the entire barrio. "These kids are proudly saying, 'I'm a Mexican and I want to learn about my culture,' " said Philip Montez, a West Coast director of the U.S. Civil Rights Commission. "When I was a kid we used to play it pretty cool about the Mexican thing." In the old days, when he went to school, students did protest, said Julian Nava, the sole Chicano of the Board of Education, elected after a barrio-wide fight. Nava, who holds a doctorate in history from Harvard University, recalled that when he attended a barrio high school, "I was told to take auto shop. And I did. I did what I was told."

Students, who led the "blowout" issued a long list of educational demands—thirty-eight in all—to the Board of Education. They ranged from "textbooks and curriculum should be revised to show Mexican contributions to our country" and "the transfer of teachers who show any form of prejudice to students," to the building of swimming pools in "all Eastside schools" and unlocked restrooms and "all campuses to be open and fences removed." Support for many of the Chicanos' proposals came from the Los Angeles Teachers Association and Local 1021 of the American Federation of Teachers. The abysmal conditions of the schools needed reform, the teachers' groups affirmed; especially did they support "more bilingual and bicultural training of school personnel, more Spanish-language library materials and textbooks," and "better cafeteria food."

But the city of Los Angeles replied by arresting the alleged thirteen leaders of the "blowout," including Sal Castro, a high school teacher. Those jailed were charged with "conspiracy" to disturb the educational process.

La Raza, the barrio newspaper, chortled that there were "thirteen Aztec gods," so the arrested ones were a select and prophetic number. It shows how "ignorant" the Board of Education is of our heritage, the editors wrote. "These are our people, the cream of the crop," declared the *Chicano Student;* and the youth did not really walk out of the schools, "they were pushed out!"

Hundreds of barrio groups came to the defense of the "conspirators." So did the Congress of Mexican American Unity, the Educational Issues Coordinating Council, the United Mexican American Students (UMAS), Cesar Chavez of the farm workers, the Council of Churches of Southern California, the Pacific Southwest Council of the Union of American Hebrew Congregations, the local American Federation of Teachers, the NAACP, and the Black Congress. Yet, when —after a year's delay, uproarious protests of thousands of barrio residents and students, and dozens of arrests—"the thirteen" were brought to trial, they were hurriedly convicted, fined, and placed on probation that forbade them to enter any barrio school, unless on official business. The probation was to last for three years.

The Los Angeles Board of Education voted to suspend the teacher, Sal Castro. In furious response the leaders of the barrios—students and parents—calmly walked into the board room of the Board of Education and staged a sit-in. For an entire week they occupied it. A young student, Paul Ruiz, was elected "temporary" Chairman of the Board; he presided over the exercise in community control. Every morning a priest offered mass, at the podium, using a tortilla as a holy wafer. He blessed the protesters, who spent the week discussing school reforms, singing Chicano songs to the music of guitars, and voting a new school system.

"Never was the Board of Education such a happy place," one of the Chicanos said.

"LIBERATED CHICANO BOARD OF EDUCATION," the barrio students and parents wrote on the blackboard. Then they went home.

The bemused members of the Board of Education returned to their silent chamber. Once seated they promptly voted to reinstate the barrio teacher, Sal Castro, whom they had suspended the week before. But in the barrio schools the rumblings have not ceased and the grievances have not changed. "What, really, did the students benefit from the walkouts?" a Lincoln High School youth writes in the *Chicano Student.* "Not a damn thing! Why can't the white man see our side of the story? We Chicanos are damn sick and tired of talking. We want action, action now!"

"Our proposals have been made," the *Chicano Student* had editorialized earlier. "The big question is, will the School Board take positive action. If so, WHEN? IF NOT—BLOWOUTS, BABY, BLOWOUTS!"

Schools had become the no man's land of the cultural conflict. They are the most visible, best known, and most exposed institutions of the Anglo society in the barrios. On the inside they are the bastions where the language, philosophy, and goals of the conqueror are taught; but to those outside they are the bastions that the conquered can most easily besiege, with common cause, so that their children may be taught the language, philosophy, and goals of La Raza.

The "community control" of the schools, for the "better education of our children," is the social issue that has united the barrios more than any other. "Education is like a god to our people," says the barrio teacher Froben Lozada. But it is more than that.

Almost by mutual consent the schools have been chosen as the battlefield. The conflict in the classrooms may be fought, and won or lost, without threatening the sources of social power. The economic and political control of the barrios will not change, even if the Chicanos were to achieve new textbooks, a curriculum based on the heritage and needs of La Raza, and a wholly bicultural and bilingual teaching system. In a sense the schools are the safest places to continue the guerrilla warfare of the cultures that began with the "Conquest" of the Southwest. They are safer battlefields than the streets or the voting booths, for both sides.

"Revolution" in the schools thus becomes a paradox that is supported by the Chicano activists and the Anglo establishment, at least federally, with equal fervor.

In the fall of 1969 the Chicano students declared a national "walkout" in celebration of Mexican Independence Day on September 17th. School officials in Denver, Colorado, acquiescing to the rebellious mood of the students, announced a special assembly in a high school where there had been a riot the previous spring, to permit "leaders of the walkout to present their views to the student body." Never before in the Southwest had school authorities given such recognition to the Chicano "revolution."

Everywhere, from rural Texas to metropolitan California, there are walkouts, "blowouts," and protest marches. The student activists demand community control of the barrio schools and an "educational revolution," based on a new curriculum that honors "the dignity of Chicano life," by teaching the language of the people and the "Mexican and Mexican-American cultural heritage."

In the barrios, where the classroom has become a battlefield, the "passive pupil" has found his voice. Schools are a common ground, most of all for the child. He sees that in the classroom he is not the minority; he is the majority. Growing up in two cultures may, at times, be precarious and absurd. But it demands agility of the Chicano. He develops survival skills in both worlds. He learns how to live "in the belly of the shark." He no longer feels he must suffer in silence or withdraw, as his father did. The Chicano is surer of himself. He is outspoken, once he starts to speak.

In *The Shrunken Head of Pancho Villa,* his play on de-education,

Luis Valdez depicts a boy of the barrios who talks back, gets into trouble, and is sent to reform school. Joaquín, the Chicano antihero, returns home in the last act as a well-dressed, well-polished anglicized youth. But, he has no head! "He seems very reformed, rehabilitated," says his brother Mingo. "A clean-cut American boy." Lupe, his sister, is equally sardonic: "I think Joaquín, Jack, is gonna be okay, Ma. He can still find a job in the fields. A man doesn't need a head to work there."

All through the play the shrunken, stolen head of Pancho Villa is symbolically off stage. When the headless, de-educated Chicano boy appears, the decapitated hero of the Mexican Revolution cries, "There's the body and here's the head. Let's get together!"

"It's time for a new Mexican revolution," Luis Valdez tells Chicano students at the University of California, in Los Angeles. "And which Chicanos are going to lead the next revolution? The ones in the belly of the shark! Nosotros! We! We're going to lead that revolution! We've got to stand up and talk straight to the *gabachos* [the Anglos] saying, 'Hell, no! I won't go!' to your whole lousy system."

XVII The Chicanos

The girl was thirteen when she tried to kill herself. She was "tired of working." But she was too inexperienced with death to die, and she lived through her death. To escape her loneliness she married, at fifteen. Her child was born that year, but her husband was sent to prison. "I got a car. The car broke down. I couldn't pay for it. They wanted to sue me. So I forged a check." In the barrios of Denver to be left with a baby, without a husband, at fifteen, was to be lonelier than death. She became a prostitute.

"I worked the town. They call it hustling. I wouldn't go for less than thirty dollars. Because I needed the money. I got it too. All you have to do is be nice," the young girl said. "But to go out and hustle I had to be under the influence of narcotics."

Diana Perea told her own life story to the National Conference on Poverty in the Southwest, held in January, 1965, to launch the War on Poverty. In the winter sun of Tucson, Arizona, the nearly two hundred delegates who had gathered under the auspices of the Choate Foundation, to hear Vice President Hubert Humphrey, were as overwhelmed by the frail and frightened girl as she was by the presidential emissary. "Go back and tell them [your people] that the war against unemployment, discrimination, disease, and ignorance has begun. Tell them to get out and fight!" the Vice President said. "The wonderful thing about the War on Poverty is that we have the means to win it. We cannot fail." He reminded his listeners, "Fifteen minutes from where we sit tonight there is abject poverty."

In the audience was Diana Perea. A few weeks later she succeeded in killing herself.

Her death was due to an overdose of narcotics, the autopsy report declared. There were some nonmedical causes. On the frontispiece of the Summary Report of the National Conference on Poverty in the Southwest there was a black border of mourning around these simple words:

DIANA PEREA
1946–1965
VICTIM OF POVERTY

Death is an ordinary thing. No one would have heard of the young girl from the streets of Denver's barrio if she had not happened to share a microphone with the Vice President of the United States.

In the streets misery is said to be so common no one notices. Life in the barrios is cruel—to outsiders, for the sons and daughters of the poor, it is said, are too hardened and brutalized to be able to do anything but fight to survive.

A young girl cries of a brown child dying of hunger in the barrios of San Antonio:

In the land of the free
and the home of the brave,
He is dying of hunger,
he cannot be saved;
Come brothers and sisters
and weep by his grave.
This is our child—

The ordeal of these youths is bemoaned by sympathetic writers. Not by the youth. Diana Perea did not weep. The Chicana was matter of fact: this is the way it is. Life in the barrio streets is just a way of life—happy, unhappy, ordinary, exciting, boring, deadly. The streets are not dangerous, they are only treacherous. It doesn't frighten youth.

Seldom do they curse the barrio. They curse themselves for their inability to survive. It is not the barrio that the Chicano fears, but the lonely and hostile world outside.

Loneliness, the coldness of urban life, is what depresses the Chicano. In his family there is a warmth and gregarious love voiced with passion, uninhibited honesty, and gusto. The city frustrates and mutes this love. Faced with a society that he feels is hostile, the barrio youth becomes lost. He tries to defend himself by forming a gang, not just to fight for his manhood, his *macho,* but for his right to be a Chicano.

"The most brutal method of birth control is the one we practice on ourselves," a young man writes in *La Raza.*

To *La Raza Chicana,* a young girl writes a bitter note: "I wish to compliment brother Perfecto Vallego and his friends for doing with Caterino B. Heredia. Keep up the good work, Baby, you and the cops [can] get together on the Chicano Annual Shoot. Your game is as bad as the racist cop who goes after Chicano's who fail to halt. You dudes don't have to kill your brothers; Uncle Sam is doing that for you in Viet Nam. You are shooting the wrong guy. *No sean tan pendejos.* If you have enough *huevos* [testicles] to shoot your brother you should be able to take on a racist cop."

The street gangs of the barrios are different from those in most ghettos. In a sense they are born not solely of poverty, but also of cultural pride. Like street-corner chambers of commerce the gangs of barrio youth defend the spirit of La Raza with bravado and youthful boisterousness.

Of the many barrio gangs the oldest and best known is that of the legendary Pachucos, who have become a heroic myth. They were born in blood that was real enough, and they not only are remembered but are imitated with awe. They began on a day in August, 1942. In the tensions of World War II, the racial hatreds of Los Angeles were about to erupt in what was to be known as the "Zoot Suit Riots." Two groups of Chicanos had a boyish fight over a pretty girl and hurt pride, in a gravel pit on the outskirts of the city. In the morning the body of young José Díaz was found on a dirt road nearby, dead. Bored newspapermen, seeking local color, dubbed the gravel pit the "Sleepy Lagoon" (it had a mud puddle in it), and an orgy of sensational headlines celebrated the boy's death.

Not one but twenty-four Mexican boys were arrested; nine were convicted of second-degree murder. All were freed later, two years later, when the Court of Appeals reversed the sentences unanimously for "lack of evidence."

The "Sleepy Lagoon" case is still remembered bitterly in the barrios, much as the Dreyfus case in France, or that of the Scottsboro Boys in the Deep South.

Amid headlines of hysteria—"Zoot Suit Hoodlums" and "Pachuco Gangsters"—the Los Angeles police raided the barrios, blockaded the main streets, searched every passing car and passer-by. Six hundred Chicanos were taken into custody in a two-day sweep that Police Captain Joseph Reed called "a drive on Mexican gangs." The Los Angeles sheriff's "Bureau of *Foreign* Relations" justified the dragnet by officially philosophizing that the Chicanos' "desire to kill, or at least let blood" was an "inborn characteristic."

The next summer the tensions exploded. When a fist fight broke out on a downtown street between a gang of Chicano boys and U.S. Navy men in June, 1943, fourteen off-duty policemen led by a lieutenant of the Detective Squad set up an impromptu group of vigilantes they named the "Vengeance Squad" and set out "to clean up" the Mexicans.

Night after night hundreds of restless and beached sailors of the U.S. Navy, bored and frustrated by their inaction in the war against Japan, seized upon the nearest available dark-skinned enemies—the young Chicanos—and beat them up. The white rioters toured the barrios in convoys of taxi cabs, attacking every brown boy they found on the streets, in bars and restaurants and movie houses, by the dozens, by the hundreds, while the Los Angeles police looked the other way. No sailor was arrested. Inspired by the inflammatory news stories about "zoot suit roughnecks," the white rioters sought out these most of all—zoot suits were an early Humphrey Bogart style Mexicanized by Chicano boys and lately revived in its classic form by *Bonnie and Clyde.*

It was a long, hot summer week. When the white rioters exhausted their racial fervor, the riots—known not as the "U.S. Navy Riots" but oddly as the "Zoot Suit Riots"—had left hundreds of injured and a residue of race hatred in Los Angeles.

The zoot-suit boys were Pachucos. Where the name came from is vague, but it may have been taken from the city of Pachuco in Mexico, known for its brilliantly hued costumes. In the riots, these gangs of Pachucos were not the aggressors but the defenders of the barrios. They were an early self-defense group. Youths who never knew the Pachucos remember them not as victims but as resistance fighters of the streets, the Minutemen of *machismo,* who fought to defend the reputation of La Raza. Wherever the barrio youth organize, the spirit of the Pachucos is evoked and revived.

"I hope you tell the story of the Pachucos," a Brown Beret says to me. "We have to learn about our heroes."

One of many Pachuco-type gangs is the Vatos. It is a fictitious name of a small gang in the San Fernando Valley of Los Angeles whose "territory" ranges from Laurel Canyon Boulevard to O'Melveny Street. The Vatos hang out mostly in the dark alleys near Acala Avenue, a poorly lit thoroughfare.

A member of the Vatos talks of his gang:

"This is the story of life in a Mexican barrio. The barrio is called 'San Fer.' The kids, so-called Pachucos, run this barrio. Life in this barrio is rough, harsh. The boys learned early to carry can openers and knives. As soon as they got a little older they graduated to switch-blades, lengths of chain, and guns, if they could get hold of them.

"Boys joined together to form street gangs, and some of them sported the Pachuco brand between the thumb and forefinger of their left hand," the Vato says. "This gang is the stuff of life, as the Pachuco knows it."

The gang member has to prove his manhood and his ability to survive. "He will undertake the most fantastic stunts to prove a great deal. He will risk his life and his freedom to maintain his growing reputation as a tough fighter, a rugged guy." These rituals are not merely rites of initiation, or idle bravado. The gang youth has to demonstrate not only that he can fight in the streets, but that he has the strength to withstand the hostility of society, to stand up to the *placa*, the police, and if he is courageous enough, to become visible to the outsider, by wearing a Brown Beret. "That is real *macho,*" a Los Angeles community leader says.

It is a new kind of political and urban *pachuquismo.* The society outside the barrio is defied by the gang. Consciously the rituals of brotherhood enforce the laws and culture of the barrio. Inside the gang the Chicano is insulated from his own conflicts. The Chicanos "find conflicts so perplexing and so full of both cultures—that of their parents and that of America—that [they] create their own world of *pachuquismo,*" says the Vato.

The Vato goes on: "The Vatos have created their own language, Pachucano, their own style of dress, their own folklore, and their own behavior patterns. The Vatos have developed a barrio group spirit. The Vatos in this area are better organized and a little tighter, due to the fact that it is a smaller group; and therefore all the Vatos participate in the activities planned by them.

"They formed a closely knit group that regarded the Anglos as their natural enemies."

In every barrio the social clubs and folk religious societies have always existed in semisecrecy, with their own rules and symbols, hidden from the world outside. Chicano gangs are the progeny of that invisible heritage—to outsiders—by which the barrio has protected itself. They re-create in their own youthful way, the society and culture of their forefathers; yet they are urban.

Eliezer Risco, the editor of *La Raza,* describes these methods of barrio organizations as "our own survival techniques. It is difficult for the culture of a minority to survive in the larger society. If we can utilize them for social action, now that we are stronger, we will surprise the country," he says. "The country won't know where our strength is coming from or how we organize."

In the dark alleyways and gregarious streets, the Brown Berets began. They have developed a political *pachuquismo.* A generation ago they would have been a street gang, nothing more. Less obvious are the barrio origins of the youthful leaders of the La Raza movements that have gained national prominence and importance. Cesar Chavez, Rodolfo "Corky" Gonzales, Reies Tijerina: these men learned their organizing techniques on the back streets of the barrio.

"They say the La Raza movements come from the universities. I disagree," says "José," the "Field Marshal" of the Brown Berets. "I say they come from the streets."

So few youths in the barrios graduated from high school in the past, or entered college, that those who achieved that miraculous feat feared to look down from their pinnacle of anxiety. If they did, the barrios beneath them seemed a bottomless arroyo. And yet, in the wholly anglicized realms of higher education they were also strangers.

"You see a Chicano [university] student is alienated from his language; he is de-culturized and finally dehumanized so as to be able to function in a white, middle class, protestant bag," the *Chicano Student News* reports. "It is damn obvious to the Chicano in college that education means one of two things: either accept the system—study, receive a diploma, accept the cubicle and the IBM machine in some lousy bank or factory, and move out of the barrio—or reject the system. . . ."

Youths who made it to the university clung to their privileged and precarious achievements: non-Mexican name and anglicized accent, an Ivy League suit, a blond wife, and a disdain for the "dumb Mexicans" left behind. "THE PURPLE TIO TOMAS" (Uncle Tom), *El Gallo* has dubbed these high achievers. "This is the middle class Tomás. He isn't a Tomás because he lives on the other side of town, but because the Purple Tomás believes he is better than other Chicanos. Purple is the Royal Color!" The would-be intellectual *patróns*—"the new conservatives," Corky Gonzales calls them.

Now the university students have begun the climb down from their lonely success to the streets of the barrios and the fields of the campesinos. They come as on a pilgrimage, seeking an identity. Los Angeles community leader Eduardo Pérez says, "I find that many Mexicans-turned-Spanish are coming back into the fold and are being identified for what they are: Mexicans." They have a "pride in being Mexican."

In the vineyards of Delano, when the striking grape pickers gathered their banners and walked north on the highway in their 250-mile pilgrimage to Sacramento to see the Governor, the university Chicanos who walked with the *huelguistas* were wide-eyed with wonder. Not only were these young people from the universities, but they were the children of the barrios who had at last escaped, had "made it." Some even had blond hair.

Here were "farm workers with dark faces, aged prematurely by the California sun, marching side by side with students with youthful faces," wrote Daniel de los Reyes in the union newspaper *El Malcriado*, the "farm workers with black hair and a determined look, by the side of blond and red-haired students with brilliant, sparkling eyes." It was "a spectacle to see, these thousands and thousands of young people" who had come "because the Farm Workers Organizing Committee had agreed to join side by side with their brothers, the students." There was a tone of wonder in the union newspaper story. It seemed unbelievable, this "brotherhood against ignorance and poverty." These were "the same students we have seen so many times on the picketlines at the vineyards of DiGiorgio, the same youth working so tirelessly on the boycotts," declared *El Malcriado*.

Still it was not to be believed. The university students respected, listened to, and obeyed the campesinos of the fields; that was what was so strange. It was as though they who were illiterate were the teachers of the university students.

The experience of the *huelga* was a strange and exhilarating one for the students as well, for it profoundly affected the lives of many who had come. Luis Valdez, who went on to found El Centro Cultural Campesino, and Eliezer Risco, who became editor of *La Raza*, were but two of dozens of student leaders whose lives were changed by their pilgrimage to the vineyards of Delano.

"I was writing my thesis," Risco recalls. "I came thinking, well, it's a way of doing my research. But it was my Graduate School."

Venustiano Olguin was a brilliant student in a graduate school of the University of California at Los Angeles and was studying for his Ph.D. The son of a bracero who had grown up in the migrant barrios of the Coachella Valley, he had worked his way to first place in his high school class and graduated with honors from the University of Redlands.

"I'd been very successful with the system." But he had begun to have the uneasy feeling he was becoming a "Tío Tomás," an Uncle Tom. "At UCLA I knew that somewhere along the line I had been betraying something." He did not know what.

One summer the young man and some of his fellow students in the United Mexican American Students (UMAS) had a meeting with Cesar Chavez. Olguin went to Delano—not to stay, just to look around and help the farm workers if he could. He decided to join *La Huelga.* He has abandoned the honors of higher education that he says were anglicizing him, indoctrinating him with materialistic values, and forcing him to reject his Mexican heritage. He lives on $5 a week strike pay. "Some people think I am crazy. But I think my life is very rich." In the campesinos he feels he has found "a special kind of courage," of manhood. "I've learned more than in all the time I was in graduate school."

University communities of Chicanos were affected as strongly. In San Antonio, Texas, a leader of the Mexican American Youth Organization recalls how the campesinos of the Rio Grande Valley became godfathers of his group. "The strike of the farm workers got everyone excited. St. Mary's University students got together to see what they could do," says William Vazquez. "And that is how we began."

Luis Valdez, whose life was changed by Delano, feels it is a necessary school for students. "In advance of their people, the Chicano leader in the cities and universities must go through the whole bourgeois scene, find it distasteful, and then strike out in new directions. This is what happened with Corky Gonzales and Cesar Chavez. Divorcing themselves from the petty aims of success, they see the middle class for what it is. Then they can see the lower class plain.

"In short, they discover there is a world out there," Valdez says.

Out of the upheaval have come dozens of new barrio and university clubs. In the last few years there has been more youth organizing than in the entire history of the Chicanos. University students have been especially outspoken and active. The United Mexican American Students (UMAS) in California and the National Organization of Mexican American Students (NOMAS, literally "No More") in Texas are but two of more than thirty groups on the campuses alone.

The university and barrio youth are talking and walking together.

David Sanchez, the prime minister of the Brown Berets, talks to students at UCLA, while the students of UMAS walk not only on the picket lines of the campesinos of Delano but also beside the Brown Berets protesting school conditions in East Los Angeles. The *Chicano Student News* reports: "UMAS is an organization of Chicano college students which is bringing the business of education back into the Chicano community"; and the headline says, "UMAS COMES HOME!"

"Old hatreds and quarrels are being put aside," *La Raza* writes, for "*Todos son Chicanos*"—"We are all Chicanos."

Several dozen Chicanos gathered at a dude ranch near Santa Barbara on the California seacoast for one of the many conferences of students and barrio youths. Eduardo Pérez, who helped run the conference, describes the occasion:

"Nowadays the young lions and lionesses have their own cars, buy their own clothes, work their way through college, and are very much on their own. Their whole thinking and outlook on life is as different from ours as night is from day.

"These Mexican American 'world leaders of tomorrow' are an exceptional breed. They can put on a *charro* [the real cowboy Mexican] costume and be proud of it. They can even put on American clothes and feel at ease. They can eat enchiladas and hamburgers on the same plate, tacos and pizza in one sitting, and possibly drink tequila with beer as a chaser and feel right at home. They have become anglicized, but only to the point that there is no excuse for them not being accepted. They take pride in being of Mexican ancestry and do not deny being what they are. These kids don't change their names just to become Spanish or European heirs. . . ."

In spite of the ease with which they seemed to go from one culture to another, the young Chicanos suffered an inner paralysis. They doubted not their emotions or their thoughts, but to create one culture out of two so different. Pérez had written of another youth conference, "The Mexican Americans attending (most of them) did not really understand themselves . . . and how they happened to be in the mess they're in."

The university and barrio youth had this in common too.

"I stand naked in the world, lost in angry solitude," the Chicano poet Benjamin Luna writes in *La Raza.* The loneliness of the urban society—impersonal, cold, efficient, foreign to his heart—evokes the feeling of a hostile world. The futility the Chicano feels is not fatalism, but a rage of frustration.

Soy Indio con alma hambrienta,
traigo en la sangre coraje,
rojo coraje en la sangre.

I am Indian with a hungry soul,
tragic in the passionate blood,
red passion in the blood.

I stand naked in the world,
hungry
homeless
despised. . . .

In the barrios, brotherhood is in the blood, the blood of La Raza. "One boy will bring beer, while others will bring *rifa;* still others bring money for the use of activities, or gas in a member's car. This is a thing that goes on every night with something different every night that can be called a 'dead kick.'" At best, their inner brotherhood is limited by the outer world of their "natural enemy," and at worst is defined by it.

A Brown Beret laments, "We are not what we were when we started out. All those TV cameras and news reporters took over our image and changed us into their image of us."

"Who am I?" asks a young woman in a suburban church of Los Angeles. "I have been afraid to speak up for my rights. Rights? What rights do we have? So many of our youth plead guilty in court when they know they are not guilty of anything. Anything but being a Mexican."

I am Joaquín,
Lost in a world of confusion,
Caught up in the whirl of an
Anglo society,
Confused by the rules,
Scorned by attitudes,

Suppressed by manipulations,
And destroyed by modern society.
My fathers
have lost the economic battle,
and won
the fight for cultural survival.

The litany "Who am I?" is echoed in the poem of Rodolfo Gonzales, the leader of La Raza community of Denver. "I am Joaquín" is at once a defiance and a requiem for the history of self-mutilation of those whom the Chicano poet calls "strangers in *their* land":

In a country that has wiped out
all my history,
stifled all my pride.
In a country that has placed
a different indignity
upon my ancient burdens.
Inferiority
is the new load. . . .

In time the act of denial becomes a self-denial:

I look at myself
and see part of me
who rejects my father and my mother
and dissolves into the melting pot
to evaporate in shame. . . .

"Soul searching," Dr. Ernesto Galarza calls it. The scholar, a sparse man of wiry thoughts and whitening hair, who talks with hard, dry words, is recognized by many of the Chicano youth leaders as the dean of the La Raza movement; perhaps the dean emeritus. "There is an incredible amount of soul searching going on among this generation. Of questioning. Of seeking," he says one midnight over coffee in a motel in Santa Barbara, where he has gone to teach a youth workshop.

"Many of these youth have been propelled into crises of considerable tension. There have been tragic losses, where some of them have been torn asunder by the conflicts, internal and external, within themselves. There has been a loss of much potential. The youth are resilient, however.

"I believe there are few phoneys in this generation. Anyone who believes this is a time for the promotion of Uncle Toms, of acquiescence, among the younger generation of Mexicans, is mistaken. Unquestionably this generation is confronted with some crippling problems. But *that* is not one of them," says the scholar.

Dr. Galarza's weary eyes light up when he talks of these youths. "I am delighted by the happenstance of the last ten years. There has been the growth of quite a small army of young men, a phalanx of potential leaders who are searching for a breakthrough. The younger generation holds much promise.

"It is too early to foresee where these movements will lead. There is little unity of thought. There is precious little cohesion. Every movement is its own little stirring of activity. In five or ten years, there may be a reckoning; a culmination.

"We will wait," the scholar says, "and we will see."

Of course, the youth will not wait. They want action now, ideology later. Having had a small glimpse of their cultural identity, they want the rest; and having had a foretaste of Chicano power, they yearn for more: "Mañana is here!" says Maclovio Barraza, leader of the Arizona miners.

"Who the hell are we? What are we? Where do we belong? Study it! Announce it to the world!" Joe Benitos, a Chicano leader in Arizona, exclaims impatiently. "Let's end this hangup about identity. We know who we are. In order to survive we have learned survival skills. Sure, but let's not confuse our survival skills in Anglo society with our culture. We have a parallel culture. We have to keep it. I say we can do it. We don't have to be one of *them!*"

His impatience with the talk of the "identity crisis" is typical of the young Chicano. Benitos feels the problem of identity is perpetuated by university study projects, "so that they will have something to study"; he has worked with several of these projects. "I've been there," he says. "And that's not where it's at.

"Yes, having two cultures creates problems. Why emphasize the problems? Why not emphasize the opportunities it gives the Chicano in the new world scene?

"There is a Chicano wave coming in," says Benitos. "I see it as part

The joyous march of campesinos led by Cesar Chavez (fourth from right), the leader of the farm workers' union. In the summer of 1965 when the grape pickers of Delano, California, went on strike, the history of American farming was altered forever.
Photo by George Ballis

On a wall near the headquarters of the farm workers' union the name of Cesar Chavez joins those of Pancho Villa, Juarez, and Zapata. Prayers are offered and *corridos* (songs) are sung to honor the union leader. *Photo by George Ballis*

The ashes of the burnt cross of Cesar Chavez mark the place, at the union's Forty Acres outside Delano, where the union leader fasted in penance for the cause of the campesinos–peace and nonviolence. His cross was set afire and then sawed off. *Photo by Stan Steiner*

Luis Valdez, founder of El Teatro Campesino (the Farm Workers' Theater), a combination of "Cantinflas and Bertolt Brecht"; his theater, composed entirely of farm workers, is part of a cultural flowering of La Raza in the Southwest—a "tough act to follow," said the *Wall Street Journal*. *Photo by George Ballis*

The story of La Raza could be told in the *corridos* of exodus from Mexico, migration to the Southwest, labor in the fields, living in the urban barrios. Danny Valdez (left) and Augustín Lira (right) sing of the *huelga*—the grape strike. *Photo by George Ballis*

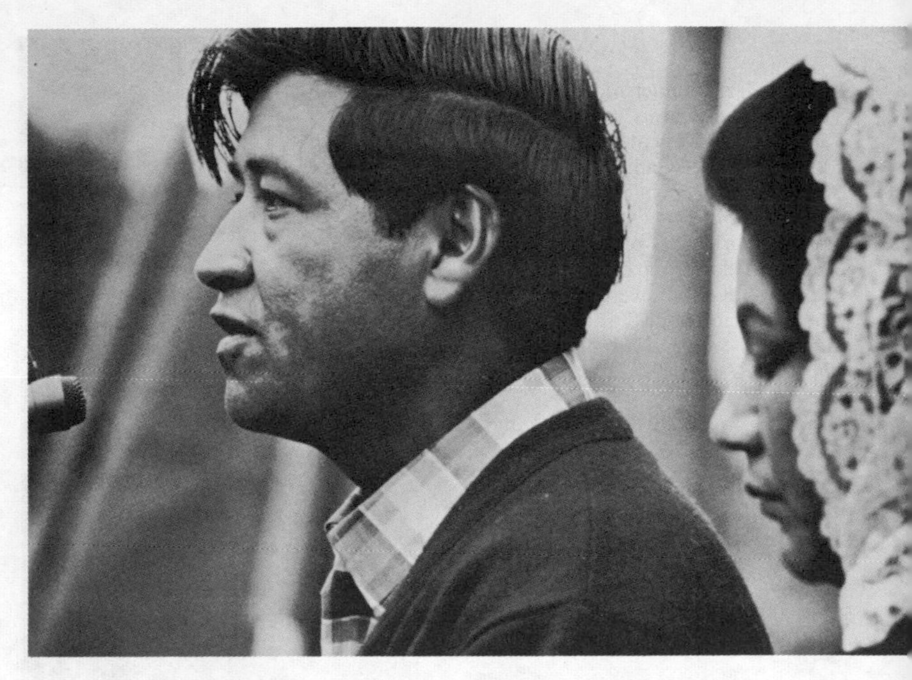

Cesar Chavez speaks to a rally of ten thousand campesinos who, together with the late Senator Robert Kennedy, came to celebrate the end of his fast and his breaking of bread. His wife, Helen Chavez, in a mantilla, stands behind him. *Photo by George Ballis*

The former national boxing champion, businessman, Democratic Party leader, and government official Rodolfo "Corky" Gonzales, who has become a leader of the Chicano revolt in Denver. His "Crusade for Justice" sponsored the National Chicano Liberation Conference that declared La Raza an "independent nation." *Photo by George Ballis*

Women have stepped to the fore on the picket lines of the grape strike and the protest marches in the barrios. This young farm worker, in Delano, is one of hundreds who have been living on strike pay of $5 per week per family. *Photo by George Ballis*

A white-gowned nun leading the rent strikers of the migrant camps and towns of the San Joaquin Valley, in California, in a march down the super-highway. "$18 IS TOO MUCH, WHY ASK $22 FOR THE HUTS?" says one sign. "GOD BLESS OUR HOLEY HOME" and "MISSISSIPPI" say others. *Photo by George Ballis*

Father John Luce says Mass–with a tortilla–to bless "the Free and Liberated Board of Chicano Education" in the "Pueblos Libre de Joaquin Murrietta." The scene: the board room of the Board of Education of Los Angeles, which Chicano students and teachers occupied for one week, in 1968, to protest the conditions of barrio schools. *Photo by "Chicano Student Movement" newspaper*

In the spring of 1968 more than 15,000 Chicano high school students walk out of East Los Angeles schools. The "blowout" started a chain reaction in barrios throughout the Southwest, and even schools in the depth of the Lower Rio Grande Valley, in Texas, were shaken by student strikes. *Photo by "Chicano Student Movement" newspaper*

In Los Angeles, a girl of the Brown Berets wears not only the insignia of a cross and crossed rifles, but also bullets crossed upon her breast, reminiscent of the Mexican Revolution. She is attending nothing more ominous than the Fiesta de los Barrios at Lincoln High School. *Photo by "Chicano Student Movement" newspaper*

of the world-wide scene. As the world shrinks everyone will have to learn more than one language, one culture. Everyone will have to be bilingual and trilingual. It will put us in a fantastic position, if we can keep our languages and cultures.

"Our experience will be a lesson for the whole world," he says.

"Chicano" is a new word, not yet in the dictionary. La Raza writers cannot yet define it except by what it is not; the Chicano is not, they say, half-Mexican, half-American, who blends two cultures in his being. He is not just one more second- and third-generation city-bred descendant of a rural villager who has learned to drive a car like a wild horse and pay for it on the installment plan. La Raza is a new people with a new culture and the Chicano is its youngest offspring. He has inherited many things from Mexico and the United States, but he imitates neither. The Chicano is a new man.

In the La Raza newspapers there appears a "Definition of the Word Chicano" by Benito Rodríguez. He is a member of MANO (Hand), a group of Chicano ex-convicts in San Antonio, Texas. Rodríguez's words, even more than his ideas, the way he writes, the style, the language he uses, give some of the feeling of being a Chicano in the barrio of a modern city. Even in the pale English translation the strong flavor of that life comes through, although it is stronger in the Spanish. He writes:

"Many designations have been used to refer to us, the descendants of Mexicans. Every ten or fifteen years, or so, we feel like searching for a new image of ourselves. First, in the time of the 'Wild West' we were 'Mexican bandits,' then 'greasers,' then 'mescins,' and now we are 'Spanish Americans,' 'Mexican Americans,' 'Americans,' etc.

"The migrant Mexicans, workers in the field, call themselves Chicapatas (short legs), or Raza (race, as in Raza del Sol, People of the Sun). City workers use the term Chicano a little more. The phrase Mexican-American is really used by the middle-class Mexicans. What is truly Mexican is covered by a layer, Chicano, to satisfy all the conditions in which we find ourselves. How shall we describe ourselves tomorrow, or the day after?

"Now they want to make us half Mexicans and half Americans, as if they were talking about geography. Well, we already know who we are. Why do we come on like a chicken with its head cut off? Why do we let them make fakes, if we are Chicanos down to the phlegm in our mouths? If you don't like the taste you'll swallow it anyway.

"Just because we've seen their marvelous technology doesn't mean we believe that those who exploit us are gods."

Benito Rodríguez concludes with a curse that is pure Chicano: "A poor man who thinks he lives in heaven is gonna get fucked, coming and going."

PART THREE

XVIII

In the Vineyards of the Lord of the Land

The Man Who Worked for Thirty Years Without Pay

On the old Montoya Ranch in the hills to the north of Albuquerque, the boy came looking for a job. It was in the summer of 1933. He was then thirteen and he was hired as a ranch hand, for 75 cents a day. Abernicio Gonzales remembers the day with wincing, distant eyes. He remembers his mother had borrowed $50 to pay for the wedding of an older brother. He worked off the debt in about three months. Yet he went on working at the ranch for thirty-three years, and he says he was never paid a penny.

In those Depression days he was happy to have any job. He had been convinced, he says, to go on working for 50 cents a day and board. He was a hard worker; the rancher liked him and promised, since he was so young, to put his wages away for him. That way he would have money to live on when he was too old to work. He reluctantly agreed to this. Whenever the boy asked to see his bank account, he was cowed into silence. He was beaten when he tried to leave the remote ranch. The boy grew to be a man, but he was afraid to run away lest he lose the years of promised savings. He was a serf in the middle of the twentieth century in the United States.

One day in 1966 Gonzales fled from the Montoya Ranch. He was forty-six, penniless, a novice in the world, bewildered by his discovery of hatred. He sued for his thirty-three years of back pay, at 50 cents a day, with 6 per cent interest, but obviously no court could repay him for his lost youth and stolen manhood.

A boy may be intimidated. But why would the grown man go on as the boy began? Year after year he lived as if he were a slave. He had enslaved himself. The habits and fears of a man who feels he has no rights bind him to servitude as tightly as if he were chained.

"There are hundreds of people kept in slavery on remote ranches throughout the Southwest of the United States," declares *El Malcriado,* the newspaper of the farm workers. "It is well known. . . ."

No man has fewer rights. The campesino earns less in wages and respect than anyone else. If he is a migrant worker "his earnings are the lowest of our Nation's work force," the Senate Subcommittee on Migratory Labor reports in *The Migratory Farm Labor Problem in the United States* (1967). In recent years these migrants averaged little over $1,100 annually from field work. And they were lucky to add $600 from odd jobs, off season. The hired hands who were regularly employed did somewhat better, but not much.

There are more farm workers in the country than steel workers, auto workers, or aircraft workers. In spite of Rube Goldberg farm machines the census counters say there are 1,400,000 farm workers. Of these over 200,000 are migrants. Since the census counters do not reach the remote ranches, the unseen alleys of the barrios, and the elusive "commuters" from across the Rio Grande, there are undoubtedly many more who are uncounted. Farm workers are a hungry army.

In the fields wages are not only "the lowest," but are getting lower. The output per man on the farm zoomed 270 per cent from 1947 to 1964, while wages increased only 64 per cent, but in the factories, during the same years, output per man went up 160 per cent, while wages increased only 107 per cent. Unlike farm workers the factory workers have unions. "The gap between agricultural and nonagricultural earnings has continually widened," reports the Senate Subcommittee. Not only that, but "between 1940 and 1964 gross farm income increased from $11.1 to $42.2 billion. Yet the average farm worker today still earns a daily wage under $9. No other segment of our population is so poorly paid yet contributes so much to our Nation's health and welfare."

> So I tell my friends
> Not to sell themselves;
> He who sells himself
> Always will be the loser.

It is a song of the campesinos by the young grape picker, poet, and singer of El Teatro Campesino, Agustín Lira. He sings:

> Look, look, look, look,
> Look, look, how they work;
> If they stop to rest
> They lose their jobs.

The campesino often feels he is trapped by his labor in the fields of a stranger. Says a campesino in Delano, "You just don't get out of the fields. I think it's very heavy. It's something you are stuck with for the rest of your life. You just can't start anywhere else because you don't have the education, you don't have the experience."

"I am nothing," says another campesino. "My children, they will get an education and they will be someone."

"We have nothing but our hands. Empty hands," a woman says.

It is a feeling of nothingness voiced in the lament of *El Malcriado:* "We have seen how they have taken the work of our hands and our bodies and made themselves rich while we are left with empty hands between the earth and the sky. We who are farm workers have been insulted. We have seen ourselves treated like cattle. We have seen our children treated like inferiors in the schools. We have seen in the face of the cop our inequality before the law. We have known what it is like to be less respected, to be unwanted, to live in a world which did not belong to us."

In a small house on the edge of town the campesino lives quietly. He bothers no one. Usually he stays as far away from the downtown streets as he can. He feels uncomfortable there.

A man says, "They want our business. But they do not like us. We do not go where we are not wanted."

He is an urban man, nonetheless. Most campesinos nowadays live in the cities. Even in the supermetropolis of Los Angeles, a state of California study of employment shows that 7 per cent of the men in the barrios of East Los Angeles are farm workers. The myth of the "foot-loose" and "shiftless" migrant eternally wandering in an old jalopy, like a poor, dirty, gypsy, no longer exists in the urban Southwest—except in old movies.

Still he does not take part in urban life. He is ignored by the city elites, of whatever group. He pays little in taxes, for his income is too low, and so he has no voice. He is unrepresented in the city where he lives.

"You see, the farm worker is an outsider, even though he may be a resident worker," says Cesar Chavez. "He is an outsider economically, and he is an outsider racially. Most farm workers are of ethnic backgrounds other than white.

"And so, with very few exceptions, they have not been part of the communities where they live. Most of them don't know how or why or by whom laws are made. Who governs them. None of these things. They don't really care," Chavez says.

It is his isolation from the sources of power over his own life that has made the campesino abject. The gap between the two sections of town, much less two societies, has seemed unbridgeable. "Our color, or our language, or our job, have kept us apart," says *El Malcriado.* "And the people who are profiting from our separateness are determined to keep it that way."

A campesino looks around and sees that he is treated as though he were nonexistent. The laws that protect other workers do not apply to him. In the fields the health codes are often ignored. In the farm towns the normal sanitation and civic services often do not reach his little house. Even his ordinary needs on the job—like water to drink and the use of toilets—are ignored. Housing regulations are not enforced in his barrios and *colonias.* "The same labor camps which were used thirty years ago, at the time of the La Follette Committee hearings, are still housing our workers," Chavez tells the Senate Subcommittee on Migratory Labor. "Nothing has changed."

Campesinos are not the invisible men of the ghetto. They are vigorous, sensuous, full of life, strenuous sinews, bright as the sun itself, and at times darkly emotional. In the bars they are boisterous, yelling "*Viva!*" to the TV; and in the churches they are reverent, passionately and publicly. They suffer few identity crises. Yet, these same men will say, "I am nothing!"

The nothingness of the campesino is the recognition of what exists, the way life is. It is not simply self-denial, nor is it the humility of the poor. His is a world of nothings. It descends on the labor camps and barrio homes from the world outside with an almost physical force. Like an impenetrable white fog, it is sometimes so dense it hides the identity of a man from himself.

"I will tell you the truth," says a young campesino in Del Rio, Texas. "When I am among you people, I am not the man I am. I am the man you think I am. A fool!"

"Who emasculated us? I say we emasculate our own manhood," says Rodolfo Gonzales. "For what? The crumbs on the table we have been promised—someday. So we stoop to lick up the crumbs on the floor, saying, 'Yes sir! Yes, sir! Thank you, sir!' "

He scowls. "It's mental stoop labor."

It is "a world of fantasy," Cesar Chavez feels, a "mental attitude" that is the remnant of the old *patrón* syndrome that enslaves the campesinos through their own sense of helplessness and servility, as much as by the power of the ranchers. "It has lot to do with paternalism. Before, when the employer came by, if the worker was dying of thirst, he would say, 'I'm not thirsty, *patrón.*' And whatever ailed him, or hurt him, he never complained. Now they come back, although they would want a union, more money, [they] keep believing these things. It's really a world of fantasy."

Not all of their fears are fantasies. There is the real fear of the invisible man who feels that he, or a relative, may be deported if he becomes too visible.

In retelling her tale of twenty years in the fields—of illnesses, deaths, hungers, and inhuman treatment—Mrs. Guadalupe Olivarez was questioned by the Senate Subcommittee on Migratory Labor:

Senator Robert Kennedy: Have you reported it to anybody?
Mrs. Olivarez: No, sir.
Senator Robert Kennedy: Why?
Mrs. Olivarez: Well, the one thing I will tell you why, we farm workers, we are afraid.
Senator Robert Kennedy: Why are you afraid?
Mrs. Olivarez: Because I have seen it, sir. Well, I wouldn't mention names. We were not contented about what they did to us in the company we were working for, so we rebelled, and this was sort of a strike. And so there was one woman, you know, who spoke for all of us, and so that woman was fired because she was called an agitator. So, you see, sir, that's why we are afraid to speak.

There is the fear of hunger. . . .

In the kitchens the hunger is visible on the bare tables, in the motley dishes of beans and cereals. The odd and battered pots on the rickety kerosene stoves have a nauseous odor that mingles with the delicious aroma of hot chili cooking. And there is the rancid smell of powdered eggs and surplus food rations. These are the aromas of hunger.

The eyes of the children grow cold in the winter, although the kerosene stoves in the campesinos' homes exude an odorous heat. The work in the fields is seasonal, and during the winter there is not much to do. Men sit and wait. In the farm towns there is little to do but sit and wait—jobs are few, the jobless are many.

It is nonsense to talk of high wages and low wages in work so seasonal. The campesino has to earn enough in the growing and harvesting seasons, his entire family working, to last all winter. His family starves if they cannot save. The income of the campesinos is disputed. Statistics are hard to get. And those that are given are inadequate and inaccurate and contradictory. It is enough to say that they all seem to show that the annual income of the average campesino is about one-third of the national family income of a factory worker.

And this too makes a man fearful. He gets no wage he dare depend on. When the season comes, he never knows what it will bring. The drought and the rain that worry the farmer are worse for the campesino. His family may starve in the winter. So he works harder, travels faster, goes farther, complains less. Once the crops are harvested, there will be little for him to do but sit and wait for the spring.

Waiting demeans a man. He becomes sullen. He is nothing who does nothing.

"People who are hungry have no spirit, have no strength to fight. People who are hungry don't care who makes decisions for them, so long as their families don't starve," Cesar Chavez says. He says it emphatically, unusually so for him, with knowing harshness. "People who are hungry have to eat first of all.

" 'Eating comes before religion and art,' " he says. "That's an old Mexican proverb."

I ask him, "Even before love?"

"No," Chavez says with a half smile, "but certainly before politics. Bread and eggs on the table are the important thing."

In Starr County, Texas, a mother of six children talks of hunger. Her name is Mrs. E. F. Gutierrez. She has been the director of a Community Action Program for farm workers, going from barrio to barrio to soothe the hungry with her words.

"There is out-and-out starvation," she says. "I have been in a home where I have seen a small, two-year-old child eating oatmeal from the original paper container, with her fingers. Dry and raw.

"And I said, 'Why don't you put it in a pot and cook it? It will taste better.'

"And the mother said, 'I don't have a stove.'

"So I said, 'Why don't you mix it with a little water and sugar to make it taste better?'

"And she said, 'I don't have a cup. I don't have sugar. I don't have a spoon.' "

In the vineyards of Delano, a farm worker talks of hunger. His lips are burnt by the sun. When he talks his words expose the scar tissue.

"When a man is hungry, he either gives up, or he becomes ruthless," he says.

"A man will kill for food. He will not kill another man. He will kill himself. If a man becomes ruthless, he destroys love. Without love there is no family. There is no life. There is nothing.

"Hunger does not kill a man," he says. "I know. The hungry man kills himself, his senses, his morals, his manhood. I know."

The Dignity of the Farm Worker

"It eats up a man's soul to beg from the government," says a young farm worker in the Rio Grande Valley. He is sitting on a dirty mattress on the floor as he talks. The hut is furnished with boxes and rags and dogs. "We are asked to sell our souls for the welfare. We must or our bodies will starve. Yes, but I say, what if our souls starve?"

The dignity of the campesino is in his pride—his *macho.* He has a harsh dignity. He sees himself as a self-reliant man, a vaquero of the harvests, on wheels. He has a free soul.

"For nearly all people there is a thing that is more important than money. It is a thing called dignity, or self-respect, or honor," *El Malcriado* writes in an editorial entitled "Dignity of the Farm Workers." "The dignity of the farm worker shows itself in many ways. This year, and in years to come, it will be shown by the man who will fight when he is insulted."

It seems a paradox. The poorest of the poor belligerently defend their honor and dignity as "more important than money," as if they were in danger of being corrupted. Of these, the oldest and poorest, who need financial aid most desperately, are the most hesitant when it comes to seeking the welfare of the government.

"My sons will help me," says an aged man living in a one-room shack in the Imperial Valley. He is insulted at the suggestion that he apply for welfare. "Beg like a wino, with my palm open?"

An old woman in a barrio of San Antonio is asked by a poverty investigator why she doesn't go for help, since she and her husband live on $5 a month. "I don't know where to go," she responds slyly. She is eighty-five.

In a barrio in Colorado, a younger woman with several children tells why she asked that her Aid to Dependent Children checks be canceled.

Mrs. Elisa Valencia says, "I heard a knock on the door at 1:30 A.M." It was a state investigator trying to discover whether her husband was sleeping with her. "Somebody had report that my husband was at my house, staying with me while I was getting ADC. I went to my case worker and told her everything and told her to discontinue my checks because my girls and myself were very embarrassed and felt terrible. So I decided to do the best without ADC. I didn't think that $107 a month was worth the nightmare we went through."

A woman who feels her husband has failed her, has betrayed her, may be too proud to weep. The pride of the poor is a cruel thing. When the woman is humiliated because her husband has lost his *macho* and run away, she may fulfill his abandoned role by becoming more independent, prouder, and stronger than he was.

The campesino believes in old-fashioned ways and values. He may accept welfare, but it is an insult. A man and a woman should help themselves. If they cannot their family should weep at their distress. But to ask the government for help is to beg of a stranger. In the hearings of the Senate Subcommittee on Migratory Labor, the late Senator Robert Kennedy asked a woman farm worker, Mrs. Guadalupe Olivarez, "Why don't you go to people who are in the government for help?" Her response was one of incomprehension.

Senator Kennedy: Do you think the government is sympathetic to the efforts of the farm workers?

Mrs. Olivarez: Sir?

Senator Kennedy: Do you think the government is sympathetic to the efforts of farm workers or not?

Mrs. Olivarez: I wouldn't know, sir.

Senator Kennedy: Well, do your fellow farm workers feel they have any friends among those in authority, or do they feel that they are by themselves?

Mrs. Olivarez: I don't know, sir. I couldn't answer that question. I wish I could. If I knew it wouldn't incriminate me, I would answer it, but I'm not sure. But I'd like to say the truth.

The truth that Mrs. Olivarez could not tell the Senator is that the campesino does not trust the government. It is not just the fear of the poor for authority—well-fed, vested, white-faced. The trouble is that ever since the campesino crossed the border, the local officials of the government, from the Border Patrol to the county sheriff, have acted as the friend of the grower, a supplier of labor, and the keeper of law and order—that is, low wages. The campesino is suspicious of the government.

"Government has found an economic way to keep our people at a mere subsistence level, through welfare," says Fecundo Valdez, the village organizer in New Mexico. "The welfare system does not help us. It cripples us. It is rather useful to the government. When we have hot wars in Korea, in Vietnam, the sons of people who are welfare recipients, who have been kept at a subsistence level, became very useful tools in the 'Fight for Freedom.'

"Our men pay dearly for every cent they receive on welfare," Fecundo Valdez explains. "It makes a man feel worthless, ashamed. He loses his self-respect.

"Let me say a word about the popular idea that our people are all on welfare. We aren't. We get very little of it. The ranchers and businessmen in the Anglo communities get ten times as much as we do through farm subsidies, oil depletions, crop parities, soil-bank programs, and whatever."

It is true that in the farm counties the growers receive many times more money from the Welfare State than do the farm workers. Even the irrigation water used by the corporate farm is "a subsidy of the federal government," charged Robert Kennedy. "With surface water the grower benefits, true, but so does the entire economy and the community and the state," Martin Zaninovich, a Delano vineyard owner, replied. The grower did not mention the $3 to $4 billion dollars that agri-business farms received in direct subsidies every year from the Department of Agriculture.

One congressional district in Texas, for instance, received $5 million in agricultural payments in 1966, for 400 farmers, while the 146,000 poor people in the district received $224,000 in food help. Carl Rowan and David Mazie, who reported this in their survey "Hunger—It's Here Too" (*Reader's Digest*, November, 1968), went on to say, "These figures reflect the priority that Congress has given to aiding large-scale farmers rather than the hungry poor."

The community groups in the barrios have civics classes to convince the poor that welfare is their right, they pay for it with taxes. But the campesinos resist. In the newspapers of La Raza there are endless columns outlining the rights of the poor in the moral labyrinth of government. But the pride of La Raza is not easily compromised. In one of the discussions on welfare rights in East Los Angeles, the group leader, an Anglo teacher, says that the welfare state is democratic. Everyone participates. "I grew up on a homestead," he says, "and now we are paying the grandsons of homesteaders five billion dollars a year not to grow things on this free land we gave them."

Immediately there is an argument in the room. A man, politely but angrily, disagrees with the teacher.

Man: "You are talking about a different thing, aren't you?"

Teacher: "No."

Man: "When the West was opened, sir, I hate to differ, you people coming from England had a different deal. *You* are not giving anything to Mexican Americans."

Second Man: "When you give something away people think you are belittling yourself."

Man: "If you think of getting your share of the economy, you accept this more easily. We give people free education. Free education is a welfare system you have to take."

Second Man: "We can't have a lot of people on welfare in an undignified manner."

Teacher: "People must be educated to accept these things. The welfare recipients are not educated to accept this money. Instead they accept it and they want to hide it."

Third Man: "When Hubert Humphrey goes to a hospital he doesn't worry about free enterprise. He goes to a navy 'socialized' hospital."

Woman: "I bet most Mexican Americans in this room have a funny feeling that this would give us that image we have of 'state aiders.' "

Man: "You have the wrong misconception."

Fourth Man: "Confused, isn't it? You say the majority of Mexican Americans. The majority! The majority! I'm not a majority. I'm a single individual, with my private thoughts. Why do I have to compete with anybody? I compete with myself."

Alicia Escalante, the chairman of the East Los Angeles Welfare Right Organization (ELAWRO), has a somewhat different view. She is a petite young woman, barely five one, who talks with the determination one might expect from a group made up of mostly mothers. "I grew up in the barrio. My fight is here with Chicanos on welfare—especially the women. You don't know the many problems of women on welfare. Too many people believe lies about people on welfare."

Her anger is something new amid the humiliation of those on welfare in the barrios. She fights "for recipients' rights against a monolithic, inhuman system," writes *La Raza*, "but her struggle is also for the basic dignity of La Raza."

The ELAWRO is one of dozens of barrio welfare rights groups throughout the Southwest. It devotes itself to "fighting for the simple essential things for recipients that are already theirs by law, but due to administrative tangles, indifference and /or callousness never reach the recipient." As *La Raza* writes: "The day of the pacifiers is gone."

Yet even among the angry urban Chicanos "the dignity of the farm worker" has been inherited. In Los Angeles a university student says that La Raza "is not seeking an abundance of money, two-car garages, and gluttonous appetites, but seeks those essential elements necessary for bodily function, while devoting its time to enriching the mind with the idea of *carnalismo* (brotherhood). *Carnalismo* is that love taught by Christianity that somehow got mangled through war, materialism, and computerization. . . . The white Americans are computerized machines . . . once you succumb to their materialism, you have taken a step towards death in life."

Gringoismo!

It is a true story, they say. There was once an orchard grower in the valleys of California who grew weary of the trouble he had every year with his farm workers. He decided to end the endless disputes once and for all. He imported five hundred monkeys from the jungles of Guatemala to harvest his crops. When the fruits were ripe, he let the monkeys loose in his apricot orchards, hoping that the monkeys would be so thankful at being freed from their cages they would shake the apricots from the trees. They did.

After a few days of frolicking and eating apricots, the monkeys disappeared into the hills of northern California. They have never been heard from since.

One of the growers who retells the story laughs. "I am not comparing Mexicans to monkeys, mind you," he says. "And that orchard man must have been an ape himself to try to harvest apricots that way. But I tell you, it's a temptation these days."

In conversations with ranchers few talk vulgarly of the campesinos. The traditional Anglo who talked of the Mexican who is "dirty and ignorant as his goat" is rarely heard. Words like "Mongrel Mexicans" that were common in the 1920's are no longer spoken for publication. The racial epithet is out of style in the era of civil rights. Even so, the campesinos say the growers "think" of them as animals. "Cattle," says *El Malcriado.*

The grower feels an affection for his farm workers such as a father feels for his own children. "We take good care of them," says Jack

Pandol, a vineyard owner in Delano. "We take care of our workers because we want to." After all, how many employers provide housing, water, electricity, and food for their workers? It is true that the cost of these is usually deducted from the farm workers' pay, but the grower does supply them. "My men get free housing," says Jack Pandol. "That's more than I get." Not only that, but the farm workers will come to the grower with their personal problems—as to a *patrón*, or a father.

When a *grower* says "my Mexicans" and "my boys," he means it affectionately. He is sentimental about the "old days," when it was "like a big, happy family here—men singing down by the camp at night. Women praying to their plaster saints. Kids playing after work."

Like a good father, the grower feels he has to be stern at times. He denies any ill intent or racial bias toward the campesinos. A father sometimes has to say no to his children, for their own good and future well-being. And like many a father, the grower feels he is kinder, gentler, and more patient than he is given credit for by his children —the campesinos. But then, children are unappreciative at times.

"The Mexican is a child by nature," a grower explains. "He has no sense of the future. He likes to enjoy himself. Sing. Dance. Drink. So he loves all those parades and flags and singing the union has. It's a fiesta to him, the damn union, and it's *Huelga!* He doesn't know anything about farm economics."

Jack Pandol, a sunny-faced and forthright man, grew up in the fields. He feels he understands "these Mexicans," beside whom he has lived all his life. "It's in the nature of these people to move from place to place," he philosophizes on the mysteries of the migrant's mind. "Most of these Mexicans like the arrangement of not working steady." The idea of a union contract, job protection, and steady work seems somehow un-Mexican to him. "Why should these men be beholden to a labor union for the right to work?" It would be "servitude." The campesino is a happy wanderer to the grower. He seems almost envious of the life of the Huck Finn on the highways that he imagines—the childlike idyl.

"Our workers have never shown any disatisfaction. They are proud to work for us."

It is this spirit that the grower basks in, as he does in the sun. There is a warmth in knowing that hundreds of men, women, and children are thankful to him for their bread and happiness. He feels proud that they pay him back for what he pays them, with admiration, if not love.

A sugar company field labor manager, J. W. Axelson, tells the sugar-beet growers they have replaced the old-style *patróns.* "Write your workers. They are proud of the letters they receive from their '*patróns.*' They carry these with them and show them off like a badge of honor," Axelson writes in the magazine of the American Crystal Sugar Company of Denver, Colorado, *Crystal-ized Facts.*

The grower is confident that "his Mexicans" are happy in their work. Pandol says, "Our men seem to be content. Happy." It is incomprehensible that they might chafe at his paternal concern for them. After all, he has always treated them with fatherly affection—sternly but fairly. No, they would not betray his benevolence. "Our employees seem to be happy," in the words of one grower. . . . "Seem to be willing to stay with us through all sorts of harassments, not only in the fields, but in their own homes."

"Just like the Southern plantation owner used to say about 'his Negroes,' " Cesar Chavez has said. "Ranchers in Delano say that the farm workers are happy living the way they are."

If the fatherly grower looks upon "his Mexicans" with the benevolence of a modern slaveowner, there is some historic justification for his view. He is not being original or malicious. Slavery and farm workers were synonymous for hundreds of years in the United States. The stigma lingers in the nation's consciousness and the national conscience.

On the plantations of Virginia the farm workers were Africans. The black campesinos of our early history plowed, planted, and harvested the wealth of the South, upon which so much of the young country's strength was based.

It was not to work as galley slaves in the Spanish galleons or to slave in the silver mines of colonial Mexico that the Africans were chained and whipped and brought in dungeoned ships to the United States. The black campesinos were slaves to the land. Whether they were kings, doctors, or village whores in the old country on the shores of

Africa, they were the founding fathers of the system of farm labor in the fields, from Virginia to Texas.

The white settlers who left Europe to escape the bonds of serfdom were not about to be enslaved on someone else's land. Indentured servants brought from England proved insufficient and unreliable as farm workers; some ran off to join the Indians, and many, taken from the jails of London, were simply untrustworthy and incapable of hard field work.

As for the Indians, they were wholly uncooperative. They would not adapt to slavery. Although the enslavement of some tribes in the South was tried, the results were unproductive. The Indians "fought and fled," an economist of farm labor has said; they would not be "tied to the plough." They died instead.

Early in our history, it was learned that farm workers had to be brought from far away, far enough so that their cultural roots were severed. They were isolated by language and color, even from one another. They were racially insulted and emasculated. When this was done, the refugees—those who survived—would work abjectly in the alien fields from which they could not escape.

In the beginning, they were brought from Africa to the East, and later from Asia to the West; and finally as campesinos from Mexico to the Southwest. In every era they were brought from the colonial countries. The people of rural villages, dark-skinned and tribal, were ill at ease, fearful, and lost in the acquisitive and successful society of the White Europeans.

Since the American Revolution the unnatural conflicts caused by the importing of colonial people to work in the fields have rent the nation asunder time and time again. The Civil War was fought largely because of the farm worker in the fields of the South; and the urban riots in the twentieth century have their origin in the migrations of farm workers to the cities.

In the Southwest, the influence of farm workers upon history is much more direct. The city of Phoenix, for instance, was originally a migrant haying camp of Mexicans set up on the banks of the Río Salado (Salt River) in 1867 to feed the U.S. Army cavalry horses at Fort McDowell. From the labor of those early-day campesinos came the city of Phoenix, and from the labor of campesinos since then has come the wealth of the Southwest.

The lands were so vast that the family farms little more than scratched the face of the endless plains and great forests. Land in the West, from the beginning of its conquest by the United States, was divided into huge tracts that needed hundreds, thousands, of hands to work them.

In 1865 the State Agricultural Society of California was warned by Dr. John Morse of "the tendency to a monopoly of soil [that] is a curse to society and dishonor to God and man. There are no monopolists so arrogant, so dictatorial, so dangerous to the peace and perpetuity of the State, as the overgrown, monopolizing, political nabobs of the soil." Five years later, in 1870, the State Board of Agriculture recognized that "land monopoly in California" had embraced "very nearly all the lands in the State."

California farming was "by nature" such that it required "a permanent supply of itinerant laborers," Professor Varden Fuller writes. "Since white people refused to perform such 'menial' tasks, such a labor supply by its very nature had to be 'un-American.'" That is, they had to be colored and colonial.

The importing of Chinese serfs was the growers' first solution to the labor problem. Although the Chinese were brought in to work initially on the railroads and in the mines, by 1886 it was estimated that there were 30,000 working as harvest hands. Ever solicitous of dark-skinned workers, the labor unions pressed Congress to exclude these Chinese laborers, and with the so-called Chinese Exclusion Act, the government obliged.

Japanese farm workers were imported instead. From 1886 to 1910 the Japanese immigrant population increased from 2,000 to 72,000. When the "bitter racial hostility" of the countryside and their own industriousness caused the Japanese to leave the fields, the hiring agents of the growers moved on to the Philippines.

Once again the fields were filled with dark-skinned men. The Filipinos were brought in at the rate of 4,000 yearly; by 1930 there were 25,000 single men alone working in the San Joaquin and Salinas valleys. But the hungers and strife of the Depression once more created racial tension. The dispossessed farmers, the Okies, coming to California, were starving for jobs, and riots against the Filipinos erupted throughout the farm country.

The "evil effects" of the hiring system of farm labor, reported to Governor H. H. Haight in 1868 by the State Board of Agriculture, had both advantages and problems. But as the California Bureau of Labor Statistics had stated in its first Biennial Report of 1883–1884, as long as the growers continued "preferring a homeless wandering heathen to a settled American," the farm labor system "could not be changed."

In desperation and trepidation, the growers cast their eyes toward the Mexican border. And so the hiring of the campesinos began.

A cotton grower, retired Major F. R. Burnham, in 1930 voiced the mixture of fear and need that impelled the hiring of Mexicans: "Cheap labor! That is the old cry. I first heard it as a small boy from slave owners. . . ." It will destroy the "purity of race," the Major said. "The Mexicans can no more blend into our race than can the Chinaman or the Negro. . . . It is old Chinese stuff, an echo of the seventies, word for word.

"I remember in my boyhood when eighteen innocent Chinese were hanged at one time in Los Angeles," the Major said. The racial nightmare will return to haunt the fields.

Why then import campesinos? It is a "greedy impulse," the Major said; he hired them himself. He was "an employer of Mexicans and at this time they are picking cotton on one of [my] ranches in California. On the whole they are the most docile of workmen. They are imposed upon both by their own employers and foreign employers as well. One wonders that they are not more resentful."

The colonial attitude could hardly be more succinctly stated. It is because of such views, expressed with more subtlety and sophistication today, that Cesar Chavez has compared the growers with the Southern plantation owners. He feels that "the idea that farm workers are a different breed of people—humble, happy, built close to the ground—still prevails."

Luis Valdez is younger and bolder. "It is gringoismo," he says.

He, too, has been a grape picker in the fields and has experienced the benevolence and severity of the growers' attitudes. "There are historical currents at work. It goes back to the Spanish Armada. It goes back to the fact that the entire Southwest once belonged to Mexico before the conquest. There is a connection between the United States taking half the territory of Mexico a century ago and the way farm workers are treated in the San Joaquin Valley. We are a colonial people. We are treated like colonials.

"As far as I am concerned, it was foreign imperialism a century ago, and it is domestic imperialism here in the San Joaquin Valley today."

El Grito of the Landless

"Now all I wait for is death," says José Gomez Gonzales. He has aged with the earth. In the dry fields of Texas his skin shrivels like dry mud. "I worked for a dollar a day until I got old. And that's nearly fifty years now. Right now I am seventy-four years old. I worked hard but never made any money.

"It was slavery for one of the poor." He does not own one inch of the earth he plowed, sowed, and harvested.

"A few own most of the land, farms stretch as far as the eye can see," says J. Trujillo, a farm worker in Mendota, California. The land is beautiful, the fields are opulent. But nothing belongs to him. The poverty of the campesino is colonial, he says. "The poverty problems aren't much different from those of South America." His grave will be the only land the campesino will own.

"Work in the earth, it is good," says a young man, Angel Vallejo, his hollow face pockmarked and dried in the sun of the Arizona deserts. "If the earth was ours—" he sighs—"ah, that would be good." He looks fifty; he is thirty-three.

The *grito* of the campesino is a cry of pain, but also of passion, full of longing for the unrequited love of the land he denies himself. He is the lover who is forever celibate. He is the *peón de tarea*, the peasant of drudgery. So deep is his hunger that he does not think of it. He has forgotten his own history.

When the mass migrations from Mexico began in the 1920's, it was the *peones de tarea* who came in exodus. In the state of Jalisco at that time, 96.2 per cent of the rural families were landless; in the state of Vera Cruz 98.9 per cent were landless; and in the State of Mexico (City) 99.8 per cent of the rural land was owned by 1 per cent of the families.

Under the guns of Zapata the peons arose in revolt primarily for the land. The land was seized for a historic moment.

On January 6, 1915, the Revolutionary Government of Mexico nullified—by official decree—every transaction in rural land of the previous seventy-five years. Lands of the landless were restored to the villages with water and forest rights. The *Ley de Ejidos*—the Law of the Common Land—was enacted in 1920, and the communal form of the village land ownership that dated back to the Aztecs was re-established.

In the years thereafter more than 100 million acres were given to the peasants. "The bulk of it [was] wrested from the vanquished *haciendas* and restored to the ancient communal *ejidos,*" Dr. Ernesto Galarza writes in *Merchants of Labor.* "The shifts in landholding brought about by the armed struggle were drastic."

Land! Land! Land! was the cry of the campesino. The lords of the haciendas of the old order fought back, for they held onto "the choicest of their land holdings," and "they moved into positions of vantage in the new revolutionary order. In the 1920's the nation was plunged into a struggle for power between rival generals, and the fighting that ensued drained the revolutionary energies." Zapata was assassinated; so was Pancho Villa. The armies of the *peones de tarea* were headless and defeated. "In this state of affairs reaction appeared in the countryside. Villages were again attacked, buildings razed, and crops burned to discourage the *ejidos.*"

A poor peon who had regained his ancestral land just as quickly lost it. He wished to live in peace, but there was year after year of war. He fled in terror. The "terror gripped many parts of the nation," Dr.

Galarza writes. It was the defeated man, the landless campesino, who fled to the fields of the north.

"Migration came only after defeat," Dr. Galarza says, "and its goal for many was California."

The campesino had little left but the dream of the land he almost had. He knew little else. "Uneducated, we have to work with our hands and backs," a farm worker, Mrs. Guadalupe Olivarez says, describing her years of stoop labor.

In the alien fields of the gringos the campesino stayed close to the earth. Not because "he was built that way," as the old joke says, but because in the earth there was solace and wages. So many of the odysseys of the campesinos go from country to country, through the rows of the fields.

Manuel Camacho says, "I'm from the state of Zacatecas in Mexico, where I worked planting corn behind two field horses. I've been here for twenty-two years and done every kind of work there is in the fields." He still dreams of those two horses.

The nostalgia of the newcomer is unforgiving. Land in the old country was poorer, but it was his. "My father had a small farm," says Luis Castro. Here he has nothing. "I came here from Mexico in March 1957, walking." He began working in the fields of the DiGiorgio Corporation (Del Monte and S&W), he says, "immediately." He works in the fields of a stranger.

"We have seen how they have taken the work of our hands and bodies and made themselves rich, while we are left with empty hands between the earth and the sky," the campesinos' newspaper *El Malcriado* quotes.

Few of the farms, ranches, vineyards, and orchards in California are owned by the Chicanos. And fewer, of course, by campesinos. In Texas and Arizona the land ownership is equally unequal. New Mexico, with its tradition of village farmers, and the ancient land grants of the San Luis Valley of Colorado are almost the sole exceptions to the landlessness of La Raza.

Crystal City, Texas, is typical. It is a farm city, the self-styled "Spinach Capital of America," in an almost wholly agricultural county. The county agricultural agent, when asked how many Chicanos own farms of the 267 listed in the 1960 census, replies promptly, "Just four. Our Latins don't do much farming. They're mostly farm workers." He is unconscious of any incongruity. Where 85 per cent of the population is Chicano, more than 95 per cent of the farms are owned by Anglos.

"It is big business farming here," the county agent says. "The Latin farmer may have a plot of beans, but he can't compete with these big outfits. He'd go bankrupt."

There is a deeper alienation between the campesinos and the growers: love of the earth divides them. It is not the exclusive passion of either, but like many who share one life, they are unequal lovers. The jealousies and hatreds of the campesinos and growers are not wholly like those of most employers and employees but are intensified by the sensuality of the earth they both love. The earth is a jealous mistress. Unfortunately she is also impartial.

Young men may laugh at this. The Chicanos say, "It's just a job." At best it is the least desirable of menial jobs, an insult to their aspiration—"the stoop labor with high school rings on their fingers," as one university student contemptuously writes.

The older men and women feel differently. It is not a humiliation to their dignity to kneel in the earth. "You have to be tough to work in the fields," the farm worker leader Gil Padilla says with belligerent pride. "It is the toughest work in the world. So you could say only the best, the people with the strongest spirits, can do farm work. And it's true."

"Our sweat and our blood have fallen on this land," says "The Plan of Delano" proclaimed almost religiously by the National Farm Workers Union. "Along this very road, in this very valley, the Mexican race has sacrificed itself for the last hundred years. . . ."

The blood of the farmers is in the earth, too. And they too talk of sacrifice and love with similar devotion.

"My father, he was a farmer, and his father, a farmer before him," says Jack Pandol, one of the vineyard owners of Delano who was among the first the union struck. "Every vine that we own here we planted. And this is our soil. This is our life. I was up this morning early until eleven o'clock, and I was under the vines, counting the berries, counting the vines.

"This is something that is in our blood," Jack Pandol says with emotion. "This is a love we have."

In the neighboring fields are the vineyards of the Zaninovich family. Like the Pandols, they came to the valley as poor peasants. "We have sweated blood here." A patriarch of the family, Martin Zaninovich, abjectly tells the Senate Subcommittee on Migratory Labor, "I am a grower of fresh table grapes in the Delano area. Like many other grape growers in this area, I have my parents to thank for the opportunity of living in the United States and becoming a farmer.

"Many of our parents came from Yugoslavia. When they arrived in this country they came as peasants," Martin Zaninovich says, just landless peasants. "The only thing they knew was how to grow grapes. But they did not complain."

His parents nourished the dry earth with their sweat. "With hard work came success," he says. Every year of his family's life, and his own, is in his vineyards. Now his father is buried there. The earth is sacred.

A nearby grower comments with equal fervor, "We've worked hard all our lives for what we have. We work now. And it hasn't been easy. I think this is probably the way the best of the growers in the area have accumulated their property." William Perelli-Minetti is the heir of another of the vineyard dynasties of Delano that the campesinos struck. He says of his ancestors, "They worked and they worked hard, because they were smart and willing to work and take the gamble."

Many of the growers say this: the hatred of those who strike is nothing but vengeance. The union of campesinos is out to destroy their vineyards and steal the fruits of their labors. It is after the land of their fathers. It is sacrilegious, an unholy conspiracy led by "outside agitators," "troublemakers," and an "invasion of riffraff."

"Somebody wants to come along after the gamble has been won and wants to take it [the land] away from them," William Perelli-Minetti says. "It isn't fair. It isn't right."

Martin Zaninovich says coldly, "We cannot in good conscience, and we will not, enter into any type of negotiations with these unions." He is adamant.

"I will hold out forever," Jack Pandol says matter-of-factly.

The growers say: What does Chavez know of growing grapes? It is easy for him to talk of unions and ruin the vines. "Chavez does not run the risk of excessive rains, or drought, or blight, that we do," says Jack Pandol. He does not love the earth!

It is a personal curse. He, the man "Chavez and his tricks," obviously is the devil who has enticed away the innocent campesinos.

Pandol says, "We have never had a walkout in our fields. And our men seem to be content. Happy."

Chavez replies, "There's a mental attitude we are dealing with here. Just the fact that one of his workers that he has been dealing with for twenty years lays down his equipment and comes to the edge of the fields and yells *'Huelga!'* at him, this shakes the foundation, the whole reason for his being."

Pandol: "I have always said that God has been good to us. The community has been good to us. And we in turn have been good to our employees. We will never cry!"

Chavez: "In some cases the growers interpret this as a challenge to their manhood."

The history of the frontier has been the history of the battle for the ownership of its incredibly rich lands. It still is.

In the barrios there is a young priest who believes there is a spiritual reason for the influence of the land on men. He says the very nature of the mystique of the West, with its cult of speed and living on wheels, has prolonged the power of the landowners. "Life is so ethereal here. Everything is transient. It's like living in quicksilver," the father says disapprovingly. "Here we do not have established values like in the East. We have no established elite, minority blocs, trade unions, entrenched industrialists. All these groups that give a material balance to society, and free the spirit to wander, have peripheral powers.

"Power is held in the hands of whoever owns the land, because the land is the only thing that seems to have permanent value," the father says. "Most of our establishment is based on land ownership. And there are still fortunes made every year on the land. Who owns the barrios of the cities? Who owns the farms of the San Joaquin Valley? I can tell you, it's not the Mexicans who once had title to the land. And it sure isn't the campesinos and Chicanos who live and work on the land. Someday the justice of this may be questioned by the poor.

"When you back Chavez into a corner," says the father, who knows the leader of the farm workers well, "he will admit that unionism isn't the whole answer. You ask him, 'Cesar, what will happen when the crops are all harvested by machines? What will happen to the farm workers then?' He gets a glint in his eyes. Especially if he's had a few to drink. 'It's the land!' he says. 'The land is the source of power! Someday we will have to get a share of the land!' "

The peasant from Europe and the peasant from Mexico face one another from opposite sides of the fence. One came across an ocean from a land five thousand miles away, and one came across a desert from a land he can almost see. But it is not this that divides them. It is the love of land they share that divides them.

XIX On a Lonely Country Road

On a deserted country road the night is lonely. In the vineyards the grapes have turned black. There are no lights. There is an eerie stillness. Somewhere, far off, the screeching siren of a sheriff's car is heard. A cock crows at midnight, frightened. In the town of Delano some men sleep with rifles beside their beds. The women say they keep their men at home at night and hide their knives, lest they be accused of violence, for blood has flowed in the vineyards this morning.

"The blood drips blood!" says a union organizer.

In the dark of midnight two young men appear. One grips a baseball bat as he approaches.

All day the *huelguistas* marched in the vineyards. There were fist fights. Four *huelguistas* on the picket lines have been beaten—one kicked in the groin, one kicked in the head. He is in bad shape. A woman has been beaten. Cesar Chavez in the union office shakes his head when word of the beatings comes. He says, "Yes, yes. Our strike against the Guimarra Vineyards will be hard." There will be more violence on the country roads.

"Who are you?" one young man whispers.

He is faceless in the night. Whether he is a deputy sheriff or a *huelguista* of the union is impossible to tell.

"Cómo estamos de cosecha?" the young man beside him says—"How is the harvest?" It makes no sense, unless the words are a trap for a scab. The voice really says: Halt!

I say nothing, for I do not know what to say. At midnight I have come to this deserted place to meet a union organizer. He told me, "Come to our union office, at the edge of town, at twelve. It will be quiet there then. No one will bother our talk." But he has not come.

"Buena noche," I say hopefully.

"Yeah," one young man mutters. "Right." His arm raises the baseball bat.

The union office is dark. It is a little pink house that looks like every other poor farm worker's house in the barrio. Symbolically the unpretentious headquarters of the United Farm Workers Organizing Committee (AFL-CIO) of Cesar Chavez is the last house on the last road on the west side—the campesino side—of Delano.

In the daylight the Pink House, as they affectionately call it, is alive with union organizers, pickets, ordinary farm workers, visiting celebrities, newspaper reporters, priests, and television cameras.

But at night it is deserted. On one side there is the silent vineyard, on the far side is a field of soybeans. No one would imagine that this insignificant house is the nerve center of a social revolution that has shaken the agricultural calm of the Southwest.

Just this morning seven molotov cocktails, in Coca-Cola bottles, exploded in the trucks of a labor contractor in a nearby town. Santos Soriano's trucks burst into flames. He had been preparing to hire grape pickers who would cross the picket lines. The local police suspect that the strikers may be guilty.

The union has denied any knowledge of the incident. It has condemned violence.

"We are committed to using the nonviolent method of organizing," Cesar Chavez told the Special Congressional Subcommittee of Labor that investigated the *huelga.* "The only reason that there has not been any bloodshed in Delano is because we have not responded to attacks on us by the opposition. Mr. Congressman, it seems to us that there will be very few people who will be against unions, but it seems to me that most of them are in Delano," Chavez said. There was laughter.

One *huelguista* was run down by the truck of a strikebreaker. The truck ran over him. His legs were broken. It happened shortly after another *huelguista* had run his car into three growers who were standing on the roadside. The battle of the cars is commonplace. Strikers and nonstrikers often run each other's cars off the roads.

"We have two cases where our cars were turned over," Chavez has testified. "In two or three cases some of our pickets were beaten up. In one case the grower ordered a spray rig to leave the fields and go out to the road and spray us with pesticide. We hope it was sulphur, and not anything worse than that, but we don't know. In another case, they drove a tractor disk back and forth right next to the picket line, so it would make enough dust to force us to leave the picket line.

"We've had five or six cases where guns were pointed at us, and we had two or three of these cases where they actually discharged the gun over our heads," Chavez testified.

"The hired guards for the DiGiorgio Corporation attacked one of our pickets, a lady picket. The police came and one of our pickets—Manuel Rosas, who was bleeding from a head wound inflicted when he went to the woman's aid—was found to have been resisting arrest at that point and *he* was arrested. He has served eight months.

"On one occasion, forty-four strikers were arrested for refusing to remain silent on the picket line. In other words, the strikers were arguing that they had a right to shout into the fields the word *'huelga,'* which means strike in Spanish. Most of the strikebreakers are from Mexico, so we yelled, *'Huelga! Huelga!'* so they would know there was a strike going on. The Sheriff's officer from Kern County came to the picket lines and said they could not use the word *'Huelga.'* They refused to give up using the word. So all forty-four were jailed.

"Justice doesn't really exist after you call a strike," Chavez said.

Now the strike against the Guimarra Vineyards—one of the largest growers of table grapes in the country—has begun. In the fields that stretch for 12,000 acres, there is the atmosphere of a battlefield.

"Oh. This will be a hard one," says Dolores Huerta, one of the union leaders.

On the lonely country road, the young men face me. They stiffen. Eying me suspiciously in the moonless night, one of them squints at my face. He grins broadly.

"I didn't recognize you," he says.

He is one of the *huelguistas* whom I had met on the picket line earlier in the day. A shy and handsome youth with a boyish face, he seems as relieved as I am that we are friends and there will be no fight.

"We have to be careful," he says almost apologetically. "We are guarding the union office. They would like to wreck it, you know."

"Oh, it's nothing," I say.

XX The War of the Flowers

It began with the "War of the Flowers," in the town of McFarland.

On the morning of May 3, 1965, at sunrise, a man rises from his knees in the fields of flowers of the Mount Arbor Nurseries, the largest grower of roses in California. He has been grafting young rosebush shoots, and his fingers are bleeding. He yells, "*Huelga!*" Strike! It is the signal. Eighty rose grafters walk out of the fields. The first strike has begun for Cesar Chavez's still unborn National Farm Workers Association, with the "Strike of the Roses."

"Here where the blood is made, here in the heart of the strike," proclaims the newspaper of the farm workers, *El Malcriado*, "here it shall be won in the hearts of our brothers."

Epifiano Camacho is the man who got off his knees. He is an intense man with black eyes and black angers, who sings of his sorrows in a *corrido* he writes for the "Strike of the Roses":

> I am the cry of the poor
> Who work in the fields
> Who water the earth
> With our sweat.

Our huts and hovels
Are always full of sorrow
For we live as animals
In the midst of riches.

He has worked on his knees all his life. The farm worker stoops in the fields. But a rose grafter kneels. He crawls from rosebush to rosebush, with his fingers torn by the thorns, as he cuts the shoots into the young plants. It is skilled work, for the plants are delicate and easily damaged. Hundreds of tiny cuts from the thorns turn the fingers of the rose grafter black with scars. The deft fingers have to work quickly, for the pay is by the number of rosebushes. At the time of the rebellion in the rose gardens, the pay was about $7 for one thousand bushes. Many of the flower workers are women and few complain loudly.

My poor Mexican race
Evil has been your lot
So many have wished
To see you downtrodden.

Awaken, oh Mexicans
Who wouldn't look up
Who work like slaves
Who don't want to know.

But now Epifiano Camacho has risen from his knees. He has been talking with three young dreamers in nearby Delano: Cesar Chavez, Gilbert Padilla, and Dolores Huerta. Quietly they organized the strike.

Long have we suffered
Being sold like slaves
Now we can all see
Our triumph is coming.

It is symbolic to Luiz Valdez, the poet of El Teatro Campesino, that the *huelga* began in the fields of flowers. "We are a people who believe in symbols," he says. "The last divine Aztec emperor Cuauhtémoc was murdered and his descendants were put to work in the fields. We are still there in the fields of America." The renaissance of La Raza had to begin again where it ended.

"History is a flower. If a single seed remains, it will bloom again," says Valdez.

In his song "Los Niños Campesinos," the "Sons of the Farm Workers," that is sung on the picket lines, he evokes the old and new symbol of the "flowers and sorrows":

> Children go to the fields of grapes, beets, and apples,
> And the children spend all day among the branches,
> From sun to sun, until the paymasters arrive,
> Giving them flowers, only flowers
> For their sorrows.

The "War of the Flowers" of the ancients was a mock battle, fought on a ceremonial plain like a football stadium with songs and rituals. But it was a battle for life. In times of peace the Aztecs staged wars as though they were plays, with marches and orations and flag waving. Like the *huelga,* the drama was real. The losers of the game, who became prisoners and victims of the victors, were sacrificed to the god of war, Huitzilopochtli, to nourish life and bless the fields. In the Nahuatl language of the Aztecs the same word may have meant a red flower and a prisoner of war. The red rose, the red poppy, was the color of life and death. In the "Song of Sorrows" the priests of the Aztecs intoned:

> Nothing but flowers and songs of sorrows
> Are left in Mexico.
> We wander here and there
> In our desolate poverty.

And so in the ancient way of the Aztecs, the ancestors of the campesinos, the modern "War of the Flowers" begins again in the San Joaquin Valley.

"Our first strike was a small one, but it prepared us for the big one," Cesar Chavez recalls.

It actually began before that. The farm workers began to organize, fifty years before, in the summer of 1915, when the Agricultural Workers Industrial Union of the Wobblies had begun in the valley. There had been hundreds of lost strikes and dozens of beaten unions and thousands of defeated men and women.

Cesar Chavez came to the valley in the summer of 1962. He had worked as a boy in these vineyards; now he pruned the grapevines once more. He dug ditches. In the evening he went from town to town, with scarcely enough money for gas, talking to hundreds of campesinos. With his wife at his side, he asked questions. He listened.

"A lot of people have asked me, Why Delano?" he says. "The answer is simple. I had no money. My wife's family lived there and I had a brother. I thought if things go very bad we can always have a meal there."

After a year of organizing they had ten dues-paying members. Chavez says, "Talk about being scared, I had to get dues in order to eat. I suspect some of the members were paying dues ($3.50 a month) because they felt sorry for me."

He begged for food. He says it was because his children were hungry, but he was hungry, too. "I went to the people and started asking for food. It turned out to be about the best thing I could have done, although at first it's hard on your pride. If people give you their food, they'll give you their hearts."

The campesinos were suspicious and cautious. Who was this stranger? They had to live in the valley and work in the fields. He could afford to talk. He could go away.

"We had hundreds of house meetings. Sometimes two or three would come, sometimes none. Sometimes even the family that called the house meeting would not be there," Chavez says.

Helen Chavez worked in the cotton fields. "If you haven't got your wife behind you, you can't do many things. We were together then and still are. I think I'm more of a pacifist than she is. Her father, Fabela, was a colonel with Pancho Villa in the Mexican Revolution."

The family of the farm worker has always worked together in the fields, the women and children beside the men. Those who are deprived of everything else are often more bound by love and need.

They were "planting an idea," Chavez says. Helen, who "was having babies," mimeographed 80,000 cards that summer which asked the simple question of farm workers: How much do you think you ought to be paid? They went from door to door in more than eighty little towns and labor camps handing out the cards. The organizing was quiet and patient. Chavez has no faith in publicity and meetings, in political fireworks and revolutionary rhetoric. "I think that groups that deal in power become impatient with groups that are strangers to power," he says. He went on "accumulating people."

"It started so slowly that at first it was only one man, then five, then one hundred," says *El Malcriado.*

Actually there were four men and two women in the beginning. There was the elfin Dolores Huerta, with the lovely face of a Mayan sculpture, who became the union's chief negotiator. "When we are deadlocked, I cry. The bosses are men, and they can't stand a woman's tears." There was the wiry Gilbert Padilla, who became the odd man out, an organizer in Texas. There was the skeptic, Antonio Orendain, who read Jefferson, Bakunin, and St. Francis, and who became the hard and efficient treasurer of the union. There was Larry Itliong, the Filipino leader, who was to join later. And there were Helen and Cesar Chavez. These six were to become the leaders of the National Farm Workers Association.

After a year they had a meeting in Fresno of about 250 people who had signed the cards and who voted to establish the NFWA.

Chavez had asked his cousin Manuel to "draw an Aztec eagle" to use as the symbol on the flag he had designed for the farm workers. But Manuel could not draw an eagle too well. He sketched a black, rough bird with squared wings. When the flag was unveiled at the meeting, the people looked at the red banner with the black eagle in a white circle and asked; "Is it a Nazi flag? Or maybe Communist?"

Manuel said, "When that damned eagle flies, that's when the farm workers' problems are going to be solved."

For three years the Aztec eagle did not stir. And then, suddenly, the red flag with its black eagle of the Aztecs was unfurled in the fields.

January, 1965, had witnessed the death of the Bracero Law, by which millions of Mexican farm workers had been imported by Act of Congress. Growers no longer needed unskilled laborers in such numbers. The mechanization of the farms, especially the cotton fields, drastically reduced the need for masses of braceros.

Braceros had been herded like cattle. They had no rights, no protections, under our laws. They were not citizens and could not join unions. One word of protest and they could be deported at whim. In the fields they worked "harder than beasts of burden," wrote one observer. It was quite "deliberate," said Dr. Galarza in his study, *Merchants of Labor: The Mexican Bracero Story.* The bracero system, like that of slavery, was designed to isolate a man from his family, in a strange country, so that he had nothing but his work.

On occasion "the typical bracero will literally work himself to death," wrote Richard Hancock in *The Role of the Bracero.* He marveled at their "uncomplaining fortitude," for "the bracero in times of trial must sustain himself with little more than stamina and spiritual resources. . . . American doctors are amazed at the animal vitality with which the Mexican worker overcomes crushing physical injuries and illnesses."

The medical files of "the bracero doctor," Dr. Ben Yellen, of the Imperial Valley, one of the rare physicians in the farm counties who treat mostly agricultural workers, are a nightmare of illnesses and deaths. "It was hell," Dr. Yellen says, "right here in paradise." The "animal vitality" of the Mexican was a myth.

None of this misery by itself would have brought an end to the Bracero Law. It was too useful in the fields, and it rendered union organizing impossible.

In the barrios of the cities, however, there were troublesome rumblings. The Viva Kennedy! campaign of 1960 had indicated the potential power of La Raza politics. Year by year the Chicano movement grew. When the Democratic party candidate for the U.S. Senate, Waggoner Carr, was defeated in Texas in 1966 by the Republican, John Tower, largely because of the switch of barrio voters, even the distant Texan in the White House voiced concern.

La Raza politicians had requested repeal of the Bracero Law for years: it reduced wages and increased unemployment in the barrios. The appeals so long ignored were now heard. Barely three months after the defeat of the Democratic Party in Texas, Congress ended the Bracero Law.

Henceforth, the Department of Labor ruled, any braceros hired in the border towns will have to be paid $1.40 an hour. The local farm workers are in no event to be paid less than the Mexicans, the Labor

Department magnanimously decreed. But the campesinos in the United States were rarely paid that much.

On the edge of the Mojave Desert, in the Coachella Valley, the local grape pickers demand the same pay as the braceros. Early in the summer of 1965 they go on strike. Within ten days the growers, fearing the ripe grapes will shrivel to raisins in the desert heat, raise wages from $1.10 to $1.40 an hour.

The grape harvest begins in Delano to the north a few weeks later, but the campesinos are offered the old, low wage rate.

"Naturally they wanted the same pay," says Larry Itliong, then an organizer for the old-style Agricultural Workers Organizing Committee (AWOC), a robust, cheerful, Filipino veteran of the labor wars, with three fingers missing. The grape pickers, mostly Filipinos, come to him and complain they will go on strike.

Itliong tells them, "If you go out you're going to go hungry, lose your car, maybe lose your wife." They insist on taking the risk. On September 8, 1965, two thousand Filipino farm workers walk out of the fields.

A young woman from the Philippines, Mrs. Luming Imutan, who was there at the beginning, tells it in her own words:

"It was the young Filipino boys that started the strike. These young boys have a lot of violence inside of them, and when they had a picket line at the field all of the workers left. Most of these boys left when it was decided that there could be no violence on the picket line. But these Filipino boys started the strike. And if it wasn't for them, the old men would never have left the fields and joined the strike."

With the grapes rotting on the vines, growers begin to hire scabs, mostly Mexicans. The farm workers are divided. Not merely do they speak different languages, but they belong to different groups. In the AWOC of Itliong are the Filipinos, and in the NFWA of Chavez are the Mexicans.

Itliong goes to Chavez for help. Both men know that if they do not get together, the strike will be lost.

Chavez is hesitant. He had not come to Delano to organize a strike. He had come to organize the barrios. The NFWA is not even a union, but an "association." He says, "The strike was not the normal function of the association." He is not an experienced union leader. "We didn't feel we were ready for a big strike," he says. He has "some misgivings."

On the Mexican Independence Day, September 16, a meeting is held in a Catholic church hall in Delano. More than one thousand campesinos crowd the hall to vote on whether to strike. Under the red flag with the Aztec eagle, and a portrait of Zapata, the band plays the Mexican National Anthem, a priest gives the invocation, and Chavez invokes the spirit of Father Hidalgo—the George Washington of Mexico—and $1.40 an hour.

"Huelga! Huelga! Huelga!" the crowd yells. The vote to strike is unanimous.

Huelga! The word means "strike," but it means much more to the campesinos. "Strike" is a cruel word that means to lash out, to attack. In the old Anglo-Saxon there is the word *strican,* that like the Hoch German, *strihhan,* means to row a boat, to strike the water, to flow and go forward. In the Spanish the meaning is different. The old word, *huelga,* meant a time of rest and relaxation and merry-making—a little fiesta. The new word *huelga* is more vigorous and joyous still.

Luis Valdez has sought to capture the new meaning of *huelga.* "*Huelga* means strike. With the poetic instinct of La Raza, the Delano grape strikers have made it mean a dozen other things. It is a declaration, a challenge, a greeting, a feeling, a movement. We cry, '*Huelga!*' It is the most significant word in our entire Mexican American history. If the Raza in Mexico believe in *La Patria,* we believe in *La Huelga.*"

"Under the name of *huelga* we had created a Mexican American *patria,* and Cesar Chavez was our first *presidente,*" says Valdez.

"We came back with flags. We came back with an utterly raw and vibrant Mexican character," says Valdez. "We shouted, '*Viva la Huelga!*' and that word became the word of life for us. That word became our hope. It reverberated throughout the Southwest."

On his old car Epifiano Camacho, of the "Strike of the Roses," painted signs in Spanish: "I TOO WAS A VIRGIN ONCE," "TO WANDER IS MY DESTINY," "WHEN I GO, I REALLY FLY," and the ebullient cry of the *huelguistas,* "I AM NOT TO BE TAKEN LIGHTLY."

The rose worker was fired from the fields of flowers after he led the

"Strike of the Roses." He has a terrible tongue, they say, and tongue-lashes the scabs in the vineyards so savagely that his friends cringe.

"Come out, you pigeon-brained sons of Satan! Why don't you foul spawn of demented chimpanzees understand what it's all about? Open your ears, you groveling pigs! Would you sell the souls of your children as well as your own to these grower swines? Are you Mexicans or what are you? This isn't Russia! Don't be slaves! Come out and join us and fight for your rights, you second-rate imitation of a female jellyfish!"

His epithets, according to farm-worker organizer Eugene Nelson, are in "the style of old Mexico." The grape pickers creep from the vineyards like dogs under a whip. Epifiano slaps them on their backs.

"Bueno!" he exclaims. "You are now real Mexicans."

The campesino bit his tongue before this. He would whisper a curse under his breath, or say nothing at all. The *huelga* has opened his lips, and his curses shouted in the valleys of California shock even him.

The growers scoff at the strike vote and ignore the telegrams of the campesinos asking for negotiations.

"There is no strike among Delano farm workers," announces Martin Zaninovich, a spokesman for the vineyard owners. "The so-called strike is pure myth, manufactured out of nothing by outside agitators who are more interested in creating trouble in the United States than in the welfare of the farm workers."

"A gross piece of fiction," Zaninovich says of the *huelga;* ". . . the public has been treated to a monumental 'snow job.' "

It is the "outside agitators" who have brought "the injection of racial issues and racial overtones" into the peaceful San Joaquin Valley, according to the dentist Dr. Clifford E. Loader, the mayor of Delano. "We have a completely integrated community here," he tells the Senate Subcommittee on Migratory Labor. "I would say that outside of Hawaii there is probably no city in the United States that is more racially mixed and lives [more] harmoniously than Delano, California." (The city fathers had referred to the town as the "Little United Nations." But that was before the *huelga.*)

The city council, in emergency session, resolves that the *huelga*, Cesar Chavez, and the outside agitators be condemned.

The violence on the country roads begins. Every leader of the *huelga* is arrested, not once but many times.

In Borrego Springs, in the desert of California, Cesar Chavez is arrested, chained about the waist, handcuffed, and locked in a steaming truck for hours. In the vineyards of the DiGiorgio Corporation, it is 110 degrees. Arrested with Chavez, chained together in the heat and dark, are Father Victor Salandini, Reverend Chris Hartmire, director of the Migrant Ministry of the National Council of Churches, and eight *huelguistas.* They are driven to jail in San Diego, hours away, accused of "trespassing." The life of the priest is threatened, but Father Salandini says simply, "I am not afraid. My faith is in God."

The vineyard owners grow nervous when the time for the grape harvest approaches. There is "the aroma of a quarter of a billion dollars in wines," that hangs precariously on the vines at the mercy of the sun and the pickers. Fortunes are made and lost in a week in the vineyards of California.

"A strike is death," a vineyard owner says. "It can kill a year's work."

The sun is the life and the sun is the death of the grapes. "In California the sun keeps up, blazing all through August, and it's the devil to keep the grapes from working up too high in sugar," Paul Masson, whose wines bear his name, once complained. "Here, you see, we have to race against the calendar."

It is true of every crop, but most of all the grapes. One week too long on the vines and the water blisters form and burst and the grapes dry up.

Arrayed against the *huelga* are the giants of agri-business. These corporate farms have a yearly gross income of more than $4 billion. "The handling, processing and marketing of California's farm products contribute over 9 billion dollars annually to the State's economy," according to the California Chamber of Commerce. In all, in this one state, agri-business and its allied industries are a $15 billion yearly complex of unquestioned power.

"We had $85 in the treasury in the beginning of the strike," Chavez says.

In the San Joaquin Valley alone there are seven corporate farms so gigantic that the cash each received from the government for lands they did not plow and crops they did not grow ranged from more than $500,000 to almost $3,000,000 in 1966. One of these, the J. G. Boswell Company Ranch in Corcoran (Kings County), received a high of $2,807,633; the farms of Griffen, Inc., in Huron (Fresno County) were paid $2,397,073 for not farming. And these "direct cash payments" for "soil bank and acreage diversion" *did not* include "any subsidy the Government may be making under the price support program" (*Congressional Record,* Vol. 113, No. 96, S.8412 to S.8422, June 19, 1967).

Corporate farming is just that. The struck Guimarra Vineyards of Delano is one of the smaller corporations. But its cash crop sales are estimated at about $12 million yearly. Its annual payroll for its 2,500 workers is about $2.5 million. Its gifts from the U.S. Agriculture Department are equally impressive. The vineyards of Guimarra received $264,882 for not growing cotton in 1966. They did even better in 1967, when they did not grow even more cotton and received $278,721. Of course, Guimarra Vineyards, Inc., grows mostly grapes.

The pastoral life is not the sole pursuit and pleasure of a corporate farm like Guimarra. Its investments are diversified far beyond its barns and packing sheds—in banking, chemicals, machinery, and Hollywood. When young George Guimarra, Jr., was thirteen he already was proud owner of a pre-teen stock portfolio of 213 shares of the Bank of America, 500 shares of Republic Pictures, and several hundred lesser stocks.

In the vineyards of Delano the romance of the tender grapes is somewhat mitigated by the corporate image. "A Texan would be at ease in these shirt-sleeved towns like Delano," writes Idwal Jones in his idyl of the wine industry, *Vines in the Sun:* "They have no romantic air. Dessert wines production goes in for vast output at the lowest possible cost. The tutelary genius of the wine fields would far more resemble Mr. Ford than Bacchus."

The week before the *huelga* begins, *El Malcriado* sets the scene by asking, "But what can one man do?"

"Everything!" it answers itself. "The roots of this country and the roots of the Mexican Revolution were established by very few men. It was one man, Gandhi, who led the huge country of India out of slavery. . . . It was one man that started the action in the Rose strike. . . ."

"You also are one man," it says.

And with that the battle against the "godless agricultural system of California" begins. In the soup kitchen that has been set up in the old Filipino Hall a sign reads:

GOD IS BESIDE YOU
ON THE PICKET LINES

By late fall the union says that 2,000 campesinos are "continuously on strike," 4,000 "have come out of the fields," 2,000 have joined the NFWA in the Delano area alone, and 5,000 have signed for NFWA or AWOC to represent them.

On a "rainy December day," Cesar Chavez says to the growers, "Sit down at the table with us." The growers ignore him.

The strike continues "into the pruning, the tying, the thinning, the suckering, and the deleafing of the vines," Chavez says. The mood grows evil in winter. In the words of a *huelguista*, "It is cold, it rains. The wet wind congeals the spirit. The gray sky afflicts me."

"Poor as we are, we have stood firm for one hundred days," they say.

The boycott of the grapes begins around the country. On the docks of San Francisco the grandson of Jack London, Bart Abbott, leads one of the picket lines. In New York City the boycott is said to be 95 per cent effective—in Harlem.

By late December Cesar Chavez says, "The name Delano is known throughout the state. It is becoming known throughout the nation."

Just before Christmas, 1965, the AFL–CIO announces it will support the *huelga.* Walter Reuther leads a march down the main street of Delano. He pledges the *huelguistas* $5,000 a month from his Industrial Union Department. The strikers and volunteer organizers are guaranteed their $5 a week strike pay. Two trailer trucks full of Christmas toys and turkeys arrive in Delano.

By March the hunger returns. The 300-mile Pilgrimage to Sacramento begins. "The theme of the march is Pilgrimage, Penitence, and Revolution," says the union. When the marchers reach the state capital they are greeted by 10,000 campesinos and supporters.

In the late spring the first large vineyard owner, Schenley, agrees to sign a union contract with a minimum wage, a hiring hall, and recognized work holidays. One of the holidays is the 16th of September, Mexican Independence Day; the 4th of July is another.

One by one the growers will now begin to sign: Christian Brothers, Gallo, Almadén, Paul Masson wines. Even the giant DiGiorgio Corporation will eventually give in.

In the fields of tomatoes and lettuce and onions, in the orchards of apricots and plums and peaches, nothing has been won. The table grape growers of Delano will hold out for years to come. Of the million and a half farm workers a few thousand have union contracts. But it is more than none.

That summer a union hiring hall for farm workers opens in the old Azteca Tortilleria in Delano. It is a historic occasion. And on the first anniversary of the *huelga* a fiesta is held. The campesinos dance to a mariachi band and a Western band; for it is also the birthday of Emiliano Zapata: What better day to celebrate the *huelga?*

On a wooden fence in the barrio of Delano a campesino has painted the names:

PANCHO VILLA
JUAREZ
ZAPATA
CHAVEZ

Zapata "died the death he had to die: betrayed, ambushed and murdered by a band of mercenary cowards," writes Gonzalo Molina in *La Raza.* "He is still with us in Mexico, in all of Latin America, and even in Delano. In every peasant or farm worker with a free mind; wherever there are people who have passion for land and for freedom; in the mind of the Indian who squats with his head covered with a sarape, thinking but not sleeping, there also lives Emiliano Zapata."

The National Farm Workers Union of Texas titles the story of its strike, "The Sons of Zapata." *El Malcriado* sells Zapata posters by the hundreds; "*Viva la Revolución!*" and the "Plan of Delano" of Cesar

Chavez proclaims: "We are the sons of the Mexican Revolution, a revolution of the poor seeking bread and justice."

"We know that the poverty of the Mexican or Filipino worker in California is the same as the Negroes' and poor whites', the Puerto Ricans', Japanese and Arabians'," says the "Plan of Delano"; ". . . the triumph of our race depends" on this, "all races that comprise the oppressed."

The words of Delano spread throughout the barrios of the Southwest faster than any teletype could have carried them. "We have our own system of human communications," Valdez explains. The migrant has to know if there is work in the next town, what they are paying, where his family can live, who is friendly and who is not. It is not something he is likely to read about in the newspapers, nor can he always read.

In a few months the legend of Chavez and the "Chavistas" is heard in the remotest migrant camps, from the Ohio Valley to the potato fields of Idaho and the Rio Grande Valley of Texas. Letters by the hundreds begin to pile up on the shabby desks at the union offices. "We have to win here first," Chavez tries to explain. "How many organizers do we have to spare? Everybody wants help. What can we do?

"Almost everywhere I go to speak somewhere in the vicinity there are farm workers. So a network is being built. There is a large and increasing demand for organization from many places around the country. It will take many years. But we know that a union of farm workers is going to be built somehow, because the workers are on the move, and they want a union.

"It is sort of a beautiful dream," Chavez says. "I hope it lasts a long time."

In September of 1969, when the grapes were ripe for harvest, the strike begins its fifth year, the longest agricultural strike in history.

On the Pilgrimage to Sacramento the farm workers sang of their unbelievable strike, in the ballad of "Ay Pero Sí, Pero No" ("Maybe Yes, Maybe No"), written by the wise clown of El Teatro Campesino, Felipe Cantu. It was originally a song sung to the scabs in the vineyards:

And I've told you not to pick
By the edge of the road
For the strikers might hit you
With the grapes you pick.

Ah, maybe yes, maybe no.
Ah, maybe yes, maybe yes,
Maybe no!

And in this way we finish,
The singing of our song;
Oh, help us win our strike;
Long live our union!

Ah, maybe yes, maybe no.
Ah, maybe yes, maybe yes,
Maybe no!

XXI The Men Without Numbers

> Know yourself and your forefathers, your history, and be proud that you are of Mexican descent.
>
> Learn both good Spanish and good English.
>
> Learn all you can about and from the gringo, so you can beat him at his own game: competition.
>
> Strive for equal position and pay with the gringo and take no less.
>
> Strive for the unity of the Mexican and Spanish American in all the Southwest.
>
> Do not criticize your own people, but direct your criticisms or hostility where it should go in a positive and constructive way at the Anglo-Saxon.
>
> Do not forget your people when you are emancipated financially; remember you are one of them. . . .
>
> Education is the key to success. . . .

This is the credo that Carlos Cansino, a former farm worker, has written for his sons. Upon the thoughts of men like this the United Farm Workers Organizing Committee has built its strength. His credo is exceptional only in that he has written it in the words of the articulate teacher that he has become.

"When the genius of the people is released, it is a powerful force," Cesar Chavez says. He sees the credos, messages, letters, personal manifestos, schemes, and programs that daily come to his desk as signs of the significant changes that are occurring in the minds of the campesinos. "Men are developing before their own eyes," he says. "It happens overnight. These things, when they get released, get translated into ideas, into acts, into demands, into struggles. They are not corrupted. They are original.

"I could sit up all night and tell of the beautiful things that happen to people," Chavez says.

Unionism is just "part of social change," to him. "If the union stops with winning the contract, stops at the job, then I think the union is not doing its job. As long as the farm workers are underpaid and overworked, have no security on the job, there is very little you can do in other areas where change is needed. The most basic thing that has to change is the economics of agriculture." But that is but the beginning of the "social revolution" he foresees. It is the foundation upon which "a more human society can be built."

He is no utopian, though. It has to begin now, he says. "Where the people are, where they work is where you have to begin. The individual is the key to social change. Nothing changes until the individual changes."

One day I ask him: "They tell me that when a man stands up in a vineyard and yells *Huelga!* he is a changed man. Isn't that a romantic idea?"

"No, it isn't romantic," Chavez says. "It's very real. When a man gets up there and yells *Huelga!* for the first time, something happens to him. He will never be the same.

"We are dealing with fear. If we get rid of the fear, then it is easier. Once we confront the fear the struggle is not hard to fight. A man will think hard, very hard, before he joins a picket line. Once he does that, he won't think twice about staying out on the boycott for a year, two years. Once the farm workers get up on their feet and strike, they are not the same people. They begin to think differently about themselves."

The words of Chavez come to life in the words of the farm workers:

"It has not been until a few years ago that I began to seriously wonder why I had been a migratory farm worker. I always come back to the fact that I was Mexican American. When I was a little boy I somehow knew that the Mexicans were poor and the Anglos were rich. This meant working for the gringos in the farms or in the city. That was a fact of life and it still is. If the Spanish soldier Juan Cansino, who came with Cortés, and the Mexican Indian maiden, daughter of a chief, would see us now, they would cry with sorrow.

"Now I wonder," he says, "why it isn't the other way around. . . ."

Chavez reflects: "This is how a movement begins. This is why the Farm Workers Union is a 'movement' more than a 'union.' "

Chavez is grateful to the unions who have helped the *huelga* with money and support. He is not one to join the contemporary chorus of disparagement of unionism. But he feels a movement has to be freer of bureaucracy and has to be closer to the people. "The movement doesn't stand still. It's like a cyclone." It's not a matter of attending a meeting. The lives of people are involved and their lives are changed. "They grow every day. And they want complete change. And they know how to get it."

A movement is the people, not merely a tool they use. He feels it is a "way of living." In these thoughts he pioneered many of the ideas of the younger generation—of the student movement and participatory democracy. But Chavez built his movement upon unionism and organization.

"For fifty years, sixty years, the farm workers have tried to organize," Chavez says. "We have been beaten every time. Beaten into the ground. Now it's like a dam where the water has been backed up, backed up for all those years, and all of a sudden there is a small breakthrough. Now we don't want just a small change. We have waited too long.

"We want a social revolution. We want to change the conditions of human life." He smiles. "Our union is not just another union. And our strike is not just another strike."

In the fields the *huelga* has already changed the way men and women think and act. Strikes are nothing new in the fields. It is the way men strike that has changed.

The campesinos have walked out of the fields year after year. Life is so abysmal and jobs are so transient that the traditional way to protest is just to walk away. Growers will simply hire new hands from the limitless reservoir of rural poor. In the next field, in the next town, there is always a new job.

"Our people have always walked out," says Eliezer Risco of *La Raza*, who has worked with the farm workers. "We walk out of the fields, out of schools, out of conferences, out of everything.

"Walkouts!" the young activist exclaims. "It's because we feel powerless to change anything."

It meant little to strike. Organizing a union was another matter. The campesinos who traveled from town to town, individualistic, full of pride and apathy, helpless as serfs, had been impossible to unionize. The old unions had tried all the old methods. For fifty years every attempt had failed.

No one had ever organized a union of farm workers that had lasted. Chavez was determined to do the impossible. "If I can't organize them," he said, "I'm finished. I'd move on. . . ."

The quixotic history of the Agricultural Workers Industrial Union of the Wobblies (IWW) was familiar to Chavez. He had studied farm labor history as a monk does the lives of the saints. He knew how the first union had arisen out of the dust of the Durst hops farm at Wheatlands, California, in the summer of 1913. More than 2,500 men, women, and children crowded into a befouled, toiletless camp of mud and tents to beg for a handful of picker's jobs at wages of 78 cents to $1 a day. The farm workers held a protest meeting, deputy sheriffs were called, a shot was fired "to sober the mob," a riot erupted, several farm workers and law officers were killed, and terror spread through the fields. There were one hundred arrests, the National Guard was called, and the first large union of farm workers was organized.

The Sancho Panzas of the IWW organized their whirlwind union in 1915. By 1916 it had 20,000 members. By 1917 its romantic leaders had been driven out of the fields, or into jails, and the union had dissolved into history.

In the turbulent thirties the Cannery and Agricultural Workers Industrial Union was organized. This time it was the Sancho Panzas of Karl Marx, the Communists, who tilted at the windmills of corporate farming. Once more the union grew to 20,000 members. Having attained that fateful figure, it too dissolved in the economic turmoil of the Depression.

After bloody and cruel strikes in the late thirties, the fledgling CIO founded yet another union of farm workers—the United Cannery, Agricultural, Packing and Allied Workers of America—in July of 1937. They proudly declared they had organized 283 locals in 24 states with 100,000 members. Labor contracts were won, the union claimed, for almost 20,000 farm workers; the magical and ominous number. Once more, in spite of its huge apparatus, its national support, and its grandiose title, the union was soon more active in its offices than in the fields.

One by one the unions of farm workers, organized and led from outside the barrios, would rise and fall. The unionism of the Anglos did not take root in the fields.

The unions of factory workers were recognized by society as bargaining tools by which the economic wealth and political power were shared. But the campesinos had little share and no power. No recognition, no laws, no machinery existed for them.

Chavez not only knew of these previous attempts and failures at organizing; he and his father had been members of some of these unions. He had learned that farm workers would be organized only if they organized themselves. The campesinos had to build their own union in their own way.

"Our goals have to be broader than the traditional goals of unions," Chavez says. "It is more than a union as we know it today that we have to build. It is a movement. It is a movement of the poor.

"We are a poverty union, a union made up of poor people. Our union will be a poor union all of its life," he says. It is not enough to give the poor more money. "So we have organized a cooperative movement, a health clinic, a gas station, a credit union, whatever those who have nothing need, a community of the poor. We are trying to create a community."

In more poetic words the union's newspaper, *El Malcriado*, elaborated on these thoughts:

"What is a movement? It is when the silent hopes of many people begin to become a real part of life. It is when a group of people care enough so that they are willing to make sacrifices. It is when there are enough people with one idea so that their actions are together like a wave of water which nothing can stop."

"Here we have a rule. We resist giving our members numbers," says Cesar Chavez of the National Farm Workers Union. "Once we do that we are frightened that we will become one mass. One ball of nothing. It's easy nowadays. We have 20,000 members. And with all the paper work and accounting that has to be done, it would be easier to use numbers. We refuse! For the sake of efficiency it would be better to substitute numbers for names. We refuse!

"Our people are human! They are not numbers!" Chavez says.

In an era of business unionism, when the assets of unions may equal those of the corporations they battle, such a philosophy seems old-fashioned. Unionism is itself a big business. Its computerized retirement funds, medical plans, and fringe benefits make many a union office resemble an insurance office. Is he suggesting a rebellion against the computers?

Chavez smiles in that gentle way he has when talking of "social revolution." "It is easy to strike. There have been strikes in the fields for fifty years. But they did not make life more human."

Just before Christmas of 1966 the union bought forty acres of land. The barren and weedy plot was on the Highway of Father Garces, in the midst of nowhere, near the city dump. On a photograph of the poor land that appeared in *El Malcriado,* the words were written, like a biblical inscription:

> *To have a piece of ground is to have roots in the community.*
>
> Emiliano Zapata

The land is eternal. Like the poor it is silent and endless. When the union decided to buy land and build on it, that was a sign that it had become one with the poor. The land it bought was poor and worthless and unwanted.

Some of the young men say the spirit of the *huelga* died that year. "The union became just a union with the signing of the DiGiorgio and Schenley contracts," they say with the poignant nostalgia of the young. "We became part of the labor establishment. We had to worry about hiring crews, working conditions, the market for grapes—that whole bit. Even the way we shouted at the scabs changed. It was quieter."

"We won the contracts but we lost our souls," is what the young men mean.

But the *huelga* had just begun. The fight against those outside had shifted to the inner struggle to build up the spirit from within, says Chavez. "The hardest thing in a movement is not to lose sight of the people you are fighting for as individuals. To not forget they are individuals. To be with them and see them grow as individuals. To listen to their individual hearts."

In a sense the buying of land was the end of the beginning of the *huelga.* The campesinos would have to build their dream with bricks and mortar, if they could.

The land they have named "The Forty Acres" is desolate. It is unbearably hot. In the monotony of the plain, where the Mountains of the Devil—the Diablo Range—are vaguely visible at the horizon, a sign says:

ON THIS SITE A MONUMENT SHALL BE BUILT HONORING THE MEN, WOMEN AND CHILDREN OF THE DELANO GRAPE STRIKE, AND THE ENDURING SPIRIT WITH WHICH THEY HAVE DEFENDED THEIR FARM WORKERS UNION.

Nearby is the city dump.

It is Easter Sunday. Hundreds of campesinos, perhaps a thousand or more, suddenly come down the road marching, singing, shouting, playing guitars and accordions, running down the road to nowhere, waving banners of the Virgen de Guadalupe, and dozens of flags of the *huelga* and the Stars and Stripes. A yell goes up. The marchers burst onto the barren field, as if this is their long-sought destination. The city dump has never witnessed so strange a pilgrimage.

A priest of Our Lady of Guadalupe Church in Delano blesses the Forty Acres. He blesses the dry land where the cornerstone of the monument will be.

Here will be "the hub of a farm worker movement that stretches for 1,000 miles," says *El Malcriado.* Where "the land is owned collectively by all the workers through their union," they will build a clinic for farm workers and a cooperative gas station ("We migrants live on wheels") and a union theater and office ("living proof of the strength and permanence of the farm workers").

Already a well has been dug. The water is "the best tasting water in Kern County," says *El Malcriado.* It has a sweet taste. The buildings rise slowly, for the campesinos are the builders. Two years later only the gas station was completed.

In the town the shopkeepers laugh at the Forty Acres—"Chavez's folly," they call it. "Come back in five years," says a druggist, "you will see the weeds and the city dump will be all that is left of that 'monument.' The Mexican has no stick-to-it-iveness."

To the improvised podium in the barren field that Easter Sunday comes Cesar Chavez. "The road has been long," he says. He is resplendent in an elegant Filipino shirt of white organdy embroidered with white flowers. The shirt is a "symbol of solidarity," for love and brotherhood are the strength of the weak. "The light of truth is the most powerful weapon," he says. "And we have it."

Evening comes and the dancing. The campesinos put on the elaborate costumes that the women have sewn by hand. There are folk dances of Mexico, the Southwest, the Philippines, and Israel. Later the dance floor is cleared of formalities and a mariachi band and a rock'n' roll combo compete loudly into the night.

In June of the year 1967 a wedding ceremony is held on the Forty Acres. Agustín Lira, twenty-two, a farm worker from Coahuila, Mexico, and one of the leading performers of El Teatro Campesino, is married to Kerry Ohta, twenty, who left San Francisco to become a teacher of art to migrant children in the Child Care Center of the union.

The wedding is performed by the Reverend James Drake of the Migrant Ministry. It is the "first activity on the new land of the union," says *El Malcriado.*

"Many people are married in a church. But I wanted to be married on this land which symbolizes the struggle of the farm workers," the young bridegroom, Agustín Lira says. "That is my church."

XXII The Coyote Talks

"When I see my father I kiss his hand. If my father walked into this vineyard now I would kiss his hand.

"I am almost forty and I don't smoke or drink before my father. My father is sixty-four and his father died just three years ago, and he never smoked or drank before his father. When I was a young man my father said to me, 'I know you smoke and drink, but don't ever let me see it.' And I never did. That's the way we were brought up. That's our family custom."

Corrilio Macias is a labor contractor who hires scabs to work in the struck fields. He is a man of unusual dignity. He is rough, but there is an unspoken formality about him. The beads of sweat blister on his forehead in the sun of the San Joaquin Valley, but he maintains his poise. In the dust and the sweaty heat, as he squats under the leaves of the vines in the vineyards of Guimarra, where he is a harvesting foreman for the company, there is a dignity even in his discomfort. The sun does not bother him.

"I have lived all my life in the sun," he says casually. "When I was fourteen I went to work in the fields."

He squats under the vines. I squat beside him saying little. At first there is an uneasy apprehension between us.

The *huelga* is all around. On the road the pickets and the police face each other. In the fields the pickers who are harvesting the grapes, in spite of the strike, are stooping low so that they cannot be seen from the road. The strikers are yelling curses at them.

Just that morning the strike against the Guimarra Vineyards was begun by Chavez's UFWOC. There is tension in the scorching sun.

I had walked up the row of vines to talk to the field workers, whom the grape strikers call *esquiroles.* On the dirt road there was a bus of a labor contractor who brought the *esquiroles* to work. I wished to see this "other side" of the dispute. Some told me it was not wise. The tempers of both sides are heated when a strike begins.

"Hey! What do you want?" someone yells.

In a bright, white El Camino ranchwagon, the company foreman, Macias, roars up to where I am walking. He screeches to a halt in a cloud of dust, inches from my shoes.

"Who are you?" he demands.

"Oh," he says, when I tell him why I have come. "I will tell you all about the grapes." He gets out of his El Camino and walks down the row and squats under the vines. "Come," he says. And I squat beside him. That was three hours ago.

"My name is Corrilio Macias. I am the field foreman for Guimarra in charge of the harvest crews," he begins.

"How is the harvest?" I say.

"Look at the grapes. It's been a bad summer. The spring was late. The last month we have the heat. Now we have the strike. The grapes have water berries from the heat. You see the little blisters on the bottom of the grapes? In the sun they break open and the grapes shrink up on the vines. If we do not get them picked they will be nothing."

Macias curses. "These grapes are ready. And these people come and strike on you. I think that's dirty."

He has a hard face. In the fields the skin becomes tanned and tough. Not like leather, that old shoe of cowboy writers, but like an impervious mask. Macias has the face of a determined man who has had the strength to survive the life he has lived and is proud of it.

"I'm from Texas," he says. "We are tough people. We have come a long way."

"There were eight in my family. I have four brothers. My father drove a truck in Texas for twenty-five dollars a week. Those were bad years. So I quit school and went to work in the fields in west Texas. My father gave me a beating for quitting school. I still remember that beating. Now I am sorry I did it. But then a Mexican boy didn't have a chance at anything. Especially in Texas.

"We heard the rumors about California. So we came. In my uncle's truck, all of us, because we didn't own a car. We went to work in the fields and we made seventy-five dollars in one day. We never had so much money before. The days weren't long enough for us. We were hungry. We picked grapes. We were dizzy."

Under the vines where we squat he opens palms and the grapes fall into them. He cups a bunch of grapes tenderly in his large hands. These are Thompson table grapes, ripe and heavy, and they fill his hands and spill over.

"Bacchus Macias," I say.

"You have to baby grapes," he says, ignoring my words, "like a little baby."

On a day in August such as this the temperature in the fields climbs to 120 degrees. Even higher. The indolent heat hovers over us like the buzzing of hornets. Sweaty, the *huelguistas* sit in the shade of their cars in the heat. It is late in the afternoon and the sun has exhausted them; the signs and flags of the *huelga* sag in their hands. The police look bored.

"Brothers!" a voice drifts over the fields. "It is shameful to scab, O brothers!"

Macias scowls. "The fools!" he blurts out. "Your strike frightens me you think? I am not a 'dumb Mexican' because I work in the fields. Maybe I like my work. Maybe I like to grow grapes."

The *huelga* does not really interest him. It is an annoyance, like the bugs that buzz under the vines. It is the grapes that interest him. The grapes, the sun, the earth, the harvesting—these are the things he lives for.

"Coyote!" is what the campesinos say of a man like Corrilio Macias. He is hated, yes, but why? "The coyote is a dirty animal," he says. He would rather be feared.

Not that they fear him—he is too familial to the farm workers to be feared; he is just despised. He is a labor contractor who escorts the strikebreakers through the *huelguistas'* cry of "Judas!" By the laws of California he is licensed as an "employer" to hire farm workers for the farmer. In time of strike that means he has to be a strikebreaker or lose his job. So they yell at him, "Coyote!" The word infuriates him.

"I am my own boss," Macias says. "Why must they call me that?" He denies he is anybody's lackey. But it is a necessary myth. A man has his pride.

The big grower doesn't know his field hands—"perhaps 2 or 3 per cent," says Cesar Chavez. He depends on the labor contractor, who hires 98 per cent of the work force. He pays the labor contractor to pay the campesinos. And he can keep his hands clean.

Chavez says, "The labor contractor, being he was a worker once upon a time, does know the work force. He is a recruiter, he is a supervisor on the job, he provides the transportation, he does the bookkeeping and so forth." He may be a usurer, as well, godfather of infants born in the camps, lay church leader, and procurer of girls for the single men.

It is a demanding job. "Like being a pimp," one labor contractor in Delano whispers to me, so softly that he cannot hear his description of himself. Another, Rodolfo Arrero, explains his ultimate powerlessness to the Senate Subcommittee on Migratory Labor. "I can only pay them [the farm workers] according to what the grower pays me."

An old-time union organizer and scholar, Dr. Ernesto Galarza, who worked futilely in the fields in the early 1950's, has called the labor contractor "a *padrón* of the classic type." That is, a type of menial tax collector. He was a lackey with the frightening power of hunger or wages in his hands. He was as humble as he was venal, for he depended wholly on the good graces of his employer, the farmer. And he was easily replaced. He went to the farmer with hat in hand in the past.

"My father always told me, 'If you are wrong and the boss is right, hang your head and admit you are wrong,'" Macias says. "But my father told me, 'If you are right and the boss is wrong, say nothing. Walk away. Just walk away. If you say something he will have it in for you. He will not forgive you for being right.'"

"Isn't that hard for you?" I ask.

"You learn to do things that are hard," he says uncertainly. "If you have to."

Now that has changed. The contractor has become essential. He has become a *patrón*, or at least a *patroncito*—a little *patrón*.

"What's happening in Delano on this strike," Cesar Chavez says, is that "the labor contractor becomes a professional strikebreaker." There are "now more labor contractors than there were when the strike started."

Thus the curse *"coyote."* He is a shrewd but mean little animal; a predatory scavenger who, when he kills, kills sheep.

" 'You hate Mexicans!' the pickets yell at me." Macias shakes his head in dismay.

" 'Hey, slavedriver!' they yell. 'What do you care about that bastard, your boss? He's making piles of money, isn't he? You hate Mexicans, your own people, if you are on his side!' " The frown on his face grows deeper. He is insulted merely by echoing the words that obviously hurt his pride. "It's not true," Macias says. "I do my job. That's what I get paid to do. If they don't want to work, I don't condemn them. It's their right. It's a free country. I am not forced to work for my boss. If I don't like it I will quit. No one can force me to do anything.

"Every man has his own right," Macias says. "I have my right."

He is a man of belligerent pride. When he talks about his work he becomes fiercely defensive. " 'You rob people,' they tell me," he says with inner anger. "They know nothing about what I go through. They don't know how rough it is for a poor Mexican to go into business. They don't know the money I owe the bank for those trucks I use in contracting. They know nothing! Nothing!"

The dignity he has earned by his years of work, he feels, is unjustly befouled by the epithets of the *huelguistas*. But it is more than that. He feels not only that the pickets insult his dignity, but that they insult their own as well.

"I tell them, don't curse people. Don't insult people," he says. "You want to strike. God bless you. You want to picket? God bless you. It's a free country. But don't call me names because I do my work."

Macias is a formal man. He believes that proper behavior is not a mere formality; it is a necessity for self-respect.

"I believe in self-respect," he says.

He is neatly dressed in work clothes that are washed and ironed. The clothes are faded by the sun, but he wears them the way a man does who has worn rags most of his life and has the money at last to buy a new suit. It is the attitude of a man who is fastidious about his old shoes because he went barefoot in his youth.

In the barrios of the farm towns and cities, the used-clothing stores are symbols of poverty. "USADA ROPA" signs are the surest guideposts, more than street signs that point the way to "the Mexican section of town." The urban peasants have clothed themselves for generations with the "used, secondhand, hand-me-downs" of the middle-class wardrobes of the Anglos.

The family that escapes from the fields and barrios immediately buys new clothes. In this they are not simply being ostentatious, they exaggerate the latest styles, wear the finest clothes they can afford, outdo the Anglo fashions they imitate. The newer the fabrics, the more obvious it is that they are far from the "USADA ROPA" stores. Even the campesinos coming to the cities indulge in this disguise.

Old clothes are the stigma of the poor man. And dirty clothes are the sign of any man who works in the earth.

"When I was a boy in Texas, they called me 'the dirty Mexican,'" says Macias. "I think we shouldn't let anyone call us that. I don't care if you have a patch on your pants, as long as it is clean. So they can't call us dirty."

The cake of soap may be a status symbol, if your parents and grandparents lived in homes without running water. Cleanliness may be a fetish. The small-town Babbitts of a few generations ago felt the same way about bathroom plumbing. It was the symbol of progress. Macias believes it is a moral matter that transcends politics. He says of the pilgrimage of the farm workers through the valley, "The march of the campesinos was all right. If they march to Sacramento to the Governor, God bless them! I'm for it. But I ask you something. Why did they have to wear dirty pants? Why didn't they wear their best suits?

"I think they kept their clean clothes, their best suits, in the trucks and dressed to fool everyone about how poor they were. Like in that union newspaper, *El Malcriado*, there was a picture of a little girl. Her face filthy, her dress torn, her legs dirty. Poor kid! That picture was a disgrace to La Raza. I don't care how poor you are, there is always soap and water.

"The mother of that little girl ought to be ashamed of herself," Macias says. He sadly nods his head.

His anguish for the girl and her mother is genuine. In his memory he knows the shame he once felt as the son of migrants, wearing torn shoes and old clothes. The photograph of a poor girl fills him with embarrassment, shame, anger.

"I say we should not beg the Anglo for anything," says a teacher in Delano. Her parents had been farm workers. "That is what these Chavez people do with their propaganda about the poor. That begging kills the pride of our people."

"We should take care of our own. Not by protests, by the Church," says a shopkeeper. "Most of all we should not let everyone see our worst people. We should show them our best."

The teachers and the shopkeepers resent the publicity given to the protests of the poor, as though it is a personal affront. It is as if they were being accused of callousness, of failure to care for their own people. *Patróns* may be old-fashioned in the barrios of the cities, but in the small towns the middle class has inherited the tradition of the *patrón*, if not the capacity to be as benevolent. And this angers them. They say: If we keep our troubles within the family, within La Raza, everything will be taken care of, and we will not have to wash our dirty linen in public to shame. They say this so often it is a litany.

Outsiders do not know "our ways," they say. It is the outsiders who cause all the trouble among the poor.

"I tell them, you are being used by outsiders," Macias says of the farm workers. "My people don't want to strike. They don't want a union. They are infiltrated with instigators in the fields. I say that's dirty. It's just these outsiders."

In the tones of a father the "Coyote" talks of "my men," "my boys," "my people." A generation ago he would have talked of "my children." He is offended at the thought that he does not speak for them.

"My men would come to me and say, 'We aren't treated right. We want two dollars an hour.' 'Boys,' I would say, 'I can't pay it.' If they walked off I would say, 'God bless them,' " Macias says. "But my people won't strike. They know I treat them right. They know I am like a father to them when they need help.

"Unions are all right," he says. "I'm not against unions. I belong to a union myself. In the winter I worked in the cotton compressors and I was a steward. But in this business the unions will ruin the small farmer. They will ruin the contractor. And what happens when the grape-picking machine is perfected? Eventually they will perfect it. Will the machine strike? It will be the grape picker who will be out of a job.

"The outsiders do not know the grapes," he says. "You have to know the grapes."

"What about Chavez?" I ask.

"He is being used by outsiders," Macias says, "by others."

In the town there are those who are more openly hostile to the union. "Local ministers have joined with the local chapters of the Community Service Organization (CSO), Latin American Citizens Associations (LACA), the Sociedad Progresita Mexicana, and other groups to fight [the] vicious and undeserved attack by [the] National Farm Workers Association," says the mayor of Delano, Dr. Clifford E. Loader. Most of these are middle-class groups of La Raza—the teachers, shopkeepers, and labor contractors. The Delano CSO has disbanded rather than obey the suggestion from its state office that it support the farm workers.

"Mothers Against Chavez" is formed to protest against the protesters. It is a women's club that visits the Governor to demand that tranquillity be restored to Main Street and the "Trotskyite flag" of the farm workers be replaced by more patriotic banners. They hold cake sales, too.

In the summer of 1968 the "Mothers Against Chavez" is replaced by the "Men Against Chavez." The leader of the new group, Al Ramirez, holds a meeting in Delano, where he denounces Chavez for engineering a "Communist plot" whereby the campesinos in the vineyards would lose their jobs to "happy hippies, beatniks, and negroids." Ramirez shouts, "Chavez is through. Chavez will be dead."

The tension in the small town is erupting with fearful and violent reactions. Nerves are becoming frayed.

Like Macias the respectable citizens of the valley are distressed by the *huelga*. The years of self-sacrificing hard work and the precarious hold they have on the edge of the small-town middle class are threatened by these "dirty, lazy farm workers" and the "outside agitators."

In opposition to the union the employers and shopkeepers organize the Kern-Tulare County Independent Farm Workers. The president, Bert Corona, is a labor contractor, and the secretary, Dorothy Christine, owns a small business in downtown Delano. When asked by the late Senator Kennedy, in the Senate's migratory labor hearings, of 1966, whether their group is a "labor organization," the secretary replies, "No, it's not. It's an organization formed of what we feel is a true worker. . . ." Rudy Arrero, an employer of nonstriking grape pickers and one of the founders of the Independent Farm Workers, tells the Senator, "I don't think we need a union."

The Independent Farm Workers does not last long. After its demise the employers form the Agricultural Workers Freedom to Work Association, the AWFWA. In a letter to California's Secretary of Labor, on February 22, 1969, the new group's president, Gilbert Rubio, admits that the AWFWA "was an outgrowth of an untitled group led by the growers," whose aim is to "enlist the aid of all growers and their foremen in enrolling workers into AWFWA without cost. . . ." The vineyard owners of Delano—Jack Pandol, John Guimarra, Jr., and others—are the behind-the-scenes instigators and financiers of the "Freedom to Work" efforts.

José Mendoza, a former poverty worker fired by the OEO, a showman and radio announcer, is hired as secretary of the new group. His flamboyant way of appearing on picket lines, dressed in an embroidered sash, wearing a straw hat bedecked with American and Mexican flags, while he burned Russian flags, wins him mass-media publicity. "A clown," the union newspaper dubs him, but he soon is sent on a speaking tour by the National Right to Work Committee. In Washington, D.C., the "representative of the farm workers" is awarded a plaque for his devotion to "Freedom to Work" by Senator Everett Dirksen.

The growers are understandably enthusiastic about their new group. Mendoza is an honored guest at the convention of the American Farm Bureau Federation, in Kansas City, where he assures the farmers that "98 per cent" of the campesinos are opposed to Chavez's union. "Seriously disturbed" by the grape strike and the union's boycott of California grapes, the Farm Bureau "strengthened its already hard stand," writes the *New York Times.* Charles Shuman, the Farm Bureau president, warns that if grapes could be boycotted today, "it can be Kansas City beef tomorrow." The farmers vote to "oppose efforts to force workers to join a union" in support of the Freedom to Work campaign.

"We have got to meet pressure with pressure, force with force," the Farm Bureau president declares.

In the valley there is an eruption of violence. The labor contractors begin to "counter picket and try to drown out UFWOC pickets wherever they picketed a grower," Rubio wrote to the state official, and to "try to get information on all UFWOC planned activities to take action to halt, or disrupt, them." One such fracas results in the arrest of Rubio himself, on the charge of waving a rifle at the grape strikers "in a threatening manner." The union accuses the Freedom to Work group of deliberately provoking violence.

Macias is indignant. He becomes a spokesman for the AWFWA. In a speech to a class in "Personnel Management" at Fresno State College, he angrily tells the students, "I'm sick and tired of Chavez knocking down Mexicans. I cannot stand still and let Chavez ruin the Mexican people. I'll fight him until there is no place to send him back to except China, because they won't accept him in Mexico."

The Delano police captain, Al Espinosa, who moonlights as a labor contractor, is just as furious at Chavez. He tells John Gregory Dunne, the chronicler of the grape strike, in his book *Delano:* "I abhor these SNCC Anglos coming in here to teach the Mexicans how to be civilized and non-violent. My people are non-violent by nature and don't need Anglos to teach us non-violence. And I don't point my finger at the Anglos. I point my finger at Cesar Chavez. He's selling his people short. If he had worked with the leaders of the Mexican American community, he probably would have forged a compromise. The scars will never heal. After this thing is over with the Mexican, American leaders are going to retaliate against these militants," he predicts. "They're not going to forget someone [has] called them Judas. . . . They've got education and breeding and they're going to get back."

In the vineyard where he squats, fondling a bunch of grapes with his fingers, Macias weighs his own anger. He is troubled by the tempers that have torn apart the quiet town. All his life he has worked for a better way of living for his family, a sense of decency, a little security. He has them now. These angers threaten everything he owns.

"Why these hatreds?" he broods. He is the man in the middle. "Every man has his own right," he says.

Corrilio Macias plucks a grape. He plucks two and offers one to me. The juice is cool and sweet in the blistering sun. Under the vines it is shadowed and pleasant. The wind is rising and the evening sun is setting. The grape pickers have gone home in the buses and trucks of the labor contractors, escorted by the motorcycle police. On the road the *huelguistas* have gone, too, and it is quiet. The leaves of the vines flutter in the evening wind.

"Who knows?" Macias says. "I can only say what I see, what I feel. That I know is so. Chavez, maybe he believes what he says. He is an honest man, I think. Maybe I'm right, maybe Chavez is right. Who knows?"

XXIII The Cross of Cesar Chavez

In the bar the young man is drinking beer. He has been in the fields, on the picket lines, all morning, and he sweats with the bodily memory and fear, even now in the cool bar. Outside the sun is an inferno. "Here," he says, "it is peace." The People's Bar on the *huelga* side of town is a *huelguistas'* hangout. It is a poor man's sanctuary. But the young man is troubled. He is silent for a moment. "You know Cesar?" he asks timidly.

"A little."

"You will do me a favor?"

"Maybe."

"My father had a heart attack," the young man says. "I have to go home for a few days. I do not want to leave the strike, but I have to. Will you tell Cesar that for me? Tell Cesar I am sorry."

"You see him every day," I say to him. "Why don't you tell him yourself?"

"He is so tired," the young man says, with a deference I hear so often. "I do not want to take his time with my troubles."

So I promise to do as he asks. We drink our beers and shake hands and go our separate ways. Later when I tell Cesar Chavez what the young man has said of his father's heart attack, of his apology, he listens but says nothing.

"A leader who does not know how to listen does not know how to lead," he says.

Cesar Chavez has the eyes of the statue of a saint. His eyes are so large and full they look hollow. "We talk with our eyes," Eduardo Pérez has said. It is not true of everyone, but it is true of Chavez.

His eyes may become the eyes of a peon's with which he looks innocently at the visiting dignitaries and newsmen who swarm about his office. In an instant these eyes may turn to charcoal, fiery, then suddenly cold as stones when there is a crisis in the strike. He has special eyes for the making of decisions.

"No, I am not fiery," he insists. "I am not a speaker. I am a listener."

In the streets people come up to him; they come to his office and his home; they talk to him at meetings and probably in his dreams. Chavez does not turn them away, or turn a deaf ear to what they have to say. He listens because he believes it is they who lead him. It is his theory of leadership.

"People know what they want. And what they don't want," he says. "It's a case of staying with them and keeping your ears open and your eyes open.

"And they tell you! They don't tell you in so many words, but they tell you with their actions. They will not so much spell it out for you. They never have a clear way of doing that. They never write it down for you. They never hold your hand. It's never tangible, but if you listen to it, it comes.

"Once you begin to 'lead' the people, to force them, then you begin to make mistakes," he says. "Once you begin to feel you are really the 'leader,' then you begin to stop being a real leader. Then a reverse process starts. The 'leader' has less and less time for the people. He depends more on himself, He begins to play hunches, to play the long shots. He loses his touch with the people.

"It happens to most leaders. . . .

"Everything!" he says, with sudden force, "Everything in *huelga* of any importance has come from the farm workers. It is a gathering of bits and pieces of what the people want. I say, Everything! Every important decision, every important program in the strike has come from the people. It hasn't come in a resolution. It hasn't come in a well-documented report. But it comes the way the people express themselves. It comes sort of in *the way they make it appear.*"

He smiles at that, knowing his thought is so clear it is cryptic. Chavez has a casual way of talking that makes his thoughts appear offhand when he is being most intense. The listener may fool himself.

"Our function is to put it all together. We get our decision from the people. It comes so easily that if you don't watch out, you begin to think that you are the one, that you are the genius, that you are making all those wonderful ideas."

I ask him, "Why Cesar Chavez and why Delano? Aren't *you* making history?"

He laughs self-consciously. "It is dangerous to make statements like that. No, I think it is like many historical events; you have to be at the right place at the right moment. To the outside world we are making history. To us it is just a hard struggle. The *huelga* is the result of a lot of effort, frustration, tears, bloodshed, and sweat no one sees."

"But *you* are leading it," I say.

"Like a composer working night and day," he says. "If there is no orchestra, there is no music. No one hears it."

He is not humble. The romantic idea of the humble campesino fits him even less than most men. Rather, he voices the concept of innate, communal democracy of the barrio, and the age-old suspicions that the farm worker has of the leader—the *gobierno*—even if he is that leader.

Cesar Chavez was born to farm work. He grew to boyhood on the poor farm of his father, who clung to a few acres of desert in Yuma, Arizona. When the boy was ten, his father lost his land. In that inferno—known as "the Sahara of the United States"—farming was dubious in the best of times, but in the Depression it was hopeless. The Chavez family became migrants. Wandering from town to town, they slept in their old jalopy, in tents, in deserted migrant camps. His father, with the obstinacy and pride of a small farmer, was not fitted for life on the road. The boy remembers fishing in irrigation ditches and picking weeds, mustard greens—"otherwise we would have starved." He vaguely remembers attending thirty or more schools by the eighth grade, when he had to drop out to work in the fields.

Estrada is his middle name: Cesar Estrada Chavez. In Spanish the word means a paved road, a highway or turnpike. Why did his parents give him so strange and prophetic a name?

In the worst of barrios in San Jose—the one they call Sal Si Puedes: Get Out if You Can—the family settled. The legend is that it was here that Fred Ross, an organizer for the Community Service Organization (CSO), "discovered" Cesar Chavez and hired him. The truth is more complex. Chavez had been a defiant youth, always attracting attention. One day when he was a boy he had refused to sit in the segregated Mexican section of a movie theater and was thrown into the street. The town was Delano. It was the year of 1943. He was seventeen.

His father had taught him years earlier the ways of protest and organization. The elder Chavez had become a union activist in 1939. "One of the old CIO unions began organizing workers in the dried-fruit industry, so my father and my uncle became members. Sometimes the men would meet at our house, and I remember seeing their picket signs and hearing them talk. They had a strike and my father and uncle picketed at night. It made a deep impression on me," Chavez reminisced in Eugene Nelson's book, *Huelga:* ". . . from that time on my father joined every agricultural union that came along. Often he was the first one to join, and when I was nineteen, I joined the National Agricultural Workers' Union."

The strikes were all lost. The unions were defeated. Chavez learned the hard way how not to organize.

Catholicism offered a faith and a permanence in those gloomy days. Young Chavez met Father Donald McDonnell, a scholarly priest who spoke seven languages, who had a passion for labor history and a compassion for the farm workers. Night after night they discussed the doctrines of social justice and the Encyclicals of the Popes. "I began going to the bracero camps with him to help with Mass; to the city jail with him to talk to the prisoners—anything to be with him so that he could tell me more about the farm labor movement," Chavez says. It was Father McDonnell who introduced the young man to Fred Ross of the CSO.

"I was working in the fields when CSO came to San Jose," Chavez says. "I was in the orchards, apricots and peaches."

For ten years after that, Chavez was a community organizer up and down California. He registered voters, cajoled mayors, dealt with health laws, organized rent strikes, handled welfare problems, dealt with death and taxes. "I was learning a lot of things," he says. He became director of the National CSO. But he was restless to go back to the fields, to organize a union of farm workers.

Unhappy with the middle-class methods of the CSO, he was ill at ease. It was "unheard of" that they meet in a cheap hall, he says: "It had to [be] the best motel in town, very expensive, and it cut off all the farm workers who couldn't afford to be there. The reason given was, 'We have to build prestige.' The politicians have to know who we are; we can't take them to a dump. I was naïve enough in the beginning to buy that. So we ended up just with farm workers who had gone to school or weren't farm workers any more.

"The officers of CSO were semiprofessionals or professionals," he says. "It became a problem communicating with the workers."

It was a conflict of styles of life, goals, attitudes, and even language, that has since divided the civil rights movement. Chavez says, "In most cases, the leadership had more to lose than the workers. They'd say, 'We should fight, but we should be moderate.' They felt that farm workers were outside the jurisdiction of the CSO. It was a 'labor' problem." He was thought to be too militant, he feels. His colleagues in the CSO do not agree with his version of history. Yet their side of the story complements his half of the conflict that has been so often repeated.

Mrs. Ursula Rios Gutierrez, a lady of distinguished gray hair and grace, worked with Cesar for three years in the National Office of the CSO. But she remembers his leaving differently. "He left for political reasons. He says we were not interested in farm workers. It's not true! One of our wealthy members offered $50,000 for Cesar to organize his farm workers.

"I was there when he came in and laid his keys on the desk and said, 'You probably read my letter of resignation. I am leaving. Here are the keys.' And I said, 'Yes, I know.' That was that.

"Like a boy," she says, hurt. "He walked out! We were good friends. His wife Helen and his children, I knew them like family." A motherly woman, she is still upset by what she feels is Chavez's lack of gratitude.

His union's tactics upset her even more. She is a disapproving mother who is not ashamed to criticize in public what others hint at in private.

"What happened to Cesar? I don't know," says Mrs. Gutierrez. "I have a lot of respect for Cesar. He is doing good work. But I don't understand Cesar.

"Cesar has the image of a Mexican peasant. He has been built up that way in the newspapers. The union has built him up that way too, as one of the campesinos. If he ever betrays that image he is finished. Cesar knows that. That is what holds him.

"On the pilgrimage to Sacramento I saw it. The way they look at him. When they began shouting 'Viva Cesar!' that was too much. As though he was a saint, a god. He is not a saint, a god."

In "The Corrido of Cesar Chavez," the farm workers sang on the pilgrimage:

> The seventeenth of March,
> First Thursday morning of Lent,
> Cesar walked from Delano,
> Taking with him his faith.
>
> When we arrive in Fresno,
> All the people shout:
> Long live Cesar Chavez,
> And all who follow him.
>
> Now we reach Stockton.
> The mariachis sing to us:
> Long live Cesar Chavez,
> And the Virgin who guides him.

Where he came from and why does not seem to interest the farm workers. He came to them, giving up all he possessed, sacrificing everything. That is all they need to know.

> Listen Señor Cesar Chavez,
> Your name is honored;
> On your breast you wear
> The Virgin of Guadalupe.

The growers, who in the beginning talked of Chavez as an "outsider" with no roots in the vineyards, now recognize him as an adversary whose strength they have to respect. "Chavez's secret is that he has the utter loyalty of the Mexican workers," one grower says. "His appeal is primarily racial--and to some extent religious. They're not a trade union. They're a racial and religious organization."

"Our biggest mistake was to think Chavez was just another 'dumb Mex,' " another grower says.

"He is no saint, he is a devil," a Presbyterian churchman tells me.

In the fields of the San Joaquin Valley, they talk of Chavez as if he were a legend, the hero of a myth. A young farm worker seriously says to me, "You know, they offered Cesar one million dollars to sell us out. He told them where to go!" The tale of the bribe of betrayal is told in a dozen versions. In every tale the money varies—from $20,000 up to $2 million. And in every tale Cesar says no to betrayal. He is faithful to those who have faith. His independence is legendary. When he has made up his mind, not even the White House can change his mind. It has tried.

When, after long months of procrastination, the White House Conference on Mexican Americans was abandoned in the fall of 1967 as potentially too explosive, the high-level Cabinet hearings were scheduled instead in El Paso, Texas, and an invitation was sent to Chavez. He was to be an honored guest. The President was to attend, as was the Vice President, and several Cabinet members, and the invitation bore the prestige and pressure of the highest officials in the nation. He would surely come to be honored.

Chavez said no. In silent protest at the barring of grassroots groups and militant leaders, such as Reies Tijerina, he stayed in Delano.

"Jesus was a troublemaker," he said to a friend. "Would they invite him?"

In the privacy of his office, Chavez later had reflective thoughts of his own. "What good do all these conferences do? Do they ever invite the farm workers in the field to attend? No! It's always the same people conferring with the same people. Everyone agrees: Let's unite. Everyone then speaks from his own narrow point of view, and everyone disagrees, and everyone goes home with the point of view they came with. Where is the unity? I think unity comes when people work together. It comes with hard work.

"So conferences don't solve the problems," Chavez says. He grins. "Maybe that's the point. If the conferences solved the problems, there would be no need to hold any more conferences. Then what would the 'experts' do?"

His sardonic words are reminiscent of his testimony before the Senate Subcommittee on Migratory Labor. Chavez began with the words: "This is a '*huelga*' button. Senator Williams, Senator Murphy, Congressman Hagen, we are meeting once again to discuss the problems of the farm worker and what might be done to correct these problems. Such meetings have been called for decades, and unfortunately, things have not changed very much in spite of them."

His patience with the problems of farm workers is one of his best-known traits. It is genuine. But Chavez has little patience with officious conferences and formal interviews. Once he led his *huelguistas* out of a meeting of a candidate he supported because he felt the officials were not "our kind of people."

Into his bare office—with its posters of Gandhi and Zapata, watched over by a statue of the Virgin of Guadalupe, where Chavez sits behind a modest, worn, old wooden desk—a delegation of dignitaries came not long ago. They were from one of the country's most influential and wealthiest foundations. Men of prominence, their mission to Delano was to invite him to serve on the Board of Directors of one of their multi-million-dollar projects. Chavez politely rejected the honor and whatever went with it.

"It's to help La Raza," the foundation men said.

"La Raza? Why be racist?" Chavez remembers telling his visitors. He smiles. "They were embarrassed. I told them, 'Our union has everyone in it—Mexicans, Filipinos, blacks, whites, Japanese, Chinese. Our belief is to help everyone, not just one race. Humanity is our belief.' " He laughs. "Their faces fell."

He retells the incident with a puckish delight, for within his gentle manner there is the muted and hidden anger of the boy on the road, in the migrant camps, in ragged clothes, hungry and unschooled and abused. It infuriates him, though he usually manages to hide his emotions, when he thinks the farm workers are being patronized. He resents the attitude of superiority of those who he feels offer pity, even in the form of desperately needed cash and good works.

But he subdues his wrath. He twits those who patronize him by patronizing them.

His disenchantment with the student activists is influenced by this feeling. In the beginning of the *huelga* the campus rebels and civil rights groups were welcomed in Delano; they were stalwarts on the picket lines and on the volunteer staff. When the union voted to join the AFL–CIO, many of the summer radicals withdrew, accusing Chavez of "selling out to the labor establishment," as one said.

"He used to call anyone who worked with politicians a 'political prostitute,' " says an old friend and former coworker. "I remember when he refused to go to a banquet honoring our Congressman. Now he goes to his own banquets. I can understand that. These things have to be done. What I don't understand is how *he* can do these things he never believed in."

Chavez says, "We were as pained as they were. We were pained that the students and others who felt this way had such little faith in the people. Every time they would bring up the merger, we would say, 'We don't think it's going to be that way,' or, 'It is the workers' choice.' But we very seldom told them what we felt. I personally felt pained to see how little trust they had in the people.

"I remember that some of the fellows that helped us in the beginning had a very strange picture of poor people," he says. "Like all farm workers were saints, you know."

The "idolizing of the poor" has the same effect as pitying them, Chavez says. "You can't help people if you feel sorry for them." He is realistic. "This kind of feeling doesn't carry you. After a little while it becomes old and there is no real basis for doing things that you're doing. There's got to be more than that."

In his mind he is still a farm worker. He sees and feels the world with the eyes of the campesino; whether it is in his gut or it is something nourished by a skillful organizer, he alone knows.

"For many years I was a farm worker, a migratory worker, and well, personally—and I'm being very frank—maybe it's just a matter of trying to even the score, you know," Chavez has said of his severe judgment of others and himself.

He has a hardness. It surprises some that this modest, soft-spoken, and mild-mannered man carries hatreds within him that are neither visible nor expected. Once, in a talk to the black militants of California SNCC, he sought to explain why he had become an organizer. He said offhandedly, "Of course, I had a lot of hatred for the cops." That casual remark, so rare in the reticent and careful words of Chavez, reveals his bitterness.

Chavez is an enigma to many. He is a different man to different people. "Who is Cesar?" says a union organizer who has been with him since the beginning of *huelga.* "He is so friendly and informal that everyone thinks they know him intimately. But no one knows him."

He is thought of as a man who grasps the infinite and remembers it in infinitesimal detail—the perfect organizer. Petty details are vital to Chavez; the most insignificant act and ordinary member is important. "When you come from the bottom up," he says, "you have to be very practical and very patient."

"From him we have learned," Lauro García, Jr., the village organizer of Guadalupe, Arizona, explains, "not only determination, dedication, and hard work, but unrelenting patience."

The patience is integral to his nature, to the farm workers. Chavez once said that he expected the *huelga* to "last for five years"; what urban union leader would calmly talk or think of striking for five years, on strike pay of $5 a week? Yet, when he is asked how long he thinks it will take to unionize the farm workers, Chavez says, "All my life."

Senator Murphy: How long have you been in this activity?
Chavez: Well, I have been a farm worker all my life.

At times, though, he becomes impatient with himself. He has that mundane dream of a public man: "Even when our work succeeds, I don't want to hang on forever," he tells Eugene Nelson. "What I would really like is to be alone somewhere—in Mexico, or in the mountains—and have time to read all the classics that there are in English and Spanish."

He is alone often. In the midst of a noisy meeting with everyone agitated and yelling, he seems quietly withdrawn, aloof, within himself.

The organizer is "an outsider," Chavez says. "If an organizer comes looking for appreciation, he might just as well stay home. He's not going to get any, especially out of a group that's never been organized or had any power before." He has to be willing to be lonely, to be nourished by his own beliefs. He came to Delano alone with his family. No organization supported him. Rarely does he ask a follower to do something he has not done, or does not do himself—whether it is working in the fields to organize, being jailed, or living on the $5 a week strike pay. He enacts his beliefs with his body.

His family lives in conspicuous poverty. A wife and eight children share a small, two-bedroom frame house in the barrio of Delano. In the era of affluent unionism, such a way of life is an anomaly for a union leader. But it is not martyrdom. The humility of his material goods is an aspect of his philosophy. He believes, as Gandhi did, that the leader of the poor has to live as the poor do, not for their sake, but for his own; the sanctity of his soul and peace of mind demand it of him.

"We will never have peace in the world until we have peace in ourselves," Chavez says. "How can we even begin to talk of peace in the world when we are not at peace with ourselves?" In this sense nonviolence is not a political tactic. Chavez talks of it as an act of purification of man. "It's what Gandhi was saying all those years. It's the most difficult thing."

Sacrifice is a principle. The poor cannot afford to suffer it, so the leader must suffer it for them.

"The poor have the biggest stake in peace," he says. "But they are the ones who can do the least because they are so busy scratching out a living to get something to eat."

I say to him one day, "If you do not win this strike soon you will have a long beard and I will be long dead."

He smiles. "That is not right."

"Why not?"

"*You* will have the long beard," he says, "and *I* will be dead."

He is not talking of the threats to his life. That is routine. He has no bodyguards. He has been hospitalized too often to talk of his illnesses. In his knowledge of himself there is only this: how many burdens of other men can one man bear before the accumulated pain becomes unbearable?

Lent is the fiesta of sacrifice, when the *penitentes* of New Mexico suffer the anguish of Christ; when the religious go on their knees to the shrine of San Juan in Texas; when in the provinces of Mexico, there are men who bodily are nailed to makeshift crosses, beside the ferris wheels of village fairs.

The sacrifice of Cesar Chavez began during Lent, in the chill spring of 1968. It was tragic and portentous. He offered his body in a "Lenten Fast for Peace and Nonviolencc" that lasted for twenty-five days. He sacrificed one-fifth of his flesh, thirty-five pounds, to "the pain and suffering of the farm workers." Except for a few ounces of bouillon and a few mouthfuls of unsweetened grapefruit juice ordered by his doctor, for twenty-five days he had nothing but water. He grew so weak he could hardly talk or walk.

He fasted because self-sacrifice was "the ultimate act of manliness," Chavez said. He fasted because "my heart was filled with grief when I saw the pain" of his people in the fields. He fasted for nonviolence.

An altar was built in the garage of the union's cooperative gas station, on the Forty Acres. Hundreds of farm workers came from the fields to pray every day. The altar, on the back of a truck, became a shrine.

Chavez sat in the unheated, unfinished garage and prayed and shivered. The Holy Mass that was celebrated every day for his sacrificial act became the scene of a pilgrimage. Women brought candles and offerings. The men knelt in the dirt by the hundreds, coming from the barrios, the remote country crossroads, the migrant camps.

On the fourth day of his fast, the land-grant leader of New Mexico, Reies Tijerina, came to pray. Chavez and Tijerina embraced.

In a rally of farm workers—though he was becoming weak—Chavez appealed for funds for the defense of the fiery land-grant leader who had been arrested for kidnaping, murder, and insurrection. The poor campesinos contributed $500 and Chavez gave Tijerina a huge, red *huelga* flag, which Tijerina draped over his shoulders like a prayer shawl.

On the thirteenth day of his fast, Chavez, by now quite pale, was himself taken before Superior Court Justice Martin Baker to reply to charges of violation of court injunctions in the strike against Guimarra Vineyards. The growers had filed a complaint of twelve charges. Well over one thousand farm workers overflowed the courtroom in Bakersfield, its corridors, and the outside plaza. Judge Baker postponed the hearing, and Chavez returned to the altar in the garage.

On the twenty-fifth day, he broke his fast by breaking bread with the late Senator Robert Kennedy, who flew to Delano to be beside his friend.

Ten thousand farm workers and their families gathered before the altar in the cold March sun. Some say it was the largest meeting of farm workers in the history of the Southwest. Beneath the wooden cross that had been carried on the union's Pilgrimage to Sacramento, and the banner of the Virgin of Guadalupe, with rows of red flags of the *huelga* whirling in the wind, Robert Kennedy rose to say that by his sacrifice Cesar Chavez had told the world that "violence is no answer."

Three months later Robert Kennedy was dead. He had just celebrated his triumph in the presidential primary of California, where the votes of the campesinos and Chicanos had been the margin of victory. In his last words he had thanked Cesar Chavez.

"I have no taste for politics in my heart," Chavez told me after Kennedy's death. In his grief, he would say no more.

During his fast, Chavez had received a telegram: "I am deeply moved by your courage in fasting as your personal sacrifice for justice through non-violence. Your past and present commitment is eloquent testimony to the constructive power of non-violent action and the destructive impotence of violent reprisal. Your stand is a living example of the Gandhian tradition with its great force for social progress and its healing spiritual powers." The telegram was from the Reverend Martin Luther King. One month after he wrote these words, the Christian leader was assassinated. "Despite the tragic violence which took your husband," Chavez wrote to the Reverend King's widow, "there is much that is good about our nation." Now both King and Kennedy were dead. Who was to be next?

"Perhaps some of us will follow the path that Kennedy was made to follow," the Secretary of the Farm Workers Union, Antonio Orendain, declared in *El Malcriado,* "but we are ready for that journey, if it is necessary."

On the site of the fast of Cesar Chavez, they erected a huge cross made of telephone poles. The cross towered for thirty feet above the barren land, vines grew up on it and flowers were attached to it. Under this cross they held religious ceremonies, open air masses, and the sunrise service at Easter. Vandals tried twice to burn the cross to the ground. Its wood withstood the fires, and the charred symbol of nonviolence remained visible for miles.

The cross of Cesar Chavez was desecrated the week before the Fourth of July. It was cut by a power saw and fell in the dust and the weeds.

XXIV Viva La Cucaracha!

A cockroach runs across the floor of the theater, toward the stage. It is more than one inch long. The foot of an actor playfully kicks the bug away, onto its back. The cockroach frantically tries to regain its feet, legs struggling in the air, then rights itself. Once more it rushes toward the stage, circling the actor's foot. The dance of the actor and the cockroach is not ungraceful. In impulsive anger the actor crunches the bug beneath his foot. And the cruel dance of death ends.

"Murderer!" cries a fellow actor.

"Why did you do that?" says a young poet, Agustín Lira, who is sitting on the apron of the stage making a rag puppet of a wolf. "It didn't hurt you, did it?"

"It hurt," the first actor says.

"How?"

"Every time I kill a cockroach it hurts me more than if I kill a dog," the actor says cryptically.

On the wall over the door of the storefront theater there is a painting of a one-foot-high cockroach. Circling the magnificent golden bug on the sign are the words, "Organize La Raza." This is the makeshift marquee of the theater of the farmworkers—El Teatro Campesino—the farthest off-Broadway theater in the country. The cockroach is the theater's mascot, its star performer, and its faithful audience.

"Cockroaches!" another actor exclaims. "Whenever we go on tour we take them with us inside our trunks."

"A town of cockroaches," says Luis Miguel Valdez, the director of El Teatro and the Centro Cultural Campesino—the Farmworkers' Center of Culture. "*La cucaracha* is everywhere. Why? Because no one cares what happens in this place."

In the abandoned drugstore on the dusty main street of Del Rey, a town of migrants and fruit-packing sheds and Mexican bars, these obstinate actors have created a Centro Cultural Campesino.

A young man with a grandiose Pancho Villa mustache, Brechtian poet, union organizer, sometime college teacher, and sometime ancient dreamer, an alumnus of the San Francisco Mime Theatre and internationally known avant-garde director ("A tough act to follow," says the *Wall Street Journal*), Luis Miguel Valdez was in his earliest incarnation a wanderer in the vineyards of the San Joaquin Valley. He is at home in towns of La Cucaracha. He grew up in the fields of Delano, a child of campesinos. He picked grapes as soon as he was old enough. He heard the night wails in the migrant camps of those whose bone-bent hands were raked by the picking, the sonorous drunken songs of those who danced in the cantinas after work. These were his lessons. He learned them as a poet will.

"I can remember that Delano was a very different sort of town than it is now," he says. "There was a street several blocks long that had Mexican shops, a Mexican show, a Mexican dance hall. There were Mexican things for sale, Mexican candy, Mexican clothes, Mexican food. It was a place full of characters—Mexican characters. Little Mexico, they called it.

"And then!" the young man shuts his fist and jabs the air with sudden anger, or is it despair? He squints at his shattered memory. "Then! Six or seven years ago our whole section of town was ripped away. The freeway came through. They told us the freeway was urban renewal. It 'cleaned up' our part of town."

It was like that up and down the valley. The freeway "cut out the Mexican hearts of these towns." Little Mexicos were bulldozed to make way "for parking lots and Highway 99."

"There were twenty-two whorehouses on one street to solace the single men who worked in the fields. Well, 'they' couldn't accept those whorehouses. So the freeway came through like a surgical knife. Urban renewal?" he laughs. "For whom?"

"A lot of people were upset," he says. "They had taken away our towns, our personality. They had shoved us across the railroad tracks. We said, okay. We lived in our own way in our part of town. We developed our unique culture. Then they came across the railroad tracks with their lousy freeway and took that away from us, too. It's not surprising that this town exploded and became the heart of the *huelga.*"

"There is contempt for Mexican things in the valley," he says, but then, "This is a society largely hostile to our cultural values. There is no poetry about the United States. No depth, no faith, no allowance for human contrariness, no soul, no mariachi, no chili sauce, no *pulque,* no mysticism, no *chingaderas.*"

He had left the valley when he was fourteen. Searching for what? He hardly knew. A freer life, perhaps, or to flee the stigma of contempt for the "dumb Mex." He went to the cities. The young Chicanos were leaving the little towns in the vineyards, hitchhiking out, joining the army, looking for jobs in the cities, doing anything to get away.

"I wanted something! I wanted *something!*" he says.

Education, everyone said, was salvation. His search led him, as it has so many bright, angered, restless young men, to the doors of a university. He entered uneasily. He suffered from "cultural schizophrenia" at the university. He describes why he was forced to flee.

"I had an aunt who had worms crawling out of her stomach. We wrapped her in clothes, every day we wrapped her in clothes, but the worms kept crawling out of her stomach. I saw those worms. Then when I went to college in San Jose, I was in a biochemistry course, and they showed us this film! I think it was an educational film about one disease or another. There was a boy with a bloated belly in the film, and there were worms crawling out of his stomach. I walked out of the class and I never went back."

His scathing laugh bursts from him unexpectedly, in a gust. It is ironic without being cynical, for he fiercely enjoys the irony. "That was no identity crisis. That was an identity catastrophe," he says. Elsewhere he has written, "It is not enough to say we suffer an identity crisis, because that crisis has been our way of life for the last five centuries."

He had to go home again. He at least knew what he was not looking for.

The odyssey of Luis Miguel Valdez led him back to the vineyards of Delano. He brought home his suitcase full of the remnants of his education in the university and Haight Ashbury, and the unfinished play he had written, *The Shrunken Head of Pancho Villa.*

"Life was absurd back then when I lived in San Francisco," he muses. "Silly and tragic. I was trying to relate to the pre-hippie Haight Ashbury, and I felt ridiculous. Moving back to Delano was a real, commonsensical act for me. I cannot begin to explain how much it was like 'coming home.' Without sentiment, you understand, only clear-headed *doing.*

"It was wonderful to come home. It was strange too. Everything had changed."

Huelga had come to the valley. The upheaval in the lives of the farmers and migrants brought about by the *huelga* had loosened a half-century of apathy that had hovered over the barrios in the somnolent and immobile heat. Like a bolt of lightning the *huelga* illuminated the valley with an ugly truth. Every town looked strangely newborn.

The prodigal was ecstatic. "You could see a new spirit in the people," he says. "Where they were shy and retiring and frightened about American society, now they're expressive, courageous and determined. The farm worker who has never said anything is now speaking."

He heard singing in the vineyards. The campesinos marched to the *huelga.* No one had sung in the vineyards when he was a boy. It was not because they knew no songs, but because there was not much to inspire singing.

On the picket lines there were rude paintings of The Virgin and biblical sayings and Spanish songs. Choruses were organized by the union, one for the men and women, and one for the children. The union newspaper of the farm workers, *El Malcriado* ("The Mischievous One," or "The Ill-Bred One") became an embryo anthology of poems, stories, and essays. In the drab, dull, dusty valley there was a "cultural revolution of those who were too uneducated and too illiterate to know they were supposed to be culturally deprived," says Valdez.

Gusty, gregarious, and full of "genius and hot chili," as he has been described, he joined the *huelga*. He was but one of hundreds of young Chicanos who came to the vineyards of Delano that summer from the cities and universities. They came as if to Mecca, supplicants.

The feeling of wholeness that comes of being one of a whole people overwhelmed him. "I was stoned with emotion," he says. "No kidding, it was a wild feeling."

Just two months after the *huelga* began in November, 1965, he "established" the *comedia del arte* of the farm workers—El Teatro Campesino. In makeshift union halls and at roadside picket lines, with no scripts, no props, no stage, no experience, no actors, Valdez created a theater. Praised from coast to coast within a few years, the troupe engaged audiences from Stanford to Howard University, starred at the Newport Folk Festival in Rhode Island and on television in New York City, had been awarded an Obie by the Off-Broadway critics, and had performed before the U.S. Senate's Subcommittee on Migratory Labor, in the courtyard of the Old Senate Office Building, at the invitation of the late Senator Robert F. Kennedy while Ted Kennedy sang strike songs.

El Teatro's "actors" were farm workers. The vineyards were their stage. The drama was improvised by the campesinos themselves. Felipe Cantu was the star. He had been an obscure grape picker who had worked, he said, at everything, from "policeman to a clown." A volatile man, the father of seven children, he "resembles a Mexican version of Ben Turpin," Valdez says. "He speaks no English, but his wild, extravagant Cantinflas-like comic style needs no words."

Yet another grape picker was Agustín Lira. He was hardly twenty, an intense and sensitive young man who became El Teatro's guitarist and poet. Lira's lyrics, "Yo No Le Tengo Miedo a Nada" ("I Am Not Afraid of Anything") and "Ser Como El Aire Libre" ("To Be Free as the Wind"), are gentle and bitter evocations of the wandering migrants:

> When I was little,
> My mother said,
> Take care, my son,
> Don't get in trouble,
> Now that I am grown up,
> These words pain me,
> For life is long,
> And I go through it crying.

There was "the Indian cowboy" Errol Franklin of Cheyenne, Wyoming, who was part black. Lean and thin, he had been a "horsebreaker, fisherman, apple picker, short-order cook, and longshoreman," before coming to the valley as a strikebreaker. He joined the *huelga* and became the mask maker for El Teatro, doubling as the stage cop.

And there were many more. "We have lost five of our best actors, really natural actors," says Valdez, "because they have gone on to leadership in the movement." But new actors always come forward: "*The Teatro* by its mere existence condemns the real loss of the human talent, the deadening of the human spirit, the brutalization of the mind and body caused by the callous feudal exploitation that is farm labor today," Valdez wrote in *Ramparts*.

"*El Teatro* is somewhere between Brecht and Cantinflas," he wrote. "In a Mexican way we have discovered what Brecht is all about. It is a bilingual propaganda theatre, but it borrows from Mexican folk humour to such an extent that its propaganda is salted with a wariness for human caprice.

"Your mind could burst at the simplicity of the acts (actos), but that's the way it is in Delano. . . . Real theatre lies in the excited laughter (or silence) of recognition *in the audience*, not in all the paraphernalia on the stage," he wrote. "Minus actors, the entire *teatro* can be packed in one trunk."

Using gargoyle masks and loud signs, they act out the *actos*. The word is one El Teatro originated, as they did the theatrical form of quick, satiric, and baroque slapsticked-together morality plays of unionism. Each actor wears a sign of his character: "ROTTEN GRAPE" says the sign on one man's chest who is picked from an imaginary vine and thrown into a garbage can by another man whose sign says, "ESQUIROL" (strikebreaker). The lines are just as burlesqued. It is "proletarian pantomime," says the critic of the *Wall Street Journal*, but that is because he could not understand the Spanish. Neither could a Spaniard. It is the patois of the campesino world of jukeboxes, fiestas, and soap operas on Mexican television. It derives from the oldest theatrical tradition on the continent, the symbolism of Aztec rituals and the evil and good, heaven and hell typecasting of the church plays of Spanish Catholicism.

Theater of this sort has deep roots in the Southwestern deserts. On these ancient lands the earliest native plays and poems and books on American themes were written. In the early 1500's the first formal theater, in the European sense, was performed in Mexico. The *Conversion of the Four Kings of Tlaxcala*, which was offered at that time to the remnants of the Aztec armies, has been called "The First American Play," by Dr. Carlos E. Castañeda of the Texas Catholic Historical Society.

"Theatrical performances began in Mexico shortly after the arrival of the conquerors," says Riva Palacio, the Mexican scholar. "In all religious and political celebrations care was taken to include some sacred comedy or Corpus Christi Play, which was usually performed in the open air. . . . In the famous festival of Corpus Christi at Tlaxcala in 1538, an elaborate *auto* was given, the subject being the sin of Adam and Eve." Indians were the actors, Palacio says, and they performed "in their own language."

And there were the fabulous horse plays of the Southwestern settlers—*Los Moros y Los Cristianos* and *Los Comanches*. In these spectacles a poetic script of romantic oratory was linked to the derring-do of a rodeo. They were performed in the fields, with armies of villagers in the cast.

Years before the Puritans set foot on what was to become the Boston Common, the native theater was born. The God-fearing New Englanders scowled upon the theater as the "work of the Devil," believing it "revilling in synn," which perhaps it did. So adamant was their intolerance of drama that when George Washington (he was an amateur actor) wished to celebrate the survival of his army at Valley Forge with a performance of a play, the Continental Congress forbade it. Any officer of the American Army who attended a stage play was to be dismissed immediately. Yet at that time the theater was already two hundred years old in the Southwest.

In 1598, the first play written on our shores was performed on the banks of the Rio Grande. This was the beginning of the theater in the fields, and in a sense it was the ancestor of El Teatro Campesino.

The illustrious Don Juan de Oñate was the producer of that play. He had that year led his pilgrimage of one hundred and thirty families of farmers, Spaniards, and one thousand Mexican Indians into the deserts to become the "father" of European settlement in the Southwest.

A man of romantic imagery, de Oñate rode into the unknown mounted on his choice of twelve saddles trimmed in black and crimson and ocelot skins. In his wagon trains, a kind of Noah's Ark of Hispanic America, he brought crates of wines, candies, rosaries, four church bells, six flutes, and "one lot of Paris trumpets"—the necessities of civilization. He was a man of two flamboyant cultures, an Español Mexicano born in Mexico. His wife was an Indian woman who was said to be the great-granddaughter of Emperor Motecuhzoma. In his sense of the dramatic, de Oñate combined the brutal beauty of the Aztecs' ascetic pageantry and the sensual passions of the morality plays of Spanish Catholicism.

Kneeling on the banks of the Rio Grande in 1598—it was Ascension Day—de Oñate intoned a prose poem, a chant, he had written. His words were as Indian as any Spaniard dared be without heresy:

". . . one, two and three times one, two and three times, and all times by right I can and should, at this Río del Norte . . ." de Oñate chanted, I do seize ". . . the mountains, rivers, valleys, meadows, pastures and waters . . . from the leaves of the trees in the forest to the stones and sands of the river, and from the stones and sands of the river to the leaves of the forest."

He then nailed a cross to a tree by the river bank in the name of the "essential sacrifice of the blood and body of Christ," and summoned his royal trumpeters to sound a fanfare for a feast and the first play in America.

The *comedia* written for the occasion by a captain of cavalry, Don Marcos Farfan de los Godos, a "Living Theater" where the actors and the audience were one and the same, was then performed before the Españoles Mexicanos farmers and Mexican Indians. Most likely it was a broadly mimed bit of pageantry in the style of the day that solemnly instructed the farmers on how to "possess, pacify and convert" the deserts.

One of the audience was the poet Gaspar Pérez de Villagra, a bachelor of arts from the University of Salamanca, whose epic poem on the pilgrimage of de Oñate was "the first poem about America" written in America. He wrote it in 1610.

It was not the beginning. Years before, in 1535, the first printer, a Master Esteban, had come from Spain. Soon afterwards the first books were printed in the New World in Spanish—one hundred years before an English press was brought ashore in New England. In 1553 the University of Mexico was founded, the first European school of higher learning in the hemisphere. Late in the 1500's and early 1600's, the Español Mexicano writers were founding literary schools to celebrate "this paradise of Mexico." The uniqueness of these writers—Francisco de Terrazas, Bernardo de Balbuena, Miguel de Guevara, Luis de Sandoval y Zapata, the incomparable Juana de Asbaje (Sor Juana), and so many more who wrote before the year 1700—was that they "mixed the Indian with the Spanish tradition," writes the Mexican philosopher and poet Octavio Paz in *Mexican Poetry,* to fuse an indigenous culture of La Raza where "the old belief mingled with the new." This was before 1700.

Even this was not the beginning. The Aztecs, long before the coming of the Spaniards, had a spectacular theater, a written language, vast libraries, institutes of higher learning, and a rich literature of manuscripts, or codices.

Miguel Leon-Portilla, the director of the Inter-American Indian Institute in Mexico, has sadly noted, in *The Broken Spears:* ". . . the

Spanish conquistadors—along with certain churchmen—burned almost all of the codices and destroyed the pre-Hispanic centers of education." So thoroughly did the conquerors do their work that only "a few codices . . . escaped the flames." Hardly fifty manuscripts remain. Yet, as Sister Dr. Angel Maria Garibay K has shown, even these few, in the words of Leon-Portilla, "offer a broad range of literary types: religious, lyric, epic and dramatic poetry, and prose history, legends, moral teachings, etc."

Books have been written on the theater of the Aztecs, and little need be written here. The awesome rituals of the Nahuatl religions, atop their pyramids, were among the most dramatic spectacles in history. If no battles were being fought, they staged elaborate and gorgeously costumed ceremonial combats known as the "Wars of Flowers," where warriors fought with mock heroics before cheering crowds. War itself was a theater to the Aztecs.

In these "Wars of Flowers," the fiestas of the saints, the rituals of joy and fertility to the Virgin of Guadalupe, the horse play *Los Moros y Los Cristianos*, the morality plays of the Church, the *comedia* of de Oñate's pilgrims, the dances of death in the Day of the Dead, the celebration of Cinco de Mayo, the Mexican Independence Day, the madrigal of sacrifice in the *corrida de toro*, the bull ring, the religious processionals in homage to the *"revolucíon,"* the peregrinations of politics: in all of these were the origins of El Teatro Campesino of Delano.

The young poet of the *huelga* knows this. He says of his theatrical origins: "Once we had our own gods. We had Quetzalcoatl. And Western civilization came with new gods. Well, what did happen to those old gods? What happened to that ancient view of life? Does it influence us? I think it does. It is still there. The conquest of Mexico was no conquest at all. It shattered our ancient Indian universe, but more of it was left above ground than beans and tortillas. Below the foundations of our Spanish culture, we still sense the ruins of an entirely different civilization.

"Most of us know we are not European simply by looking in a mirror—the shape of the eyes, the curve of the nose, the color of the skin, the texture of the hair; these things belong to another time, another people. Together with a million little stubborn mannerisms, beliefs, myths, superstitions, words, thoughts—things not easily detected—they fill our Spanish life with Indian contradictions."

But then, "The old Aztec universe was a universe of contradictions."

His grin becomes a grimace. "Somehow, away from this chaos, away from this American life, back in my memory, there's a different sort of life. There is a more stable life, full of traditions, of beauty, of a human view of people. And I sometimes look back at this with a great deal of nostalgia. It's kind of foolish. How can I have a memory of the Aztecs, of Mexico? It's impossible because I was born in Delano."

Where does his memory come from? "It's a feeling more than a memory though it feels like a memory. I am thinking, I guess, of what should have been. Life in the country should have had its own traditions of lasting value for us. Reaching out for something like this is what is behind the *huelga* thing, the Delano thing, the farm workers thing."

The young man with the big cigar—he is a chain smoker, or chewer, of long Cuban-style cigars—takes the cigar out of his mouth to think aloud. "Culture? What about culture? It is akin to a political act. It is when a man stands up and takes his life in his hands and says, I am going to change my life. That's what culture is all about. I feel that before you get any political act out of a man that man has to feel a certain pride in himself. He has to touch his own dignity, his own destiny. La Raza needs the arts to tell itself where it is.

"The arts are largely prophetic. Even the Teatro. Many of the things we do on stage now prefigure the course of social action that La Raza will take in the future. We have been organizing the organizers. Let me explain that: The blacks have a tradition in the arts that is as old as the country—theater, poetry, novels, essays, paintings, music; they have been expressing what they feel for a long time. Good and bad ideas, but articulated thoughts nonetheless. Ideas about the black people's relation to the white society that oppresses them. Marcus

Garvey, Booker T. Washington, W. E. B. Du Bois, Malcolm X, James Baldwin, Richard Wright. Some of their ideas have suggested integration, some segregation, some a complete return to Africa—but they have all suggested *something.* Black liberation is predicated on ideas that have gone before.

"We don't have that," he says. "There is no Chicano leader who has put his finger on our problem because we have lacked the poets, novelists, and essayists that prefigure the appearance of such a leader of leaders."

The belief in the power of the arts to remake man is as old as that of the Aztecs. Luis Valdez's faith is like that of the ancient artists who thought of art as the "flowers and song" through which man talked to "the Giver of Life," to the gods. It was never an entertainment to them; it was a wholly religious act.

The "true artist," the Aztecs believed, "is master of himself. He is whole." Unlike the "false" artist who "scorned his destiny," and who "held himself above others, which meant he grew conceited and insolent," and who "thereby ruined his happiness—he lost it," the true artist was a "creator of life."

"His destiny," the Aztecs wrote of the artist, "is to humanize the desires of the people."

"Now we must seek our destiny," says Valdez, "and Delano was only the beginning of our search." In the wake of his wandering troupe, El Teatro Campesino, have come a caravan of newborn Chicano theaters; there is the Teatro Chicano itself in the barrios of Los Angeles, which is composed of university students and street youth; El Teatro Rebelde, a musical theater group from Visalia in the San Joaquin Valley; the Teatro Azteca of Fresno; and the Teatro Urbano, created by the rebellious college students of San Jose State College.

In Colorado, New Mexico, and Texas there are Chicano theaters where there were none before. The search of Luis Valdez for an indigenous art form for La Raza has been joined by a generation of young artists and wanderers.

His search leads him deeper into the vineyards of the valley. Once more the poet and his troupe have joined the migrations of the poor campesinos, going north to the village of Del Rey, the village "of the king," near Fresno.

It is a tiny village of one thousand. Poor and unknown, it lies hidden from the highway in the midst of the region where the grapes of the raisins grow. Some say it is the village of the Swineherd. That, too, is the meaning of Del Rey. Near the village there are two dozen more villages of migrants. Their names describe these dots on the map of California: Raisin, Malaga, Conejo (Rabbit Wire), Orange Cove, Naranjo (The Orange), El Nido (The Hen's Nest), and a place named Tranquility. In the harvest season the countryside is home to tens of thousands of migrants living in the camps, by the roadside, under the bridges. The poorest of the poor.

Why bury his theater in so godforsaken a rural ghetto?

His voice is weary with the reply he has so often given: "We are not aspiring to Broadway. We are aspiring to build a theater among our people. That's the whole bit about the Teatro. We are not a theater *for* farm workers; farm workers are our theater," he says. "Besides, we are trying to build something bigger than a theater. In English you could call it La Raza Folk Cultural Center. But it will be more than that. Someday it will be a center for Chicanos all through the Southwest."

The building is dilapidated and threadbare. In its inauspicious interior, hardly 50 feet by 50 feet, "We have our art classes: Life Drawing and Children's Art. We have guitar lessons. We have our Teatro. We have 'history happenings,' every two or three weeks, dealing with the history of La Raza. We have *actos* about La Conquista [The Conquest], the Alamo, Gold Rush, the Cisco Kid and Pancho Villa."

Workshops for farm workers are envisioned in the making of woodcuts, murals, and sculpture; photography and language classes; and the writing of a "primer and coloring book" to teach "the young Mexican American his 20,000-year-old heritage." These workshops are to be free to the campesinos and their families.

"Campesinos are far from 'culturally deprived,' " says a brochure of the Centro Campesino Cultural. "They possess and live within a 'culture'—one which is, however, largely unfamiliar to the mass of English-speaking North Americans. It is a culture native to a great part of the land mass of the United States and has been for the last 400 years. It is an untapped resource of human experience. . . . The Mexican American farm worker in the Southwest has long been denied the tools of [his] cultural expression. . . . El Centro Campesino Cultural is an attempt to hand over these tools—the tools of the Arts—directly to the Spanish-speaking people of the Southwest. . . ."

"We know we have our own culture. Culture of the migrants," Valdez says. "It's just that there has been nobody to express it—until now. We will change that. We are on the verge of it. The whole country will be amazed!"

The poet says little of the poor. He laughs. "Everyone knows the poor are poor. That's no news. It's our way of life."

He talks of the "bourgeois *chingaderas*": "I go along through American life and I see the homes of the poor Mexicans with the broken down TVs, radios, beds. We have the bits and piccces of your technology in our homes. The refuse. The broken artifacts.

"*Chingaderas!*" he exclaims. "Here in the United States La Raza is confused by the bourgeois *chingaderas* all around them. The car, the house, the furniture, the TV—all these things are *chingaderas*, because they are the poor, secondhand, used objects that were handed down from the genuinely bourgeois life of your prosperous middle class. I am using Octavio Paz's definition of *chingada*, meaning not merely the 'Great Whore,' but a place of broken-down things, faraway and distant.

"Look, we don't need your broken-down TV sets. We don't need the scraps of your culture.

"They say this is the melting pot. I wonder who invented the melting pot. Horrible term! You melt people down, God! It shouldn't be that way. Our country should be a place where the individual is sacred. We have so many different sorts of people. Every man has his own heart. Who gives you the right to cut out a man's heart and put it in a melting pot?

"There are beautiful things in our lives. We have had them in our past and we will have them again. We will create our own 'flowers and songs.' "

In the Centro Cultural Campesino there are few songs and fewer flowers, but many cockroaches. Luis Miguel Valdez sits down to write a letter. "The roof is leaking again," he writes. "I mean the ceiling. The neighbors upstairs pour water all over the floor in an effort to drown the cockroaches. The water is flooding part of my desk. Viva la cucaracha!" he writes, in the summer of 1968.

One year later the troupe of El Teatro Campesino is on the road again, migrating with its props and its actors to Fresno, to San Jose, to Los Angeles, to Paris. The cockroaches have the stage to themselves, in the empty theater of Del Rey.

XXV The Unfrocked Priests

"I will never put on those faggoty robes again." The priest is bronzed, intense. "Priests are men. Why do we hide our manhood behind the skirts of the Church? So many of the young priests I know have a woman in another parish. Why do they have to support two households? On a priest's salary no man can afford the luxury of hypocrisy."

Father Robert García laughs abruptly and sharply.

We are in a village bar. It is one of those cafés at a country crossroads, high in the valleys of the Sangre de Cristo Mountains of New Mexico. The name of the village has vanished. It is not far from Santa Fe, but it is a century away. Who comes here? No strangers sit at the bar, its wood aged and carved by time, but the priest and I. Whispering in the feudal Spanish of the mountains, two very old men sit in an unlit corner and insult us with their suspicions. The head of a stag is molting above the bar. In Spanish, the priest yells back a taunting joke. He was once the priest of a mountain parish and knows the dialect.

"Here a man is a man," the priest says. "What do they care if I am a priest? Or a pimp! Look at what Saint Augustine was trying to tell us: the way to God is through the flesh of man. And what about the Holy Martyrs? What about Christ? He took the flesh of man for His own body."

In the liturgy of martyrdom and manhood there is an echo of the early desert fathers. "For who is without sin, save God himself?" St. Ephraim of Edessa wrote in his *Life of St. Mary the Harlot.* The severity of these words seems oddly appropriate to the Catholicism and climate of the Southwestern deserts of the United States, as it was for the deserts of the Old World a thousand years ago.

Father García swigs his beer and wipes his lips. "I say, God is not on earth or in a church. He is not in the Bishopric. He is not in a priest's robes. Let us confess, a man is nothing but a man."

"Ah, *macho* in the church," I say. "You talk like a true Spanish man."

"Spanish!? We are not like those effeminate Spanish men. The priests of the villages have *macho,* sure; but it's Indian. It's Mexican Indian. We are the Mexican Church. We are Mexican priests, maybe a bit Americanized. But not enough to be effeminate. Yet."

On that summer day in August, 1967, there is no hint in his voice that he will leave the priesthood, but he will. He is then a dynamic, controversial, and respected young priest, the state director of New Mexico's Office of Economic Opportunity, appointed by the Governor with the sanction of his Archbishop. Within a few months he will leave his Church career to marry a divorcee, one of the 711 Roman Catholic clergymen known to have left the Church in 1966 and 1967. "Obviously, this report is an undercount," according to the Reverend Joseph Fichter, a Jesuit sociologist at Harvard.

"It is not the Church I am leaving but the hypocrisy," Father García later says. We do not meet again, so I judge his decision by his talk of that day in the café. He is not talking of celibacy. He is talking of humanity. Celibacy, that "agonizing" doctrine, as the liberal theologian Father Peter Riga refers to it—that "delicate question"—has historically been less an issue than a conjecture to the clergy of Mexico. It was so from the time of the conquest. In his *Verdadera Relación: The True History of the Conquest,* written in 1568, Bernal Díaz del Castillo, the companion and chronicler of Cortés, tells of the typical case of a Father Benito Martínez, the chaplain to the Governor of Cuba, who brought his mistress, Maria Rodríguez, with him from Spain. Journeying to Mexico, the priest simply took her with him, as did many others. It was the "accepted custom," wrote Jorge y Santacilla and Antonio de Ulloa in the *Noticias Secretas de America.* "Both the regular and secular clergy live licentiously, scandalously and as they please." Some of the bolder prelates kept their *barraganas* (concubines) in their cells, the Spanish historians noted. Hundreds of journals and contemporary accounts celebrate these Rabelaisian urges of the early Spanish fathers of the Church.

"The climate is not favorable to chastity," was the dry observation of Sir Richard Burton, a British consular officer in Latin America in the nineteenth century.

As recently as 1899 the Plenary Council on the Latin American Clergy, meeting in Rome, was reported to have estimated that of 18,000 priests, almost half were married, living in concubinage, or "in relationship" with women. Still more recently, the scholar Dr. Manuel Gamio has written that in Mexico "generally priests live conjugal lives."

"A man need not stop being a man to serve God in Mexico," says Father García.

What then is a priest to a villager? He baptizes the infants, weds the lovers, buries the dead. He performs rituals, not miracles. It is a wholly human way of viewing a man of God.

In the mountain village of San Cristobal, New Mexico, the earthy, humanistic attitude toward priests is voiced by Cleofas Vigil. He is an ex-*penitente* and a wholly religious man. But of the priests he says critically:

"I believe in God. But not in priests. If you go to confession to the priest, he forgives you. Who is he to forgive you? It is not for him to forgive, but who you have sinned against. Maybe I do something wrong. If I steal your watch how can the priest forgive me? Was it his watch?

"No, I have to confess to you. To ask forgiveness of you who I have wronged.

"And I will say, 'Stan, I have stolen your watch.'

"And you will say, 'Why did you do that, Cleofas? Why didn't you ask me for it?'

"And I will say, 'Well, I was ashamed.'

"And you will say, 'But I need my watch. It cost me a lot of money. What did you do with it?'

"And I will say, 'I sold it.'

"And you will say, 'That was wrong.'

"And I will say, 'Yes, it was wrong. I know it. But I needed the money. I will pay you back when I can. Will you forgive me?'

"And you will say, 'Yes, Cleofas, I forgive you.'

"Maybe I will never pay you back. But I have confessed to you and you have forgiven me. That is being Christian. That is Christ's way. Who the hell are the priests to tell us that if we do this we will go to hell? Aren't the poor living in hell now?"

Man is his own confessor. He is his own priest. "The most individualistic of humans," says Fecundo Valdez, a village organizer, of the man of La Raza whose self-respect is not a matter of pride but of his well-being. "We bring our individualism from the villages to the barrios. In religion we are individualists to a degree the Anglos cannot comprehend. We do penance when we decide to. We atone for our own sins." If a supplicant kneels before the shrine of his name saint, it is not by the obligation of a priest. He does not pray by ritual.

"You do not ask the priest to talk to God," says a young girl in the barrio of the Seven Hells in El Paso. "You have to talk to Him by yourself."

An old man in the barrio of San Antonio, Paul Rodríguez—who some look up to as "the humble patriarch of La Causa," and some look down upon as "that fool, he's a damned mystic in politics"—says of God, "I fear the Lord. I am a deeply religious man. Religion to me is not going to church or attending ceremonials. Religion to me is what you do with what you have, to look out for your fellow man."

Cleofas Vigil says, "I know who God is. God is kindness. God is sweetness. God is love. To respect man is to love God. It is not hard to know God. I have searched for Him and I found Him."

Father So-and-So, a parish priest in the barrios of East Los Angeles, says the same thing, but differently. He is anguished by what to his parishioners might be an ordinary truth. He says, "Sometimes I ask myself: Where is God? He doesn't seem to be in the institutionalized Church. He is not manifest by the majority vote of men, no matter how they vote. No, God exists in the individual soul of man, not in the institutions of men."

In the village adobe and the barrio home, the statuette and tinted print of the Virgin of Guadalupe or Jesus on the Cross is almost as omnipresent as the television set. A family that is religious has its own homemade shrine. Often in the bedroom there is a niche with a candle burning for a martyred saint, or the late John F. Kennedy.

Some of the statistics show that barely 10 to 15 per cent of the men go to Mass, though many more say they are religious and Catholics. Why go to church? God is in your deeds. He is not in the sermon of the priest. Let the women go and weep.

Unlike the Indian priest the Church priest is not believed to possess mystical powers. He knows no magic. He "has influence," the parishioners say, with the civil service and "the welfare," and he knows how to talk to those people downtown. But that is all. Like a civil servant in the Church he may be helpful or bumbling, kind or callous; but he cannot perform a miracle. Church is a social occasion where you go to meet friends and to celebrate the fiesta of the Mass. For a miracle you pray to your saint, or go to your *curandero*—the curer.

In a church in the Rio Grande Valley after a sermon, a man tells an interviewer: "These priests are good and educated men and we must respect them. But they do not understand everything. Their learning comes from books. . . . The priest's duty is to say Mass. He runs the machinery of the church. He does not see into the trouble of one's soul.

"But take Doña Toribia, the curer," the man goes on. "Where does she get her wisdom? Straight from God Himself. She can talk with God, so there is no need for her to read the inaccuracies of men's words." (*The Mexican-Americans of South Texas,* by William Madsen.) The priest does not have that power. He is respected, but he is not feared.

The God of La Raza to some seems confined and circumscribed by the church denominations. He is too personal and too universal. Abelardo Delgado, the Catholic writer, poet, and barrio martyr of El Paso, says, "We are mostly Catholic. But our religious spirit is too great to stay within the walls of any church."

Anticlericalism in the barrios, as in old Mexico, is rarely atheistic. Radicals in social liturgy curse the Church for not being religious enough. Even priests who leave the Church usually go no farther than the other side of the altar.

It was the universality and romantic humanism of the Spanish Catholic Church that originally appealed to the Mexican Indians; the Gods of the Aztecs were deities who embraced the universe. Everyone is Catholic; everyone was Aztec. In the religions of man there have been few as terrifying, awesome, and beautiful as that of the Plumed Serpent. There have been no religious states built upon more virile religiosity—from the War of the Flowers to the Pyramid of the Sun. And the Gods too were conceived on so vast, so complex, a design that they embraced their opposites within themselves.

Ometeotl, the Lord of Life, was thought to be male and female, near and far, darkness and light. His duality became the living Passion of Christ, of life in death. Coatlicue, the Mother Earth, the womb of life common to all religions of the Aztecs, was the Mother Famine as well, the tomb of hunger and earthquakes. Tlazolteotl, the Goddess of fertility and the lover of Quetzalcoatl, to whom men prayed for forgiveness of their sin, was at the same time maliciously the Lady of Filth and Eater of Feces.

It is sorrowfully said that the Spanish Catholic Church destroyed the Aztec gods. The ancient temples were desecrated and ruined, the holy libraries were burned, the Indian priests were slaughtered in a blood sacrifice that made their own pale by comparison.

Yet the Gods of the Aztecs were to embrace their opposites once more. Gods of such potency were not to be forgotten easily. The Indian religion adapted to Catholicism, but Catholicism also adapted to the religion of the Indians.

"We took your Virgin Mary and made her our Virgin of Guadalupe," says Luis Valdez of the Teatro Campesino. "It meant more than making a white statue brown. It meant making her Mexican. And *Indio!*"

The Virgin of Guadalupe was a miraculous vision of the poor shepherd Juan Diego. He was an Indian who was tending his flocks on a hill where coincidentally there had been a shrine to the Aztec Goddess of Motherhood, Tonantzin. It was at that sacred place that the mother of Christ appeared; and she looked like an Indian to Juan Diego. She was the Aztec mother reborn as a brown madonna. Long ago, Tonantzin was in fact depicted as black in basalt statues. In the mountains of Mexico some Indians still pray to the mother symbol of both religions whom they have named the Virgin of Guadalupe-Tonantzin. Ever since then, Our Lady of Guadalupe, the Patroness of Mexico, has been dark-skinned. Her personality, even more than her skin, is Mexican, the Virgin of the Indians is thought of as warm and fecund rather than pure and immaculate.

On my desk I have a statue of the brown madonna. I bought her in a religious store in East Los Angeles. She wears a Spanish crown and her gown is leafed in gold. In her brown hand she holds her child, the Infant Jesus, who is white.

Cleofas Vigil says, "Some of the priests and ministers in the church don't even know who God is. They think God is a white man. Is God white, by the way? I don't think God is white. He is clean, yes. Who knows who He is? God may be an Indian."

If the Virgin is Mexican and God is Indian, or half-Indian, what about Christ? The Christ of La Raza appears in every shade and nuance of culture and color. He is a microcosm of humanity. He may be white, or he may be black. It does not matter to the La Raza worshipers, unless they attend Anglo churches.

The village of Chimayo, near Santa Fe, New Mexico, is famous for its Holy Sanctuary of Our Lord of Esquipulas, to which thousands of pilgrims come every year. In a spring that is enshrined beside the altar, there is a mudhole of curative waters. The wafers of mud eaten by the pilgrims come from this mudhole. It is these cakes of mud that cure. On the altar, in the Sanctuary, worshipers pray to the black wooden body of an emaciated Christ. He is Our Lord of Esquipulas, known as *El Cristo Negro*—The Black Christ.

In the jungles of the Mayans there is a shrine quite like that of Chimayo, with its Black Christ. Built for the Indians four centuries ago by the conquistadors, it, too, is known as the Sanctuary of Esquipulas. There, too, the pilgrims among the Mayans eat wafers of mud dug from a holy spring at the site of an ancient temple, and their Christ too is a Black Christ. Earth eating was, and still is, a religious devotion of the Mayan and Mexican Indians, much as Roman Catholics eat wafers of grain. It is still so in the pueblos of New Mexico, as well as among the Hispanos of Chimayo. But why is Christ a black man? No one knows. The shrines of the Black Christs that exist almost three thousand miles apart are one in ritual. They unite the Indian and Catholic rites.

The religions of the Indians and the politics of the Spaniards created the unique beliefs of Mexican Catholicism. The conqueror and the conquered have been wedded in one church more Spanish than Roman and more Indian than either. In the visible structure of the buildings and doctrines of the Catholic Church of Mexico and the Southwest, the Spanish influence seems dominant; for the Kings of Spain were powerful. But that too is more apparent than real.

Joaquín García Icazbalceta, the historian of the origins of Mexican Catholicism, in his classic work on the great bishop of the conquistadors, Don Fray Juan de Zumarranga, described the power of the Spanish kings "in the ecclesiastical government of America" as being "pontifical." "Without the king's permission, no church, no monastery, or hospital could be constructed and no bishopric or parish erected. No priest or friar might go to America without his express license. The king named the bishops, and without waiting for confirmation by the Pope, sent them out to administer their diocese," Icazbalceta wrote.

So absolute was the religious authority of the kings of Spain in the Catholic Church that no papal bull or edict could be enacted, or even read, from any pulpit of a parish church in all of the Americas without the permission of the crown. When, in fact, Pope Alexander VI sent a papal nuncio to the Island of Española (Cuba) in 1493, the Spanish king was so enraged that he demanded and secured the immediate recall of the Vatican's emissary. The Pope "meekly capitulated." It was three hundred years before another personal representative of the Popes dared to set foot in New Spain.

No wonder a Catholic historian has written that the Church was "an appendage of the State." The Spanish Kings won their power over the popes through the doctrine of *patronato real*—the King's patronage—

granted to Charles V of Spain in 1484 by the Bull of Pope Julius II. Happily and conveniently for the Spanish Empire this bull was issued just eight years before the first voyage of Columbus.

In Europe at that time the hegemony of the Vatican was threatened by the oncoming Reformation. The heresies of King Henry VIII in England, and Martin Luther in Germany, were grievous losses to the power of Roman Catholicism. The diplomats of the Vatican wisely sought to mediate any such national apostasy in Spain by concessions to the kings, in the hope of retaining their spiritual dominion. Historically, the outcome of the compromise was ambiguous. In time "the Church in Spanish America was, from an administrative point of view, more a Spanish, national Church, controlled from Madrid, than a Catholic Church controlled from Rome," writes Dr. Frederick B. Pike, a church historian at the University of Notre Dame.

Out of the national and independent nature of the priesthood of Mexico, a political reformation was born. The "Father of Mexican Independence" was inevitably a parish priest—Father Miguel Hidalgo y Costilla, a Rousseauian, thought by the hierarchy to be a heretic, as he was. On the sunny morning of September 16, 1810, he walked to the steps of his little Church of Dolores and proclaimed his famous El Grito de Dolores to his Indian parishioners: "Long Live Our Lady of Guadalupe! Long Live Independence!"

Within a week Father Hidalgo was an unwilling *generalisimo* of an insurrection. He sought out another parish priest, the frail and handsome Father José Maria Morelos, who had been one of his students when the old man was rector of the College of San Nicolas, and he chose the young prelate to lead the revolutionary armies of Indians and peons. Soon enough both priests were to die the deaths of martyrs; the old Father Hidalgo, after months in chains, crying to the Lord for "the pores of my body [to bleed] the blood of my veins." The young Father Morelos, convicted by the Holy Office of the Inquisition, in 1815, of heresy, treason, blasphemy, and lesser sins, was unfrocked and killed. The Spanish rule of Mexico was to die soon after; few societies have long survived those whom they martyr.

The independence of the national church, built by the kings of Spain to rule their empire, was to have a doubly ironic end. Its colonial walls guarded and nourished a newer national church within the old—that of the Mexican Catholicism of the Indians, and the religious nationalism of the native-born barrio priests.

In the wilder territories of the Southwest, the village priests were equally the leaders of the independence battles. Father Antonio José Martínez was such a man, born in the hamlet of Abiquiu, a man of obstinate and strong beliefs. The "Padre of the Poor," he founded the first coeducational school in the Southwest (in the 1830's), was publisher of one of New Mexico's earliest newspapers, *El Crepúsculo de la Libertad,* of Taos (The Dawn of Liberty), and was thought to be involved in the uprisings of 1837 and 1847 against Mexico *and* the United States, in turn. Later, in 1854, the rebellious padre was unfrocked, too, by the newly appointed bishop of Santa Fe, John Lamy from Cincinnati, Ohio, who arrived soon after the conquering U.S. Army. Lamy, immortalized in Willa Cather's *Death Comes for the Archbishop,* was welcomed to his diocese by the native priests with cold hostility. Father Juan Felipe Ortiz, the *vicario* in charge, refused to recognize the zealous bishop's credentials.

Bishop Zubiria of Mexico's Catholic Church unwillingly gave up his claim to the conquered parishes of the diocese. In triumph Lamy began a "Church Rebuilding Program," reconstructing the old historic missions, building eighty-five new churches, dismissing the defiant native priests, like Father Gallegos of Albuquerque, from their pulpits, and excommunicating Father Martínez. The "Padre of the Poor" was accused, not unreasonably, of "opposition to Church authority."

It was a conflict that echoed and re-echoed through the years between the poor priests of the villages and the opulent bishoprics. The native-born and Spanish-speaking clergy and the Anglo and English-speaking hierarchy were united in the Mystical Body of Christ that was the Church, but they were in every other way divided by a way of life and cultural inheritance, religious ritual, and practice. Rebellions were frequent, as they were predictable.

Father Robert García was not as rebellious as was thought. He was born into a tradition. In fact, he was born in a mountain village not too far from and not too different from the birthplace of his unfrocked ancestor, Father Antonio José Martínez.

The unfrocked priest in a sports shirt, who lives in the barrio as one of the poor, is not extraordinary. He is one of many. In his church duties he may not defy the hierarchy, but obey the word and canon of religious authority with a nod and genial acquiescence. But his style of life and his day-to-day Catholicism is quite different from the urban Roman Catholicism of his chancery office. Curiously, though the faithful of the barrios are the largest ethnic group of Catholics in the country, there has never been a La Raza cardinal or archbishop in the history of the Church in the United States.

"Our Church has been two Churches," says a barrio priest in Texas. "We have always had a conservative hierarchy, first from Spain, then from the Anglos. In the poor parishes we have had revolutionary priests, like Fathers Hidalgo and Martínez. It is nothing new."

Cesar Chavez, the campesino unionist, who is a devoted Catholic, says of the dichotomy: "On the one hand we have the Church which is part of the power structure; on the other hand we have the churches of the native priests who want to apply the teachings of the Church to our movement, who come to Delano, walk on the picket lines. They are few in number. Still they are a larger number than ten years ago.

"We are just beginning to understand the Church. Especially in our case the Catholic Church," Chavez says. "There are priests who will go almost anywhere in the country for a meeting to discuss social justice, who are very concerned with it, but who fail to understand how social justice comes about. We have large numbers of people, in and out of the Church, who are for social justice, theoretically. Good people, fine people, moral people, who aren't realistic enough to understand.

"The Church has to minister to both sides. We realize that," says Chavez. "We do not criticize the Church for ministering to the upper class, to the power structure. But we want the Church to minister to us as well—to the poor."

There are those who do not talk as kindly of the inner conflict in the Church. Paul Rodríguez, an elder of the barrios of San Antonio, is one of these. He says flatly, "The Church has conspired with those in power. Why? To keep the poor people ignorant. Why? Because in every barrio the Church owns slum property, tenements, rat-holes. Why? Not in the name of Christ, I know.

"Our Catholic Church in San Antonio has not behaved in a very Christian way. Here we have a neighborhood where the people had no sewers and no gas. I did a lot of hollering and complaining and agitating to get the city to install sewers. These people had been deprived of the elemental needs of civilization. They had pit toilets in the backyards. Close by this neighborhood is a great big beautiful convent—the Convent of the Sisters of the Holy Ghost. In the last few years, they built an addition to the convent; a planner told me it cost $700,000."

"I asked the people, 'Why don't the priest and nuns help you? Don't they come around?'

"They said, 'No, they seldom come. But they come to collect.'

"I asked, 'Collect what?'

"They said, 'When they were building the convent they came to us for donations.'

"One lady I talked to, she was ragged, she had nothing, no stockings, her hair was stringy, she was not very clean, which I don't blame her for, because she didn't have hot water or anything like that. She told me when the Church came to collect money, she gave them sometimes 35 cents, sometimes 50 cents.

"It shows the depth of degradation to which part of our Church has fallen. To take money from these people who are so poor.

"I feel that the Church in San Antonio has been grossly derelict in its Christian duty. Especially I condemn Archbishop Lucey, I wish I could do it in person. Sometime, maybe, the Lord will give me the opportunity. He has persecuted the few priests who have fought for the poor, who have sacrificed their priesthood. In my own parish the priests say: We can't get involved in politics. The Archbishop doesn't like it. It's not politics. It's religion. It's Christianity."

The feeling of frustration has opened the doors of the storefront sects—fundamentalist tents and Protestant churches—to the religious faithful of the barrios. Evangelism and the Pentecostal sects are gaining converts. It is not only the most anglicized—those who wish acceptance by society—who convert, but the poorest of the poor and most Mexicans who feel the Church has betrayed their devotions.

" 'Christianizing' Mexican Catholics" was the caustic title that Archbishop Lucey gave the proselytizing of the Protestants back in 1947.

In the once wholly Catholic parishes, the faithful are fragmented by an urban array of churches. The Protestant influx runs the spectrum of the denominations: Reies Tijerina, the land-grant leader, is an evangelical preacher; a leader of the San Antonio barrio, Father Henry Casso, is an Episcopalian.

Catholicism in the traditional Mexican way may seem old-fashioned and superstitious to the youngest generation. At a "Burger-Taco" Drive-In on North Broadway, in East Los Angeles, two Chicanos sit and munch the ice of Coca-Colas. One of the boys has just returned from a trip to Mexico. He tells of seeing the religious pilgrims crawling through the streets on their knees.

"On their knees?" his friend says.

"Yeah, they scrape themselves bloody!"

"In the streets?"

"Listen, I saw the blood."

"Why?"

"It's penance."

"Oy, veh!" says his friend. "That's super-superstition! If someone asked me to crawl on my knees . . ." He wags his head. And his voice trails off, unable to even contemplate the thought of that supplication.

> Christ, your cross sure ain't
>   impressing nobody no more,
> Get a new one, run, don't walk,
>   to your nearest store.

In his lyric, "A New Cross," the singer of the Barrio of Seven Hells in El Paso implores Christ for a modern crucifix that will attract "the turned-on generation." Abelardo Delgado, the poet, suggests a cross of gold, but decides that's too old. How about "one made of petrified dollar bills," he says to Christ. "You always looked well in green." Better still, a cross "of cemented birth-control pills to signify your power over life," or "a psychedelic one with neon," or with "hot and cold running blood":

You always did go for the poor
So maybe we can find
A slum shaped like a cross
To fit you on. . . .
But let's face it,
A wooden cross leaves us cold.

Abelardo Delgado is the organizer of a juvenile-delinquency center. The boys are his "flock," he says. He is one of the new "priests" of the urban barrios who has never worn the cloth of the Church. He is a mystic, they say. With rosy cheeks and the gentle manner of a boy and that sudden sadness, he is a Mexican mystic. He seeks a "New Christ," he says.

On the first day of Lent he drinks a glass of water with two teaspoons of sugar for breakfast, lunch, and supper. He has decided to suffer the Passion of Christ, with a "Fast for Love." He will fast for forty days, in the barrio of Seven Hells on the borders of the red light district of Juarez. He sits in his tenement room on a narrow, worn, bed, weakly staring at the green paint that peels from the walls, and he says: I fast for the children "so they do not have to grow up in tenements"; I fast for "love of neighbor"; I fast for "tenement owners"; I fast for "both strikers and management"; I fast for "peace in Vietnam"; I fast for "the churches to get involved with us instead of making statements to the press." He wrote in his poem "The Fast":

Maybe my empty belly
Will serve as a drum
On which I can drum messages
To a distant God.

In the evenings he goes into the streets. Hundreds of people pray with him every night in his Rosary Service at the neighborhood altars he sets up on the street corners of the barrios.

"For too long we have been told that poverty is a blessing and that we should be content with what we have," he prays. "These are myths! I don't believe Our Lord wants it that way. Some people think I will tell them to use force." In his hand he holds a peculiar crucifix with three prongs, "like the branches of a tree." Abelardo Delgado says cryptically, "This is the New Christ." He says little more, but an old man says the three-pronged cross is a "good luck thing" he remembers from his youth in Mexico. "It is an Indian cross," the old man says.

Wherever Delgado walks he is guarded by fourteen boys wearing bright-red bandanas and wide straw sombreros. It is an incongruous sight in El Paso. They say they are "Los Dorados"—The Golden Ones. It is a revolutionary name remembered from the days of Pancho Villa.

Palm Sunday comes finally. In the Barrio of the Seven Hells, a white card is handed out in the churches:

You are cordially invited to attend
HOLY MASS
officiated by our Most Reverend Bishop
Sidney M. Metzger
on Sunday, April 7, 1968 . . .
to end the 40 day Fast of
ABELARDO DELGADO
who fasted for Better Housing
for the poor of the Southside
and their general welfare.

In an empty lot where a single tree grows amid the rubble and broken bricks, two thousand worshipers have gathered. The old women in black shawls fall to their knees. Men in business suits kneel on an abandoned railroad track that cuts through the vacant lot. Before the open-air altar the Bishop intones the Holy Mass. In the wind above his head are the flags of the United States, of Mexico, of the City of El Paso, and of the Church.

Abelardo Delgado sits under two umbrellas guarded by Los Dorados. He is touched by the worshipers.

The frocked priests and the frockless poet of the barrios link arms. On a pilgrimage they march, under the colorful flags of two cultures and the Church, the sombreros of Los Dorados, and the yellow umbrella protecting the head of the martyr as he leads the two thousand worshipers through the streets of the Seven Hells. The muffled sound of shoes on the pavement is heard. Soldiers on a weekend pass from Fort Bliss walk by on their way to the red light district of Juarez. "Love is more powerful than violence," Abelardo Delgado has said. The boys in uniform look bewildered.

XXVI Of Blood and Death

The Region of the Damned

On the empty streets of Rio Grande City, Texas, a gray dust covers everything, like a patina of death. The faces of the people are as gray as the walls. In the old cowboy hotels and empty bars, with their antique and wheezing fans, no one talks to a stranger.

"It's a town of ghosts," a gaunt man says. He is called "The Skeleton" by some.

"Who haunts it?" he is asked.

"The devil," says the gaunt man. "Or maybe the Texas Rangers."

Gilbert Padilla, a taut and intense farm worker from sunny California, had come to the region of the damned to lead the *huelga* of the cantaloupe pickers and to organize the Farm Workers Union if he could. No one in this "feudal town," as Padilla calls it, has ever organized a union, and the *huelga* will be lost in beatings, jailings, and fear.

"We are afraid," a migrant worker says. His look is part of the death.

In the yard of his union office, the rotting house of a campesino, Padilla looks at the dusty town, the muddy street where the scraggly chickens peck futilely at the dry, caked tire tracks. "Cesar Chavez said to me, 'There's some problem in Texas. Go and see what's wrong.' That was in January, 1967. I have been here ever since." He smiles so slightly that his lips hardly quiver. "We do have 'some problem.' One problem we have is that the Rio Grande Valley is still in the Middle Ages. South Texas is a place of lords and serfs. Or maybe slaves."

A bony cow munches weeds in the wreckage of a junked car. Barking dogs fight over garbage. In bare feet a little girl in sackcloth plays in the mud of the road. Her lips and feet are covered with sores. It looks like any town in Mexico, without the exuberance and bright colors. Nowhere in the United States are there more dead and decayed towns than those of the farm workers in the beautiful valley of the Rio Grande.

"This is the poorest place in the whole country," says Froben Lozada, a local schoolteacher.

Clusters of shacks in the hidden edges of the fields resemble the back country of Guatemala. These are the *colonias* of the poor. Unseen from the highways, the *colonias* are ignored by the towns and counties; they are less tended than the town dump.

An ordinary *colonia*, like any other, is that of Madero (Timber). It is a cross between a Hooverville of the Depression and an Indian village of a century ago.

In a thicket of bushes and trees are huts built of straw and mud, old boards, and road signs. Some of the huts have outhouses. Some have compost heaps in the bushes. Flies swarm by the thousands. On the abandoned cars, where children sleep, chickens squat. Under the trees are old beds with sagging mattresses. There is no room in the huts. There are no stoves. In the winter the people burn wood in washtubs and carry the ashes and coals into the huts for warmth when the temperature drops below freezing, as it often does.

Half of the "houses" in the Lower Rio Grande Valley—46 per cent —have neither plumbing nor hot water, estimates Professor Claude Arenas, of the Department of City and Regional Planning of the University of Texas. At a conference, "Housing Problems in the Valley," sponsored by several federal, state, and local governmental agencies, in the summer of 1968, he tells the audience that 35,000 new houses are needed. But he is pessimistic. "I suspect the situation will get worse. The only question is the rate at which it will get worse."

Across the Rio Grande in Mexico it is the same. Carlos Nuno, an engineer employed by the Mexican Government in the bordertown of Reynosa, tells the conference that 50 per cent of the houses in Mexico have "only one room, 60 per cent lack water, and 39 per cent have no windows." Nuno might be describing any of the *colonias* of Texas.

In the Lower Rio Grande Valley wages have been so depressed they resemble those of the Depression. The random survey of seventy-two farm workers in twelve barrios and *colonias* revealed that forty-six who labored in the cotton and vegetable fields, on hoeing, earned 45 to 75 cents an hour; twenty-six received 45 to 50 cents. The cantaloupe harvesters did better, earning 50 to 85 cents an hour, while the skilled tractor drivers were paid 60 to 90 cents an hour. One man, a cantaloupe picker, reported he earned $1 per hour. His was the highest wage reported. This was in the summer of 1967 when Padilla came to Rio Grande City.

And in Starr County, of which Rio Grande City is the county seat, 75 per cent of the families, in 1960, lived beneath the poverty line of $3,000 a year. One-third of the families earned less than $1,000; one-third subsisted on welfare and surplus food.

"Many of the migrant farm workers in the lower Rio Grande Valley were living under conditions close to peonage or slavery," Father Theodore Hesburgh, the chairman of the United States Commission on Civil Rights, and president of Notre Dame University, was reported to have said (the *New York Times*, December 13,1968) after an investigation of the plight of the *colonias*. That winter "180 rural slum villages with no roads or utilities" were studied. Father Hesburgh was appalled. He instructed the Commission's staff to determine whether the federal antipeonage laws were being violated.

Colonias are a separate world. The irony and anger of their names describe them: Blue Town, Ojo de Agua (Eye of the Water, or Whirlpool), Rancho Alegre (Happy Ranch), Campo Alto (High Field), Relampago (Lightning Bolt), La Paloma (The Dove), La Tijera (The Scissors), La Feria (The Fair).

There are dozens of the *colonias* in the valley, and there are hundreds in southwest Texas. Unseen and uncounted, the families that live in these *colonias* are not even statistics.

Into the region of the doomed comes the union of farm workers, and the Migrant Ministry of the Texas Council of Churches. The Reverend Edgar A. Krueger, a boyish-faced, soft-spoken evangelist of the United Church of Christ, who has worked for eight years in the fields with the migrants, is sent into the valley. He helps found the Colonias del Valle, a "weedroot organization," of twenty-three of the poorest colonies. He begins a self-help program, to build up the communities. "I really believe in self-determination," the young minister says, "so the people in the *colonia* can speak for themselves."

The *Noticias de las Colonias del Valle* (The News of the Colonies of the Valley), a single mimeographed sheet, is issued by the Reverends Edgar Krueger and Nehemias Garcia, the "migrant ministers." "In some areas 70 to 90 per cent of the people are without work and without money," reports *Noticias.* "The vast majority of farm worker families have no welfare payments, nor any other financial support when they are without work. Farm workers are excluded from unemployment insurance."

When Christmas comes, the men of the *colonias* who are blessed by charity distribute boxes of food to the hungry families: ten pounds of beans and two pounds of lard for every four to eight people, a box of salt, a can of tomato sauce per person, and two cans of milk for each child under the age of two years. It is a "real Christmas spirit," says the *Noticias.*

"It's worse here than on the Mississippi Delta," says the teacher, Froben Lozada, who has lived and taught in both regions. "The people here are poorer than the poorest blacks. And they are even more thoroughly forgotten by the country. Who ever heard of the *colonias* in the East? Who cares about these people? No one! No one!" Unless you live in the *colonias* you cannot imagine "what a hell hole it is," Lozada says.

A woman organizer for the National Farm Workers' Union in the Rio Grande Valley says, "It's hot here. The weather drains all your strength. The water is bad and the scorpions drive me buggy. They have quite a few of them here, as well as rattlesnakes and rats.

This evening Ishmael came in with his little kid who had been bitten by a rat. Tamar was bit by a scorpion yesterday."

The lemon-and-blue sky illuminates the *colonias* with brilliant light. Old carcasses of cars become iridescent. In contrast to many colors of the sun, the stately palms, and the lushness of the farms in the valleys, the gray hunger seems even more like death.

Under the palm trees the tourists bask in the sun. Come to vacation amid the "palm-lined citrus groves and fresh vegetables in superabundance as far as the eye can see," says a brochure of the Lower Rio Grande Valley Chamber of Commerce. "This is the Fun Coast of Texas." Civic pride has named it "The Magic Valley.""Ever pick a sweet, juicy, ruby red grapefruit or an orange right off a tree?" asks a tourist come-on.

Froben Lozada says,"It would be more accurate to call it the Tragic Valley."

"The Valley, for all practical purposes, is an underdeveloped country," Professor Claudio Arenas says, ". . . similar in economic problems to African and Asian countries. The best solution for the Valley is to model itself after Puerto Rico, or possibly Israel."

Gilberto Padilla, "the Skeleton," is the appropriate man for this ghostly, forgotten valley. On the Day of the Dead, the union newspaper jokingly printed a *calavera*—"skull song"—dedicated to the lean organizer:

> The skeleton came
> And said,"What a shame
> This poor Gil Padilla
> Is so skinny and tame."
> But Padilla arose
> And gave such a fight
> "The devil," he said,
> "I'll come another night."

On the door of his union office there is a black and red flag. He holds it in his hands, The colors are those of the flag of nonviolence of the *huelga* but without the Aztec eagle; it is just black and red, the colors of anarchy and revolution. Is that what the colors mean?

"Here, I think," Padilla says, looking at the flag carefully, "the red stands for blood and the black stands for death."

Blood and Death

In the Valley of the Rio Grande the murder of Mexicans at least equaled, if not surpassed, the lynching of Negroes in the South during the late nineteenth and early twentieth centuries. Many thousands of men, women, and children died. No body count was ever taken.

Up the road from Rio Grande City, across the Texas badlands, there was a court where these wholesale killings were legally approved. In the town of Langtry, Judge Roy Bean, known as "The Law West of the Pecos," dispensed frontier justice from his porch. One day a Texan was brought before him accused of murdering a Mexican. The judge could find "no law in his books against killing a Mexican." Case dismissed!

On the Pecos River so many Mexicans were casually killed that "Pecosing a feller" became West Texas slang for murdering a man and getting away with it. The bodies of the victims were weighted with rocks and dumped into the rivers.

In his *My Reminiscences as a Cowboy* the Victorian vaquero Frank Harris tells how in the 1870's his Texas cronies would cross into Mexico to rustle cattle and shoot up the villages for the fun of it. The "bunch of greasers" who came looking for their stolen cattle would be shot for their troubles, Harris says. Then the Texans would sue those they had just shot for attacking *them.* "The idea of punishing the Mexicans for getting shot while trying to recapture their own cattle, appealed to us Americans as something intensely humorous," Harris writes.

The killing of a Mexican was a popular game. It was a sport, a murderous joke, to be recounted in saloons, or in black folk humor.

In South Texas there was an old saying: "Every Texas Ranger has some Mexican blood. He has it on his boots."

Hunting Mexicans was legal. The Texas Rangers who were traditionally chosen to enforce law and order in West Texas, after "The Conquest," were "cold blooded where Mexicans were concerned," wrote a friendly chronicler of their deeds. That was so the Mexicans "can be properly handled," he explained. The reporter George Marvin, writing in *World Work* in those horse-and-buggy days, was less friendly: "Some of the Rangers have degenerated into man killers. There is no penalty for killing [Mexicans], for no jury along the border would ever convict a white man for shooting a Mexican," he wrote. "Reading over the Secret Service records makes you feel almost as though there were an open season on Mexicans along the border."

The dawn of the enlightened twentieth century did not stop the flow of blood. "From 1908 to 1925 the whole border was aflame again as revolution engulfed Mexico," Carey McWilliams writes in *North from Mexico.* In those brief years the dean of Texas historians, Walter Prescott Webb, estimated that anywhere from 500 to 5,000 Mexicans were killed by Texans in the Rio Grande Valley.

In the early 1920's the Rangers "executed" from 100 to 300 known Mexican residents of the border towns, without trials or formal charges, according to Jovita Gonzales, a distinguished Texan writer. President Venustiano Carranza of Mexico offered evidence documenting the murder and lynching of 114 "Mexican citizens" who were "mistakenly" killed in the Rio Grande Valley. His charges were diplomatically acknowledged and regretted. Secretary of State Charles Evans Hughes suggested that the Governor of Texas afford some protection to Mexicans along the border, lest there be international repercussions from the killings.

The murders went on. In dismay the *New York Times* commented editorially in 1921: "the killing of Mexicans without provocation is so common as to pass unnoticed."

Once the valley was a peaceful Shangri La. When the settlers came from Mexico in 1749 to build towns like Rio Grande City, they named the tree-lined river banks the Seno Mexicano—the Mexican Hollow.

The grassy meadows were a refuge from the harsh desert that surrounded them.

Long before the American Revolution there were cities in the Rio Grande Valley as large and prosperous as New York City was then. The fertile and green land was among the richest in the Southwest. The water was clear and so swift they called it the Rio Bravo, the River of Courage, or the fierce river. It was a river "like the Nile," settlers wrote. Along its banks were little lakes known as *esteros* and *resacas.* Herds of cattle, the first great herds in Texas, fattened on its meadows. On the ranches of the Mexican settlers there were 3 million head of cattle when the United States Army invaded the valley in 1846. The cattle industry of Texas began with the stealing of these herds.

The art of the vaquero, the cowboy, was introduced into Texas by the Mexicans, as were the cattle and horses. "After God, our only security was the horses," Cortés wrote during the conquest of the Aztecs. It was an ancient pride of the Spaniard and Mexican. One historian has said that "the Spaniard always had the Arab's fondness for his horse." He had the Arab's horse as well. And he brought his horse to Texas. The words of the cowboy's language reveal his Mexican ancestors: bronco, rodeo, lariat, ranch (from rancho), chaps (from chaparral), poncho, sombrero, hoosegow (from *juzgado),* mustang, ramada, patio, plaza, and a hundred more, are all borrowed from the Mexican. Even the Alamo was Mexican, in Spanish it means poplar.

The first cowboys in Texas were these vaqueros of the Rio Grande Valley. Frederic Remington, the great Western artist who rode with the vaqueros, once said of them: "When he mounts his horse, all men must bow and call him master. My imagination had never before pictured anything as wild as these leatherclad vaqueros."

But the vaquero paid homage to the Indian. In *The Vaquero,* the old-timer Arnold R. Rojas puts it plainly: "When a vaquero was especially skilled, and he was asked how he reached such a degree of proficiency, his answer would invariably be, *'Me crie entre los Indios'* —I was raised among the Indians. Contrary to a lot of false statements a man took pride in calling himself *'Indio.'* "

In the Valley of the Rio Grande, the Indians "were neither exterminated in the English manner, nor enslaved, according to the usual Spanish way," says Americo Paredes. "The Indians who began as *vaqueros* and sheepherders were absorbed into the blood." Paredes, a professor of English at the University of Texas, whose *With His Pistol in His Hand* is a study of the history and *corridos* of the valley, notes that this was to haunt Texans. The late Walter Prescott Webb found that "there is a cruel streak in the Mexican culture," which "may and doubtless should be attributed partly to the Indian blood." Unlike the Indians of the Great Plains, whose blood Webb thought noble, the Mexican Indians had blood "like ditch water."

The "ditch water" flowed into the Rio Bravo. In time the river grew red and brown as the earth and became known as the Rio Grande. And the towns were to dry up.

On the border the crevice of turgid water runs sluggish and reddish in the Texas sun. The water of the Rio Grande becomes muddy as the mud on its banks, day by day wasting away the land of the Southwest for a thousand miles. It is like a deep wound.

In the gash in the earth the young Republic of Mexico, which had just won its independence from Spain, fought and lost its Thermopylae against the "Colossus of the North." Of that "most unjust [war] ever waged by a stronger against a weaker nation"—as General Ulysses S. Grant said of it—the goal was "the occupation, separation and annexation [of Texas], from the inception of the movement to its final consummation, a conspiracy to acquire territory out of which slave states might be formed."

"We were sent to provoke a fight," the Union Army Commander, who was a lieutenant in the invading army, wrote in his *Memoirs*. "But it was essential that Mexico should commence it. . . . Mexico showed no willingness to come to the Nueces [River] to drive the invaders from her soil [and] it became necessary for the invaders to approach to within a convenient distance to be struck. Accordingly, preparations were begun for moving the army to the Rio Grande. . . ."

James K. Polk in the White House promptly declared the country had been attacked. In his diary the President was less rhetorical, for the entry of May 30, 1846, a few weeks after the Declaration of War, reads: "I declared my purpose [in the Cabinet meeting] to be to acquire for the United States California, New Mexico, and perhaps some other of the northern provinces of Mexico whenever peace was made. In Mr. ——'s secret instructions last autumn these objectives were included. Now that we are at war the prospect of acquiring them is much better."

The nature of the war sickened even the commander of the U.S. Army, General Winfield Scott. His troops "committed atrocities to make heaven weep and every American of Christian morals blush for his country," the general wrote. "Murder, robbery and rape of mothers and daughters in the presence of tied-up males of the families have been common all along the Rio Grande."

If the war against Mexico was an almost classic example of a colonial war, then the conquest and occupation of the Southwest understandably gave rise to an almost classic example of colonialism. But it was a very difficult conquest to maintain. The conquered country was not only within the borders of the conqueror, but it bordered for 1,500 miles on the edge of the mother country from which it had been dismembered.

"Mexico is so far from God and so near to the United States," laments the old folk saying.

From the time of the rule of Spain and then of Mexico, the people of the Southwest had been treated like colonials. They were considered to be uncultured, boorish rurals, the ruffians of the frontier. Although the Southwest constituted one-third of Mexico, it was known by a separate name—the Borderland, as if it was on the edge of purgatory. The seat of government was in Durango or Mexico City, Seville or Madrid. Economic control and political power were imposed from the outside, as they were by the absentee landlords and Eastern investors after the conquest. It was a colony of mines and farms that produced raw materials for the high culture and wealth of its governors, Spanish, Mexican, or gringo.

In spirit the people of La Raza were kin to the farmers and frontiersmen of the American Revolution who rebelled against the colonialism of the British Empire. The history of the Southwest is one of endless rebellions, largely unwritten; for the settlers were an Indian and Mexican people who thought of themselves as a rigorous, brazen, free, and independent breed. They are the unsung pioneers of the West who fought the rigors of mountains and deserts with wooden plows and ancient muskets and lances. In the sparse and rugged villages of mud houses there was not much need for the splendor of the baroque haciendas and ducal palaces of Mexico. The villagers were contemptuous of the luxurious life of their rulers—a gracious society their forefathers had abandoned to suffer the wilderness. It was irreconcilable to their sacrifice.

The colonial bonds that held Mexico together under the Spanish Empire were strained, and they snapped when the colonials won their independence from Spain in 1824. The inexperienced Republic of Mexico was too weak to hold its poor relations in the Borderland in bondage any longer. Warfare erupted all along the border.

At the time of the conquest of the Southwest by the armies of the United States much of the territory was in varying states of revolt against Mexico, ranging from open civil war that raged for a decade in New Mexico, to political subversion of Santa Ana in Texas, and economic defiance in California of the government authorities. So insistent were the voices of independence of *Mexicans* in the Southwest, that one leader of the Government of Mexico, José Maria Tornel, berated those "liberals" among his fellow countrymen who had created a state of "constant anarchy" in the border regions and had "left us powerless against the attacks and invasions of the modern Rome [the United States]." Tornel was prophetic.

Mexican warred upon Mexican. The Army of the United States thrust itself between the divided nation.

The independence of the Republic of Texas was won in part by Mexicans fighting for their own self-determination. It was not merely the Davy Crocketts who turned the old Mission Church of the Alamo into a fort and who died upon its altars and parapets, but Mexicans, too. Santa Ana's army was made up mostly of Mayan Indian recruits and professional soldiers, while the most experienced military men fighting for the independence of Texas were a group of former officers of the Mexican Army. At least two battalions of Texas troops were composed of La Raza Mexicans—that is, Mexicans who were *Tejanos*, the first nonnative settlers of Texas, and who died for the Republic of Texas.

In the valley of the Rio Grande, the resistance to outsiders was long-standing. Of these people, Americo Paredes has written that their "principal offense was an independent spirit." So strong was the resistance that, before the War against Mexico, General Santa Ana ordered that the local militia be disarmed and prohibited the possession of firearms by the citizenry—an act of repression he was to regret when the United States overran the unarmed towns.

But the memory of the bloodshed did not dry. It was to be fed through the years by endless guerrilla wars and warriors.

One of the most dashing was Juan Nepomuceno Cortina, "the red robber of the Rio Grande," a rancher and wealthy landowner who, in 1859, began a land war to drive out the invaders. Cortina led his private army into Brownsville with the cry "Viva Cortina! Viva Mexico! *Maten los gringos.*" From 1860 to 1875 his guerrillas "liberated" the entire valley from Brownsville to Rio Grande City. He raised the Mexican flag once more. In Mexico, President Juárez appointed Cortina a General of the Army. "Our enemies shall not possess our land until they have fattened it with their gore," the border Robin Hood proclaimed in triumph.

"ASTOUNDING NEWS FROM THE RIO GRANDE! THE MEXICAN POPULACE ARMING TO EXTERMINATE THE AMERICANS AND RECONQUER OUR COUNTRY TO THE COLORADO RIVER! ACTUAL WAR ON THE BORDER!" said the headlines in the San Antonio *Herald*, less troubled at the time by the report of "a riot at Harpers Ferry."

There were some who thought of Juan Cortina as a John Brown. Not all of these were Mexicans. One U.S. Army officer, a Major Heintzelman, who fought against him, said, "He was the champion of his race—the man who would right the wrongs of the Mexicans and drive the hated Americans to the Nueces."

Once more the blood flowed in the Rio Grande Valley. The Cart War of 1857 and the Salt War of 1877—in which the Mexicans of El

Paso, led by Father Borajo, briefly occupied that city—were but two of hundreds of skirmishes fought along the border that continued until the Mexican Revolution broke out.

"Our Southwest" is threatened by a "Mexican Indianista Movement," Lothrop Stoddard wrote in 1921 in *The Rising Tide of Color: Against White World Supremacy.* "In Mexico the last decade of revolutionary turmoil has developed a complicated race war of meztisos against white, or near white upper class, and of Indian fullbloods against both whites and meztisos. One bond of union is the dislike of the gringo which often rises to fanatical hatred. During the early stages of the European war our military unpreparedness and apparent pacifism actually embolded some Mexican hot-heads to concoct the notorious 'plan of San Diego.' The conspirators plotted to rouse the Mexican population on our southern border . . . by means of a 'reconquering, equitable army.' "

The near hysteria of landowners from Texas to California, evoked by the Mexican Revolution, is reflected by the fears of Stoddard, who wrote, "Our Southwest was to be rejoined to Mexico, while our Southern states were to form a Black Republic."

Historically there has been an equation between the fears that the Mexicans might seek to "reconquer," or legally reclaim, their lost lands, and the bloodiness of the strife along the border. The revolution in Mexico provoked these fears. So do the contemporary movements of La Raza in the dusty border towns and counties.

On the earth there is no sign of blood. As the sun is absorbed by the earth, so is the blood of man. But a man does not easily forget the blood and death of his ancestors that is buried under his feet.

In the summer of 1967, when the *huelga* of the melon pickers—who wanted only a few cents more an hour—began, the guns reappeared in the valley. Rifle in hand, the Texas Rangers were summoned to Rio Grande City. The dusty streets were occupied like an armed camp. Fear of violent fighting spread up the valley. A prominent lawyer wrote that the union organizers of the farm workers were "ruffians and agitators who vowed that no growing crops would move out of the area even if they had to burn bridges, and use any force, legal or illegal. . . . It is my opinion that had the Texas Rangers not come into the area and enforced the law as they did, we would have seen rioting, the burning and destruction of property, and possible loss of life as a result of those who were terrorizing the community."

There *was* violence. The railroad bridge outside of Rio Grande City *did* burn.

"The men wanted to carry their guns on the picket lines," says Gilberto Padilla, the union organizer. "You know, a pistol in their belts to protect themselves. In the beginning of the strike everyone thought the Rangers would shoot them. But I told them, 'When you carry a pistol that means you're scared.'

"But they said, 'We'll be killed!'

" 'No guns!' I said. 'Be a man with your own body.'

Padilla says he convinced the men. "You know, Texans are supposed to be *muy bravo.* It is not true. Oh, they'll carry a gun and strut. Like the Rangers. But take away their guns? And the Texans are chicken.

"Now we have fifty men who got guts, without pistols," he says. "It's a beginning, yes?"

The Quiet Revolution

At night the silence of a border town is broken by the howl of a dog, or an unknown cry, or a shot. "Loud rapping on the door . . . the shuffling of booted feet on the wooden porch . . . harsh, guttural commands shattering the night stillness . . . the fear that the next gun-butted head will be one's own . . ." Unfamiliar noises in the rural quiet. These are the sounds of the night in the towns of the valley of the Rio Grande, where the Texas Rangers ride forth on what may be their last ride, in the summers of the *huelga*—the strike of the melon pickers.

Late one evening in 1966 four carloads of Texas Rangers pull up abruptly in front of an empty movie house—the old Mexico Theatre—in Rio Grande City. Inside, beside the silent screen and shabby seats, the United Farm Workers Organizing Committee (UFWOC) has set up strike headquarters. The melon pickers of the La Casita Farms, one of the country's cornucopias of cantaloupes, have walked out of the fields. For the first time since the "Cowboys' Strike" of the turn of the century the bucolic sloth of South Texas is threatened.

Into the dilapidated theater the Rangers burst with leveled shotguns. They hold their weapons at waist height, aiming low. But there is no shooting. Everyone freezes.

His face set, Captain Alfred Y. Allee, the commander of the Rangers, a tall and imposing lawman, wearing his impervious Stetson hat and chomping a cigar, demands to know the whereabouts of Magdaleno Dimas, a "troublemaker." One of the Rangers barks, "Where's that son of a bitch, Dimas? We're going to get him." It is a scene from an old western flick, but the shotguns are real.

The young man with the sad name, Magdaleno Dimas, had gone hunting that afternoon for doves. Jim Rochester, the manager of the struck La Casita farms, who is also a deputy sheriff, charges that Dimas threatened him with his hunting rifle and yelled "*Viva la huelga!*" to his face. The yell is illegal, for there is a court injunction against the cry of "*Huelga!*"

Randall Nye, the Starr County Attorney, who is also the lawyer for the La Casita Farms, later was asked by Federal Judge John Robert Brown why he had a union member arrested, charged with "disturbing the peace," merely for yelling, "*Viva la huelga!*"

"He said it loudly, Judge," Nye replied.

Magdaleno Dimas is obviously a headstrong young man. He is bearded, besides, and has a prison record for "assault resulting in murder"—a young man of disastrous temper.

In the cantinas they say that the Rangers "have it in for Magdaleno. He hates the *rinques* [Rangers]! He talks back." On the brick wall of the Mexico Theatre in Rio Grande City, under the list of *Héroes de la Huelga,*" the name of Magdaleno Dimas is written. One of the Rangers reportedly tells a newsman, "I'd like to hold my foot on

Dimas' neck until his eyes bulge out like a toad."

Dimas is not in the theater. They corner him in the house of a fellow striker. Rangers surround the house, smash the front door, break the lock, and burst into the room, shotguns cocked.

In the jail of Edinburg, Texas, a woman farm worker who has been imprisoned for picketing hears what happens from an eyewitness. She tells the story without telling her name. Like many of the Mexicans in the valley her identity is anonymous. "When they saw the guns," she says, "[the men] put their hands in the air. They thought the Rangers—especially Captain Allee—were drunk. [They] were told to lay on the floor. They [the Rangers] were cursing them the whole time, saying they were going to kill the bastards. Then they proceeded to kick Magdaleno and smashed the back of his head with the shotgun barrel. He is in the hospital in a critical condition, with a broken rib, concussion, blood clot near the spine."

The broken body of Magdaleno Dimas is taken to a hospital in McAllen, Texas. He is treated by a local physician, Dr. Ramiro Casso, who tells the newspapers, "It is the worst beating I have ever seen given by the police. The Rangers are a bunch of thugs."

But Captain Allee denies that he or his officers roughed up their prisoner. In leaving the kitchen the two men fell over each other and that may have caused any bruises they had.

"I just cracked him [Dimas] slightly on the head," says the Ranger captain, with a gun butt.

Unconvinced, the farm workers' union brings suit against the Texas Rangers in the U.S. District Court for Southern Texas. The union charges twenty-three counts of harassment of its members and asks the court to restrain the Rangers and Starr County officials from "selectively arresting and prosecuting" the striking melon pickers. In a further action the union challenges the constitutionality of the Texas statutes concerning mass picketing, the use of "abusive language"—that is, yelling *"Viva la huelga!"*—and laws against "unlawful assembly." Sixty of its members have been jailed on such charges, it says.

It is unheard of that poor farm workers, and Mexicans at that, take the Texas Rangers to court. Gilberto Padilla remembers. "When I took the Texas Rangers to court, everybody told me I couldn't do that.

State Senator Joe Bernal, of San Antonio, said to me, 'You can't do things like that in Texas.'

" 'You can do these things,' I told him."

In the hearing before the federal judges the unswayed Captain Allee testifies that he is not opposed to the union. "They can strike from now until doomsday. I don't care as long as it's done peacefully. I'm not prejudiced."

He was simply doing his duty in making the arrests, the Ranger captain says. Dimas had a gun. Under the circumstance he was quite lenient with the strike leader. "I could have broken his neck if I wanted to," Allee tells the judges. "I could have shot him three or four times. I could have killed him if I wanted to, and maybe I should have."

Law and order is not a church tea, Captain Allee has said on another occasion. "I've always said if a man really wants to lose his religion, and lose all he's got, just get him to be a peace officer." He has been in several "shoot-outs." He has killed men, but "I hated to do it," he says. "I've never killed unless I had to. It isn't pleasing to take somebody else's life. If you can keep from killing a man, well, I think you can sleep a little better at night, so that's what I've always tried to do."

"Like lawmen of old, Captain Allee is the law in Rio Grande City and the only thing twentieth-century about him is that his 'peacemaker' is an automatic pistol and not a six gun," comments *Inferno*, a barrio newspaper in San Antonio.

According to the frontier ethic of Alfred Y. Allee one talks straight and shoots straight. As he says, "I have never been a man to flower anybody up." He voices a family tradition that is in his blood, for his father and his grandfather were Texas Rangers before him. The aging lawman is sixty-four, worn by the years but hard-handed as ever, and unflinching in his dedication. "I took an oath," he says simply. "I guess I'm just dedicated to the State of Texas."

"One of the finest men I've ever known," says Homer Garrison, Jr., director of the Texas Department of Public Safety, which nominally is responsible for the work of the Rangers.

But the poor of the *colonias* and the dusty towns of the valley see a different legend. "The Rangers are pigs!" says the anonymous woman farm worker in her jail cell. "I have been in jail three times. Twice roughed up by the Rangers and the third time a State Senator was present. Everyone who is arrested is beaten and has his arms twisted and is thrown against the walls and cars. . . . Even the judge stands by while you're being pushed around. Once in jail, you're liable to be beaten by the jailkeeper.

"Say a prayer for all of us here," the frightened woman pleads. "It's like being somewhere and you have nowhere to appeal."

"The Rangers are regarded with great resentment and distrust by many Mexican Americans," declared the staff report *The Mexican American*, prepared for the United States Commission on Civil Rights.

State Senator Joseph Bernal of San Antonio, who witnessed some of the arrests and beatings, rises to the floor of the Texas Legislature to request an investigation of the Rangers' behavior. The legislators are in an uproar. "A shouting match quickly ensued among a number of Senators before Bernal was voted down," reports *Inferno.* In Texas the one thing more sacrosanct than the Alamo is the Rangers.

In Washington, D.C., Senator Ralph Yarborough of Texas denounces the ordering of the Rangers into the Rio Grande Valley as strikebreakers. He urges that the Rangers be withdrawn, and swipes at his old political opponent, Governor John Connally, in the process. But Bexar County Commissioner Albert Pena goes further—the Rangers ought to be disbanded and retired to the pages of history, he declares.

Once or twice before, Texas legislators have sought to curb the Rangers. In 1902, John Garner, who was to become Vice President of the United States under Franklin D. Roosevelt, suggested that the Rangers be abolished. He considered them outdated. In 1913, State Representative Cox of Ellis tried to eliminate the budgetary appropriation of the Rangers, saying, "There is more danger from the Rangers than from the men they are supposed to hunt down," and "they are the most irresponsible officers in the state." All attempts to curb, censure, or disband the Rangers failed; so did Bernal's.

For the Texas Rangers are more than a living legend. They reflect the community's mandate—nonetheless real for being unstated—to subjugate La Raza in the Rio Grande Valley and in all of Texas.

Randall Nye, the County Attorney, was succinct and honest when he explained to the federal court hearings why he had called for the Rangers. "The situation became electric in early May, 1967. The harvest season was about to begin. Evidence indicated to me that something was about to happen. I felt the situation needed the attention of the Rangers." The "situation" was the strike of melon pickers on the La Casita farms, one of the largest melon growers he represented.

Men are even arrested for praying on the courthouse steps (the prayers "disturb the peace"). The Reverend Edgar Krueger, migrant minister of the Texas Council of Churches, is seized by a Ranger and his face held inches from a speeding freight train. "That preacher was ramrodding the whole thing," says Captain Allee. In all, scores of striking farm workers are jailed.

On the picket lines of the melon pickers new signs appear: "RANGERS NEEDED IN VIETNAM" and "RANGERS GO HOME."

"Most who work for La Casita would like to join the union, but they're afraid," a migrant worker tells Peggy Simpson of the San Antonio *Express*. "But the strike has already helped us. La Casita wages have risen. The farmers treat us kindly just seeing those pickets around. Sometimes they would push us hard, make us work fast. And now they're more reasonable."

A woman farm worker says, "I don't think the union will succeed. We are afraid to join it. Here you lose your job like . . ." and she snaps her fingers.

But the union does not succeed. The *huelga* drags on to defeat. In two years of bloody organizing, only a handful of growers, each of them a small Chicano farmer, signs a union contract; not one of the large corporate farmers.

Southwest Texas is a rigid society, unbending and divided. Although the people of the barrios and *colonias* are an overwhelming majority of many towns and counties, they have been relegated to the periphery of political patronage and the fringes of the professions. The seats of economic and political power are tightly held. In many ways it is still like a conquered country.

Here is "the perfect place for a people's war," a union organizer reports. "But we're nonviolent, and we believe it, because we would have all been dead by now any other way."

In the barrios some nod their heads in agreement; some do not. Violence has been more frequent than nonviolence, and the frustrations of the younger men are equaled only by the angers.

The schoolteacher Froben Lozada says, "Who the hell has always been violent? It's the white who have always been violent. Preach nonviolence to them, not to the Mexicans. Why teach nonviolence to the Mexicans? So they can get their heads banged up by the Texas Rangers? As if nonviolence is going to cushion the blow.

"I don't see any change coming. If there is going to be change, it won't come through the election thing. That'll just dish out a little more money and buy a few more Mexicans with street-cleaning jobs."

His skeptical view of achieving change by voting is widespread. In southwest Texas elections have often seemed a *fait accompli* of a one-party system and a one-party vote. Politicians come and go, but social inequity stays. The county seats—whereby, through the peculiarity of the Texan political system, the power of the county judge is unchecked—further solidify the status quo. Then, too, the irregularities in vote counting have created a distrust of the ballot box.

"It's not our bag," says a young farm worker. The resident of the barrios and *colonias* tends to look at the elections as a game played by the gringos and the respectable *venditos* for high stakes. He just votes.

Elections in Starr County are a feudal pageant and an elaborate ritual. Wherever there is a ballot box, the opposing political parties set up ornate tents, sometimes tassled and decorated, sometimes of canvas, sometimes a wooden booth. The voters, by an old custom, visit the tent or booth of their party before going in to cast their ballot. It is an ancient tradition that has no legality in election law but has been going on for fifty years. And it is rigorously adhered to. By the custom the secret ballot is rendered redundant, for everyone knows how everyone else will vote.

Neither the Democratic nor the Republican Party is on the ballot for Starr County posts. The old party is called the Old Party. The new party that has ruled the county for twenty years is called the New Party. And then there is the perennial upstart, the New New Party. Between themselves the Old Party, the New Party, and the New New Party have dominated political life for generations.

Yet in the election of 1968 an independent party—called, of course, the Independent Party—enters the pageant for the first time. It has the support of those people jarred by the old and new parties, acquiescence in the fear the Texas Rangers have introduced into the county. The union is one of its strong backers. And its prime purpose is the defeat of Randall Nye, the County Attorney, who had summoned the Rangers.

To everyone's surprise the Independent Party sweeps out the old regime. Not only does it elect its own man County Attorney, but its candidate, C. C. Valle, wins the *jefe político* job as County Chairman. La Raza activists have for the first time upset a reigning dynasty in Texas politics.

The Valley Evening Monitor, a conservative newspaper, begins its story, "Starr County voters staged a 'quiet revolution' . . ."

"We were trapped between the economic power of the growers and the political structure of the law. Maybe now we have a chance," says Gilberto Padilla, weighing the election in his mind. "I am optimistic now."

"I think maybe the *huelga* was not lost after all. We will win."

"You know, I'm a mild guy. I don't hurt a fly. If it doesn't get in my way. What motivates me to stay here? Same thing as people here. I'm real mad—even so, it will take a man's whole life to change Texas. But, it *is* my life now."

He says these things matter-of-factly. There is no bravado, and his eyes are calm. Padilla is stating a fact of his life, like the hour of the day.

"What makes you think you can change Texas?" I ask.

"Because I will change it," he says.

Nothing changes. On the dusty roads of the dusty towns the dust rises. The dust falls. The dust settles as it was before the elections and the strike. Into the poverty of the valley come reporters, investigators,

Senators, and tabulators of the U.S. Commission on Civil Rights, congressional committees, and the Citizens Crusade Against Hunger and Malnutrition. They come and they go.

The years go by. After two years in the valley, Gilberto Padilla packs up his hopes and leaves. From California the union sends a new organizer, Antonio Orendain, to begin again. Where has "The Skeleton" gone?

"He is sick," they say. "In a hospital in California."

"What is wrong with him?"

"He is sick," they say, "with frustration."

In the courts the farm workers' suit against the Texas Rangers is lost in a legal labyrinth. The case is never tried. "Who, I don't know, but someone is holding it up," says Reverend Krueger. His own suit against the Rangers, brought by the Texas Council of Churches, is dropped. His church superiors have three times asked the young minister to sign a "compromise agreement" that absolves the Rangers. It reads, in part: "The parties of this lawsuit, whose signatures are affixed below, are desirous of bringing the lawsuit to a peaceful conclusion, without fixing blame therefore."

Reverend Krueger refuses to sign. He "can't pretend these things didn't happen," he says. He is fired from the Migrant Ministry of the Texas Council of Churches.

"He made a lot of trouble," regretfully explains Dr. Harold Kilpatrick, the executive director of the church body. "We're tired of fighting city hall, courthouse, school boards, and things that look like the establishment. If we are to get anywhere we have to enlist [the help of] the power structure."

"IS THE CHURCH FOR THE POOR?" questions a sign carried by one of scores of pickets outside the meeting where the young minister is dismissed. "THE CHURCH IS FOR JUSTICE, WHERE IS JUSTICE FOR REV. KRUEGER?" and "IS THE TEXAS COUNCIL OF CHURCHES UNCHRISTIAN?" read others. The pickets come from the colonia del Valle, PASO (the Political Association for Spanish Organizations), MAYO (the Mexican American Youth Organization), and even the conservative League of Latin American Citizens, whose San Antonio leader, Frank

Gonzales, condemns the "wholesale surrender to these forces of oppression that have kept Mexican Americans in the Lower Rio Grande Valley in the condition of servitude."

"We have lost the only arm we had with the Texas Rangers," says Reynaldo de la Cruz, the president of the Colonia del Valle. But on the picket line Reverend Krueger is said to be arm in arm with the protesters.

"I told him not to get involved in revolutionary situations," says a high official of the Texas Council of Churches. "Krueger represented militancy. I am taking a strong stand against militancy. I'm getting a very favorable reaction in the valley, especially from the Anglos. . . . The rich have problems as well as the poor, maybe more." As for the poor, "We'll continue our Band-aid measures. It may be a twenty- to twenty-five-year job."

The young minister smiles and says, "I was fired by those who want a more paternalistic Christmas basket approach. But it's too late for that.

"In the *colonias* the men are eager to work, but there is no work. These men are fed up. Our government better become aware of the extremely volatile situation that exists here in the valley. We're asking for real rebellion if more jobs are not forthcoming."

A gray-haired man stands up in a *colonia* meeting and quietly says that if things get worse, "We will have a revolution." He reflects a growing frustration, Reverend Krueger says.

It is not the gray-haired men, the polite and patient older generation, who expect no change, who accept defeat, who will resort to violence, he believes. "The youth are becoming more and more impatient, and they won't wait for another generation for life to change; they are explosive," Reverend Krueger says. "It is the Vietnam veterans returning to the valley who could cause an explosion. These young Mexican Americans, with their medals and sacrifices, won't accept closed doors, and a society that won't accept them.

"They are coming home now. They and the high school and college youth are an explosive generation. And they are accustomed to violence.

"Something has got to give," the Reverend says. "And it will."

In the dark heat of the summer nights in South Texas the melon pickers once more meet and talk. Now they are alone. They have been forgotten by the rest of the nation. They have nothing but their hungers and angers. They wait for the dawn, when the morning sun explodes over the Valley of the Rio Grande.

When dawn comes the sun is a ball of fire. And the river is red as blood.

EPILOGUE: The Poet in the Boxing Ring

He "lurked like a cat for the kill." The ritual lingo of the boxing ring described the fighting style of a young intellectual who read Lorca in the dressing room, and who fought seventy-five professional bouts and won sixty-five of them. He fought with the desperation of a kid from the barrios. The crowds savored the blood that dripped from his eyes, his lips, his bronzed face. "A crowd pleaser," one boxing buff recalls.

"Rodolfo is a gentle man," his wife says. "He is a poet."

In a poem he wrote later, an epic of the "La Raza revolution" that he titled "I Am Joaquín," the lyrical fighter remembered his own bleeding as a symbol:

> I bleed as the vicious gloves of hunger
> cut my face and eyes,
> As I fight my way from the stinking barrios
> to the glamor of the Ring
> and lights of fame
> or mutilated sorrow.

The Championship of the World was almost his. *Ring Magazine* hailed him as one of the five best boxers of his weight. He was rated the third ranking contender for the World Featherweight title by the National Boxing Association. When Gonzales was still in his teens he had won the National Amateur Championship and the International Championship as well. In the Lysoled corridors of the pugilistic kingdoms of the Mafia he was fingered as the coming "King of the Little Men." He was a "hungry fighter," the connoisseurs of flesh wrote in the sports pages. They did not know he was a poet.

He is a "poet of action" in the ring, the boxing writers wrote unwittingly. Lithe, his mind as quick as his body, he reacted like the reflex of a muscle. He was later to write of a young boxer, Manny, in one of his plays, "His movements are smooth, casual, and catlike." It may have been a self-portrait.

The Golden Boy of the boxing legend, he was to become the new voice of the Chicano movement. He was the idol of his generation, and he shared their frustrations. He was the embodiment of the confused barrio youth, the urban Chicanos.

He quit the ring. In his poem of self-discovery he wrote of the odyssey he embarked upon:

> I am Joaquín
> Lost in a world of confusion,
> Caught up in a whirl of
> Anglo society,
> Confused by the rules,
> Scorned by the attitudes,
> Suppressed by manipulations,
> And destroyed
> by modern life.

Where was he going? He did not know. "It's a long road back to yourself when the society has made you into someone else," he now says. "But I was determined to find my way, to rediscover my roots, to be the man I am, not the emasculated man that the Anglo society wanted me to be."

Rodolfo "Corky" Gonzales lived all the lives that "divide our hearts and emasculate our souls." In his young manhood he became an insurance salesman, a romantic poet, a big-city politician, a campesino in the fields, a soldier, a lumberjack, a playwright, the landlord in the ghetto, the leader of the Poor People's March on Washington, D.C., a high-ranking government official, a lone crusader, the father of eight children, the hero of the newspapers—and the villain, the All-American Boy, the victim of police riots, the descendant of the conquistadors, the "foreign Communist agitator," a political ward heeler, a successful businessman, and a revolutionary.

"The young Chicano is the most complex man in the country." He smiles, self-effacingly. "I guess that means me, too."

He was born in the barrios of Denver, a kid of the streets. Yet he grew up on the earth as well as the cement pavements, for his father was a Mexican emigrant, who worked as a campesino and coal miner in southern Colorado. As a boy he worked in the sugar-beet fields, beside his father, at the age of ten.

"Yes, I am a city man," he says. "But I did a lot of farm work. I have relatives in the villages in the San Luis Valley. Every spring and summer, as a boy, I worked in the fields. Every fall and winter I lived in the city slums."

Schools did not educate him. He learned of life in the fields and barrios. "The teachers taught me how to forget Spanish, to forget my heritage, to forget who I am," he says bitterly. "I went to four grade schools, three junior highs, and two high schools besides, because of our constant moving to the fields and back to the city." Even so, he graduated from high school at sixteen. He remembers working in a slaughterhouse at night and on weekends, so he could afford to go to school. He walked in so much blood that his shoes were always stained.

"I became a fighter because it was the fastest way to get out of the slaughterhouse. So I thought." He laughs.

The fictitious fighter in his drama *A Cross for Maclovio,* which Gonzales was to write some years later, has a family fight with his sister that has an autobiographical ring. It was a familiar scene:

MANNY: I can't understand people who knock themselves out for someone else. If you don't make it on your own, ain't nobody gonna help you.

LITA: If you ever get it through your thick head that this world can be changed . . . you might see things differently.

MANNY: Horseshit! What's wrong with a Cadillac, a big diamond ring, sirloin steak and fur coats?

LITA: You're afraid. You're a coward.

MANNY: Yeah, I'm a coward. That's why I won the Nationals. That's why I've already whipped every lightweight in this state. . . . Mama, you won't have to worry about the future. Cause this is the hand that's going to shake the world. *(He shakes his right fist in the air.)* Manny Galegos, the Lightweight Champ of the world. Furs for Mama, two-buck cigars for Papa. Vacations in Mexico. We'll give them peons a sight to behold. . . . I'll send them tickets to watch me fight in New York City. Then I come home and be their leader. I'll scale the City Hall walls and throw a blonde to all my buddies. I'll tell them how they come from proud chiefs, kings, Revolutionists, winos, tricks, addicts, and . . ."

He was doing this in derision of his father who was working for La Causa.

He came home to "be their leader." A hero, Gonzales went into politics, opened a free boxing gymnasium for ghetto youth, was befriended by the mayor, became an after-dinner speaker on inspirational themes. "Like all boys growing up in this society, I identified success by wanting to be an important person loved by everyone."

He became a businessman. In one year he was owner of an automobile insurance agency and owner of a surety-bond business. Within three years, by 1963, he was General Agent for the Summit Fidelity and Surety Company of Colorado.

Once again he was too successful. He was the pride of the barrio. "Corky beat the Anglos with his fists, then he outsmarted them with his brains," a neighbor says. The fair-haired boy wherever he went, the "different" Mexican, he was beckoned with offers of political jobs. Los Voluntarios, a political action group, had been organized in Denver with Gonzales as chairman. "The sleeping giant was awakening."

The poet with scarred eyelids became a ward heeler. He was the first Chicano ever to be a district captain in the Denver Democratic Party at the age of twenty-nine. "Corky has charisma," says a City Hall hanger-on. "He zooms. That boy was a comer." In the presidential election of 1960 he was Colorado coordinator of the "Viva Kennedy" campaign, and his district had the highest Democratic vote in the city. He was rewarded for his victory. On a table in his old barrio office, beneath a flamboyant mural of the Statue of Liberty, her breast bared as she lay half-naked and raped by corruption, there was an array of bronzed and golden sports trophies, in the midst of which there was a photograph of the late President standing beside the ex-featherweight, and inscribed, "To Corky—John F. Kennedy."

In no time he was a one-man directory of poverty agencies. He was on the Steering Committee of the Anti-Poverty Program for the Southwest, on the National Board of Jobs for Progress (S.E.R., a major funding group for the barrios), on the Board of the Job Opportunity Center, President of the National Citizens Committee for Community Relations, and Chairman of the Board of Denver's War on Poverty.

Gonzales was rumored to be in line for state or even national office. The line was long. The Chicano was last in line. On the rising aspirations of the young and pugilistic barrio go-getter there was a political ceiling. And he was not yet poet enough to celebrate his frustrations. The poverty programs had disappointed him, much as party politics had disenchanted him. In the barrios the jobs were just as scarce, the poor just as poor. He attended conferences by the dozens, perhaps feeling the same as he imagined the delegates to the White House's Cabinet Committee hearings on Mexican American Affairs in El Paso, Texas, felt: "well-meaning, confused, irate, and insulted middle-class Chicanos who knew they were being had when they were asked to swallow and digest the same old soup and cracker disks fed by the politicians, with Johnson and Humphrey at the head of the line. Lacking was any positive direction or militant action. . . . What resulted was a lot of brave words, promises, motions—and no action."

Conferences and more conferences; how many times can he talk about poverty? The young man has heroic daydreams.

> I am Joaquín.
> I rode with Pancho Villa
>   crude and warm.
> I am Emiliano Zapata.

On the bus going from Denver to El Paso to hear the President and his Cabinet, he envisions a mirage of revolution looming out of the gas-station desert towns: "We could have been a guerrilla force riding to keep a date with destiny, if only the time and place and emotions of the people were right." But there is soup and crackers awaiting them.

I ride with Revolutionists
against myself.

"The politics of the Anglo emasculates the manhood of a man of La Raza. It makes him impotent, a Tío Taco, an Uncle Tom. I was losing my cool," Gonzales says.

"I was used by the Democratic Party. I was used because I had a rapport with my people. Working in the two-party system I found out one thing, and I found it out very late. My people were exploited and men like I was are . . ." he falters, biting off the sentence. "But I was never bought. I could have accepted a number of payoffs from politicians and administrators. I never accepted them. Our people who get involved become political monsters." He pauses again and says, "Whores."

In his play, *A Cross for Maclovio*, the hero complains, "They're afraid, now they want to buy off our leadership. You stir up people, get them ready for a revolution, and the establishment comes running with a suitcase of pesos." And in his poem, "I Am Joaquín," Gonzales writes:

I sometimes
sell my brother out
and reclaim him
for my own when society gives me
token leadership . . .

The Golden Boy was ending his odyssey. When a Denver newspaper attacked him as "almost a thief," it was an insult to his dignity, a betrayal, he thought, of his "manhood." The poverty officials in Washington defended him, denying the accusations, but his friends in City Hall were strangely still. His scathing letter of resignation to the Democratic County Chairman, Dale R. Tooley, reverberated in the barrios of the Southwest:

> The individual who makes his way through the political muck of today's world, and more so the minority representatives, suffers from such an immense loss of soul and dignity that the end results are as rewarding as

> a heart attack, castration, or cancer! . . . You and your cohorts have been accomplices to the destruction of moral man in this society. I can only visualize your goal as complete emasculation of manhood, sterilization of human dignity, and that you not only consciously but purposely are creating a world of lackeys, political boot-lickers and prostitutes.

He resigned from the boards and councils of the War on Poverty one by one. He went "home again," he says. "Now I am closer back to home than I ever have been in that I am financially just as bad off as any Chicano," he says.

> And now!
> I must choose
> Between
> the paradox of
> Victory of the spirit
> despite physical hunger
> Or
> to exist in the grasp
> of American social neurosis,
> sterilization of the soul
> and a full stomach.

The odyssey was ended. In an old red-brick building in the condemned barrio of downtown Denver, in 1965, the ex-almost-champion and past-president-of-everything founded *La Crusada Para la Justicia*, the Crusadc for Justice. Gonzales declared this was "a movement born out of frustration and determination to secure equality with dignity."

In the politics of the Crusade for Justice there would be no wheeling and dealing. There would be no compromise with stereotypes. "To best serve our particular ethnic and cultural group our organization must be independent, and must not be dependent on the whims and demands of private agencies which are establishment-controlled and dominated. The services offered will not have the taint of paternalism, nor will the feeling of inferiority be felt when securing need, help and guidance."

In a few years, the Crusade was so influential that "the Anglos come to us for our help," Gonzales says. He tells how Archbishop James Casey of Denver came, uninvited, to the Easter "Mexican Dinner" they held. The Archbishop donned a tourist sombrero, told the guests, "Cherish your history, your culture, and preserve your wonderful language," and donated $100 to the Crusade's Building Fund.

The Crusade bought an old church in downtown Denver that resembled a miniature U.S. Treasury. In the colonnaded edifice there is "the most unique Mexican American center in the country," with a school of "Liberation Classes," a nursery, gymnasium, Mayan Ballroom, Chicano Art Gallery, Mexican shops, library, community dining room and community center, job "skill bank," legal aid service, Barrio Police Review Board, health and housing social workers, athletic leagues, a barrio newspaper [*El Gallo*], a bail bond service, a kitchen, and a "Revolutionary Theatre."

"No government money, no grants, no rich angels, no hypocrisy, no begging, no handouts" created El Centro Para La Justicia, boasts Gonzales. "We did it. We can do it. The Crusade is living proof of self-determination. The Crusade is not just an organization; it is the philosophy of nationalism with a human form.

"Nationalism exists in the Southwest, but until now it hasn't been formed into an image people can see. Until now it has been a dream. It has been my job to create a reality out of the dream, to create an ideology out of the longing. Everybody in the barrios is a nationalist, you see, whether he admits it to himself or not. It doesn't matter if he's middle-class, a *vendito,* a sellout, or what his politics may be. He'll come back home, to La Raza, to his heart, if we will build centers of nationalism for him."

In the Southwest, "nationalism is the key to our people liberating themselves," he says.

"Colorado belongs to our people, was named by our people, discovered by our people and worked by our people. We slave in the fields today to put food on your table. We don't preach violence. We preach self-respect and self-defense . . . to reclaim what is ours.

"I am a revolutionary," he says, "because creating life amid death is a revolutionary act. Just as building nationalism in an era of imperialism is a life-giving act. The barrios are beginning to awaken to their own strength. We are an awakening people, an emerging nation, a new breed."

Rodolfo "Corky" Gonzales feels that he has found himself among his people. He is a unique revolutionary in a time of ugliness and hatred in that he devotes his efforts to building his community. He is the happiest revolutionary in the country.

"Now I am my own man. I don't need to prove myself to the Anglos," he says.

"*Machismo* means manhood. To the Mexican man *machismo* means to have the manly traits of honor and dignity. To have courage to fight. To keep his word and protect his name. To run his house, to control his woman, and to direct his children. This is *machismo*," Gonzales says. "To be a man in your own eyes.

"If you are afraid of the Anglo he is like an animal. The human being is an animal; when you are afraid he attacks you, he punishes you, but if you are not afraid of him he respects you. The Anglo respects you only when you have power and respect yourself.

"We have been withdrawn. We have been quiet. And this has been mistaken for being afraid. We are not afraid. Look at the Congressional Medals of Honor our people have. It shows that when it comes to *machismo* there is no match for La Raza. We have been withdrawn from this society to protect our culture, the values we have—not because we were cowards. Now we have to show them that we are strong. We have to use more forceful methods."

Gonzales is not talking of violence and nonviolence. The luxury of that choice he feels exists for those who have power to control and order their environment. It is meaningless in the barrio, as in the boxing arena, where violence is a normal act of everyday life that people are powerless to halt.

"Power is respected in this society," he says. "The black militants say the Negro needs black power to offset white power, and we need brown power to offset Anglo power.

"Are we endangering the economic system, the political system, by saying that? I think the system should be endangered. It is a system that is built upon racism and imperialism. That is why the low-income people and the minority people across the nation are rebelling. Unless the system changes, there will be more rebellions. Those who advocate change will save the country, not destroy it. Those who are resisting change are destroying the country.

"If there is no change by peaceful assembly, by demonstrations, by sitting down to discuss changes, then there will be frustration. Out of the frustration will come real violence, not riots. Unless everyone gets an equal share in this country, there won't be any country."

In Washington, D.C., during the Poor People's March, where he and Reies Tijerina led the Chicanos of the Southwest, Gonzales created a plan for the future, "the Plan of the Barrio." His words became the poetic demands of the Crusade for Justice to the Government of the United States:

> I am Joaquín
> in a country that has wiped out
> all my history,
> stifled all my pride.

"We are basically a communal people . . . in the pattern of our Indian ancestors. Part of our cultural rights and cultural strengths is our communal values. We lived together for over a century and never had to fence our lands. When the gringo came, the first thing he did was to fence land. We opened our houses and hearts to him and trained him to irrigated farming, ranching, stock raising, and mining. He listened carefully and moved quickly, and when we turned around, he had driven us out and kept us out with violence, trickery, legal and court entanglements. The land for all people, the land of the brave became the land for the few and the land of the bully."

> My knees are caked with mud.
> My hands callused from the hoe.
> I have made the Anglo rich.

"Robbed of our land, our people were driven to the migrant labor fields and the cities. Poverty and city living under the colonial system of the Anglo has castrated our people's culture, consciousness of our heritage, and language. Because of our cultural rights, which are guaranteed by treaty, and because the U.S. *says* in its constitution that all treaties are the law of the land . . ."

> Here I stand
> Poor in money
> Arrogant with pride.

"THEREFORE WE DEMAND: HOUSING."

"We demand the necessary resources to plan our living accommodations so that it is possible to extend family homes to be situated in a communal style . . . around plazas or parks with plenty of space for the children. We want our living areas to fit the needs of the family and cultural protections, and not the needs of the city pork barrel, the building corporations or the architects.

"EDUCATION: We demand that our schools be built in the same communal fashion as our neighborhoods . . . that they be warm and inviting facilities and not jails. We demand a completely free education from kindergarten to college, with no fees, no lunch charge, no supplies charges, no tuition, no dues.

"We demand that all teachers live within walking distance of the schools. We demand that from kindergarten through college, Spanish be the first language and English the second language and the textbooks to be rewritten to emphasize the heritage and the contributions of the Mexican American or Indio-Hispano in the building of the Southwest. We also demand the teaching of the contributions and history of other minorities which have also helped build this country. We also feel that each neighborhood school complex should have its own school board made up of members who live in the community the school serves.

"ECONOMIC OPPORTUNITIES: We demand that the businesses serving our community be owned by that community. Seed money is required to start cooperative grocery stores, gas stations, furniture stores, etc. Instead of our people working in big factories across the city, we want training and low-interest loans to set up small industries in our own communities. These industries would be co-ops with the profits staying in the community.

"AGRICULTURAL REFORMS: We demand that not only the land which is our ancestral right be given back to those pueblos, with restitution for mineral, natural resources, grazing and timber used.

"We demand compensation for taxes, legal costs, etc., which pueblos and heirs spent trying to save their land.

"REDISTRIBUTION OF THE WEALTH: That all citizens of this country share in the wealth of this nation by institution of economic reforms that would provide for all people, and that welfare in the form of subsidies in taxes and payoffs to corporate owners be reverted to the people who in reality are the foundation of the economy and the tax base for this society.

"LAND REFORM: A complete re-evaluation of the Homestead Act, to provide people ownership of the natural resources that abound in this country. Birthright should not only place responsibility on the individual but grant him ownership of the land he dies for."

On Palm Sunday, 1969, in the secular temple of La Crusada Para la Justicia the elated Rodolfo "Corky" Gonzales convened a national gathering of barrio youth. He called it, with a flourish, the Chicano Youth Liberation Conference. The young campesino activists, university graduate-school Chicanos, barrio gang members, *vados locos* from the streets, clever young government "Mexican Americans" incognito, and the wealthy children of the descendants of Spanish dons came to the temple-like building in downtown Denver to attend workshops in philosophy, self-defense, poetry, art, and identity. In all, more than 1,500 Chicanos come from as far away as Alaska, where no one thought there was any La Raza, and from Puerto Rico, and from all the states in between. They came from one hundred youth and student groups.

The conference of "music, poetry, *actos, embrazos,* tears, *gritos,* and the Chicano cheer: *'Raza, Raza, Raza, Raza,'* " went on for five days and nights. Afterward a youth wrote, "The building is just an ordinary building, but what counts is when you step through its doors. In this building we are not separated by the gringos. We are one."

" 'Conference' is a poor word to describe those five days," wrote Maria Varela, in *El Grito del Norte.* "It was in reality a fiesta: days of celebrating what sings in the blood of a people who, taught to believe they are ugly, discover the true beauty in their souls during years of occupation and intimidation. Coca-Cola, Doris Day, Breck Shampoo, the Playboy Bunny, the Arrow shirt man, the Marlboro heroes, are lies. 'We are beautiful'—this affirmation grew into a *grito,* a roar, among the people gathered in the auditorium of the Crusade's Center."

In the streets of Denver there were cries of youthful pain. The week before the Liberation Conference began some teen-agers walked out of the city's West Side High School to protest the insults of a teacher who had told his class, "Mexicans are dumb because they eat beans. If you eat Mexican food you'll become stupid like Mexicans." Students objected to his sense of humor and requested that the teacher be transferred. After a rally in the park the high school boys and girls tried to re-enter their school to present their demand to their principal.

Two hundred and fifty policemen barred their way.

Soon there was "a riot." The ex-boxer hurried to the school. "Fearing the police were going to hurt the students I rushed forward to take a bull horn," Gonzales recalls. "I shouted to the young people to leave. The police were beating men, women, and children, indiscriminately." Gonzales' young daughter was one of those caught in the melee. "I heard my daughter Nita Jo scream. She was being mauled by a six-foot policeman." There were thirty-six Chicanos arrested.

Denver's barrios had never seen the kind of riots that had been desecrating ghettos in other cities. The people of the community walked to the school the following day to protest, in dismay as much as in anger. Some two thousand came, kids and parents, brown and black and white, teachers as well as students.

When the demonstration was over the police began to move in on those who lingered. There were curses hurled. In moments a battle erupted and dozens of police cars, riot police equipped with chemical Mace and a police helicopter, were ordered into the fray against the taunting teen-agers. "Some say it was a riot. It wasn't. It was more like guerrilla warfare," says one eyewitness. The helicopter dropped tear gas on the youths. "But the wind was blowing the wrong way and they [the police] ended up gassing their own men. This also happened with the Mace. The police were practically Macing their own faces," says another eyewitness.

George Seaton, the Denver Chief of Police, reported that twenty-five squad cars were damaged, "some extensively," and at least "seventeen police were assaulted, injured, and hospitalized." It was the worst street fighting in the modern history of the city.

"What took place after many people left was a battle between the West Side 'liberation forces' and the 'occupying army.' The West Side won," said Gonzales. He told the high school students, "You kids don't realize you have made history. We just talk about revolution, but you act it by facing the shotguns, billies, gas, and Mace. You are the real revolutionaries."

It was barely a year before that the Crusade for Justice leader had told me that he thought there would be no riots in the barrios. "The riots across the nation lead to the self-destruction of man. He acts like an animal," Gonzales had said. "I don't think it is in the Mexican temperament to riot, or to hurt your neighbor that way. Our way would be to pinpoint our enemy, where we wanted to attack him—not to riot."

Riots were "circuses," Gonzales had said then. He described the urban upheavals as the products of the "dehumanized cities," where life itself was riotous and people had no hope. "Why do blacks riot? Because they see no way out, because they feel trapped in the ghettos, because that is how mass society acts. I respect the suffering of the blacks. We have both suffered. We work together. But we work differently because we are a different people.

"Our culture is such that we don't like to march, to protest. We don't like to be conspicuous. We don't like to seem ridiculous in the public eye. That is *machismo*. That is a man's sense of self-respect. We are not nonviolent. But in the barrio self-determination means that every man, every people, every barrio has to be able to take care of themselves, with dignity.

"We are men of silent violence," Gonzales had said. "That, too, is *machismo.*"

He voiced these thoughts in the summer of 1968, not in the spring of 1969. In the streets of the barrios of Denver something new had happened to the young Chicanos.

In the fiesta of the Chicano Youth Liberation Conference there emerged the "Spiritual Plan of Aztlán" that opened a new road for the odyssey of Rodolfo "Corky" Gonzales. The name of Aztlán had been that of the ancient nation of the Aztecs. Now the young Chicanos who had come from throughout the Southwest of the United States voted, almost unaminously, to revive the spirit of that defeated nation.

On the flowered and festooned platform the ex-boxer, former politician, and once-successful businessman, who had not so long ago sought so desperately to escape from the barrio, was the heroic host to the "Spiritual Plan of Aztlán":

> In the spirit of a new people that is conscious not only of its proud historical heritage but also of the brutal "gringo" invasion of our territories, we, the Chicano inhabitants and civilizers of the northern land of Aztlán, whence came our forefathers, reclaiming the land of their birth and conse-

crating the determination of our people of the sun, declare that the call of our blood is our power, our responsibility, and our inevitable destiny.

We are free and sovereign to determine those tasks which are justly called for by our house, our land, the sweat of our brows, and our hearts. Aztlán belongs to those who plant the seeds, water the fields, and gather the crops, and not to the foreign Europeans. We do not recognize capricious frontiers on the Bronze Continent.

Brotherhood unites us, and love for our brothers makes us a people whose time has come and who struggles against the foreigner *"gabacho"* who exploits our riches and destroys our culture. With our heart in our hands and our hands in the soil, we declare the Independence of our Mestizo Nation. We are a bronze people with a bronze culture. Before the world, before all of North America, before all our brothers on the Bronze Continent, we are a nation, we are a union of free pueblos, we are Aztlán.

March 1969

Por La Raza Todo Fuera de la Raza Nada

Sources

It was a dry, hot afternoon. On the plains of the Texas panhandle the summer sun burns up the air. Seven migrant farm workers and a boy who was hitchhiking to nowhere sat in the back of an open truck, on the sacks of potatoes—dusty, sweaty, hungry. His lips parched, one of the men tore open a sack, took out a raw potato, brushed off the dirt, and dug his teeth into the pulpy meat. The raw potato was hard, acid-tasting. But it was cool. When you are drying in the Texas sun even that is better than nothing.

He offered everyone a raw potato. We laughed and ate, chewing and sucking up the juices. Since the migrants were Mexicans who spoke no English, and I had failed high school Spanish, the raw potatoes were our means of communication. I was roaming, that summer, in the barrios of the Southwest, aimlessly. That was twenty-five years ago.

That day this book may have begun, although at the time I had no thought of writing, merely of surviving.

The potato eaters on that farm truck were unknowingly one of the "sources" of what I have now written. As were the thousands of men and women of La Raza whom I have known through the years. Neither I nor they would have imagined this book. Yet, is this not how life becomes literature?

Long, long before this book had been begun, it began. The "sources" of what I have written are the people who appear in its pages. Not the books in libraries, reports of the government, university studies, or even my own stubborn ego. In seeking to subdue these abstract, pedantic, extraneous ideas and images the people who have been written about were asked to read, comment upon, and edit what was written about them. Wherever this was impossible, those who knew them well enough performed this critical role. Is it a difficult way to write? Yes, it is. There are some chapters that were read by several people of differing views, who participated in the story told there.

Why have I written this way? It seems a long way home.

This book is not a study. It is not a survey. It is about real people, who have been re-created in their own image. Like every work of literature it attempts the impossible: the creation of life through the use of words—"the word was made flesh," says Ulibarri—by depicting the joys, pains, fears, angers, hopes, and fantasies of people. My pursuit is for the truth, as it exists in their hearts and minds. Whether it is your truth is unimportant. Whether it is mine does not matter either. It was the truth for me at the moment of writing, which is the moment of truth for every writer.

I am not a writer of information or social science. I am a man, not a social scientist; but then, I think, so is the social scientist, no matter how well he hides behind his methodology.

And so, the "sources" of this book were the people in it, first of all. The "sources" of this book were my own heart and the heart of La Raza. The "sources" of this book were living history.

"Our history has been lost. Lost!" cries Luis Valdez, the poet/director of El Teatro Campesino. "People ask me: What is Mexican history in the United States? There is no textbook of the history of La Raza. What really happened? No one can tell you."

It is true and it is not true. The history of a people exists outside of the textbooks. History, in a scholarly sense, is the written chronicle of events. The textbooks merely institutionalize what is remembered. That is, they recognize what has had prior and independent existence in the lives of a people and a nation, by the subjective decision of historians who choose what they believe to be important, what they understand, what they can accept. For this reason the history of the past is constantly changing, being rediscovered, revised, and reinterpreted. Although history is a fact of life, the historians have a godlike power of death, after the fact. They may consider it worth redeeming, or they may condemn it to oblivion.

Those who have written the textbooks of the Southwest have for one hundred years suppressed the history of La Raza. Why? Perhaps because the memory of "what really happened" jars the rationale of Manifest Destiny, disputes the recurring epithets that La Raza has always been "impoverished, bigoted, uncivilized, and degenerate," and denies the ethnocentric concept of those scholars who see their own civilization as the measure of human significance and progress.

What is "the reason for including a study of Spanish America in a series concerning the history of the United States?" asks a historian, Warren Dean, of the University of Texas, in the *Southwestern Historical Quarterly* (vol. LXXI, no. 1, July, 1967). His annoyance is due to Charles Gibson's pithy and trenchant *Spain in America* (Harper & Row, 1966), which surveys the colonial policy of "Spanish imperialism" and its influence in the Borderlands (the Southwest). The Texas historian objects: "The account of the Spanish Borderlands [has] almost total irrelevance to the national history of the United States."

In similar disdain King Philip II of Spain, in 1577, dismissed the writings of Fray Bernardino de Sahagún on the history of the Mexican Indians. The Royal Cedula of the King decreed with feudal fiat, "It is not proper that this book be published and disseminated . . . make sure that no original or copy is left there [in Mexico]. . . . And you are warned absolutely not to allow any person to write concerning the superstitions and ways of life of these Indians in any language, for this is not proper to God's serve, and to Ours."

The medieval methods of suppressing the history of the Mexican Indians were harsher than the modern methods of omitting the history of the Mexican Americans. But the effect did not differ greatly. Walt Whitman prophesied the triumph of ignorance, in 1877, when he wrote, "I have an idea that there is much and of importance about the Latin race's contributions to American nationality in the South and Southwest that will never be put with sympathetic understanding and tact on the record." And Charles Lummis pleaded in vain, at the turn of the century, for "a real history of the United States; a history not written in the closet; a book which will realize that the early history of this wonderful country . . . began in the great Southwest."

In the Beginning—The Mexican Indians

Actually, no people in the New World have an older written history than the Mexican Indians. The Olmecs were known to have a system of writing that has been dated back, at least, to 600 B.C. But the fratricidal wars and the burning of books and libraries by the Spaniards turned much of this history to ashes.

Enough was saved, in hidden codices of Aztec scholars and by the verbal memory of Nahuatl priests, to indicate the richness of the lost literature. The *Pre-Columbian Literatures of Mexico*, by Miguel Leon-Portilla (University of Oklahoma, 1969), is a panoramic survey of what has survived, enlivened with fragments and a comprehensive bibliography of known codices. Leon-Portilla's *Aztec Thought and Culture* (University of Oklahoma, 1963) is a companion work, which concentrates on textual analysis and interpretation; while his *The Broken Spears: The Aztec Account of the Conquest of Mexico* (Beacon, 1962) presents the chronicles and poems of the Nahuatl writers themselves.

The *Historia de la Literatura Nahuatl*, by Angel Maria Garibay K (Mexico City, 1953), and the magnificent, six-volume, *Colección de Documentos para la Historia de Mexico*, edited by Antonio Penafiel (Mexico City, 1897–1903), are a must for the reader of Spanish.

Interpretive works are plentiful. The ones I found especially interesting were: *The Aztecs: People of the Sun*, by Alfonso Caso (University of Oklahoma, 1958); *The Aztecs Under Spanish Rule*, by Charles Gibson (Stanford University, 1964); *The Aztecs of Mexico*, by George C. Vaillant (Doubleday, 1944); and Laurette Sejourne's *Burning Water: Thought and Religion in Ancient Mexico* (London, 1957).

And then there are the illuminating works of the conquistadors, monks, and heretics of Spain, whose origins and prejudices should be remembered. *The True History of the Conquest of Mexico*, by Bernal Díaz del Castillo, written in 1586 (issued in 5 volumes in London, 1908–1916, and later abridged by Irving A. Leonard, in New York, 1956), is surpassed only by Fray Bernardino de Sahagún's *Historia General de las Cosas de Nueva España*, begun in 1547, of which there are four editions, all in Spanish, and Fray Bartoleme de Las Casas' *Historia de las Indias*, which is at last being translated for publication in English. *Life and Labor in Ancient Mexico*, by Alonso de Zorita (Rutgers University, 1963), is a lesser work, written in 1590, that offers details about ordinary life.

The Making of Mexicans

The impact of Spain on the New World and that of the New World on Spain are comprehensively viewed in William Lytle Schurz's *This New World* (Dutton, 1964), valuable to the lay reader for its eclectic reference to contemporary documents and accounts. Schurz's approach is kaleidoscopic, as is Herbert E. Bolton's and Thomas M. Marshall's in *The Colonialization of North America, 1492–1783* (Macmillan, 1936), and Clarence E. Haring's *The Spanish Empire in America* (New York, 1947).

In the opinionated and insightful style of the Spanish essayist/philosopher Salvador de Madariaga's *The Rise of the Spanish American Empire* (New York, 1947) and *The Fall of the Spanish American Empire* (New York, 1948), Lewis Hanke's *The Spanish Struggle for Justice in the Conquest of America* (Philadelphia, 1949), and Silvio Zavala's *The Political Philosophy of the Conquest of America* (Mexico City, 1953), there are more probing and provocative thoughts. I prefer these works, though students seeking facts and deaths had best turn to the texts.

If one could read no other book on Mexico it ought to be Octavio Paz's *The Labyrinth of Solitude* (Grove, 1961), a celebration of the furies and silences, brilliance and shames, of "the cosmic race." These dissonances are sounded as well in Samuel Ramos' *Profile of Man and Culture in Mexico* (McGraw-Hill, 1962), which might have been subtitled "Middle-Class Man and Culture." *Is the Mexican Revolution Dead?* edited by Stanley R. Ross (Knopf, 1966), elaborates on these themes, pointedly in the essays of Luis Cabrera, Jesús Silva Herzog, Moises Navarro, and Gilberto Loyo; while an earlier collection, *Renascent Mexico,* edited by Herbert Weinstock and Hubert Herring (Covici-Friede, 1935), exemplifies the inner conflict in Luis Cabrera's plea for homogeneity, "The Key to the Mexican Chaos," and Moises Saenz's defense of the indigenous Aztec dichotomy of "Indian Mexico."

The history of modern Mexico is more conventionally depicted in Leslie Byrd Simpson's *Many Mexicos* (University of California, 1967). From the Conquest to contemporary affairs Simpson writes accurately of events and sardonically of people. His style is abrasive, but his scholarship rewarding. The dispassionate studies of Howard Cline, *The United States and Mexico* (Harvard, 1953), and Victor Alba, *The Mexicans: The Making of a Nation* (Praeger, 1967), complement the Simpson work. More *simpático* is Frank Tannenbaum's *Peace By Revolution: Mexico After 1910* (Columbia University, 1966), John Reed's journalistic tour de force of the Pancho Villa era, *Insurgent Mexico* (International, 1969), and *Zapata and the Mexican Revolution* by J. Womack, Jr. (Knopf, 1969).

After the Mexican Revolution several of the country's dismayed intellectuals sought for an ideology beneath the rubble. They found one literally written in blood. It was as though some purpose, some lesson, had to be learned to give life to the deaths.

Unfortunately for those readers who do not understand Spanish, few of their works have been translated. The influential *La Raza Cósmica* (The Cosmic Race) by José Vasconceles, published by the Agencia Mundial de Libreria in 1925, still influences the La Raza movements; its ideas are reflected in Tijerina's New Breed, the Los Angeles New Race, and the Chicano Liberation Conference's resolution, in 1969—"We are a Nation. We are Aztlán." Vasconceles, a former Minister of Education, wrote dozens of works including the classic, *La Cultura en Hispano-America* (The Culture of Spanish America) (La Plata, 1934). Yet only one of his books has been translated into English: *Aspects of Mexican Culture* (University of Chicago, 1926), which he wrote with Manuel Gamio.

The works of Antonio Caso, "*el Maestro* of contemporary Mexican thought," have not been translated at all. Even his pivotal work in the growth of the La Raza philosophy, *El Problema de Mexico y la Ideologia*

Nacional (The Problem of National Ideology in Mexico) (Mexico City, 1924), and his famous *Principios de Estética* (Esthetic Principles) (Mexico City, 1925) are all but unknown to the non-Spanish reader.

Conquest of the Southwest

The literary journey into the Southwest must begin with Gaspar Pérez de Villagra's *History of New Mexico,* written in 1610. Although the poet's poor verse has been translated into worse prose by Gilberto Espinosa (Quivera Society, 1933), the work of Villagra had earned the undeniable honor of being the first creative book of "American literature."

Letters and journals of the conquistadors fill the archives. Excellent bibliographies of these treasured documents appear in Herbert E. Bolton's *Coronado* (University of New Mexico, 1949) and Oakah Jones, Jr.'s *Pueblo Warriors and Spanish Conquest* (University of Oklahoma, 1966). The most useful one-volume translations are still *Spanish Explorers in the Southern United States, 1528–1543,* by Frederick W. Hodge and T. H. Lewis (Scribner's, 1925), and George P. Winship's *The Journey of Coronado* (Grabhorn, 1933). The popular history, written with lucid prose and a dramatic flair that illuminates, rather than clouds, the events, is Paul Horgan's *Conquistadors in North America* (Macmillan, 1963), but most popular books are too romantic and too stereotyped, and are to be avoided.

A fascinating sidelight into the history of La Raza may be glimpsed in the works of Fray Angelico Chavez, particularly his *Origins of New Mexico Families, 1598–1821* (Historical Society of New Mexico, 1954).

The older histories of the Southwest are still the most thorough: Herbert E. Bolton's *The Spanish Borderlands* (Yale University, 1921), Hubert H. Bancroft's *History of Arizona and New Mexico* (The History Company, 1889), *History of the North Mexican States and Texas* (San Francisco, 1884), Ralph E. Twitchell's *The Leading Facts of New Mexican History* (Torch Press, 1911), and Charles E. Chapman's *The Founding of Spanish California, 1687–1783* (Macmillan, 1916). However, these works do tend to detail external clashes—Spaniard versus Indian and Mexican versus Anglo—rather than delineate the formation and growth of the culture of La Raza.

One seeks in vain in this array of books for a history of La Raza. There is none. There have been published bits of folklore, reminiscences, and documents, but the historians have yet to recognize La Raza as an historical entity. There is not one comprehensive biography of any of the major figures, statesmen, or thinkers of La Raza: such men as Father José Antonio Martínez, who published the first newspaper and opened the first free school in New Mexico, in the early 1800's; José Gonzales, the revolutionary Governor of that state; Joaquín Murietta and Tiburcio Vásquez, the

Robin Hoods of California; General Juan Cortina, the "Liberator of the Republic of the Rio Grande," in the 1870's; and those men of La Raza who helped write the constitutions of California and New Mexico, who blazed the cattle trails across the Southwest, who were the first cowboys, who fought to defend the Alamo.

The history of La Raza has been thoroughly suppressed. Carlos E. Castañeda, the Latin-American librarian of the University of Texas, sought to balance one aspect in his *The Mexican Side of the Texas Revolution* (Turner, 1928). Yet, these documents, including the impassioned indictment by José Maria Tornel, were largely ignored. And Castañeda himself has had to privately publish most of his historic research. Recently, the war against Mexico has been re-examined by historians. And works like Glenn W. Price's *Origins of the War with Mexico* (University of Texas, 1967), with its documentation of President Polk's intrigues, the Polk diaries themselves, and the Texas State Historical Association's *The Republic of Texas* (American West, 1968) have all indicated a return to Ulysses S. Grant's view of that "immoral war." The *Personal Memoirs* of General Grant (Webster, 1886) and General Winfield Scott's *Memoirs* (Sheldon, 1864) might be read for contemporary accounts. Among the more objective histories are Albert K. Weinberg's *Manifest Destiny: A Study in Nationalist Expansion* (Johns Hopkins, 1935), and Otis A. Singletary's *The Mexican War* (University of Chicago, 1960).

However, the most important document in the Conquest of the Southwest by the United States, *The Treaty of Guadalupe Hidalgo,* was "almost impossible to obtain by the general public" from its signing, in 1848, until it was reprinted by the Tate Galley, of Truchas, New Mexico, in 1967.

If the formal history of La Raza has been arrantly recorded, the memories of its participants have been rich with detail. Reminiscences by Arnold R. Rojas of the cattle herds, cowboys, and *Indios* on the rancheros of old California, in *The Vaquero* (McNally and Loftin, 1964); Fabiola Cabeza de Baca's tales of the sheepherders, Texans, and Comancheros on the plains of the Llano de Estacado of New Mexico, in *We Fed Them Cactus* (University of New Mexico, 1954); Jovita Gonzales' folk tales, *corridos,* and historical essays from South Texas, in the *Annals* of the *Texas Folklore Society;* Americo Paredes' nostalgic and defiant memory book of life in the Lower Rio Grande Valley, *With His Pistol in His Hand* (University of Texas, 1958); and George I. Sánchez's gentle and scholarly depiction of the life of New Mexico's *Taosenos, The Forgotten People* (Calvin Horn, 1940, 1967).

The memories are unending. In the files of the Federal Writers' Projects alone there were thousands upon thousands of stories of the living history of La Raza, told by the people who lived it. And the unwritten histories await discovery.

La Raza: Rebirth and Renaissance

After the Mexican Revolutions the migration of millions of refugees from the frustration and poverty in southern Mexico changed the complexion of the Southwest. The studies of Manuel Gamio were chronicles of that exodus: *The Mexican Immigrant: His Life Story* (University of Chicago, 1931), and *Mexican Immigration to the United States* (University of Chicago, 1930).

In the face of the influx of Mexicans into the Southwest the restrictive "Immigration Lobby" launched a political and literary counteroffensive. *The Rising Tide of Color*, by Lothrop Stoddard (Scribners, 1921), accused the "Mongrel-Indians" of Mexico of plotting to "invade Texas," "rejoin" the Southwest to Mexico, and massacre "the entire white population." Later, in the early 1930's, *The Alien in Our Midst*, edited by Madison Grant (privately printed), urged the total exclusion of the "Mexican half breed Indians."

Emory S. Bogardus *Immigration and Race Attitudes* (Heath, 1928), Charles C. Alexander's *The Ku Klux Klan in the Southwest* (University of Kentucky, 1965), and Cecil Robinson's meticulous diagnosis of literary stereotypes, in *With the Ears of Strangers: The Mexican American in American Literature* (University of Arizona, 1963), analyze the varied forms of anti-Mexican racism. Earlier attitudes are represented by the gently patronizing *On the Trail of the Immigrant*, by Ernest Steiner (Revell, 1906), and Peter Herzog's lynch-rope jokes and frontier humor in *The Gringo & Greaser* (The Territorian Press, 1964).

The travail of Mexican workers who migrated into this culturally hostile terrain is told in the works of Paul S. Taylor, a dean emeritus of the University of California, and of La Raza history. His pioneering books include: *Mexican Labor in the United States: Imperial Valley* (1928), *Mexican Labor in the United States: South Texas* (1930), *Mexican Labor in the United States: Chicago and the Calumet Region* (1932), and *Mexican Labor in the United States: Migration Statistics* (1929–1934), all published by the University of California, Publications in Economics.

"Songs of the Mexican Migration" that appeared in the Texas Folklore Society's *Puro Mexicano* edition, in 1935, is yet another product of the labors of Paul S. Taylor.

In the fields where so many of the migrants settled there have been disparate rows of books. The farming textbooks, such as *The Yearbook of Agriculture*, issued annually by the Department of Agriculture, hardly concern themselves with farm workers. Until the late 1930's, when Carey McWilliams entered the field, there were few studies of migrant life and working conditions. His *Factories in the Field* (Little, Brown, 1934), *Ill Fares The Land: Migrants and Migratory Labor in the United States* (Little,

Brown, 1942), and *Brothers Under the Skin* (Little, Brown, 1944) are modern classics. In those years the statistical and political tracts were numerous but serious study was rare. One of the soberer books of radical ideas, upon which much of the labor organizing in the fields was then based, is Anna Rochester's *Why Farmers Are Poor* (International, 1940), an outdated work that does contain a history of farm worker's unions from the IWW of World War I. Also see *Farm Labor Organizing: 1905–1967* (National Advisory Commission on Farm Labor, 1967).

In the inventive and penetrating *Politics and Minorities* (University of New Mexico, 1969), edited by Henry J. Tobias and Charles E. Woodhouse, there is one of the salutary essays on La Raza politics—that of the Alianza of Reies Tijerina. Dr. Francis Swadesh not only writes with personal knowledge of the land-grant movement but also includes the testimony of Manuel Mejida, a journalist for the Mexico City newspaper *Excelsior*, who sees the conflict of Anglo and Hispano politics as a battle against "final extinction."

The upsurge of the campesinos in recent years has been recorded by La Raza itself. *Huelga: The First Hundred Days of the Great Delano Grape Strike*, by Eugene Nelson (Farm Workers Press, 1966), is a thin and hastily written tract that expresses the views of Cesar Chavez's union through the voices of the campesinos. *Basta!* [Ēnough] *The Tale of Our Struggle* (Farm Workers Press, 1966) is an even more evocative photo essay, by George Ballis, that contains the words of the *Plan of Delano*. Ernesto Galarza's *Strangers in Our Fields* (Washington, D.C., 1956) and *Merchants of Labor: The Mexican Bracero Story* (McNally and Loftin, 1964) are the definitive works on Mexican immigrants in the fields, together with José Lazaro Salina's *Emigración de Braceros* (Mexico City, 1955). Compared with these indigenous stories, even John Gregory Dunne's stylistic verve and hard reportage, in *Delano* (Farrar, Straus, & Giroux, 1967), seem shallow.

The United States Government reports also draw their strength from the campesinos' voices. See *Hearings Before the Subcommittee on Migratory Labor*, of the 89th Congress, "Amending Migratory Labor Laws," 1966, U.S. Senate, and of the 90th Congress, U.S. House of Representatives, Subcommittee on Labor, 1967. *The Migratory Farm Labor Problem in the United States*, U.S. Senate, Committee on Labor and Public Welfare, 1967 Report, provides the statistical background from these hearings.

The land-grant movement in the Southwest is too new to have produced an extensive literature. Peter Nabokov's *Tijerina and the Courthouse Raid* (University of New Mexico, 1969) is the first major study. But there is much background material: *Land Title Origins: Force and Fraud*, by Alfred N. Chandler (Schalkenback Foundation, 1945); *The Public Domain in New Mexico: 1854–1891*, by Victor Westphall (University of New Mexico,

1965); Westphall's unpublished *The Land Grants of New Mexico;* Aaron M. Sakolski's *The Great American Land Bubble: The Amazing Story of Land Grabbing* (New York, 1932); W. W. Robinson's *Land in California* (University of California, 1948); Elgin Williams' *Animating Pursuits in Speculation: Land Traffic in the Annexation of Texas* (New York, 1949); Betty F. Dobkins' *The Spanish Element in Texas Water Law* (University of Texas, 1959). Westphall's *Public Domain* and Chandler's *Land Title Origins* are noteworthy for their bibliographies.

Of all the accounts of the raid on the courthouse of Tierra Amarilla none has as much sense of immediacy and accuracy as the tape-recorded interviews of eyewitnesses and participants issued under the title *Shootout At Tierra Amarilla,* by Rubio Salas of Albuquerque. Salas, a schoolteacher, interviewed those on the scene while the incident was still alive in their memories. His document is living history.

And then there is the small, succinct booklet *The Spanish Land Grant Question Examined,* issued by Tijerina's Alianza Federal (Albuquerque, New Mexico, 1966), which raised the issue like a dusty ghost from the lost archives.

Clark Knowlton, director of the Center for the Study of Social Problems, University of Utah, has written widely on the history of the land-grant movement. Of especial interest is his *Land Grant Problems Among the State Spanish Speaking* (New Mexico Business, June, 1967) and his explosive *Recommendations for the Solution of the Land Tenure Problem,* presented to the President's Cabinet Committee Hearings on Mexican American Affairs in October, 1967.

Village life in New Mexico and elsewhere has been analyzed into the dirt. The list of books, studies, and reports is overwhelming. Since the *Revised Bibliography* of the Mexican American Study Project (University of California, 1967) and the older and larger *A Guide to Materials Bearing on Cultural Relations in New Mexico* by Lyle Saunders (University of New Mexico, 1944)—and a dozen other bibliographies—list almost all the extant materials, I shall not be redundant. In any event the village studies are mostly written by outsiders, from the romantics (Charles Lummis' *The Land of Poco Tiempo* [University of New Mexico, 1966]), to the dispassionate anthropologists, (Nancy Gonzales' *The Spanish Americans of New Mexico* [Mexican American Study Project]). The villagers have yet to speak for themselves.

In South Texas the problem of survival has overshadowed the problem of land. *Starvation in San Antonio,* 1940, is the title of a study by the local Social Welfare and Fact Finding Committee; long before *Hunger/USA* (Beacon Press, 1968) chronicled the continuing starvation in the city. *The Mexican Americans of South Texas,* by William Madsen (Holt, 1964), and

Across the Tracks: Mexican Americans in a Texas City, by Arthur J. Rubel (University of Texas, 1966), document the social poverty of the region, though both books are prone to the mythology of social science methodology. Two quite different books, Pauline R. Kibbe's highly moralistic and facile journalism, *Latin Americans in Texas* (University of New Mexico, 1946), and Sister Frances J. Woods' emotionally sympathetic *Mexican Ethnic Leadership in San Antonio* (Catholic University, 1949) attempt to tell of La Raza's response to poverty and discrimination.

Life in the urban barrios is equally proscribed by outside writers. *Urban Politics in the Southwest,* edited by Leonard E. Goodall (Arizona State University, 1967), and *American Ethnic Politics,* edited by Lawrence H. Fuchs (Harper Torchbooks, 1968), do not have a single La Raza author; the latter work does even have a chapter on the barrios. *La Raza: Forgotten Americans,* edited by Julian Samora (University of Notre Dame, 1966), is one of the few works on modern, urban life written entirely by Mexican-American writers. The only comparable book is *The Mexican American: A New Focus on Opportunity* (Inter-Agency Committee on Mexican-American Affairs, Washington, D.C., 1967), which consists of the reports of nearly fifty La Raza leaders to the President's Cabinet Committee Hearings.

In no field is there more to write about and fewer books than in that of the arts of La Raza. Until the publication of *El Espeso* (The Mirror) by *El Grito,* in 1969, there was not a single anthology of Chicano stories and poetry. *The Southwest in Life and Literature,* edited by C. L. Sonnichsen (Devin-Adair, 1962), is an excellent collection but does not have one La Raza author; while *Southwest Heritage: a Literary History,* by M. Major, R. W. Smith, and T. M. Pearce (University of New Mexico, 1948), apologizes for its meager chapter "Spanish Folk Drama, Songs and Tales" by hoping that "some day we shall attain the breadth of vision." Anyway, the authors add, "the dominant strain seems clearly to be Anglo-American" in the Southwest, and it will "absorb its competitors."

The works of La Raza culture that have been published are mostly folk culture. At this writing there is not a single collection of Chicano poetry, plays, essays, or stories that has been printed by a major textbook or trade publisher. Nor has the vast and intriguing "lost literature" of the Spanish colonial period been found, or even sought. Although not devoted to the literature of La Raza alone, the monumental volumes of *The Literature of Spanish America* by Angel Flores (Las Americas, 1969) are a tribute to the breadth of "Hispanic-Indio" culture in this hemisphere. Divided into four books—Vol. I: *Colonial Period;* Vol. II: *1825–1887;* Vol. III: *El Modernismo and Post-Modernismo;* Vol. IV: *1930–1967*—Flores' anthologies contain hundreds of works from throughout Latin America, text in Spanish and notes in English. There is an excellent bibliography, in English, as well. Unfortunately no comparable work devoted to La Raza exists.

Education is fittingly the field in which there are the most books. *Concerning Segregation of Spanish Speaking Children in the Public Schools,* by George I. Sánchez (University of Texas, 1951), Herschel T. Manuel's *Spanish Speaking Children of the Southwest: Their Education and Public Welfare* (University of Texas, 1965); and *Disadvantaged Mexican American Children and Early Educational Experience,* by Charles B. Brussell (Southwest Educational Development Corp., 1968), are three of the basic studies. They detail educational deprivation of the schoolchildren and the subsequent low scores and high dropout rates. But they do not deal with the de-education of children whose schooling is aimed at the replacement of La Raza culture.

The forthcoming *Bilingualism* by Vera P. John and Vivian M. Horner (Modern Language Association, 1970) is a cogent and comprehensive study of de-education. It surveys every major bilingual school program in the Southwest. Statements before the Special Subcommittee on Bilingual Education, U.S. Senate, May, 1967, offer background material, especially the testimony of Joshua A. Fishman.

Statistics on the tragic effects of de-education are summarized in the brief booklet *The Mexican American: Quest for Equality* (Office of Education, Washington, D.C., 1968), while educational activism in the barrios is the subject of a special issue of *American Education* (November, 1968), "Mexican American Education." The *Proceedings* of the Texas conference for the Mexican American (San Antonio, 1967) highlights the educational struggle in that state; *The Schooling Gap: Signs of Progress,* by Leo Grebler (Mexican American Study Project, UCLA, 1967), presents a statistical survey of educational retardation; and *The Invisible Minority: Pero No Vencibles* (National Education Association, 1966) indicts the education "laws of the Anglos" and pleads for "bilingualism: a valid objective." It should be noted that none of these studies represents the Chicano students, whose opinions are voiced in the *Chicano Student Movement, Inside-Eastside,* and similar student newspapers, as well as magazines such as *El Grito* (Berkeley) and *Con Safos* (Los Angeles).

The outstanding and most thorough study of the social history of La Raza is the panoramic *North from Mexico* by Carey McWilliams (Lippincott, 1949). Although outdated by some twenty years and suffering from an honest outsider's focus—"of the head, not the heart—" the book is nevertheless an "important source for students of Mexican American affairs," writes Rafael Guzman, a Cal State professor who helped carry out a four-year Ford Foundation study of Mexican Americans.

Curiously there is, as yet, no published voice from the barrios that "tells it like it is" with the veracity of W. E. B. Du Bois' *Souls of Black Folk,* Richard Wright's *Native Son,* James Baldwin's *The Fire Next Time,* Claude

Brown's *Manchild in the Promised Land*, or Eldridge Cleaver's *Soul On Ice.*

In the pages of the Chicano Press the *grito* of the barrio youth echoes. But the verbal outcry of manifestoes, *cholo* tales and poems, and protest journalism has yet to be distilled into the literature of La Raza that is bound to blossom forth eventually. While that cultural rebirth is awaited, the Chicano Press itself remains the most vital source of the new voices of La Raza. Some of the barrio newspapers are:

LA RAZA
P. O. Box 31004
Los Angeles, California
90031

EL MALCRIADO
P. O. Box 130
Delano, California
93215

EL PAISANO
P. O. Box 155
Tolleson, Arizona
85353

EL GALLO
1567 Downing St.
Denver, Colorado
80218

CHICANO STUDENT MOVEMENT
P. O. Box 31322
Los Angeles, California
90031

EL GRITO DEL NORTE
Route 2, Box 5
Espanola, New Mexico
87532

EL PAPEL
P. O. Box 7167
Albuquerque, New Mexico
87104

CARTA EDITORIAL
P. O. Box 54624
Terminal Annex
Los Angeles, California
90054

BRONZE
142 Pickford Ave.
San Jose, California
95127

LADO
1306 N. Western Ave.
Chicago, Illinois
60622

INFERNO
321 Frio City Road
San Antonio, Texas
78207

LA RAZA NUEVA
2815 W. Commerce
San Antonio, Texas
78207

INSIDE EASTSIDE
P. O. Box 63273
Los Angeles, California
90063

COMPASS
1209 Egypt St.
Houston, Texas
77009

LA VOZ MEXICANA
P. O. Box 101
Wautoma, Wisconsin
54982

LA REVOLUCIÓN
Box 1852
Uvalde, Texas
78801

CORAJE
% Mexican American
Liberation Committee
Tucson, Arizona

NUESTRA LUCHA
110 NW 5th Avenue
Delray Beach, Florida
33444

EL DEGUELLO
P. O. Box 37094
San Antonio, Texas
78237

THE FORUMEER
990 Elm St.
San Jose, California
95110

EL YAQUI
P. O. Box 52610
Houston, Texas
77052

CON SAFOS: REFLECTIONS ON LIFE IN THE BARRIO
P. O. Box 31085
Los Angeles, California
90031

LA CAUSA
4715 East Olympic Blvd.
Los Angeles, California
90022

EL CHICANO
% 4021 First Avenue
San Bernardino, California

EL GRITO
Quinto Sol Publications
P. O. Box 9275
Berkeley, California
94709

LA VERDAD
P. O. Box 13156
San Diego, California
92113

In the years of my writing this book these La Raza newspapers and the young men and women who write them have been one of the "sources" of my inspiration, and trepidation. They are the living history of Chicano life.

My "sources" have been, as I said in the beginning, more human than scholarly. There have been many hundreds and thousands of people. But there has been one above all others, the "source" of my life, Veronka, my wife.

Index

70 71 72 73 12 11 10 9 8 7 6 5 4 3 2 1